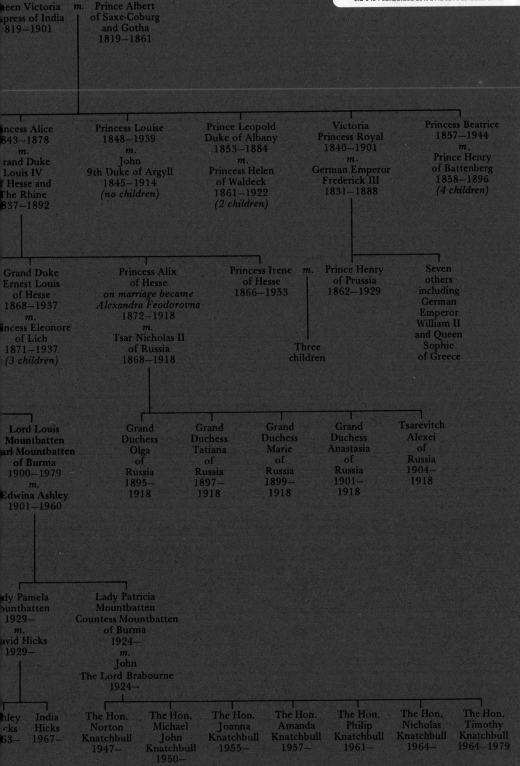

MOUNTBATTEN

MOUNTBATTEN

Hero of our Time

RICHARD HOUGH

Weidenfeld and Nicolson
London

To his memory

CONTENTS

ILLUSTRATIONS

Between pages 50 and 51
Princess Victoria of Hesse, 1884 (*Bassano & Vandyke*).
Prince Louis of Battenberg (*Radio Times Hulton Picture Library*).
Dickie in 'naval uniform', age 4 (*Radio Times Hulton Picture Library*).
The naval Battenbergs, father and sons, 1913 (*Bassano & Vandyke*).
Winston Churchill as First Lord of the Admiralty and Prince Louis as
　First Sea Lord, 1914 (*Radio Times Hulton Picture Library*).
Winston Churchill (*Bassano & Vandyke*).
On board the Russian Imperial yacht, *Standardt*, in the Baltic
　(*Keystone*).
The Russian Imperial family, 1905 (*Radio Times Hulton Picture Library*).
Mountbatten's favourite portrait of his cousin, the Grand Duchess
　Marie (*Keystone*).
Mountbatten and the Prince of Wales at play on the Prince's world tour
　(*Central Press*).
Mountbatten and the Prince of Wales at work on board HMS *Renown*,
　1920–22 (*Central Press*).
King George V considered this widely printed photograph of his son and
　cousin unsuitable for the general public (*Central Press*).
Edwina Cynthia Annette Ashley (*Topical Press*).
Edwina with her grandfather, Sir Ernest Cassel (*Popperfoto*).
Lieutenant Lord Louis Mountbatten, age 21, shortly before his wedding
　(*Bassano & Vandyke*).
Edwina – Lady Louis Mountbatten – in 1925 (*Radio Times Hulton
　Picture Library*).
'The wedding of the year', 18 July 1922, St Margaret's, Westminster
　(*Radio Times Hulton Picture Library*).
The honeymoon. Edwina and Mountbatten embark in the *Majestic* for
　New York (*Radio Times Hulton Picture Library*).

Hollywood, 1922. Charlie Chaplin breaks the news to Dickie that he will never make an actor (Reproduced with permission of *The Bodley Head*).

Edwina 'held up' in the film *Nice and Friendly* which Chaplin made for them as a wedding present (Reproduced with permission of *The Bodley Head*).

Dickie and Charlie recovering after a hard morning's 'shooting' (Reproduced with permission of *The Bodley Head*).

Instant and lifelong friends: Edwina and Chaplin, 1922 (Reproduced with permission of *The Bodley Head*).

Between pages 146 and 147

Edwina, age 27 (*Rex Features*).

Goodwood Races, July 1926. On Mountbatten's left is his sister-in-law Nada, Marchioness of Milford Haven (*Radio Times Hulton Picture Library*).

Mountbatten, Edwina and her sister Mary at the Highland Gathering, 1923 (*Radio Times Hulton Picture Library*).

Mountbatten with his first Rolls-Royce (*Popperfoto*).

Douglas Fairbanks, Patricia, Edwina and her father, Colonel Wilfred Ashley (*Popperfoto*).

Discussing tactics with the Duke of Gloucester before a chukka, June 1937 (*Fox Photos*).

The Royal Navy Polo Team, 1937 (*Fox Photos*).

Pranks at Balmoral Castle, August 1936 (*Popperfoto*).

The Penthouse, Park Lane, in 1937 (*H. V. Joel*).

Mountbatten and his senior officers of 5th Destroyer flotilla in jovial mood (*Keystone*).

The destroyer commander, Captain Lord Louis Mountbatten on the *Kelly*'s bridge, 1940 (*Keystone*).

The *Kelly* torpedoed and listing, off the Dutch coast, 1940 (*Fox Photos*).

The *Kelly* saga as heroic film fiction, with Noël Coward acting the part of Mountbatten in *In Which We Serve*, 1942 (*National Film Archive*).

Three generations of Mountbattens (*H. V. Joel*).

Mountbatten the Chief of Staff with Field Marshal Alan Brooke, Air Chief Marshal Peter Portal and General 'Pug' Ismay (*Keystone*).

Mountbatten the orator, with assembled troops on the quayside at Bombay (*Central Press*).

General 'Vinegar Joe' Stilwell and Mountbatten at Kandy, 1944 (*Fox Photos*).

Mountbatten, General R.A. 'Specs' Wheeler and the Chiang Kai-sheks, 1944 (*Keystone*).

Between pages 210 and 211
The new Viceroy and Vicereine arrive at Delhi airport, 22 March 1947 (*Keystone*).
1947: the last Viceroy and Vicereine (*Fox Photos*).
In full rig, India 1947 (*Popperfoto*).
With Mahatma Gandhi, 1947 (*Keystone*).
With Pandit Nehru at Delhi (*Keystone*).
Communal riots, Calcutta, 1947 (*Keystone*).
The solemn acceptance of Partition for India: Nehru, Ismay, Mountbatten and Jinnah (*Keystone*).
The Christening of Norton Knatchbull, Mountbatten's first grandson, November 1947 (*Keystone*).
With his nephew, Prince Philip, October 1948 (*Popperfoto*).
Second grandson, Michael John, June 1950, with Edwina, Princess Elizabeth, Mountbatten, Lord Brabourne, Norton Knatchbull and Patricia, Lady Brabourne (*Keystone*).
c-in-c Mediterranean Fleet, 1951 (*Keystone*).
Grand Harbour, Malta. At the termination of his Mediterranean Fleet and NATO command, Mountbatten is rowed in his barge by six of his admirals, December 1954 (*Central Press*).
With Edwina, Princess Anne and Prince Charles, Malta, April 1954 (*Central Press*).
Mountbatten as First Sea Lord, 1955, with Edwina at Broadlands (*Camera Press*).
Edwina at her last London home, Wilton Crescent (*Popperfoto*).
Edwina's bedroom at Wilton Crescent (*H.V. Joel*).
Mountbatten's study at Wilton Crescent (*H.V. Joel*).
The Board of Admiralty, February 1959 (*Popperfoto*).
The Suez crisis, 1956. An anxious Mountbatten arrives at 10, Downing Street (*Fox Photos*).

Between pages 242 and 243
Another family occasion: the wedding of the Mountbattens' second daughter, Pamela, in January 1960, to David Hicks (*Fox Photos*).
Mountbatten kisses, then casts into the sea, a wreath of lilies after the burial of Edwina (*Popperfoto*).
With President John F. Kennedy and General Lemnitzer at the White House (*Keystone*).

FOREWORD

I first met Lord Mountbatten in 1971, appropriately at sea, and for several weeks had the opportunity of discussing naval history with him from time to time, more especially eighteenth-century naval history, upon which I was then working. Later, he invited me to write his family history and a dual biography of his remarkable mother (Queen Victoria's favourite granddaughter) and his naval father, Prince Louis of Battenberg, who was First Sea Lord in 1914 and worked in harness with the young Winston Churchill.

Lord Mountbatten was unstinting in his help over *Louis and Victoria* and made available to me much manuscript material relevant to the life of his parents. For this purpose I also had access to the Royal Archives, Windsor, and enjoyed the privilege of interviews with members of his family, old shipmates and others.

Lord Mountbatten gave me equally willing and generous help over several of my more recent books. But my suggestions from time to time that I should write a one-volume informal biography of him were invariably met by the reply that he did not wish any biography to be written or any official biographer to be nominated until after his death. Given that the official biography is still several years away, I feel that there is now room for an informal study of Lord Mountbatten's life.

RICHARD HOUGH
March 1980

THE MURDER

Classiebawn Castle is a turreted, early Victorian stone mansion built on his Irish estate in County Sligo, now the Republic of Ireland, to the order of the English statesman and Prime Minister, Lord Palmerston. Its situation on the highest point of a promontory overlooking the sea is dramatic in the extreme. From the tall neo-Gothic windows you can see north and north-west across the bay to the saw-tooth silhouette of the Donegal mountains, while below the Atlantic rollers unfold themselves against the shore.

From the other side of the castle, to the east and south, and beyond the green coastal strip of bog and meadow, stand the peaks of Benbulbin, Truskmore and Ben Weskin, sculpted by volcanic upheaval and millennia of gales into grotesque configuration. Beyond are more peaks, and, unseen, the loughs of Fermanagh, Cavan and Leitrim.

It is wild, savage country, nowhere more savage than along this coast of County Sligo, which has seen as much killing and suffering as anywhere in Ireland. Among the sand dunes to east and west of Classiebawn (the white hollows) are the graves of Bronze Age warriors. Countless ships have been thrown on to these shallow, shelving, carboniferous sandstone cliffs, which themselves are like the crank-tilted hulls of scattered wrecks.

In September 1585 three Spanish galleons, survivors of the Armada, were wrecked on this shore. 'I numbered in one strand above eleven hundred dead corpses of men which the sea had driven upon the shore,' reported Sir Geoffrey Fenton to Lord Burghley at the court of Queen Elizabeth I. Other Spanish sailors and soldiers by the hundred were stripped and clubbed to death as they staggered ashore along the coasts of Donegal Bay.

Lord Palmerston was born two hundred years after these infamous killings. As a young man he travelled from Dublin across Ireland to inspect for the first time his inherited estate. 'It commences at about six or seven miles north from Sligo,' he wrote to his sister, 'and continues with scarcely any interruption for

*five or six miles along the coast, bounded on one side by the sea and on the other
by bog and high craggy mountains.'*

The young man was bursting with idealism, was eager to improve the sorry
state of his tenants, to build good school houses and roads, and 'to put the Parish
Church in a state of repair so as to make it fit for service'. The local peasants
were fortunate. Unlike most absentee English landlords, Palmerston came frequently to his estate, ensured that it prospered, and where the sand blew and
threatened the pasture, planted coarse grass 'to hold the land'. On the sheltered
side of the promontory near Cliffony he built a harbour.

'It is nearly completed,' he wrote in 1826, 'and will be an excellent one for
my purpose, with enough depth to admit vessels of 300 tons, and as much as
any harbour on the west coast of Ireland.' He named it Mullaghmore (the Great
Summit) for the hill above it, upon which he now built his castle.

As the harbour never prospered, so the building is a castle only in name. It
is not even very big, only gauntly prominent in its isolation, so that on a clear
day it can be seen in all its ridiculous ostentation clear across Donegal Bay.

From his visits to Classiebawn, Lord Palmerston in his compassion and wisdom
recognized the evils of civil strife among these poor people, and the terrible
dangers of the suppression of the Catholics. In 1829 he made his famous speech
in the House of Commons on Catholic emancipation, predicting the terror and
bloodshed that would one day stem from the 'suppressed pugnacity', like 'over-
charged thunderclouds bursting with accumulated fire' upon this land. 'Let us
not exercise a suicidal fury on ourselves,' he ended with awful prescience.

Classiebawn Castle and the Palmerston estate came into the property of Lord
Mountbatten through the seventh Earl of Shaftesbury, stepson-in-law and private secretary to Palmerston, and thence through the Ashley family to Mountbatten's wife, Edwina, who died in 1960.

Nineteen-and-a-half years later, shortly before 11.30 on the morning of 27
August 1979, a Mountbatten family holiday party of six walked down the four
wide front steps of this castle. Besides Lord Mountbatten, there were in the party
his elder daughter Lady (Patricia) Brabourne, Lord (John) Brabourne, his
eighty-three-year-old mother, the Dowager Lady (Doreen) Brabourne, and the
fourteen-year-old identical twin sons of the Brabournes, Timothy and Nicholas.
Patricia Brabourne and her father had agreed only a few minutes earlier that
they should not waste such a lovely morning, and that it was time to lift the
lobster pots they had set the previous day.

The rest of the house party, including Mountbatten's younger daughter, Lady
Pamela Hicks, and her husband, and Hugh Tunney, the Irish meat millionaire,
had decided not to join them. Mr Tunney, who leased Classiebawn and its 1,500-
acre estate from Mountbatten, with the stipulation that the family could stay

there for one month in every year, had already expressed anxiety about Mount-batten's annual August holiday so close to the strife-torn border with Ulster. But Mountbatten shrugged off these warnings, and insisted that the bright, many-coloured family flag – 'In Honour Bound' – should fly from the castle's mast as always.

At dinner the previous evening he had said, 'I can't think of a more wonderful thanksgiving for the life I have had than that everyone should be jolly at my funeral.' His funeral, as elaborate as for any monarch, had been prepared by himself down to the last minute detail, though he had discussed it only with his private secretary, in the utmost confidence, the Queen and the closest members of his family. To pore over the invitation list and revise it from time to time, as people died or fell out of favour, was a favourite occupation. He had completed his obituary television film for the BBC.

Shortly before he left for Ireland he told the columnist Audrey Whiting, 'I can't go on for ever. I'd rather snuff out in a hurry.' Earlier that evening, while it was still light, he had asked the castle's domestic staff of twenty to gather together to be photographed with him and his family.

Now, before getting into the car, Mountbatten said 'Good morning' to Garda Kevin Henry and his fellow officer on protective duty that morning since 6 am. They had small arms and two pairs of binoculars in their Ford car, which was a well-named Escort model. Mountbatten's news that they were going out in his boat came as no surprise to the Gardai. Shadow V, twenty-nine-foot, clinker-built motor cruiser, a converted fishing boat, lay at its mooring in the harbour of the holiday and fishing village of Mullaghmore less than a mile distant. Concealed beneath its decking, between the cockpit and the engine, was a plastic tube of gelignite. It weighed five pounds, was seventeen inches long and two-and-a-half inches in diameter.

The old lady got into the front passenger seat of the car, John Brabourne was the driver, and the rest climbed into the back, Mountbatten last. He was wearing well-creased blue lightweight trousers, sand shoes, and a long-sleeved jersey specially knitted for him and displaying on the front the badge of HMS Kelly. This wartime destroyer of his had been blown up and sunk by a single 1,000-pound bomb. A hundred and thirty men of the ship's company had died on that occasion thirty-eight years earlier.

The car containing the Mountbatten party drove down the winding narrow drive between open pasture land, through the little spinney by the lodge gates (the emblems of Mountbatten and his dead wife, carved upon the pillars, were already covered in lichen), and on to the public road leading to the village.

This short run to Mullaghmore reveals the modern prosperity of this Irish estate beyond Palmerston's most sanguine dreams. The slopes of Classiebawn's promontory are scattered with holiday chalets and caravans, and the few surviving old bothies are newly whitewashed, with bright curtains in the windows and children's toy scattered in the trim gardens, television aerials towering above. No one tills the soil round here any more, except to plant out nasturtiums, and the children are plump, and barefoot from choice. On this beautiful Bank Holiday Monday, they were streaming up from the curved sweep of sand with their parents, many in bright swimming costumes, for their mid-day meal.

The Gardai's Ford Escort slowed down behind the Mountbatten car. In the bay there were sailing boats, inflatable dinghies, fishing boats and motor boats. The sea was calm, with a gentle north-west breeze blowing. Here was a panorama of summer holiday fun and relaxation, the perfect scene for a postcard – 'Having a smashing time – sea lovely....'

Lord Brabourne turned off right, leaving the Gardai behind, and on to the narrow pier which encloses two sides of the harbour – the harbour itself on the left, the sand dunes, green-tinted from Lord Palmerston's grass, stretching away to the right. On the seaward side a high wall protects the harbour and the pier from easterly gales, and at its base lay scattered tackle, rope, lobster pots and all the paraphernalia of sailing and fishing.

Across the harbour are the few buildings contemporary with its construction – the grey, gaunt 'Star of the Sea Public Oratory', J.P. McGloin's bar with its curious sign of three fish in a circle, the village store and Post Office, the Beach Hotel and Pier House Hotel, both doing full business, the bright Mazdas and Peugeots, Fiats and Opels, parked outside. Below the second of these hotels is a slipway, and a fishermen's store dug like a cave from beneath the jetty.

Lord Brabourne parked the car beside Shadow v, which was moored five berths from the end of the pier. There were several fishermen about, some working on tackle, among them young Paul Maxwell from Enniskillen, just across the border of Ulster, which is only twelve miles away. The regular boatman for Shadow v could not come this year, but everyone had taken a fancy to the fifteen-year-old boy. He knew that the Mountbatten party were likely to visit the lobster pots they had set the previous day.

A number of the holidaymakers, and locals, had already recognized Mountbatten, and many eyes followed him. He was liked by the villagers for his cheerfulness, friendliness and the trade he attracted. They saw him now step out of the car, an impressive figure, six feet two inches tall, fourteen stone, a long, aristocratic face with a long, slightly hooked and distinctive nose – the Mountbatten nose; a well-shaped mouth that seemed as enquiring and responsive as the blue-grey eyes – seamen's eyes that missed nothing. Ears long, too, on a big head, with fine hair, white now but almost as full as a half century ago when he was the most handsome man in London.

He walked towards the boat, feet wide-splayed, stooping a little, talking and laughing with the twin grandsons – sixty-five years younger – at his side. Paul

Maxwell had the diesel engine turning over. The boys helped their grandmother on board, then their mother. Lord Brabourne remained on the pier to photograph the party, and then joined them. Less than a quarter-hour had passed since they had left Classiebawn Castle.

Lord Brabourne sat on a swivel chair, the three boys stood in the centre of the boat, the old lady sat on the starboard side, Lady Brabourne on the port side. Mountbatten was at the wheel. He opened the throttle and steered Shadow V out between the mole on the north side of the harbour and the pier head, decisively and with the authority of an Admiral of the Fleet who had been handling boats since he was five years old.

As the boat turned to port to follow the line of the coast, its new white and green paintwork glinting in the sun, the Gardai's Ford Escort joined the traffic along the narrow coast road. Garda Kevin Henry followed the progress of Shadow V through a pair of binoculars. Until recently the boat had been guarded night and day, and an officer had always gone out with Mountbatten. But he had asked for security to be relaxed – 'Whoever would want to murder an old man like me?'

Among the steady stream of cars along the coast road was a yellow Ford Cortina containing two members of the Provisional IRA. One of them had a remote control device, of the kind used for controlling model planes, concealed in his lap.

Mountbatten eased back Shadow V's throttle to bring the boat alongside the lobster pots. They were just two hundred yards from the shore and three hundred yards from the head of the pier. The boys in the boat had cast handlines, and Lord Brabourne was leaning over the gunwale to haul up the first pot.

A number of people on shore and in boats were watching Shadow V as she slowed, besides the two Gardai, and, only a short distance from them, the two men in the yellow Cortina. Kevin Henry told his driver to halt at the roadside. In his own boat, David Mulligan, a retired Irish Army officer, was taking a party of German holidaymakers for a day's fishing. A Mr Brian Wakeley was a few hundred yards farther out to sea than the Mountbatten boat.

The explosion, when it came a minute later (at exactly 11.45, according to one member of the Garda) was more a tearing crack than a boom, like an ultra-loud rifle shot close to the ear. The boat disintegrated in a cloud of smoke and spume, and countless fragments of timber and metal, rope and cushions, life-jackets and shoes, filled the air and fell in an oval pattern of splashes in the sea, which had been thrown into a spasm of agitation about the area where the boat had been.

The gelignite had been only a few inches from Mountbatten's feet when it had been detonated. He was thrown high into the air, along with everyone on board, many of them losing everything they wore in the blast.

A number of nearby boats, including David Mulligan's and Brian Wakeley's, converged on the area. Wakeley managed to haul one naked body into his boat. It was Paul Maxwell, horribly mutilated and already dead. The Brabournes were dragged from the water into an inflatable boat, both conscious. One by one the rest of the party were taken from the sea.

Everyone in the village had heard the explosion, and the news of its origin raced through the beach parties, and among those in cars, chalets, shops and caravans, almost as fast as its shock wave – which came near to toppling a builder from the roof of a house.

'They've blown up Lord Mountbatten's boat....!' The barking of many dogs, much shouting and several screams could be heard, and fear chilled everyone in the harbour and village as if this was only the beginning, as if they were all at risk from more explosions that must inevitably follow.

The first of the injured were brought ashore and up the slipway on stretchers. Crowds pressed round, enterprising young men with cameras jostling them. Besides Maxwell, Nicholas was dead too, and blankets covered their young faces. The other twin was injured about the face and body, the old Dowager fatally hurt. The Brabournes had their legs broken and lacerated badly, and injuries elsewhere.

They found Mountbatten's body some distance away, face down, his head and body peppered with wood splinters, his left leg shattered, and the ankle joint almost destroyed. Most of his clothes had been ripped off by the blast but his rescuers could still make out the Kelly's emblem on what was left of his jersey. According to the pathologist's report, he had been rendered unconscious and incapable of saving himself.

When the Kelly had been blown up, Mountbatten had led his men in singing 'Roll out the Barrel!' and other cheerful songs as they awaited rescue from the sea. After the last echoes of this explosion, and the few screams that followed it, faded away across the sea, there was only the sharp sound of orders and complaint, protest, rebuke and breathless dismay, of children's voices demanding to be held up (some were), of dogs still barking; and then the distant chatter of a rescue helicopter (its crew found Nicholas' body), and the howl of sirens as the first ambulances from Sligo tore through Cliffony, turned left at the sign to Mullaghmore, past the lodge gates of Palmerston's castle....

It was a hundred and fifty years since the noble Lord had spoken of this land where 'men, naturally kind and benevolent, are brought up from their earliest infancy to hate with all bitterness . . . and not satisfied with the disputes of the days in which they live, rake up the ashes of the dead for food to their angry passions.'

As a boy, Mountbatten had dreamed of dying at sea, like his hero Nelson, while leading a great fleet in a great victory. He had never commanded a fleet in battle, and in war his little destroyer was always in trouble, and was eventually sunk by the enemy. But if Shadow v *was no more than a leased old converted fishing launch, he had at least been killed while in command as an Admiral of the Fleet.*

Within minutes, the news of the Admiral's death was known all over the world, creating shock and grief as great as the Provisional IRA assassins had hoped for. What was the reason for this? It could not be because he was cousin to Queen Elizabeth II, had once been Viceroy of India for a few months, once leader of a 'Forgotten Army', once married to one of the richest women in the world.

1
THE BOY SAILOR

LORD MOUNTBATTEN had been born seventy-nine years, two months and two days earlier, on 25 June 1900. He weighed eight pounds precisely. On hearing the news, his great-grandmother, Queen Victoria, ordered her carriage and drove to see him. In spite of her own too numerous labours, and those of her children and grandchildren, the delivery of a new child never failed to interest her. 'He is a beautiful large child,' she noted. He was also, as it happened, the last great-grandchild of her lifetime, and her last godchild. 'Will you please call him Albert?' she asked the baby's mother. The Queen's consort had been dead thirty-nine years, but his name was still frequently on her lips.

On 17 July, an unusually hot day, the Queen was driven from Windsor for the christening. She was eighty-one years old, frail, small and bowed. She had reigned for sixty-three years. She was infirm and almost blind. The dignity and authority of this aged Queen-Empress, who ruled so much of the world and so many of its people, had in no way diminished.

Recounting the family story, Mountbatten used to tell how the old Queen sat holding him in her arms throughout the ceremony, in spite of his hefty size, when he was named Albert Victor Nicholas Louis Francis; and then had her spectacles pushed off by her godson. He bellowed throughout but the Queen thought he behaved very well.

The family returned to London, and six months later the Queen's remarkable resilience and strength of will at last began to fade. Mountbatten's parents, His Serene Highness Prince Louis of Battenberg and Her Grand Ducal Highness, were summoned to Osborne House where the Queen was lying mortally ill. She died at 6.30 on the evening of 22 January 1901, surrounded by her children and grandchildren, a silent multitude of kings and queens, princes and princesses, grand-dukes and grand-duchesses; and by her first grandson, the Emperor of Germany, Kaiser Wilhelm II, whose good right arm – his left had been withered at birth – lay under her pillow in support as she passed away.

One of those closest to her in mind and spirit for so many years, and closest to her bedside as she died, was Mountbatten's mother. 'Look on me as a mother,' the Queen had instructed her grandchild when her own mother had died more than twenty years earlier. The Queen was 'her true friend'. No one about that bedside was more grief-stricken.

The consequences of the death of the old Queen, neatly at the turn of the new century, were profound and numerous. One of the least important results, but with a certain subtle bearing on his life and on the image he presented to the world, was that the name Albert was quietly relegated now that the future Lord Mountbatten's godmother was no longer able to take offence.

'My brother and sisters', said Mountbatten, 'always wanted to call me Nicky but my parents pointed out that it would lead to confusion with the Tsar. They then for some curious reason suggested Dickie, and my mother was most amused because they obviously didn't know that her private pet name for my father was "Dickie bird".'

Perhaps his older brother and sisters were not so naive as their mother supposed, and realized that the endearment that they overheard in supposed privacy was somehow associated with this new infant brother. It turned out to be apt, too. For Dickie grew up to be much closer in character to his father than to his mother. He was also, like many late children, terribly spoilt.

'My brothers and sisters treated me as the baby and forgave me for everything. I'm afraid that I was the favourite. I was spoilt and no one minded.' Not long ago, Mountbatten was having tea with the present Queen and his elder sister Alice, who lived out her last years in Buckingham Palace, and as the Queen was holding the teapot he was impelled to exclaim, 'I don't like China tea. I hate your tea, and you never serve Indian tea.'

Princess Alice interjected, 'Dickie doesn't like China tea, he always had Indian tea as a boy.'

The Queen, laughing but mock-outraged, replied, 'Are you telling me that Dickie always had a special pot of tea? That's entirely his upbringing. He's always been spoilt, and he's spoilt to this day. I suppose that's what his mother did to him – I can see that now.'

Born a Serene Highness, scion of the oldest traceable Protestant reigning family in the world, young Dickie Battenberg, as he was then called, looked out in childhood on a world that might have been shaped for his delight and for the fulfilment of all the ambitions that crowded into his mind in later years.

Mountbatten as a young man was very close to his father, and resembled him in many ways, something that his mother recognized while he was still a very young boy. 'I was a great father-worshipper', Mountbatten would often say, 'because I did think he was wonderful.' It was a statement that accounted for a great deal in his character and performance in life.

Mountbatten defined himself as a 'semi-royal'. A few years before his death he was puzzled to find himself placed on the right of the hostess at foreign embassies, and later, on being shown a copy of the diplomatic list, saw that it was because he was defined as a 'royal' instead of more correctly as an earl. 'I am a sort of hybrid. My grandfather married a commoner, and I was born a Prince, became a lord and second son of a marquis, then an earl with a lot of letters after my name.'

Randolph Churchill complained in a postscript to a letter to Mountbatten he had just signed: 'You have fourteen letters after your name! Really, Dickie, more than your father.'

What caused Randolph, son of the great statesman who shaped the life of Admiral Prince Louis of Battenberg and his son, Admiral Lord Louis Mountbatten, to exclaim at the number of honours and decorations earned by these men? And what made it so important to the Admirals, father and son, that people should notice them? You have to go back more than a century to find the answers.

The oldest ruling Protestant dynasty in the world is the house of Hesse, set on the River Rhine in Germany. Their roots go back to Charlemagne. The present Queen married a Hessian ('Where did they get all that talent?' she asks), so did her great-great aunt Alice, Queen Victoria's daughter and Lord Mountbatten's grandmother.

The Hessians, great soldiers, married into the Greek, Russian, Spanish, Danish and Swedish royal families, too. They brought with them versatility and great misfortune: they inherited haemophilia from the British royal family, were assassinated by the Bolsheviks, met frequent catastrophe long before Lord Mountbatten and his grandson were murdered in Ireland.

Mountbatten was born a Battenberg instead of a plain Hesse because of another piece of ill-fortune, or ill-judgment. His grandfather, Prince Alexander, eloped with a mere countess, no better than a commoner, so he was stripped of his titles and rank. He became a mercenary, and eventually – solidarity being a first priority in sustaining ancient dynasties – he was accepted back into the fold, but only as a Serene Highness instead of a Royal Highness and only if he took the name Battenberg, which was considered inferior to Hesse by that royal *Who's Who* of the nineteenth century, the *Almanach de Gotha*.

The Battenbergs were an exceptionally gifted couple, and they had a number of children, the first of whom was called Prince Louis. He was born in Graz, Austria, on 24 May 1854. When he was eight his parents took him to stay at Windsor Castle in England with Queen Victoria. The links between the English Hanoverians and the German Hessians were very close. Young Louis fell in love with England, and above all fell in love with the British Navy, which was curious for a boy from a land-locked German state. When the Queen's sailor son, Prince Alfred, came to stay at the Battenberg palace in Darmstadt, Louis asked him, 'Would it be possible for a foreign Prince to serve in your Navy?' Prince Alfred thought it an admirable idea. So did Queen Victoria, the most important person of all. And so the sentimental, home-loving Louis, at his own wish, detached himself from his family and was prepared by a tutor for entry into the Royal Navy, with all its ancient traditions and customs, its special language and protocol, its clubbish exclusivity and harsh practices.

Louis was a pretty boy, with a lot of dark brown hair, a vulnerable demeanour, a German royal title and, of course, a strong German accent. Here was ripe game for bullying, and he was bullied relentlessly. His position was made worse because, at once, he was obliged to accept special privileges. Even his first ship was a royal ship, a frigate prepared for a Mediterranean cruise and tour of Egypt with the Prince and Princess of Wales as passengers, and a suite of titled people on board. Louis longed to conform with the established training routine and way of life of a naval cadet, for all its harshness and strictness. Instead, he found himself alternately mollycoddled and treated roughly in the gunroom by cadets keen to teach this young German upstart a lesson or two.

At one time during those early years, Louis was tempted to throw it in and return to Darmstadt. The rough treatment was one thing, and he learned to stand up for himself. But, brought up in a household in which the arts were cultivated and curious minds and conversation about science and philosophy encouraged, Louis found the philistinism of his fellow officers almost intolerable. But to resign would be to admit defeat, which was contrary to Hessian tradition. Louis overcame his misery and loneliness, and was sent to North America in a two-decker battleship. There he had a chance to travel, and to fall in love, frequently and ardently. But his greatest love affair was with the USA. Like his son later, Louis revelled in the freshness, the open-mindedness, inventiveness and the warm hospitality of the people he met in Detroit and Chicago. He was to come back many times to New York and enjoy the people and the way of life.

But, while he loved America for all his lifetime, it was to England that he surrendered himself over the early years of manhood. He affected the latest fashions and became known as something of a dandy, cultivated English mannerisms, read the latest English books, became an authority on genealogy and titles; and, as his friends would remark, 'became more English than the English'. He grew a full beard, which was almost as standard as the uniform in the Royal Navy, and was generally regarded as one of the most handsome and eligible bachelors, and a Serene Highness too.

The structure of Victorian society made it almost mandatory that his friends were naval officers and the titled and grand. His closest royal friend was the Prince of Wales. Louis became one of 'Bertie's' fast-living 'Marlborough House Set', though he rarely drank or gambled to excess. He accompanied the Prince on a great tour of India, and no doubt shared his mistresses. He certainly had a passionate and long affair with Lillie Langtry, and had a daughter by her.

In spite of his grand connections, and in part because of them, Prince Louis still did not 'fit into' the Royal Navy. To the end of his career he had few friends. The famous Admiral 'Jackie' Fisher, wrote that Louis had only three friends, including Churchill and himself. This was typical Fisher exaggeration. But Louis did not have many. Those friends he had tended to be close ones. The vast majority of serving officers, from the upper middle classes and aristocracy, tended to choose more orthodox friends, more British friends.

Another barrier was Prince Louis' unashamed professionalism, which was very German and very un-British. When Prince Louis entered the Royal Navy he was appalled at the conscious encouragement of the cult of the amateur. He did his best to conform, tried to learn the 'language' and imitate the style. He acquired the nickname 'old soul', a popular contemporary endearment for a male friend, but so overworked by Louis in an effort to conform that the name stuck. Like his future son, he could not help being a professional to the core.

It is a truism that the further one is detached from the harsh, petty realities of life, the less exercised are the imaginative processes. Thus Louis came to take for granted the special privileges of his rank and title, his social life with the Queen and her family on the one hand and the Emperor and Empress of Russia on the other. These royal connections were slightly discomfiting to his fellow officers, and obstructive to the forming of friendships.

Prince Louis made insufficient effort to cure his German accent, and failed to see that regular visits to his German castle and his German naval relations – his brother-in-law was an officer in the German Navy, which was growing in size and hostility – could be misinterpreted. If it was not lack of imagination, it was incredible stupidity in a man of superior intelligence that he failed to recognize the danger signs.

When at last this in many ways extraordinary, clever and charming German-naturalized Englishman decided he had had enough of mistresses, and that he needed a steady wife, he formed a love affair with another German, his own cousin and fellow Hessian, Princess Victoria of Hesse.

Mountbatten's mother, Princess Victoria, was the first child of the future Grand-Duke Louis IV of Hesse and Princess Alice, and was born in Windsor Castle in 1863, the first of the Queen's grandchildren to be born in England, and destined to be her favourite grand-daughter. The Queen herself assisted during the long labour. She had only recently lost her husband (at the Queen's insistence, Victoria's second name was Alberta), and wrote, 'Oh, could my adored one have only seen her, lying so happily with her little Baby in her arms!'[1]

Princess Victoria gave early signs of brilliance, and when she was only six, her mother wrote of her wonderful facility in learning. She was tomboyish, physically vigorous, endlessly curious, a fanatical reader. Even as a girl her face was more interesting than beautiful. Later, she was to say, 'I just had my mind. I accepted that I was not beautiful.'[2]

Princess Victoria was only ten when there occurred the first of the Hessian tragedies which scarred her life. Queen Victoria had unknowingly been a haemophilia agent, a disease that is transmitted through females but only strikes males. One of her sons, Prince Leopold, suffered from it. Two of her daughters, Alice and Beatrice, were also carriers, and both passed this blood disease on to several of their male Hessian children. 'Our poor family seems persecuted by this disease!'[3] the Queen once cried in despair.

Haemophilia was early diagnosed in Princess Victoria's second brother, Prince Frederick. He suffered greatly through his brief childhood. At the age of three he had a bad fall. It might have proved fatal to any child; the unstaunchable bleeding ensured his death.

Tragedy on a greater scale struck the unfortunate family five years later, in 1878, when Princess Victoria contracted diphtheria. The disease rapidly spread to all but one of the family. Teams of nurses and doctors fought to save their lives. Queen Victoria, frantic with anxiety, despatched Sir William Jenner to Darmstadt. But nothing could save the little Princess May, and her mother, Alice, herself succumbed.

The Grand-Duke was among those who recovered. But, since he was a bluff military man with no knowledge of bringing up children, new and heavy responsibilities were suddenly thrust upon Victoria's fifteen-year-old shoulders. There were, of course, nursemaids and teachers in the palace, presided over by an Englishwoman, Miss Mary Anne Orchard. But Victoria was, in effect and at once, a replacement for her mother. Mountbatten said, 'She was the head of the family in every sense because she was much older than any of the others. She really acted as Grand-Duchess to her father, and ran the household. My mother inherited an extraordinary position. She ran the whole place from top to bottom, and ran her own father completely. He just sat at her feet and did as she said.'

Victoria accepted these responsibilities with the equanimity of one born to rule. Supported from afar by her grandmother, Queen Victoria – 'Look upon me as a mother' – and visited frequently by the Queen's children, especially the haemophiliac Uncle Leopold whom they all adored, Victoria continued to run the Darmstadt palace, until she fell in love with Prince Louis of Battenberg and agreed to marry him. He was twenty-eight, a handsome lieutenant, worldly-wise, world-travelled, charming, bronzed, tall – a fairy-tale prince. Victoria was nineteen, quick-witted, showing no signs of the burden of responsibility she had carried since her mother's death. And, unlike Louis, she was in love for the first time.

She had met her English naval cousin several times before. Once, she remembered, he had rowed her about the lake at Buckingham Palace, dressed in morning clothes. She thought him fascinating. Now, in the beautiful spring of 1883, they became engaged; and Louis wrote to his cousin, great naval friend and shipmate, Prince George (the future George v):

My dearest Georgie,
   I have a great piece of news to tell you. Our mutual cousin Victoria has promised to be my wife....

The wedding in April 1884 in Darmstadt was a grand occasion indeed. Even Queen Victoria, who hated visiting Germany, agreed to come.

The Battenbergs' first child was born at Windsor, and Queen Victoria again gave comfort during the long labour. The infant was a girl, Victoria Alice Elizabeth Julie Marie, to be known as Princess Alice. Some five years were to pass before it was learned that she was deaf. (This beautiful and brilliant princess was destined to marry into the Greek royal family and experience more unhappiness and tragedy than her mother, but also to bear four girls, and then – like her mother, much later – a boy, the future Prince Philip, Duke of Edinburgh.)

By the nature of their father's profession, the Battenbergs led a nomadic life, often in rented houses in England or at the naval base of Malta, broken by long visits to the Russian and Hessian courts, at Darmstadt, the summer residence Schloss Wolfsgarten, Heiligenberg, Balmoral or Windsor with the Queen. Like that of most naval people, theirs was a life of trunks, of train and carriage rides accompanied by ladies-in-waiting and servants.

There were two more Battenberg children, Louise in 1889, and George three years later. Victoria, and her ageing grandmother, assumed that that was the end of the family. By June 1899 Louis was a senior captain, with much work of reform and organization behind him, who had just been appointed Assistant Director of Naval Intelligence at the Admiralty.

Victoria was enjoying a summer visit with her family at Wolfsgarten. Two of her sisters had married into the Russian royal family, Ella to Prince Serge, and the solemn, mystical and utterly beautiful Alicky to the Tsar himself. Another sister had married the Emperor of Germany's brother, Prince Henry of Prussia; and the woods and lawns of the schloss rang with the cries of numerous princes and princesses, from crawling infants to leggy adolescents.

The Battenbergs returned to London in October. The South African War had just broken out, and the streets were filled with marching troops singing jingoistic music-hall songs, and bands playing 'Soldiers of the Queen'. Louis had rented a house in Grosvenor Gardens, close by Buckingham Palace. By mid-December Victoria learned for sure that she was expecting another child. She let herself in with her special key to a back gate of the Palace and told the Queen, who was delighted. Then the family took the train to Sandringham where they stayed with the Prince of Wales, himself destined to become King-Emperor in a year's time. Uncle Bertie was thrilled. He loved children. When they returned to London, he took them all to the pantomime.

The Queen lent the Battenbergs Frogmore House in the grounds of Windsor Castle in the New Year, 1900. Louis travelled up to London to his work in Whitehall. Alice was fourteen, Louise ten and Georgie seven. And it was Frogmore House, a short carriage-ride away for Queen Victoria, that became the birthplace of Admiral of the Fleet Earl Mountbatten of Burma. It was a swift labour, and he gave his mother little trouble.

Infant photographs show an irresistibly attractive face, with the clearest eyes and the long, strong nose already evident. In most of them, he is being held by one of his sisters or by Georgie. Walking precociously early, one can imagine the strut, even at little over a year old. Later, when he was two, his mother wrote: 'Baby has been more defiant and swaggering than ever lately, and he and his father have had some serious differences, productive of much loud howling.'[4]

Mountbatten never liked being corrected or proved wrong, and when scolded as a small boy became moody and sulky. He was still under six when he was seen to be marching about the house, after being rebuked, with a cardboard sign hung round his neck with 'IAO' scrawled on it.

'And what does that mean?'

'It stands for "I am offended". I shall wear it every time I am offended.'

In a household in which everybody talked, mostly at the tops of their voices and incessantly – especially his mother and younger sister – Dickie listened thoughtfully, something he always did, although no one ever enjoyed talking more, too. But at first he was inclined to be quiet, and cautious. As a little boy he was not daring. Later, he was quite sure that the story about his choice of future career was true. His aunt, the Empress of All the Russias, had asked him what he wished to be, suggesting in turn 'a sailor like your father', 'a soldier like your uncle', and finally 'perhaps an engine driver?'. All were turned down peremptorily and in turn as too dangerous, for ships always sink, soldiers are shot, and 'the engine might go over the embankment'.

Incarcerated in a clothes cupboard by his mother for some misdemeanour, he was told he would be released only when he was good. Later, his mother became anxious and insisted that he must be good now, and let him out. 'I am not good yet,' he said defiantly, repeated the offence and marched back into the cupboard commanding to be locked in again.

Half an hour passed before he shouted, 'I feel I am good now.'

Dickie was deeply attached to his pets, of which he always had a great number, from a lamb and a squirrel and white mice, to more orthodox ponies and dogs. He idolized his elder brother, and when he learned that Georgie had lost a £5 tip at Osborne Naval College, he saved up his pennies and hocked all his toys to his mother. He could not bear to hear of the suffering of others, and natural catastrophes filled him with undue concern.

Dickie loved uniforms and dressing up and acting in pantomimes. His interest in the theatre and music-hall and amateur theatricals came early, and lasted throughout his life. 'I suppose I've always been a bit of a showman.'

At the age of nine we can see a perky, passionate, sentimental, spoilt but thoroughly engaging little boy. Apart from a short period at a day school in Eaton Square, his only formal education had been given him by his mother. Victoria loved teaching, had taught her older children at home, and always wanted to be a teacher. 'My mother taught me everything. I had a proper school desk, with my weekly timetable pinned up inside. She was a far better teacher than one could hope to find in any expensive private school. What is more, lessons were fun. I never dreaded them, I couldn't wait to get back to them. Every lesson was interesting, and there was nothing she didn't know about.'

Victoria had a special interest in history. 'She always taught me history in an international context. It was parallel history, not vertical history. Kings and Queens and dates were much less important than movements and social trends.' It was the same with geography. 'Not rivers and climates and cities and exports, but people and places. As to languages, we were such an international family that they were no problem, except French. I never learnt

German. I spoke it at the same time as English. My nurse was German, and I never knew which language I was talking, and was completely bilingual until I was about thirteen. At Heiligenberg my aunt Alicky, the Tsarina, talked English to me and the rest of the family, Russian to her servants, German to our staff. So did Uncle Nicky, the Tsar, and all the children. It was completely natural and taken for granted.'

This multi-lingual fluency posed problems to Dickie's eldest sister. When it was finally realized that Alice was deaf – due to thickened eustachian tubes and therefore inoperable – her mother taught her to lip-read as if it were just another subject in her curriculum. She was an unusually intelligent and quick girl and soon learned to lip-read in German, French, English and Greek so that she could keep up with any conversation. If she missed anything, she was told firmly, she was to give no indication of it, and certainly never ask anyone to repeat what they had said. 'You'll soon pick up the flow of conversation again.'

Just as Dickie was a 'semi-royal' boy, so was his education partly like those of male members of the royal family at that time, and partly orthodox. Where it differed from both was in its strongly feminine influence. His mother and sisters, and his governess, and the adoring housemaids, figured far more in his life than his brother and father, whom he tended to admire from afar.

This indulgence that he enjoyed, and the femininity of his surroundings, for the first nine years of his life, were to have a powerful effect upon him. It was one reason why he found it difficult all his life to see his fellow men on an equal level. They tended to be over-admired by him, like his father and brother, and other of his male relations, or seen as protagonists who had to be defeated, and nearly always were.

But Mountbatten was always convinced that he had the best possible initial education. When he went to school at nine years, he was not ahead of his contemporaries. Latin average, mathematics just about adequate. 'But I knew far more about things that don't get marks in exams, and my understanding of history and my knowledge of the world was far ahead of everyone else's,' he would claim, with characteristic immodesty.

This included such special skills as how to address those who were very grand yet closely related, like Russian grand-dukes, German princes and the King of England, still an additional subject on the curriculum of young members of the royal family today. The King was to be addressed in a letter as: 'His Majesty the King, Buckingham Palace, London', and it should begin: 'Dear Cousin George' and end: 'I remain Your dutiful and obedient cousin, Louis Francis Battenberg',[5] the 'of' before Battenberg not being necessary.

Locker's Park, whose headmaster was Percy Christopherson, was a preparatory school for the rich and well-born near Berkhamsted in Hertfordshire. The school motto was 'Do well and be happy.' It was a sound and steady establishment, accustomed to managing royalty. Dickie's elder brother had been there, and so had a number of his princely cousins. But here he came up against his first serious rebuffs from the outside world, and his over-feminine upbringing so far had not equipped him to deal with them. There was a certain amount of mild bullying, and no doubt he over-reacted to it. There are references to punch-ups and bruises in his letters at this time, and to a severe cut on the chin from a fight with a future admiral. He was poor at football, which counted against him, and only average in his lessons. He got across his French teacher, a Frenchman called Craig, of seemingly modest accomplishment and understanding, or perhaps as a good republican he was prejudiced against royal princes, especially one with a German-born father – the French defeat in the war against Germany only forty years earlier still rankled.

At length, Dickie complained to his mother about a particular incident with Craig. She wrote back a wise and understanding letter. She was not over-protective towards her younger son. Nor did she always take his side. Dickie may have been spoilt by his brother and sisters and family and the staff, and often by his mother, too, but she could be firm with him, moulding his character into a blend of the best qualities of her own and her husband's: kind without being patronizing, behaving with all classes equally, talking to them naturally no matter what their background and upbringing and education, evincing interest in everything. Apathy and idleness were two of the worst sins, compassion and understanding two of the worthiest characteristics to cultivate.

Victoria herself had benefited, on the English side of the North Sea, from the puritanism and severe self-discipline of her grandmother's reign, and on the German side from the emancipated liberalism and appreciation of the arts of the Hessian court. For example, she detested English cooking but admired English novelists, Dickens especially; hated English acceptance of discomfort and cold in winter but admired English inventiveness and parliamentary democracy. Her lucidity, her enquiring mind that never ceased questioning everything, her enthusiasm and determination to convert others to her way of thinking, her natural acceptance of leadership – all these she passed on to her younger son.

She wrote to him at school regularly, expressing her love unselfconsciously and accompanying it with advice on a wide range of subjects. 'Do not talk to the other boys too much about it,' she told him before the funeral of his uncle, King Edward VII, when he would be taking a privileged part in the proceedings. Also, 'You will try hard not to think about it when your thoughts are needed for your work.'[6]

His mother's influence and love were strongly present all through Dickie's life, until she died at the ripe age of eighty-seven. Until he left Locker's Park, she remained the dominant parent. It was Victoria who ran his life. His father was an admired but more distant figure, often absent at the Admiralty or abroad, engaged on affairs of state and security at the highest level. It was not always a case of admiring from afar. Dickie would see him when he was ashore at Dover, where they stayed at the Burlington Hotel, or Sheerness, on board his flagship in the Mediterranean where Dickie was the idol of the ship's company, and – now in civilian clothes – in London when he went to the Admiralty as Second Sea Lord at the end of 1911.

But the emphasis of parental influence shifted inevitably and naturally when Dickie entered the Royal Naval College at Osborne on the Isle of Wight, donned the cap and round jacket of a naval cadet, and left childhood behind as Cadet Prince Louis of Battenberg; or, to avoid confusion, 'the young Prince Louis'.

'It never at any remote moment ever entered my mind – it never even occurred to me – I had no other plans whatsoever – than go into the Navy.' With his father nearing the top of the Navy, his brother already a midshipman, the family solidarity as strong as it was, no other career was conceivable. The Royal Navy was, in his eyes, quite simply the greatest service in the world, and he was destined to remain on active service duty, from cadet to Admiral of the Fleet, for fifty-two years, until 1965.

Life at Osborne was tough for all the cadets. It was part of the process of 'knocking off the rough edges', of 'bringing down to size', and the other convenient contemporary clichés that covered the shaping of pliable youth to a common pattern for a life demanding discipline and initiative, self-restraint and responsibility, self-assurance without arrogance. Bullying was the crude beginning of the process, the first hacks with a blunt blade. It was not actively encouraged, nor was it discouraged, unless outside reasonable limits. It was, then, considered inevitable as today it is universally condemned. Certain new cadets could at once be picked out by the older cadets as particularly ripe game; and who riper than this Serene Highness, slim in build and vulnerable in appearance, with a German-born father who was also – now – First Sea Lord?

They went for young Dickie, this little prince with the pretty smile, and bloodied his nose. Dickie was ready and forewarned, by his father and brother. 'They'll try to knock you about, Dickie. You know what to do. If you don't stand up for yourself....' Dickie did. Sixty years later he recalled, 'Admiral Sir Percy Scott had an odious son called John d'Urban

Scott. I had known him at Locker's Park and disliked him very much. He was a term senior to me, and started to bully me at once, and knocked my cap off. So I knocked his cap off and we had a fight, and I won.' At the time, he wrote to his mother jubilantly. 'A lot of chaps in second term egged me on to fight him, which I did ... and I've become a hero.'[7]

Osborne taught him no more useful lesson than that it pays to make your mark firmly and at the outset; a lesson that he applied in every command, from his first to Supreme Commander South-East Asia. But the period as hero was brief. Some of his fellow cadets found his style brash and cocky, others were fearful of being thought ingratiating to the King's cousin and the First Sea Lord's son. On the first of many occasions in his service life, Mountbatten was lonely.

One day the young First Lord of the Admiralty came on an official visit to Osborne. Winston Churchill was already nationally famous as the son of Lord Randolph Churchill and grandson of the 7th Duke of Marlborough, as a hero of the South African War and a dynamic politician. At present he was working effectively in harness with Dickie's father in preparing the Navy for the coming Armageddon. In another generation, and another war, it would be Dickie's turn to work with Churchill and no one would have a deeper and more profound influence on the shape of his career than the portly statesman who now stood up to address the assembled cadets before leaving.

'Do any of you have any request to make?' he asked at the end.

Dickie was the first on his feet. 'Please, sir, may we please have three sardines for Saturday supper instead of only two?'

'I'll see to that,' Churchill assured him.

These were the first words they ever exchanged. The sardines were never forthcoming. In later years Mountbatten said, 'From that time I never trusted him.'

Dickie was not doing any better academically than at Locker's Park. By contrast with Georgie, Dickie was considered slow. Mountbatten always said that his older brother was much cleverer than he was. The difference rested more with the approach to learning than to the relative intelligence of the two sons. Georgie was regarded as the bright one by Louis and Victoria because he went straight at a subject, and did indeed have a very considerable brain and always came out top. But Dickie's mind had a profundity lacking in his elder brother's. He inclined to walk round a problem, to survey it from every angle, and consider the implications and the consequences of each approach. Later, he became very quick at this assessment process but he never missed it. He may not have been as clever in the literal sense, but his mind was broader and more imaginative.

The contrast between term-time at Osborne and holidays at the Russian or German palaces and castles, or at Mall House in the Admiralty, the First Sea Lord's official residence, was striking. One week it would be 'show a leg' at 6.30 am, a naked race to a cold bath, exercises, a spartan breakfast, a series of lessons in mathematics, signalling, seamanship and knot-tying, interspersed with games, at which Dickie still did not shine. Then, the next week he might be with his family in the fairy-tale splendour of Heiligenberg: adoring servants, rich German food, visits to and from loving relatives, rides and dances and fancy dress parties.

The last summer at Heiligenberg in 1913 stood out in Mountbatten's memory, with the visual assistance of photographs of smiling young faces – seemingly all of them attractive and intelligent – and princes and princesses, grand-dukes and grand-duchesses: Prince and Princess Henry of Prussia, the Emperor and Empress of Russia, all with the stance and stamp of authority; and so many, alas, destined for assassination, exile, or at best the loss of home and title.

The photographs show the boys in sailor suits, the little haemophiliac Tsarevitch in Russian sailor's uniform, pale and slim, the girls in flounced, high-necked frilly silk dresses and wide-brimmed straw hats against the sun, like naval sennit hats. There are babies in big prams with nurses, little children holding the hands of older children, numerous pets, and in the background of what appears to be an eternal summer scene of joy, waiting open carriages for a visit to Darmstadt or Wolfsgarten.

Another photograph taken on the same day of the same faces will reveal quite different clothes and uniforms, as if this party is a fancy dress pageant of many acts. Dickie himself – already fascinated by uniforms and medals and decorations and orders and badges of rank – might be wearing the uniform of one of the Evzon Guards given him by the King of Greece, or the Cossack uniform presented by his uncle the Tsar, or the miniature Hessian Life Guards uniform, a present from another uncle, the Grand-Duke of Hesse and by the Rhine.

'At Heiligenberg,' Mountbatten recalled, 'there were tennis courts and all sorts of games like diabolo, and we went on picnics up into the hills and forests, and we had ponies to ride. And then in the evenings we had more games. I remember I wore my cutaway coat for the first time, and it was much admired by my cousins and I was terribly proud. There were a lot of us, and it was really just like any other family.'

The Russian family were there in full strength, and Dickie fell seriously in love for the first time. He was just thirteen, and utterly susceptible to the looks and charm of the Tsar's daughters. Olga was eighteen, Tatiana sixteen, Marie fourteen and Anastasia twelve. 'Oh, they were lovely, and terribly sweet, far more beautiful than their photographs show. I was crackers about Marie, and was determined to marry her. She was absolutely lovely. I keep her photograph on the mantelpiece in my bedroom – always have.'

Then there was Nicky, the Tsar, looking so much like Louis' old ship-mate, Georgie, now King, but much gayer and more irresponsible, simple and family-loving. And his behaviour to his son, the pale, vulnerable, laughing little Tsarevitch, nine years old and the spoilt darling of them all, was very different from George V's to his sons.

This was well known among all the party at Heiligenberg, as was the story about Lord Derby approaching the King and asking him if he could not be more friends with his children and make them less afraid of him. After some thought, he turned round and said, 'My father was afraid of his father, I was afraid of my father, and I don't see why my children shouldn't be afraid of me.'

There was none of that Hanoverian nonsense at Heiligenberg in the hot summer of 1913, or at any other time. It was all love and happiness. The Grand-Duke of Hesse, Uncle Ernie, who had succeeded to the title eleven years earlier, had had one disastrous marriage but was now happy with 'Onor', the former Princess Eleanore of Lich. Their first child, Don, the heir to the title, was just seven – one more Hessian destined for tragedy. Of the families at Wolfsgarten and Heiligenberg, Mountbatten recalled: 'They were all charming, every one of them. Even that crazy lunatic my aunt the Empress [of Russia] was absolutely sweet and charming.'

Mountbatten also at one point overheard his father say to his mother (for Victoria was always expected to put everything right), 'Alicky is absolutely mad – she's going to cause a revolution. Can't you *do* anything?' And Dickie's mother replied, 'Well, I am doing all I can,' knowing only too well the hard line that Alicky was forcing her husband to take towards any sort of reform, and the influence Rasputin held over her. But, alas, for once it was not enough. And it was the last time that Dickie would see his beautiful Marie, or the rest of the Russian royal family.

Another portent of doom for the Hessians was the new invention – flying. Both Dickie's father and the Grand-Duke were great enthusiasts. As early as 1906 the Grand-Duke had taken up the family in a Parsifal airship from the grounds of Wolfsgarten. Dickie had been told he was too young for flying, but at the last minute Uncle Ernie found they were short on ballast, and had reached down and dragged the boy into the sketchy gondola.

There was more flying after that. Three years later, Dickie had been taken to an international exhibition of heavier- and lighter-than-air machines at Frankfurt. In that same year, 1909, Messrs Wilbur and Orville Wright wrote to the British Admiralty to enquire if they might be interested in their flying machines. When Louis, who did so much to support the creation of a Fleet Air Arm, went to the Admiralty in 1911 as Second Sea Lord, he found a copy of the reply, which he later enjoyed quoting as an example of the refusal of the Navy to move with the times: 'Gentlemen, I am commanded by my Lord's Commissioners to the Admiralty to acknowledge your letter in which you enquire whether you can interest the Admiralty in aviation. I am to reply that their Lordships can see no possible advantage that aviation could have for the Royal Navy.'

In 1912 Uncle Ernie took up many parties from Wolfsgarten in the Zeppelin *Victoria Louise* for flights around Hesse, with champagne and caviare. Dickie had already flown for the first time in an aeroplane, a very primitive naval machine of the first unit formed, in which he sat straddled across the fuel tank, clutching two wire struts. Many years later, Mountbatten could not help looking back to this time. He wondered how his parents would have reacted if they had known that in one Anglo-German war Zeppelins like the *Victoria Louise* were to drop bombs on London, and, in the next, descendants of Dickie's first British machine were to wipe Darmstadt virtually clean off the map.

The last summer of peace for Europe and for the Hessians at Wolfsgarten and Heiligenberg faded into early autumn. In one final pilgrimage, the families moved north, with great quantities of luggage containing their dresses and suits and hats for all occasions, their guns and rods and racquets, their uniforms and orders and decorations. (Dickie already had his first of the countless number of decorations he was to acquire: the Coronation Medal from King George, which he wore proudly and for which he got mercilessly teased at Osborne.)

With them came their ladies-in-waiting and servants and their pets, the smaller held in arms, the rest in special cages. They stopped first at the family seat of Prince Henry, now a Grand Admiral of the German Navy, and in twelve months' time Louis' bitter antagonist. There was plenty of naval talk – there always was – and the latest types of ships were discussed. But it was all immensely friendly, in spite of the fact that Germany now had almost as great a fleet of Dreadnoughts as Britain, built in scarcely more than a decade, and with only one enemy in view.

Prince Henry, a Prussian through and through, brother of the Emperor Kaiser Wilhelm II, had married Dickie's Aunt Irène, who, like the Russian Empress, had one haemophiliac son and had already lost an earlier one at the age of four.

Then it was Kiel. Dickie saw the Russian royal yacht, *Standardt*, anchored in the harbour among a host of German men o'war from grey, great battle-ships to dark little torpedo boats. 'It was a beautiful yacht, with every con-ceivable comfort. We all went on board and were given the most lavish cabins – very different from Osborne where we slept forty to a wooden hut.'

It was a last fairy-tale cruise in a fairy-tale vessel, through the Kiel Canal which had been constructed to facilitate the German Fleet's passage from the direction of one future enemy in the east to the other in the west. The Russian yachtsmen, who spoke no English but were hand picked, played with the children, and took special delicate care of the haemophiliac Tsare-vitch, for whom one small fall could bring weeks of pain and anxiety. There were boat rides, swimming and paddling on the Baltic coast.

Then the party broke up. The *Standardt* proceeded up the Baltic, the Germans returned to Germany, the Battenbergs to England.

Even before he had entered Osborne, Dickie had been aware of the dangers that threatened Europe. In the evenings and at meals, the talk was often of the political and defence manœuvrings of the nations that were to align against one another as the Allies and the Central Powers. And it was highly informed talk. No one was better connected to the top politicians and defence chiefs than Prince Louis. 'I remember standing in the main hall of Buck-ingham Palace', said Mountbatten, 'before all the really important people left for the coronation of my cousin, George V, in 1911. My father turned to me and said, "Now pay attention. I am going to introduce you to a very great man, Field Marshal Lord Kitchener. Have a good look at him, because in the war that is inevitably coming, he will be the great soldier because they will call him back to run the army." I remember looking up and seeing this great figure and shaking the hand that was offered to me. My father and Kitchener got on very well, far better than Churchill and Kitchener.'

After Louis became First Sea Lord, Churchill was often at Mall House. Dickie remembered the plump figure with the clever, pixie-like face, the darting eyes, the slight lisp in his brilliant conversation, and inevitably the cigar. 'He seemed incredibly young even in my eyes, but he and my father were marvellous together. They complemented one another so well – my father with his unsurpassed knowledge of the service of which Churchill was political head, and Churchill the canny political animal, very devious, bursting with energy and determination, learning as hard as he could go.'

Dickie frequently heard his father declare that there must inevitably be a great war. As night follows day, Europe would be convulsed in a bloody upheaval. Louis knew the Kaiser too well to believe anything else, had pleaded with him many times to restrain his hell-bent course to Armaged-don, had – under the instruction of King Edward VII – mediated with his

German nephew over the 'Tangier incident' in 1905, which had already brought the two powers close to conflict.

War was inevitable, and imminent. But the immediate demands and events of life at a naval college filled Dickie's mind in the months ahead. While his father hastened to develop a proper naval staff which he had brought into being belatedly and against a reactionary tide in the Navy's hierarchy; while he developed a scheme for insuring merchant shipping in time of war; while he gave his blessing to the development of an air arm, and the further development of new fighting ships like the submarine and new weapons like the mine and torpedo, and dealt with the multitudinous tasks of running the greatest navy in the world and the greatest navy of all time; while all this was being conducted in the corridors of Whitehall and in the fleets and squadrons and naval bases, his son was working at mathematics and seamanship, navigation and pilotage, algebra and small arms practice, on the Isle of Wight.

Dickie was doing better, but his marks were still not brilliant, and he was generally regarded by his instructors as slow and dreamy. 'I got beaten yesterday with some cow-hide for passing out water at lunch before Grace,' he wrote to his mother jauntily. 'It warmed my stern up a bit.' There are references to falls and cuts and bruises – an unusual number even for his age. Some of these were no doubt a consequence of fights. Certainly the bullying continued, and certainly he defended himself stoutly. Long before the crisis of the high summer of 1914 developed, the innuendos about his father's German origin were being hurled at Dickie. On 21 June he wrote bleakly to his mother, 'I have got only one real chum left now, Graham. Stopford got so ragged about being chums with me that he has chucked it.'[8]

Dickie would be thankful when the term was over, when, after a test mobilization of the Navy's reserves and an inspection of the Fleets by the King, he would be going to Russia again with his father to join Victoria and his sister Louise who were already there. While his father conducted preliminary negotiations for a naval treaty with the Tsar and his naval advisers, he could renew his affair with darling Marie.

That was the plan. And then three days after Dickie's fourteenth birthday, the Archduke Franz Ferdinand of Austria and his wife were assassinated at Sarajevo; and from then the crisis deepened, and it seemed less and less likely that they would be going to Russia after all. The mobilization, the first for years and an uncannily prescient piece of planning by Louis, went ahead; and, this time, it included all the cadets at Osborne, and their seniors at Dartmouth Naval College.

Amidst all the hurly-burly of transporting some twenty thousand civilian part-time sailors from all parts of the country to their allotted ships, and of assembling these ships at Spithead – fifty-nine battleships and battle cruisers and a hundred and thirty-three cruisers and destroyers and countless smaller craft – a single very small but well-oiled cog spun into motion and ensured that Cadet Prince Louis of Battenberg found himself on board the great battle cruiser of his elder brother Lieutenant Prince George of Battenberg, and sharing his cabin.

From the decks of the *New Zealand*, Dickie participated in the royal review, the greatest since the coronation. 'It took more than six hours,' wrote Churchill, 'for this armada, every ship decked with flags and crowded with bluejackets and marines, to pass with bands playing and at fifteen knots before the Royal Yacht, while overhead the naval seaplanes and aeroplanes circled continuously.'[9]

'Men o'war were to be a part of the fabric of my life for the next half century,' Mountbatten recalled, 'but I would never again see a sight like this. No one had beaten us at sea for centuries, and how could they now, against all this might? That's what was going through my mind.'

His account written at the time to his mother in Russia was more prosaic. 'Papa arrived and we had church, after which we had lunch with the skipper. After lunch we went on board the *Enchantress* [Admiralty yacht], and saw Winston Churchill, Mrs and Miss Hogier [Hozier] or something, also Admiral Jellicoe and the Fourth Sea Lord, and Admiral Hood etc. Georgie took the female Winston Churchills back to the *New Zealand* for tea.'[10]

For all his fourteen years, Dickie had observed life 'at the top', among kings and emperors, prime ministers, presidents and grand-dukes. Now, a mere fourth-term cadet with an undistinguished record, he was observing the navy 'at the top', and by reason of his exalted station would have access to the highest in the service as well as the highest in the land for the rest of his life.

His father returned to the Admiralty to face a series of decisions as crucial as those which had confronted Lord Barham in the Napoleonic Wars. Not only was he certain that there would be war; he knew that it was imminent. Nerves were on a knife edge in all the chancelleries of Europe, and every decision had to be closely examined for any possible sensitive reaction from abroad. The Navy's reserves were due to be demobilized and to return to their homes on 27 July. Without them, the Fleet would be gravely weakened if – as many feared – the German Navy sprang a massive surprise attack.

On Sunday 26 July Louis was alone in his office at the Admiralty. Churchill had gone to the seaside to join his family. The Prime Minister and Foreign Secretary and most of the cabinet were absent from London, too. ('Ministers with their week-end holidays are incorrigible,' Louis exclaimed

to Dickie a few days later.) On Friday the Austrians had sent a threatening
ultimatum to Serbia. For Britain to cancel the demobilization of her Fleet
reserves would inevitably be seen as an overture to war.

After an unsatisfactory telephone conversation with Churchill – the line
was bad – it seemed that the decision was left to the First Sea Lord. When
the telegrams arriving in London suggested a heightening of the crisis,
Louis took the calculated risk of reversing the demobilization. The vast
machinery of sending out the messages, of cancelling trains and reversing
the dispersal of all the personnel, and the recovery of some who had already
left, snapped into motion. Louis then informed the Foreign Office of his
decision, and on the next morning drove to Buckingham Palace to explain
to George v what he had done and why he had done it. Later, on Churchill's
return, Louis was praised for his timely action. The Fleet, told to 'stand fast',
was ready for war, and hostilities could be only days away.

Dickie arrived in London from Osborne a few days later. The older Dartmouth cadets had remained on board their ships, and many were to die in
one of the Navy's early disasters, but the junior Osborne cadets were considered too young and inexperienced for war. It was an exciting time to be
in Mall House, but from the family point of view, it was disappointing.
There would now be no visit to Russia, no Marie. His mother and sister
were already on their way home via Norway. His father was even more concerned with great affairs than ever. Feeling at a loss for companionship
and occupation, Dickie took the bus to Selfridge's, and in the store's pet
department bought some white mice and a cage with his pocket money. Pet
animals had always been a comfort.

On the evening of 4 August 1914, father and son, admiral and cadet, with
forty-six years between them, dined alone at Mall House. The silver, and
the mahogany table at which they sat, glinted in the candlelight. The butler
silently supervised the single naval servant in his white jacket as he waited
on them. They could hear the sounds of cheering and shouting from the
Mall and Trafalgar Square, muffled by the heavy curtains. The people of
London were celebrating the start, at midnight, of a war with Germany that
would result in the death of a million soldiers from Britain and the Empire
alone, and the maiming of a million more. For Louis it was the blackest day
of his life. His adopted country would be fighting his own homeland, and
he knew from his highly informed position that this was going to be a long
and cruel war.

'I felt half excited and elated, half sorry for my father and very sorry that
I was only fourteen,' Mountbatten recalled. 'All the boys at Osborne knew
that it was going to be a quick, crushing victory over Germany, and that

there would be a huge battle in the North Sea which we would easily win.'
Dickie looked forward to Georgie's account of it: that was the best he could
hope for.

Now he learned from his father the real truth. That it would not be over
by Christmas, that the German Fleet was very powerful, in some ways more
powerful than the British one. They discussed the political situation that
had led up to the crisis, the progress of the German army against France
and Belgium, of the organization of the Navy to transport safely the small
British army across the Channel to join in the fight, the likely use of submarines. It was a typically masculine conversation, with Dickie – as always
– encouraged to say his piece. Then the Admiral arose to proceed to the
Admiralty War Room, to check on the latest situation and issue a series of
last-minute orders; and Dickie withdrew to his room and played with his
white mice.

The Osborne cadets, with their cocky assumptions, were of course quite
wrong. But no one had predicted that the first three months of the war at
sea would bring so many setbacks, losses and disasters. While the cadets
were still on their summer leave, the Navy won its only victory in Prince
Louis' term of office, in a chaotic skirmish close to the German coast, when
three German light cruisers and a destroyer were sunk. After that, and after
the term began at Osborne, the news was bad. Already two powerful German
men o'war, the *Breslau* and the *Goeben*, had evaded a vastly superior British
force and reached Turkey, which promptly came in on the German side.
There would be many recriminations. Then three big cruisers were sunk
by a single submarine on the same day in the North Sea, with grave loss
of life. A powerful force of German cruisers in the Pacific was causing havoc
to shipping, and the *Emden* had begun her long and famous cruise of destruction. The same force was soon to destroy the greater part of a British squadron sent out to find it.

The Press, at first restive at the absence of another Trafalgar, with Jellicoe
the new Nelson, began to ask questions about the management of the war
at sea. Inevitably, fingers pointed at the German-born First Sea Lord. Spy
stories were rampant. The nation was seized with anti-German fever, which
the newspapers and gossip-spreaders encouraged. Was there a German spy
at the very top?

Prince Louis had made many naval enemies among those who were jealous
of his powers and his influence in royal circles, were irritated by his German
thoroughness and accent, neither of which was sufficiently concealed. It was
recalled that he had made frequent trips to Germany almost up to the outbreak of war, that he had visited his relative, Prince Henry, Grand Admiral

of the enemy fleet, that he even had the ear of the Kaiser. Once a German always a German, it was said by those who were ignorant or envious. A Hun running the Admiralty, when the nation was fighting for its life!

The campaign of suspicion and denigration built up rapidly, and found eager ears at Osborne, where almost every cadet had relatives high in the Navy, and not all of them Prince Louis' men. Dickie was at first stunned by the implications, and then outraged. 'What do you think the latest rumour that got in here from outside is?' he asked of his mother in a letter. 'That Papa has turned out to be a German spy and has been discreetly marched off to the Tower, where he is guarded by beefeaters. ... I got rather a rotten time of it for about three days as little fools insisted on calling me a German Spy.'[11] Others called him 'a bloody Hun'.

Dickie's mother was not surprised to receive this letter. At Mall House, she was in the heart of the political storm raging about the Admiralty. She had observed, with distress, her husband's suffering on seeing the assaults of the gutter press and the ever increasing numbers of anonymous and venomous letters. He was being broken on the rack, and she knew that the campaign was seriously affecting his ability to run the war at sea. Churchill, recently returned from Belgium, where he had been supervising the defence of Antwerp ('Our friend must be quite off his head!' George v's private secretary commented) recognized that his partner would have to go, for his own political future was at stake as well as the Royal Navy. On 27 October a highly valuable modern Dreadnought battleship was sunk by a mine – another blow among so many and one which brought the German battle fleet almost to equality in numbers.

Even the Prime Minister, who admired Prince Louis so much; even Victoria herself, recognized that there was no alternative to resignation. 'With uncomplaining dignity worthy of a sailor and a Prince,' as Churchill described his going, Louis did as he was told and resigned with a letter which began, 'I have lately been driven to the painful conclusion that at this juncture my birth and parentage have the effect of impairing in some respects my usefulness.'[12]

But in his heart he was hurt and bitter. 'The hurt showed in his tired, lined face,'[13] commented the Prince of Wales. He had given his whole working life to his adopted nation and her first arm of defence, and he was being tossed aside at the supreme moment of crisis.

'It is the penalty of serving a democracy,' wrote Victoria, for whom the humiliation was almost unbearable, 'the "man in the street" is mighty.' But she did not spare her words on the government which 'with the exception of Lord Kitchener, few greatly respect or trust'.[14]

Letters of sympathy and outrage poured into Mall House from shipmates

– ratings to retired admirals – and from friends and relatives and people of eminence with unprejudiced minds. The mood was summed up by Lord Selborne, recent First Lord, who described the end of Prince Louis' career as 'nothing short of a national humiliation'.

The dismissal of his father had the same long-range effect on his younger son as a plunging salvo of shell-fire upon one of Prince Louis' Dreadnought battleships. It marked one more of the catastrophes that have plagued the Hessian dynasty.

Churchill's dismissal of Prince Louis was also as fatal, if less sudden and violent, as the bomb which killed his son. The Admiral lingered on for seven years to die prematurely of a heart attack. That was the medical diagnosis. But his family knew that his heart had been broken on that October day, when the German armies were still marching on Paris, and the threat of the German Fleet was even more dangerous than that of the French Fleet had been in Nelson's time.

When, forty-one years later, Winston Churchill, complaining bitterly, appointed Lord Mountbatten First Sea Lord, justice, it was said, had been done; a great wrong righted. Every newspaper had its own cliché for the occasion, except for Lord Beaverbrook's *Daily Express*, still in the full throes of its vendetta against Mountbatten. In company with the clichés came the anecdotes, some apocryphal, others true. There was, inevitably, the story of young Mountbatten, in 1914 Cadet His Serene Highness Prince Louis of Battenberg, seen standing at attention on the parade ground under the flagpole at Osborne Naval College. He has just heard the news of his father's resignation. As he salutes, the tears are pouring down his cheeks.

Mountbatten loved stories about himself. His appetite for them was insatiable. 'Oh yes,' he said about this one, and many others that may appear as equally absurd yet romantic, 'yes, that's right – perfectly true.'

But when asked about a special power, a special vengeful thrust, that drove him on to become a post-captain at thirty-six, a great war leader at forty-three commanding all three services – American, British and Imperial – in the Far East, and First Sea Lord at fifty-four, he would say, 'It's a curious state of affairs. I must obviously have had a great urge, impelled on me by my father's example, and the fact of his tragic resignation. Too many people say they have heard me say in the past, "I am going to right a great wrong" or something like that, for it not to be true.'

Mountbatten might then divert into some anecdote, a practice he always enjoyed. But he would come back to the original question again, for, like the multitude of tasks he took on, he completed everything to his satisfaction: 'I don't want it to be thought that I was trying to avenge his fate.

I think words were probably put into my mouth. People kept on saying, "After all those terrible things they said about your father, you must be searching for a chance to put things right, to wipe the slate clean. Oh, yes, you'll be First Sea Lord." And then I probably grinned and said, "I hope so." It was something wished on me. It wasn't really resentment that drove me on through my naval career.'

Without doubt, Mountbatten's appointment as First Sea Lord was the culminating point of his professional life; more important than his appointment as Chief of Combined Operations, achieved by leaping over the heads of countless British and American senior officers to become Commander-in-Chief South-East Asia Command; a greater moment than the acceptance of the Japanese surrender in Singapore, and, later, his appointment as the last Viceroy of India with supreme power over hundreds of millions of people. Towards the end of his life, when presented with proofs of the family history containing a bare list of chief characters (representing a cross between *Debrett's Peerage* and the *Almanach de Gotha*) against his own name, he firmly added: 'First Sea Lord 1955'. That was all he wanted.

If Mountbatten found it uncharacteristically difficult to express the reason for his lifelong determination to achieve this appointment, and his satisfaction in its fulfilment, it is possible for others to do so. It was not to right a great wrong nor to avenge an injustice. It was to restore the family honour and its name in the annals of history, and to complete an interrupted tour of family duty.

'We are not going to mope or hang our heads,' declared Victoria. But the psychological shock for her husband was profound and he never fully recovered. From working sixteen hours a day at the very centre of the war machine, bearing as great a burden as anyone in high command, he was reduced to idleness and impotence, with little more than the promise of reinstatement, and the chance to hoist his flag again when it was all over, to support him. He retired to the Isle of Wight where they had a house, from which he emerged from time to time to go to London on family business, or perhaps to visit the wounded in hospital. He took up medal-collecting as a hobby, and painted – he was a good artist. Victoria, who never could bear idleness, worked with maniacal energy on the garden.

Churchill did not survive for long without his partner. He and Louis complemented one another ideally and had worked in harmony – two aristocrats with wide-ranging, progressive minds, the older admiral instructing yet restraining the clever young politician's excesses. Ironically, Louis' 'German view' and his understanding of the German mind had been invaluable to Churchill and the Board of Admiralty.

Like his mother, Mountbatten always loved speculating on the 'ifs' of history. 'What would have happened if my father had been an Englishman?' he once said. 'To begin with, he would have suffered under no pressure, for he was made completely on edge by these attacks and very nearly had what we now call a nervous breakdown. If he had been English the two of them would certainly have survived those early months. Don't forget that the annihilating victory at the Falkland Islands took place only five weeks after his resignation – and it was he who urged the sending of battle-cruisers after von Spee. He and Winston would have worked hand in hand for the duration. What's more, he would have worked marvellously with Kitchener, who was the world's most hopeless administrator. There would have been no Dardanelles nonsense, no "wilderness" for Winston, and success and honour for them both. . . .'

Some years ago Mountbatten had a talk with Lady Soames, Churchill's youngest daughter, which was not an 'if' historical discussion, but touched on the relationship between their fathers and was highly revealing. 'My belief,' said Mountbatten, 'is that in 1911 your father was young and immature but full of dash and go, and when he went to the Admiralty was full of desire to do things, but was at first frustrated by "Tug" Wilson, Bridgeman and Co. But he fell for my father in a big way when he was appointed Second Sea Lord. The Admiralty was in an almighty mess, but he saw that my father was progressive and open-minded, and above all his ideas were in tune with your father's.'

Mary Soames expressed agreement with this; and Mountbatten continued, 'I believe, too, that your father recognized that mine had a direct link with the royal family, which was always useful. Now, when war became imminent, my father must have discussed the dangers of his position if there was a war with Germany. I am quite sure he said, "Look, I think I should be replaced now." But your father would not agree. Why not?'

Mountbatten was not satisfied with Mary Soames's belief that it was because he liked him so much. 'I know he did,' Mountbatten persisted, 'but that's not a good enough reason. I think you've got to search deeper. I think Winston realized that my father was the sort of person who would allow him to operate without causing a mutiny in high quarters. He knew that he could leave the Admiralty in his safe hands when he went off on those ridiculously long cruises. This he could not have done with any other Admiral at that time. He was essential. And when war came, he begged my father to stay. And my father was flattered and made the very great mistake of staying on. And the moment my father went,' Mountbatten continued, 'Winston had to find someone else in a hurry, and went back to that old has-been, Jackie Fisher, which was an act bordering on lunacy.'

Prince Louis' comment was: 'They will blow each other out of office.' And he was right. Within a few months, the young politician and old salt were at loggerheads over the Dardanelles. Churchill got his way, and they floundered on the beaches of Gallipoli. By mid-1915 they were both out.

When Dickie heard the news, he wrote plaintively to his mother, 'What are things coming to? Do you think they'll want Papa back?' But like Jackie Fisher, Prince Louis was out for all time, and now it was up to his sons to put the family record straight.

2
THE GOLDEN COUPLE

'A YOUNG NAVAL OFFICER, injured and in hospital,' wrote Dickie, 'desires correspondence.' Then he signed the letter 'Battenberg' and sent it off to the local newspaper.

In a way, it was true. He had had another accident, this time breaking his ankle while making one of those valiant efforts to master a new sport in half the time anyone else had achieved. This time it was skating. He was in bed in the sick quarters, his foot in plaster, bored, deprived of attention. The letters came pouring in, some proposing marriage. He sent them off to his brother, suggesting that they should be distributed about the *New Zealand*'s wardroom. In this way, some of them were, presumably, answered. Mountbatten recalled the incident with amusement as a boy's prank.

There is no early evidence of the cadet's eagerness to forward his career after the dismissal of his father and the distress it caused him. This was something that built up slowly and progressively, and did not come, as some later believed, in the form of an explosion. 'I was a slow starter,' he said.

At Dartmouth, he failed to become a class captain, a rank suggesting good potential officer qualities. He had passed out finally from Osborne thirty-fifth of eighty in his term: a mediocre rating revealing no augury of future greatness. At Dartmouth, he was distinguished only for his single-stick fencing, an unpopular sport in which he figured second. A contemporary described him as 'very hard-working, passionately interested in military decorations, and rather worried about the condition of his complexion'.

The Dartmouth course was reduced from two years to one in the emergency circumstances of war, but Dickie – to his chagrin – was still at the college when the Battle of Jutland was fought on 31 May–1 June 1916. His brother, lieutenant of a heavy gun turret in his battle-cruiser, had already fought at Heligoland Bight and at the Battle of Dogger Bank in 1915, and was in the thick of this massive engagement.

The Germans had inflicted the greater damage but were thankful to escape.

Georgie told his envious, admiring younger brother how his was the first big ship to sight the enemy, how they had disabled two and sunk one of Hipper's battle-cruisers, and how lucky the *New Zealand* had been to escape unscathed in the prolonged gunnery duel, at one time steaming through the falling debris of the 26,000-ton *Queen Mary* after her magazines blew up.

The battle-cruiser commander, Admiral Sir David Beatty, was Dickie's hero, and Dickie had no time at all for the insignificant commander-in-chief, John Jellicoe, 'without style and looking like a frightened tapir. Beatty had dash, elan, and loads of style,' Mountbatten claimed. 'I loved the man, his cap jauntily aslant, really going for the enemy, giving the order to close Hipper's ships after two of his own had blown up.'

Dickie's father was more cautious in his opinion of Beatty. He had appointed Jellicoe as supreme commander, and admired his coolness, judgment and exceptional intellectual ability. But it was the Battle-Cruiser Squadron that saw most of the action, and, in answer to Dickie's pleas, Louis pulled strings to ensure that he was appointed to Beatty's flagship, the *Lion*, when he had qualified.

Dickie had another accident before his final examinations – a broken leg this time. He took them lying in plaster and passed eighteenth out of eighty. Then there was a last 'crash' course of three months at Keyham; and, now showing his true mettle, he passed out top. 'This is the proudest moment of my life,' remarked Prince Louis when Dickie entered the room wearing his midshipman's patches for the first time. And suddenly one sees a jaunty, handsome boy looking out at the world with eyes that are bright with intelligence and enthusiasm for what life has in store for him, with none of the unease of later years.

After her battering at Jutland, the *Lion* was under repair. Dickie joined her on the day she came out of dock, and almost at once was in action to prevent the German Fleet from bombarding Sunderland. This was not to be another major battle, but the desperate pursuit, the gunfire and the brushes with danger were all that Dickie could ask for. At sixteen, he had seen naval action in the North Sea, something few could claim. On that 19 August he also saw the new face of warfare at sea, an experience that was to prove invaluable during a later war in which he was to command at the highest level. The Air Arm took a considerable part – they sighted half a dozen German Zeppelins – and the danger was less from shellfire than from mines and torpedoes.

Daily life, and its risks, in the *Lion*'s gunroom were altogether less pleasant. Gunroom bullying was as old as the Navy, and the beatings were more serious than at Locker's Park or even Osborne. 'Things had not changed much since Nelson's day. We slept in hammocks, of course, and we slung them wherever we could find room – mine was six inches under a bright police light, but you can survive anything. I just slept with a handkerchief over my face.

'Then, there were still "stunts", when we became the playthings of the sub-lieutenants in the gunroom. Suddenly one of them in the middle of dinner would stab his fork into the table or a beam, which meant every snottie had to get out quickly. But before most of us could do so, the subs were at the door with canes, beating us out, and hard, too.' Beatty was made aware that his flagship was particularly notorious for bullying when one snottie, suffering the popular 'sport' of cutting hammock ropes, broke his back on the steel deck and was permanently crippled. 'Things got better after that, but it was still not a soft life.'

The war at sea changed its nature in 1917. The German Navy, despairing of ever beating the British Fleet in a full-scale gunnery action, now that the disparity in numbers had become so great, turned increasingly to submarine warfare against Allied shipping. An earlier and very effective U-boat campaign against merchantmen and passenger liners had been halted by the pressure from neutral America after powerful protests at the loss of American lives and trade. Now the campaign was reopened, with devastating results. Methods of fighting the U-boat were still primitive, and many hundreds of thousands of tons of shipping were sunk and many thousands of lives needlessly lost before the Admiralty could be persuaded to make use of the old safety measure of sailing in convoy. In the month of April 1917 alone, 545,000 tons of merchant shipping were lost, bringing desperately needed food and arms, or reinforcements from the Empire.

Jellicoe was now at the Admiralty, Beatty had become the commander-in-chief, flying his flag in the *Queen Elizabeth* and Dickie was still serving with his hero. But, just as many of the German big ships' crews were seconded to the U-boats, so Grand Fleet personnel were being transferred to the new small craft designed to destroy these U-boats. Dickie was appointed to the new 600-ton *P31*, armed with light guns and depth-charges, for patrol and escort work. Sub-Lieutenant Lord Louis Mountbatten was now second-in-command over a crew of fifty petty officers and ratings.

Why was Dickie now a Mountbatten and no longer a Battenberg, no longer a Prince? Not only had the war at sea changed in 1917. It was a year of desperate fighting on the Western Front – Arras, Aisne, Passchendaele. The Americans had ceased to be neutral but it would be many months before the effect of their support would be felt, and meanwhile the Russians were virtually defeated and close to revolution. The French armies mutinied in

May. In Britain the frustration of failed offensives, of ghastly casualties, of seeming impotence against German air raids, was leading to an unhinging of rational judgment and national hysteria. No end to the suffering appeared to be in sight, and only the rich seemed to be getting enough to eat.

It was a terrible year for everyone in Britain. A mixture of hopelessness and fury was everywhere evident. Decorated heroes on leave out of uniform were scorned and given white feathers. Worse than in 1914, everything German was vilified. While some called for peace, others called for the abdication of the 'German' King. In 1914 a 'German' had run the Navy: he had been got rid of, but could he not still be a seditious influence? And what of the German Tecks, Queen Mary's family, and the King, whose grandfather had been pure German?

The Prime Minister recognized the growing danger, and made known his anxieties to the King. This was hardly necessary. George V knew what was going on, and was properly outraged. Socialists were loudly proclaiming against 'an alien and uninspiring court', and agitating for its extinction. 'I may be uninspiring,' complained the King, 'but I'll be damned if I am alien.'

A change of name, ruling out all German connotations, was clearly called for. The trouble was, no one was sure what the royal family's name was at present. The King was a Saxe-Coburg-Gotha, but that was not his name. Perhaps Wettin? There was, however, no doubt of the origin of the names Battenberg or Teck.

It was the King's secretary, Lord Stamfordham, who in an inspired moment produced a name that no modern public relations firm could have improved upon. Windsor: so English, so safe, so steady, already traditional upon inception. As solid as the castle. And Prince Louis, summoned to Court from the Isle of Wight by his cousin, simply anglicized his family name to Mountbatten. 'I have very serious news of far-reaching effects on us all to tell you,' Louis wrote to his children, concluding that 'all this is very terrible.'[1]

Dickie did not appear to take the news very seriously. 'Will my children be misters or honourables?' he asked his mother. As always he was in a fever of interest about titles and protocol. 'Can I marry without asking the King?'[2] Yes, he was not even a Peer of the Realm, just Lord Louis Mountbatten, younger son of the First Marquis and Marchioness of Milford Haven, the new title of Louis and Victoria, no longer a prince, no longer a serene highness. The Battenberg line, created to deal with a dynastic embarrassment, had been short-lived.

For Louis, so proud of his title and breeding, it was 'a terrible upheaval and break with one's past'. His wife grieved for him. But for herself, she attempted to show indifference. It was a confusing situation to cope with. She had been brought up under the enlightened liberal philosophy of the Hessian Court, and in England had become a keen socialist. Bernard Shaw was her god, but she had no difficulty in reconciling this with her rank and support of the monarchy.

Why should she not be a plain 'Mrs'? 'I would prefer to be a "citoyenne",' she wrote to her lady-in-waiting on the news of the name change. But she thought it her duty to think of her descendants, and gave up only her German titles so that she became simply a peer's wife, along with all those wives of 'bankers and lawyers and brewers',[3] as she referred scathingly to these jumped-up title-grabbers.

Dickie shared his mother's anxiety about their relatives in Germany, and especially those in Russia after the revolution and surrender. At about the time of the name change in the family, Victoria and her sister Irène, the wife of Grand Admiral Prince Henry, thought it politic to exchange their maids, Victoria's being German, Irène's English. This was effected through neutral Holland, and each brought news to their new mistresses. The sisters' admiral husbands now also had two sons fighting at sea against their cousins. There is nothing on record to show that Victoria thought this extraordinary.

Her German sister, Victoria learned, was growing thin. Of her Russian sisters, she heard little, and feared greatly for them, although she was supported by the belief that the Prime Minister, or perhaps the King, would intervene to rescue them. At one time, early in 1917, the Foreign Secretary, Arthur Balfour, proposed to send Louis to Russia to see and reason with the Tsar before it was too late. Louis, she believed, would have done a marvellous job, perhaps even have forestalled the revolution; and would have brought back news of Ella and Alicky. But the Prime Minister vetoed the idea and sent Lord Milner, who was a disaster.

Two months later, in March 1917, Dickie wrote to his mother, 'How awful about what has happened in Russia. I suppose Uncle Nicky is quite safe, though I can't understand why he has abdicated.'[4] And Marie? The beautiful Marie he planned to marry after the war? She was under guard, he had read, along with her mother and the other children.

But Victoria was relieved that the Tsar had abdicated, for 'no one can tell how far the revolution may go', and her sister was less likely to be assassinated as an ex-Empress. After the murder of her husband, Prince Serge, twelve years earlier, Ella had founded a religious nursing order and given her whole life to her convent. Surely she would be spared.

Rumours of the fate of Dickie's Russian relations multiplied as hard news diminished, and it was not until September 1918 that Victoria, 'in a kind letter from George Rex', heard that her sister and brother-in-law and their entire family had been murdered, 'removed for ever from further suffering'. Like his mother, Dickie continued to retain some hope for blameless, saintly Aunt Ella. But two days before the war ended, news of her horrible, long-drawn-out death at the bottom of a mine shaft reached England.

Queen Victoria had done all that she could to dissuade her grand-daughters from 'going to terrible Russia'. And now both of those misguided princesses, and all their families, were dead; marking one of the worst in the long record of Hessian tragedies.

Many years were to pass before Dickie learned how bitterly his mother felt about the failure of Prime Minister Lloyd George to raise a finger to save her Russian relations and his determination to dissuade George V, whose position was still weak in spite of the change of name, from interven-ing on their behalf. A politician's fear of losing trade union and working-class votes by showing support for the victims of communist revolution had caused this tragedy, 'Just because the poor man was an Emperor,' the King commented. As Victoria never forgave Churchill for dismissing her husband, so she never forgave Lloyd George for staining his hands with her family's blood. Nor did the King forgive himself for his weakness and his failure which haunted him and Queen Mary for the rest of their lives.

Always enthusiastically interested in politics, Victoria was confirmed by these two events in her belief that all politicians were devious, the successful ones criminally dishonest. 'Lloyd George and Wilson coquetting with the Bolsheviks,' as she put it – the Bolsheviks who had committed mass murder!

Lloyd George also judged it politically inadvisable to make any friendly gesture towards Louis, a foreign-born prince, at the end of the war. He ensured that he was not invited to the formal surrender of the German Fleet, and a few days later Louis was asked if he would like formally to retire, in spite of the promise made when he resigned.

Later, Dickie heard his father exclaiming bitterly to his mother, 'But they promised me. It was a condition of my resignation. I said that I would go if they made me a member of the Privy Council to show that I still had the trust of Cousin George and the government, and if I was allowed to hoist my flag again – preferably in the Mediterranean.'

'Yes, I know dear.'

'The first was a request, the second a condition. You know how much it meant to me – the Mediterranean, the premier command. That's what I so much wanted.'

His wife replied soothingly, 'But that was not four years ago, it was four hundred years ago. Everything has changed in that time, you must see that.' And she enumerated them – the end of dynasties and empires, the revolu-tions, the old map of Europe. He had to admit it.

Louis was only sixty-four but the repeated blows to his sensitive German pride had beaten him about badly, physically and mentally. 'I think he is beginning to show his age rather,' wrote Victoria. Dickie had noticed it too. The admiral with the quick, decisive mind whose fleet always won at manœuvres, the steady, painstaking First Sea Lord of 1913, had grown old before his time. Dickie had got permission to take him on a routine anti-U-boat patrol across the Channel shortly before the end of the war, proudly showing him all the new gadgetry the *P31* boasted. Louis loved the experience, always loved being at sea, but Dickie had to recognize that this was not the same man who had stood so proudly on the bridge of his flagship, the *Prince of Wales*, and directed evolutions of the Atlantic Fleet. But when Dickie heard a few weeks later of the duplicity of the government and the Board of Admiralty, he loyally wrote, 'I do think it is disgraceful!'

While his father was aged by the long, hard war through inactivity and injured pride, his younger son had become a man, even if he was still only eighteen. (And we shall now drop the familiar nickname and call him Mountbatten.) He was over six feet, taller than his father, had filled out, and grown unusually strong. His complexion, which had so bothered him as a cadet, was clear and attractively bronzed by his long periods at sea. He was, in the expression of the time, 'quite crashingly handsome'.

As Sub-Lieutenant Lord Louis Mountbatten, full of brightness and practical jokes and quick repartee of a rather schoolboy nature, he was already developing the winsome appeal – part vulnerable, part boyish cockiness – that caused people, and especially women, to be drawn to him in any gathering. The magnetism of the mature man of achievement was already there – visible but still undeveloped.

The voice had the fashionable timbre of the upper classes of the 1920s, but characterized by its speed instead of the more common drawl. He was quick to pick up nuances, and the eye that was always eager to recognize a pretty girl was already on the main chance, too. He drank the usual, quite considerable, amount for his generation but rarely got drunk. He would drop the most amusing and interesting conversation if something relating to his profession came up. It was already apparent that the Navy came before everything in his life, but that did not exclude his having a very good time.

Like most sentimental young men, he fell in love easily and broke his heart easily. He could be teased up to a point, so long as it was frivolous. If it hinted at some failing on his part, he did not like it and let it be seen, by an expression or gesture. In his social and his professional life, it was clear that to be a winner meant more to him than to most people. The days of dreaming and absent-mindedness were over. Everything he did – taking up a new game, learning to operate new equipment, studying photography, improving his French (still his only weak language), driving fast – he did as if his life depended on his doing it better than anyone else. No one had seen a young man so competitive. His determination to win was so powerful that he almost always did. But some shrewd observers murmured the word 'insecure'.

Why? Surely here, above all, was a young man with everything on his side, except a great fortune: looks, rank, brains, future, all of the best. Who could be insecure with all this stacked on the credit side at the outset of his life? Especially when most people thought he was already very well endowed with self-confidence.

Any suggestion made to him in old age that he was in the least insecure at any time in his life, would be brushed irritably aside. Yet Mountbatten's swashbuckling style always concealed doubts about his abilities and achievements. This uneasiness can be explained by the fact, of which he was only too well aware, that during his most susceptible years he saw so many of his great and powerful relations brought down – the Tsar, the Kaiser, the Grand-Duke of Hesse and the King of Greece; and even, nearly, Cousin Georgie, George v, King-Emperor.

But far above all these rulers in its effect upon him was the fate of his father, whom he so hero-worshipped and who had been so publicly and appallingly humiliated and destroyed by slow degrees. The evidence that even the best and most powerful could be defeated by the chances of fate and the injustices perpetrated by man was a cataclysmic revelation for a young man whose worst fear was of defeat and humiliation.

Did he ever acknowledge this fear, even to himself? It is unlikely. It was not in the nature of the young man to toy with this sort of self-analysis which might weaken his resolve to be totally self-confident one day. As an old man, he believed that he had succeeded so well that he could actually say:

'Many people express surprise that I accomplished what I did with my background. What they don't understand was that my upbringing and background were far more liberal, progressive and far-seeing than any average British aristocratic family's.' He added as an afterthought, 'As for the Royal Family, they were off in the *opposite* direction.

'When I was a boy I thought that the intelligence of all those about me was normal in life. It came as a great shock to me when I went out into the world and discovered that this was not true at all. This led me from quite an early age to feel a lack of reverence towards, say, great politicians with their supposedly great brains. This made it much easier for me to feel at least their equal when I was in their company.'

Mountbatten may have felt their equal, or their superior, but there were those who knew him well who could still discern a flicker of uncertainty in his eyes from time to time. He could have ruled the world and it would still have been there. But Mountbatten faced his first royal review, at the age of nineteen with complete equanimity. This was the sort of thing for which he felt no doubts at all. The King had expressed a wish to come on board and inspect his little *P31*, so the ship was smartened up at Sheerness and steamed up the Thames to Whitehall. The King's movements were always news, and so, already, were Lord Louis Mountbatten's. Reporters and photographers swarmed over the *P31* – 'Interviewers are assailing her already,' reported Victoria, 'and Dickie is in agonies at every scratch.'[5]

George V, 'our sailor King' who always dearly loved any man o'war, came on board at eleven o'clock one morning, went everywhere below decks and asked about all the anti-U-boat gadgetry ('didn't have those in my time') and expressed satisfaction with ship and crew.

Threatened with the loss of his *P31*, Mountbatten preserved her commission with characteristic devious ingenuity. At Portland naval base in 1919, she lay awaiting 'c & m' – care and maintenance. The Admiral was due to inspect her and check that, like the others of her kind tied up alongside her, she was ready to go into 'mothballs'. Just before he arrived, Mountbatten ordered the entire company into a locked boiler room, and hung a warning notice on the door, 'Wet Paint'.

The Admiral, seeing the *P31* apparently unmanned and silent, did not even come on board. 'So your ship is in "c & m" is it?'

Glancing at the *P32*, Mountbatten confirmed. 'She's next door to it, sir.'

By this means, and an administrative hiccup, the *P31* remained in commission and took part in the Baltic operations of 1919–20. But not with Mountbatten as her second-in-command. He was ordered ashore; the next appointment could not be fiddled.

A great number of junior regular naval officers were axed at the end of the war and all the defence economies that followed it, the first to go being those with private incomes. By happy chance, or intervention (Mountbatten would never say), he and his brother were not affected. But it was decided by the Board that a select few, whose education at Dartmouth had been cut short, should go up to university for a year to polish their brains while the peace following 'the war to end wars' set in.

Christ's College, Cambridge, in the beautiful autumn of 1919, with the Backs and the willows and the ancient grey colleges looking their loveliest, was as remote a world as anyone could imagine from the dangers and discomforts of the war at sea which had seemed everlasting. Smart young Mountbatten, always in uniform and already sporting the first row of ribbons

– one day there would be ten – threw himself into the parties, the Union debates, and his chosen subjects, History of Geographical Discoveries, and Ethnology. But no one seemed to do much work in the aftermath of the dreadful and debilitating war. Cambridge was full of young men like himself who had escaped with their lives and even younger men who had just been too young for the trenches. There was an air of unreality and over-excitement among the undergraduates.

Mountbatten had a £300 a year allowance from his father, five shillings a day pay, and a small car. It was ample for a good time. Besides parties, he was elected to the Pitt Club and the Union. There was to be a debate with Oxford on the motion: 'The time is ripe for a Labour Government'. Mountbatten, defending the motion of course, was allowed to invite a guest. Characteristically, he telephoned Winston Churchill, now Secretary of State for War, who agreed to come. The Duke of York (the future George VI) and the Duke of Gloucester sat on the cross benches. This was to be no commonplace debate. Mountbatten's contribution at the end was forceful and direct. 'Sir,' he began, addressing the President of the Union, 'in my humble opinion, what previous speakers on both sides of the House have said up to now is tripe.'

Churchill liked it. 'I trust', he remarked, 'that the last speaker will show as great facility in dealing with admirals on their quarterdecks as with his opponents on this platform.'

Mountbatten fell in and out of love at parties in London and Cambridge and the great houses. His greatest love, 'far surpassing all the others', was for Audrey James, the most popular debutante of the season. 'I saw her photograph in the *Sketch* one day, and thought she was the most beautiful girl I had ever seen. I met her at a dance soon after, and we both fell madly in love. We were engaged in two weeks.'

His mother watched these affairs with a worldly but wary eye and a good deal of indulgent amusement. But she did not in the least approve of the engagement. 'You are far too young and poor, Dickie.' The family had lost all their Russian possessions, worth several hundreds of thousands, and when Louis was reduced to selling Heiligenberg, the mark had crashed, inflation was wild, and he received only a nominal amount for it.

The love affair prospered through that autumn and winter, and they made firm plans for their wedding. Mountbatten was certainly head over heels in love, but even through this passion he kept a steady nautical eye open for advancing his career. Emulating his father in cultivating the friend-ship of his cousin and the future sovereign when he was a lieutenant, Mountbatten had warmed to the company of David, Prince of Wales.

The Prince had been born just six years before Mountbatten, the first

son of the future heir to the throne. After the usual confined 'family' upbringing – no school, few friends, many relations – he had been hurled
into the harsh and spirited life at Osborne, where – like Mountbatten – he
was quite severely bullied and found life difficult, and to the chagrin of his
father produced indifferent results. His fear of his father developed early
and, even by the standards of his generation, it grew to a threatening size,
although mixed with respect. After graduating from Dartmouth, he had
served at sea in HMS *Hindustan*. To his distress, because he was now
enjoying the navy, this was his only commission, and a brief one at that.
His grandfather died in 1910, and the new King made him Prince of Wales.
Instead, there was educational travel about Europe, the study of statesman-
ship and politics, a time at Oxford.

He experienced great loneliness. His nearest brothers were away at school
most of the time. In the months before the outbreak of war, he acquired
a strong taste for parties, from small intimate ones to great balls, when he
'danced the night away'. The taste never left him.

Then came the Great War. At first, as he put it, 'my trophy value
exceeded my military usefulness',[6] and he was not allowed even to go to
France. But by sheer persistence, he first got a staff job at HQ, and then
got appointments nearer to the Front, so that several times he was close
to the fighting and risking his life. He was appalled by what he saw,
responded warmly to the comradeship. He really felt one of the people at
last, and the experience was to colour his whole attitude to his unusual role
in life.

On the night war was declared, while Mountbatten was dining with his
father alone at the Admiralty, a short distance up the Mall another prince
dined with his father, at Buckingham Palace, also discussing the political
and military situation. It was not until after the war, when the age gap
seemed so much narrower, that Mountbatten and David came to know one
another better. They laughed at the same things, talked a great deal about
girls and parties, their time during the war, and their future. Mountbatten
loved the young Prince with his strong penchant for enjoying himself, his
shy smile and nervous ways, his infectious laugh. The fact that he was
heir to the throne and his father not very fit was a factor in their relationship
that was never discussed, that Mountbatten would not accept consciously
to himself as being important, but was undeniably the case all the same.
To cultivate powerful people was a part of the competitive game of life,
coming as naturally as a golfer's urge to improve his handicap. It lasted to
the end, and even included a call on Mrs Thatcher when she became Prime
Minister shortly before his death.

Soon after the end of World War I, when the Prime Minister was

David Lloyd George, he consulted the King about the desirability of telling the Empire how much Britain appreciated its recent support and
sacrifices. From these discussions, the plan for sending the Prince of Wales
on a series of tours was worked out. In addition, as the traveller himself
put it, 'I was required to show myself to the people in order to make my
character known, and at the same time to fill the Prince of Wales' traditional role of the leader of society.'

In 1919 he went to Canada, and then on to the United States because
it seemed a pity to miss the opportunity. He loved both countries. On
his return he met Mountbatten, who asked him if he could accompany
him on any future tours as his naval ADC. The Prince thought this an
admirable idea, but then appeared to forget all about it. Plans went ahead
for a longer tour in 1920 to the West Indies, New Zealand and Australia.
At the end of the year, Mountbatten had heard nothing more of the proposal and was becoming anxious though not wishing to appear too 'pushy'.
Then he learned that the Prince would be at a ball to be given by the famous
society hostess, Lady Ribblesdale, to which he, rather surprisingly, had not
been invited.

At the last minute he telephoned a friend he knew to be going and asked
him if he knew his hostess very well. 'If you do, can you arrange to have
me invited tonight? It's very important that I see David before he goes
away.'

'What do you want to see him about?'

Mountbatten said he would tell him later but that it really was important.

The matter was arranged, with some difficulty, and Mountbatten was
thus able to corner the Prince of Wales, now a Post-Captain RN, and bring
the subject round again to the now imminent world cruise. In this way,
Mountbatten was invited to share the tour with his cousin, not as ADC but as
flag-lieutenant to the Prince's chief of staff, Rear-Admiral Sir Lionel Halsey,
in the great modern battle-cruiser, Renown.

There was a farewell dinner at Buckingham Palace, and on the morning
of 16 March 1920 Mountbatten called at Mrs Dudley Ward's house to
collect the Prince and accompany him to the station. The Prince of Wales
was in the throes of his deep love affair with this kind, understanding and
utterly discreet woman, the wife of a Liberal MP and Party Whip, William
Dudley Ward. Now his imminent departure with the prospect of a long
separation was too much for him.

The Prince was in tears on the way to Victoria Station. 'Have you ever
seen a Post-Captain cry?' he asked Mountbatten.

'I don't think I have.'

'Well, you'd better get used to it. You may see it again.'

The streets were lined with cheering crowds who knew nothing of their 'gay young Prince of Wales'' grief, and there were more at the station, who broke through the barrier to give him a rousing send-off.

From that March morning until their return seven months later, Mountbatten's constant presence and support, his cheerfulness and ebullience, were a blessing for the Prince. A friendship was cemented that lasted until the Prince of Wales' death as the Duke of Windsor. At nineteen Mountbatten was, in the words of the Prince, 'a vigorous and high-spirited young man who became the instigator of many an unexpected diversion outside the official programme'.[7]

There is a typical photograph of him with Dudley North (whose unjustifiably blackened reputation in the next war Mountbatten was later to help recover) and the Prince's private secretary, all on pogo sticks. Mountbatten is the only one to have clearly mastered the stick, the only one grinning from ear to ear, and the only one actually airborne.

But it was not only his cheerful effervescence that was such a tonic for the Prince during the longest and most arduous tour any member of the royal family had ever made. Besides his misery at the separation from his beloved Mrs Dudley Ward, the Prince of Wales was subject to fits of depression and uncertainty in himself. He could easily be overcome by a desperate loneliness and he often said that he would do anything to change rank and place with Mountbatten. The King had always found it difficult to show his approval of anything his eldest son did, and even far from Windsor Castle, in the middle of the Pacific, the Prince would receive disapproving letters from him. Something was always wrong; it always had been. If it was not the over-informal poses in which he allowed himself to be photographed, it was something else. Mountbatten jollied him along, gave him fresh encouragement, told him he was marvellous. In this way Mountbatten made the first of his numerous contributions to the quality and happiness of the British monarchy. And he enjoyed every minute of it.

'You've no idea what a friend David is to me,' Mountbatten wrote home. 'He may be six years older, but in some respects he is the same age as me. How I wish he wasn't the Prince of Wales and then it would be so much easier to see lots and lots of him! He is such a marvellous person, and I suppose the best friend I have ever had.'[8]

At sea, it was nearly all fun, with endless games and high-spirited pranks; 'crossing the line' was a formidable and furious ceremony of pills and lather and shaving with an outsize razor and ducking and pronouncements by King Neptune. On land, however, it was nearly all gruelling work. Everybody wanted to meet the handsome young Prince, above all the ex-servicemen for whom the tour had largely been arranged. Everywhere the Anzacs – the old Australian and New Zealand Army Corps – were out in strength, and with handshakes so strong that the Prince was obliged to resort to using his left hand.

The New Zealanders were quieter and warmly hospitable. The Australians proclaimed their welcome loudly and roughly with much chi-iking – 'Oh Percy, where didya get that hat?' – and touching, rough touching that left the Prince and his party painfully bruised. There was a strong anti-monarchist and extreme left element in Australia that had to be coped with, too, as well as the proverbial Australian sensitivity to criticism and sup-posed patronizing. 'The Australians must be handled with care,' was how the Governor-General had greeted the royal party, no matter how roughly the Australians might handle the royal party. That was not always easy, but the lusty welcome left the right overall impression with both young men. 'I had a fine time,' concluded the Prince. 'I liked its bigness and its courage.'[9] Mountbatten liked the country for the same reason, and in later life returned many times, eventually buying land in Western Australia which he enjoyed visiting.

Mountbatten arrived home in mid-October 1920. He had been away 210 days, travelled 46,000 miles, arrived at countless destinations, shaken tens of thousands of hands, played tennis in Trinidad, surfed off Waikiki Beach. 'I learned a tremendous lot on this tour,' he remembered, 'I think really that I came of age though I still wasn't twenty-one.' This was because, he claimed, he had met so many people far outside his usual circle, had seen so many places, and had also carried responsibility on his shoulders.

Mountbatten had found time (he always did) for a number of passing flirtations on his cruise, but now he was determined to make firm plans for his wedding. Young Audrey had other plans. Her fiancé had been away too long, long enough for her to brood on the respective charms of great wealth or a title. She had chosen the first, as represented by the cotton king Major Dudley Coats. She broke off her engagement to Mountbatten, who soon discovered that the story going the rounds of London was that Audrey James had preferred the arms of Coats to coats of arms. At first Mountbatten took the rebuff badly, while enjoying the joke, but as one of the most eligible bachelors in the country it was easy to soothe the wound with more affairs.

Mountbatten fell in and out of love, as he did most things, with amazing speed. 'It does not matter how often you are in that state,' Mama advised, 'as long as somewhere in your heart you keep the knowledge of the difference of a love which I hope may come to you only later on and which is one of head and heart together for a girl you want to make your wife.'[10]

Then in July 1921, at a Claridge's ball given by Grace Vanderbilt,

Mountbatten met a girl quite as lovely as Audrey James 'and about ten times more lively and intelligent'. She was introduced as Edwina Ashley, the part-Jewish grand-daughter of Sir Ernest Cassel. He was the mountainously rich international banker, promoter of industry, railways, dams (the Aswan, for example) and projects of all kinds that had made great profits in a time of boom and rearmament in the late nineteenth and early twentieth century.

Cassel was one of those shrewd and amusing Jews whom King Edward VII had loved, ennobled and then milked for his favourite charities. His wife had died young, leaving him with a daughter who married Wilfred Ashley, a grandson of the Earl of Shaftesbury. Ashley joined the Army, became a colonel and later, having entered politics, was created Baron Mount Temple. They had two daughters, Edwina Cynthia Annette in 1901, and Mary four years later. Their mother was always delicate, and died in 1911.

Edwina had led a restless and often unhappy childhood, for the first sixteen years at Broadlands, the great family estate in Hampshire. With her full and open heart, her uncertainty in herself, and her vulnerability, she desperately needed a mother, and the nursemaids and governesses and later her schoolteachers found her difficult to handle. Her father got married again, to a vicar's daughter, Muriel Spencer. She was certainly no surrogate mother for Edwina, and turned out to be more like the wicked stepmother in a fairy tale. 'A wicked woman, a real bitch,' Mountbatten called her.

Life became impossible at Broadlands, and it is extraordinary that Edwina did not take against the place for the rest of her life. She became a wilful, highly-strung, temperamental and very bright adolescent, and begged to be allowed to live with her old grandfather in London. Cassel gladly agreed. He loved the idea of his grand-daughter about his house, in spite of the responsibility. With some relief, Colonel and Mrs Ashley said goodbye to the child.

Cassel had four country estates, and in London lived in a gigantic and hideous edifice in Park Lane called Brook House, whose echoing interior was largely of marble, and most of that dark. Edwina did not care. She adored her grandfather and he doted on her. She was already a very practical organizer, and as he frequently gave large parties, she became his social secretary.

Later, after her coming-out ball – Edwina breathlessly lovely in a simple gold dress – she followed the usual social ritual of balls and dances and dinners, country-house parties and the season's progression. The ball given by Grace Vanderbilt at Claridge's was an appropriate venue for her introduction to Mountbatten. They danced and talked, and the fusion of minds and hearts was (they both later agreed) instantaneous.

The scene might be stereotyped, but there was nothing standard about Edwina's beauty. The wide-apart, clear, intelligent blue eyes, the shape of her mouth, the rapidly changing expressions that crossed her intriguing face, the set of her head on the loveliest of necks: even an undiscerning eye must at once recognize that here was no standard debutante beauty taking a commonplace view of a confined social world. Mountbatten saw that he was dancing with an exceptional young woman, to whom he increasingly warmed as they talked.

At this time Edwina was rather shy and introspective by contrast with the extrovert Mountbatten. She found his decisiveness and firm views, his ambitiousness, his compulsive need for fun and action, marvellously complementary to her own needs. His Hessian breeding, her own measure of clever middle-European Jewish blood, their exalted backgrounds with so many royal associations, stood them mutually a little apart from the usual run of aristocracy with whom they so freely moved socially, and together gave them an edge on anyone else. Brains, beauty, youth, – everything, and not an impediment in sight. Or was there?

For Cowes regatta week, Edwina was invited to stay with Sir Godfrey and Lady Baring. The instantaneous flash of love between her and Mountbatten was at once recognized by many other people, too. Parties were rearranged to ensure they were both present, every hostess hoping to claim that she was the real matchmaker of the greatest romance of the year. Cornelius and Grace Vanderbilt had invited Mountbatten on a ten-day cruise in their schooner, *Atalanta*. Edwina joined the party at the last minute, and so, for the first of countless times, the future Mountbattens went sailing together.

'It was a wonderful cruise in this huge yacht,' Mountbatten said, 'a very happy time. But what happened after was better still. My parents were living at a house called Fishponds at Netley Abbey. The Crichtons [Nona Kerr, Victoria's lady-in-waiting, had married an Army officer she had nursed in the war, Richard Crichton] lent it to them. I took Edwina to meet them and my father fell head over heels for her. She fell for him, too. He took me aside and said, "Edwina is the most remarkable and charming girl of this generation that I have met. She's got intelligence, character, everything. Now, you're very young, but if you do decide to marry her, you have my whole-hearted approval. She'll make a wonderful wife for you."'

In view of what was shortly to happen, Mountbatten was always thankful that he had, at this comparatively early stage of their courtship, 'taken her home'. Victoria had approved, too, in spite of her prejudice against titled bankers. 'Between them, this strongly influenced my decision to go ahead.'

Above: Princess Victoria of Hesse, Mountbatten's mother, as a young woman before her marriage at the age of 21 in 1884.

Above right: Prince Louis of Battenberg, now a naturalized Englishman and 'buck about town' as well as a rising naval officer. He was 46 and a Captain RN when Mountbatten was born.

Right: Dickie in 'naval uniform' at the age of 4 in company with his tattered but beloved teddy bear 'Sonnenbein'.

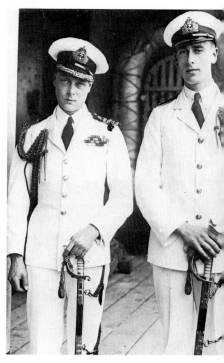

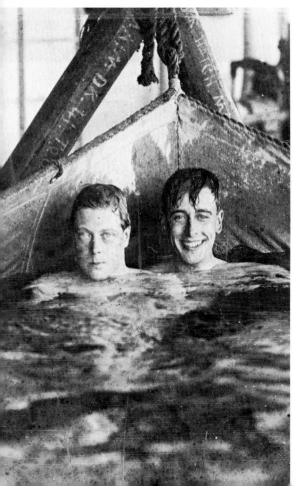

Above left: Dickie and David at play. A characteristic 'snap' of Mountbatten and the Prince of Wales while on the Prince's world tour.

Above: Dickie and David at work. The Prince of Wales as a Captain RN, Mountbatten newly promoted Lieutenant RN in uniform for one of the numerous formal occasions connected with their world cruises on board HMS *Renown*, 1920–22.

Left: King George V considered this widely printed photograph of his son and cousin unsuitable for the general public.

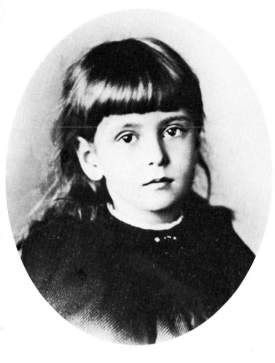

Left: Edwina Cynthia Annette Ashley.
Above: Edwina with her grandfather,
Sir Ernest Cassel.

Lieutenant Lord Louis Mountbatten, age 21, shortly
before his wedding.

Edwina – Lady Louis Mountbatten –
in 1925.

Above: Dickie and Charlie recovering after a hard morning's 'shooting'.

Left: Instant and lifelong friends: Edwina and Chaplin, 1922.

The old Admiral, who had known Queen Victoria when she was still quite a young woman, and like the Prince Consort, had offered everything he had to his adopted country and received little enough in return, went to sea again in the late summer of 1921, and for the first time as an Admiral of the Fleet. The King had approved of this gratifying promotion and also awarded him a second GCB. Now his son had his Captain's approval, as a celebration, to invite him on board the *Repulse*, sister battle-cruiser to the *Renown*, for a bracing North Sea cruise.

It had been ten years since Louis had felt the vibrating deck of a great Dreadnought beneath his feet, and watched the dip of the prow as the forecastle 'took a green' and the spume was swept as high as the bridge. He loved every minute of it, the camaraderie, the war reminiscences, the 'salty stories' so beloved of his cousin, the King, told over the port after dinner, and the wardroom pranks among the junior officers. All this had been such an important part of his life, which had been so different from those of his Hessian ancestors in their palaces or on their long military campaigns.

'We had delightful weather and I think Papa thoroughly enjoyed himself,' Mountbatten reported to his mother. 'I know the Ward Room here have thoroughly enjoyed having him,' adding ominously, 'Papa succeeded in catching rather a bad cold', and 'during the night Papa got lumbago'.[11]

When he was well enough, Mountbatten put him on the train from Invergordon and returned to his ship. That weekend he was to see Edwina again and propose to her. It was to be spent in the usual exalted company, this time at Dunrobin Castle, with the host and hostess the Duke and Duchess of Sutherland (George and Eileen), the Prince of Wales, his brother Bertie (the Duke of York), the Archbishop of Canterbury, the Dudleys, Charlotte 'Baby' Demarest and her sister Hélène Leveson-Gower, and several others.

It was marvellous to see Edwina again, looking lovelier than ever, her clever, pure blue eyes shining with excitement at the fun, the Prince of Wales describing some of the more outrageous incidents on his last tour – 'They called me Cobber and nearly poked me to death....'

It was Sunday 11 September when, late in the afternoon, a telegram arrived for Mountbatten with the news that his father had died at 1.30 pm from a heart attack following influenza. He had not been at all well when he arrived in London and went to his club, the Naval and Military in Piccadilly. His wife and daughter Alice had delayed their departure for Paris, and had visited him again at the annexe to the club to be told that he had just been found dead by a chambermaid.

Mountbatten burst into tears as he read the telegram. 'I loved him deeply, and it was the most terrible shock. Everybody was marvellously kind, especially David and Edwina. Somebody telephoned the station and found the only train of the day had already left, and I wanted to set off right away in the car, but Edwina said, "You can't possibly – it's 600 miles." And of course she was quite right, it was only a small car, too.

'Later in the afternoon,' Mountbatten continued, 'I remember the Prince of Wales saying again how sorry he was and how cut up I must be. "How lucky you are to have had such a marvellous father!" Then he added, "If I heard my father had died I wouldn't be able to conceal my delight."

'The Archbishop said, "We might have a short service before dinner in your father's memory – what do you think of that?" So I said, "That's very kind."

'We didn't say anything to the servants, and I got a couple of cushions for David and Bertie to kneel on as they were wearing kilts, and we knelt down. Then when we were in the middle of the service, the doors were flung open and in marched the butler with a cocktail shaker followed by two footmen with the ingredients. It was six o'clock. Everyone was rather put out but I thought my father would have approved.'

So Mountbatten never proposed that weekend. By an extraordinary coincidence, Edwina's grandfather – who enjoyed from her the same respect and affection as had Louis from Mountbatten – died ten days later. The consequences of this death were infinite in the lives of both the bereaved.

Mountbatten read of Cassel's death in the newspaper. It was a few days after his father's funeral, and the whole family was still shattered. 'There it was, in cold print,' said Mountbatten. 'Death of multi-millionaire. Edwina Ashley, great beauty of the year, now richest heiress. Over seven million pounds. Result: the question I was going to pop that very day, I didn't pop. Marriage now was out of the question. My mother, when I asked her, also thought I shouldn't marry her. She said, "It never really works when the woman has so much more money than the man." From being all for the marriage, she turned against it.'

Mountbatten later said that he had no idea that Edwina was going to be so rich, and that she did not either. Mountbatten knew that Cassel was a very rich old man. But the inheritance, he claimed, never crossed his mind. 'She never seemed to have much money. She told me she had £300 a year.'

Many people, some of them close to them at the time, and others who were merely cynical or jealous, refused to believe that Edwina and Mountbatten were quite as innocent as they claimed to be. The extent of Cassel's fortune was well known. He was, quite simply, one of the richest men in the world, and his possessions and style of living demonstrated that he did not care who knew it. Edwina's father was rich in his own right, so it was unlikely he would receive any share of the inheritance. His two grand-daughters were the obvious likely beneficiaries, and Edwina was especially close to him. Cassel was older than Mountbatten's father, and not in good health. Even if Edwina was not to be sole beneficiary, even if, as her biographer suggests, 'Dickie and Edwina were at this stage totally unaware of the disposition of Sir Ernest's fortune'[12], it seemed unlikely that her income would remain for ever at £300 a year.

Cassel had kept the promise he had made on his wife's deathbed that he would become a Roman Catholic, and was buried according to the rites of the Church of Rome at Kensal Green.

Mountbatten saw Edwina twice more, the last time to tell her that he was leaving the country for many months. 'David has asked me to go to India and Japan with him – he says it will take my mind off my father's death.'

Could their friendship survive the huge disparity in their wealth, and the additional burden of a long separation. 'You must come out and join me – cheer things up,' Mountbatten suggested lightly, imagining her chartering a luxury liner if she came at all. Then they parted in the last week of October 1921.

It did seem likely that this second Empire Tour might need cheering up. The Prince of Wales, who had still not fully recovered from the rigours of the last voyage, was reluctant to leave England again so soon and face another long separation from Mrs Dudley Ward. Cheering New Zealand schoolchildren, six thousand of them forming the word WELCOME, were in strange contrast with a sub-continent in a state of sullen rebellion, and, under the influence of Nehru and Gandhi, hardly any longer the 'brightest jewel' of the British Crown.

The Prince of Wales had been sternly enjoined to do as he was told this time. 'You seem to have evolved a new technique of your own in the carrying out of your Commonwealth missions,' George v told him, and while I do not altogether approve your informal approach, I must concede that you have done very well. But you must not forget that India is entirely different from Canada, New Zealand or Australia. What went down well with the white people in those three Dominions will not go down at all in India. You are to do exactly as *they* tell you.'[13]

At Aden a huge banner above the cheering crowds asked the Prince to 'Tell Daddy We Are All Happy Under British Rule.' It was immediately evident that this was not so in Bombay, where the *Renown* dropped anchor and the welcome was formal and lavish but little supported by the natives. Gandhi had ordered a strike, there was rioting, and the police opened fire on the mob. In other cities there were only a few people out to welcome the royal party.

'I must at once tell you that I'm very depressed about my work in British India,' the Prince wrote home to the King, 'as I don't feel that I'm doing a scrap of good.'[14] Even Mountbatten found it hard to keep the Prince's spirits up in the face of boycott and violence. 'The pomp and ceremony,' Mountbatten reported, 'could not disguise the desperate poverty, the prevalence of disease and the regularly returning nightmare of famine.'

Mountbatten said to his cousin one day, 'Why don't we go and talk to Gandhi? It would show that we understood and sympathized. Between us, we could convince him that we should be friends.' The Prince of Wales agreed and the idea was put to the government officials. It never got up to Viceroy level. Officialdom was outraged – a twenty-one-year-old lieutenant telling them how to run the country! Why, the fellow had been in India only a few days. When Mountbatten, undismayed, asked if he could go alone to see the prophet, this, too, was firmly refused.

Years later, Mountbatten wrote, 'I wonder whether a meeting would have done any good? We *might* have established a useful contact.' It was a subject he was able to discuss twenty-six years later with Gandhi when Mountbatten himself was appointed Viceroy. In the event, with the continuing troubles Gandhi was clapped into prison. And that did not do any good either. Later, in Allahabad, the authorities locked up Jawaharlal Nehru, already a strong supporter of Gandhi and a Congress Committe member, and his associates too. The result was a total boycott of the royal processions and formal events. The city might have been abandoned. 'It was a spooky experience,' said the Prince.

It was better in the princely estates, of which there were more than five hundred. Here the welcome was spontaneous and enthusiastic, and the hospitality of the maharajahs and nawabs the most lavish that Mount-batten had seen anywhere. Mountbatten bagged his first tiger in Nepalese Terai in December, and learned to play polo.

Three loves, which lasted all his life, Mountbatten said, stemmed from this four-months-long tour of India. One was for India itself, a deep and abiding love, for the contrasting lifestyles from massively rich maharajahs down to the starving untouchables, the smell of the shrubs and flowers, burning dung and hot dust, and the sounds of the vast open countryside and the packed, squalid cities.

The second love was for polo. Polo was an expensive sport, and the opportunity to play it had never arisen for him at home. Now he had all the ponies and facilities he could ask for. The Prince watched his first efforts with amusement. 'He was determined to learn,' he wrote, 'and his initial appearance on a pony startled the Indian cavalry officers and my staff. But Dickie was nothing if not analytical; and undaunted by his inexperience, he persevered.'[15] This unselfconscious determination was typical of him, and one can be certain that the Prince's is an accurate picture. Quite inaccurate, however, was the Prince's conclusion that 'his interest in the manifold problems of India was confined to that part of the country bounded by the white boards of polo fields.' It was to be Mountbatten's fate all his life to have his ebullient and light-hearted enthusiasm for whatever he was doing off duty mistaken for a frivolous attitude towards duty itself, which he invariably took very seriously indeed.

And the third love? Mountbatten had kept up a steady correspondence with Edwina since his arrival in India. Her letters, and the memory of her, helped to weaken his decision that marriage between them was impossible, and encouraged him to beg that she should join him. Life was no longer supportable without her. 'Come out! This is a marvellous country.' He was further encouraged by the Prince. David was fascinated by Edwina, and always pooh-poohed the idea that her great wealth was an impediment.

In fact, Edwina was flat broke, and it was lack of money that was the first impediment to a reunion with Mountbatten. No wonder she had not understood the reason for the evident cooling down of Mountbatten's ardour! Cassel had laid down that her allowance of £300 was to continue until she was twenty-one, or she married; and this allowance was almost exhausted. He had been relentless in his efforts to ensure that she would not be spoilt: she even had to pay for her own laundry out of her £6 a week.

It never crossed her mind that, with the imminent expectation of millions, she might be able to borrow enough to pay for her passage. In the end, Cassel's sister obliged, but only to the extent of £100. Then she had to get her father's permission, reluctantly given and only on condition that she was chaperoned. She had booked on the cheapest ship she could find, and for that reason it seemed unlikely that any of her friends or relations would be on board. They were not. But 'discovering a likely cicerone, she promptly communicated with the lady, who said she would be delighted to "look after" Edwina'.[16]

But it was kind brother Georgie, now the 2nd Marquis of Milford Haven, who took Edwina to Southampton to see her off and cheer her up before the long (and as it turned out very primitive) passage to the East. Georgie was all for the match and, like the Prince of Wales, had tried to persuade Mountbatten to forget his scruples about the millions and marry this adorable, intelligent girl. Georgie himself had married during the war Countess Nada de Torby, daughter of the Grand-Duke Michael of Russia, and was no longer short of money.

'I'm so miserable,' said Edwina. 'It all seems to have gone sour. I don't think I ought to go.'

Georgie would have none of this. 'He absolutely worships you. Everything will be all right, you see.' And he kissed her goodbye.

Edwina never minded roughing it. Like most young women of her class, she had experienced the full rigours of boarding school. But it was not only childhood training that led her to ignore physical discomforts. She possessed a fakir's physical detachment from pain and exhaustion, which proved of inestimable value in her mature life but was to kill her prematurely in the end.

Her voyage was extremely uncomfortable and it was burning hot in the Red Sea. She loved it all. She had never travelled out of Europe before, and the magic of Malta, which she was to come to know so well, the mysteries of Alexandria, the hot smell of sand in the Red Sea and at Aden, all fed her newly acquired appetite for strange places.

It was out of the question that she could tag on to the royal party, so she had to find somewhere cheap to stay in India. Young as she still was, it was typical of her style and of her determination that she should at once telegraph the Viceroy on the strength of an old invitation to her grandfather. Lord and Lady Reading, still in the throes of the royal visit and the problems of nationalism, said yes.

The Prince of Wales and his entourage had reached Delhi when Edwina arrived at Bombay. She had still 750 miles to cover and enough money left for only a third-class rail ticket. She was prepared to travel fifty-natives-to-a-compartment, along with bedding and animals, but she was told at the station that it was quite impossible.

'She telephoned me from her hotel,' Mountbatten said, 'and the line was very bad, but she seemed to be telling me that she was coming to Delhi on a third-class ticket because she was broke. I said "That's impossible. You simply can't do that." And she said rather sadly, "That's what everyone says."'

More suitable arrangements were made through the Viceroy's office, and Edwina arrived in Delhi at last in early February. The Prince's duties in the capital were more gruelling than in any of the other cities, and for much of the daytime Edwina had to amuse herself in the magnificent temporary Vice-Regal Lodge. In the evenings she joined in whatever was going on. 'She got on marvellously with David, of course, and everybody loved her,' Mountbatten recalled. 'She loved dancing, and there were balls or dances most nights. David was flat out for us to get married, so, out of courtesy, he telegraphed the King for his permission and I told my mother that I intended after all to pop the question.'

Mountbatten's diary entry for 14 February 1922 read, 'After dinner there was a small dance. I danced 1 and 2 with Edwina. She had 3 and 4 with David, and the fifth dance we sat out in her sitting-room, when I asked her if she would marry me, and she said she would.' It was St Valentine's Day, the windows were open and looked out on to the magnificent gardens. The air was heavy with rich scents.

There was a mixed reception to the news of the engagement. The Prince of Wales was, of course, the first to congratulate them, and agreed to stand as best man at the wedding. Lady Reading, the Vicereine, was doubtful. 'I am afraid she has definitely made up her mind about him. I hoped she would have cared for someone older, with more of a career before him.'[17] Inevitably there were those both in India and in English society who commented on the advantage to a 'penniless' young naval officer, known for his ambitiousness, of claiming a pretty young girl so soon after her inheritance of a vast fortune.

There were, too, uncharitable comments in wardrooms of HM ships, where most officers lived on their meagre pay. But to the great masses, who read about the engagement in the popular papers, this was a fairy-tale romance. 'The friendship of the young couple has been remarked upon for some time,' ran one gossip column. 'Both were guests of Mrs Ronald Greville at Polesden Lacey last October, not long before Lord Louis sailed for India.' For a number of the more sophisticated people, and especially the London 'smart set', it was too good to be true, and caustic comments were *de rigueur*.

But for the present, safely out of earshot of the jealous, ungenerous attacks that were later to follow them like a baying chorus of denigration throughout their lives, Mountbatten and Edwina delighted in each other's company, publicly and also in the privacy of a bungalow prepared for the Prince of Wales, the key to which was slipped to his cousin as a practical gesture and as a token of his joy at their happiness.

Mountbatten's mother, concealing her earlier doubts, wrote to say that the news was no surprise. 'I am really and truly happy at it as I think you both know your own minds now. May much happiness be in store for you.'[18]

In fact, Victoria Milford Haven and Edwina quickly formed a close, affectionate and mutually compatible relationship. Edwina admired the older woman's courage, pragmatic intelligence and wide knowledge of the world, of history and philosophy, and found in her the surrogate mother she had subconsciously been searching for. Victoria was attracted by the freshness, depth and openness of Edwina's mind, and (later) her sensible attitude towards her new wealth. Both the woman of fifty-eight who was Queen Victoria's favourite grand-daughter and once a royal princess who knew all the crowned heads of Europe, and the richest young woman in the land, were socialists by instinct and conviction for most of their lives, which became another object of unfavourable comment. As a naval wife who had also married young, Victoria felt it necessary to offer advice on that rôle. It was not always an easy one, she told Edwina. 'I hope you will be able to take much pride and interest in his career.'[19]

Edwina now had to part from her fiancé – the first of so many partings. The Prince in the *Renown* continued the tour, first to Ceylon, then to Singapore and Hong Kong, arriving in Yokohama on 12 April 1922.

Mountbatten was fascinated but disturbed by what he saw and heard in Japan. Since that nation had opened its doors to the world in the previous century, it had become a traditional friend and ally of Britain. When the Japanese began flexing their muscles, it was the British Navy to which they turned for knowledge, training and tradition, and British shipyards for their men o'war. A treaty of friendship had for long existed between the two nations, and the Emperor had recently made a state visit to Britain. But now Mountbatten observed new tides flowing in Japan. Nationalism was unhealthily rife on the one side, and bolshevik-style unrest was growing among the industrial workers. Japan had been rearming at sea in competition with the United States Navy for a decade, and now possessed the third most powerful navy in the world. The treaty with Britain had not been renewed.

Mountbatten was naturally curious about the Japanese Navy's organization and the new ships pouring from the new shipyards. All official suggestions that one or two of the new big ships might be inspected were rebuffed in chilly tones by the Japanese authorities. But Mountbatten's unofficial attempt to examine the battleship *Mutsu*, the most powerful afloat, surprisingly succeeded. 'Perhaps they thought I was too young and silly to matter,' he commented. 'But, in fact, I compiled a most secret report for the Admiralty on her armour and underwater armament.' The figures were impressive. Everything he saw relating to this new and aggressive nation's defences impressed him. He noted in his diary the warlike mood of the rulers. 'This,' he wrote prophetically, 'is the war I fear.'

When the *Renown* docked in Plymouth on 21 June 1922, Mountbatten had travelled over 40,000 miles with his cousin, and had logged impressions and experiences that were to be of priceless value when he faced, in the East, two of the greatest challenges in his life.

Edwina was there to meet him, vivacious, excited, 'lovelier than ever', as Mountbatten described her. 'We were determined to get married as soon as possible, and we had already made the arrangements for 18 July. That was a date that seemed to suit everyone.'

What else could the event be called except 'the wedding of the year'? For an hour or two on this wet, chill, summer day, it seemed as if there had been no Great War, no royal assassinations and abdications, no dynastic toppling, no revolution. It may have been a hollow deception, but it was a good one.

George v was present, of course, and Queen Mary, the King's mother, Queen Alexandra, Tsar Alexander iii's Dowager Tsarina, who unlike the rest of her family had been rescued by the British Navy, the Prince of Wales, as best man, and his younger brothers, princes and princesses, representatives of defunct grand-dukedoms, Princess Alice's four girls, Margarita (born in 1905), Theodora (1906), Cecile (1911) and Sophie (1914), acting as bridesmaids in delphinium blue dresses. The Houses of Windsor and Hesse, of Denmark and Saxe-Coburg-Gotha, of Teck and Greece – all were present at this grand celebration of the half-truth that dynasties could not be toppled as easily as all that.

During the short period between Mountbatten's return and the wedding, photographers and reporters had stalked the couple from the box at Newmarket racecourse to the gates of Buckingham Palace, from Broadlands to Brook House. Now, as the *Illustrated London News* austerely headed pages of drawings and photographs, 'The occasion aroused great public interest owing to the bridegroom's relationship to the royal family, and the great wealth of the charming young bride.' The tabloids screamed that it was 'The Wedding of the Century'.

The wealth was reflected in some of the wedding presents piled up at Brook House for the massive reception after the couple in a bridal car had been pulled by a gun crew from the *Repulse* from St Margaret's. A diamond pendant with the royal cipher in diamonds came from Queen Alexandra, and there were many more diamonds from her family, a platinum and diamond brooch from the Aga Khan, and a silver figure of Atlas supporting a silver globe from the Prince of Wales, with the routes of their world tours traced upon it.

Edwina had been allowed just one pearl necklace before her wedding. Now she insisted on taking all the jewellery with her on the honeymoon. Mountbatten took a revolver. He also took six months' leave on half-pay, which he could now reasonably afford, and they decided to take their honeymoon in two halves, the first in Europe, the second in the USA.

It all started with a drive from Brook House to Broadlands, which had been made available for them, in the Rolls-Royce Edwina had given her husband, a Barker-bodied cabriolet Silver Ghost model. 'I was mad about it.' They were both worn out after the reception for 800, and Mountbatten enjoyed recounting how, for the only time in their marriage, neither of them was able to talk. 'I had to refill the tank at a garage on the way,' he recalled, 'and by chance a mutual friend of ours pulled up at the same time.

So I said, "D'you know my fiancée, Miss Ashley?" I saw Edwina holding up her hand with the wedding ring, and with a resigned expression on her face. But I was still so stunned I didn't realize it.'

After Broadlands, they took the car across the Channel. 'We drove 700 miles through France and Spain to Santander, to stay with my cousin Queen Ena and King Alfonso. Then we drove across to Germany to stay with my Uncle Ernie, the Grand Duke of Hesse. ...' Even in the 1920s, it was still possible, for the right people, to tour from palace to palace.

In addition to being passionately in love, the couple experienced an un-surpassed sense of liberation. Both, in their different ways, had led circum-scribed lives: for Mountbatten, Navy discipline since the age of thirteen, and the restrictions imposed by his rank and background; for Edwina, the social confinements of her class and upbringing – she was still not yet twenty-one. Now, touring about Europe, they felt utterly free, relaxed and emanci-pated. Mountbatten had, in his usual thorough way, planned a detailed itinerary with the aid of Baedeker guides. Edwina asked him to throw it away. She said she had had enough organization and discipline to last a lifetime. For Mountbatten, it was like asking a German general to go into battle with-out a map, but he agreed in order to please her. The first night out of Paris they ended up with a single bed in a murky attic.

As the gossip columnists described it, 1922 was a golden year for the golden couple, the Mountbattens. From July to December, Edwina and Dickie, beautiful and handsome, rich, almost royal, charming, intelligent, amusing and privileged, moved about the world by Rolls-Royce, luxury liner and private luxury railroad car, trailing a golden streamer announcing that this is the jazz age, this is the way we must all live. They were, in the eyes of the public, the personification of fun and life and materialism after the four years of austerity, fear, suffering and death. 'They were, quite simply, the most glamorous and sought after people in society. Everyone loved them,' one of their contemporaries said.

Edwina fell in love with the USA on the first sight of New York's sky-scrapers from the East River. Their introductions were limitless. 'We were treated as VIPs and met important people wherever we went,' Mountbatten said. 'I was invited to visit the President of the United States [Harding], and I was one of the principal speakers at a Navy League dinner in Wash-ington, packed with admirals and senior officers – very disconcerting for a young lieutenant!'

He was, of course, not in the least disconcerted. From the earliest age, Mountbatten never had any trouble on a platform. Nor did he have any trouble with the American reporters who followed them everywhere. 'What d'you have to say about political conditions in India, sir?'

'It's not the Navy's business to talk, you know,' he replied with that charming, intimate smile.

'What do you think about the conduct of the modern woman and divorce, ma'am?'

'Oh,' said Edwina blandly, 'I just believe in being an old-fashioned wife.' And her smile was equally disarming.

Dinner with Jerome Kern on the first night. The Ziegfeld Follies, a baseball game to meet Babe Ruth, dinners, theatres. Then the trans-continental train, the Topeka, Aitchison and Santa Fé, in their private car.

Hollywood. They were met at Los Angeles and whisked off to Pickfair, the famed home of America's sweethearts, Douglas Fairbanks and Mary Pickford, who were to become lifelong friends.

In addition to an abiding curiosity to see movieland, Mountbatten was keen to learn more of the technical side of film-making. He had been given the customary box Brownie as a boy, learned to get the best from it, and became fascinated by photography. During his first voyage with the Prince of Wales, he had learned about movies from the *Renown*'s ciné-cameraman, and in collaboration they had made a film to teach fleet manœuvres to the service.

The Admiralty were not interested in this early effort, but Mountbatten was not in the least discouraged. He bought one of the very early 35mm ciné cameras for his own use. And now he was determined to be the most proficient of cameramen – better than anyone else.

In Hollywood he received the best technical instruction from the best cameramen in the world. Cecil B. de Mille and Charlie Chaplin taught him how to direct and how to act. From this stemmed their most unusual wedding present, a film directed by Charlie Chaplin, starring Jackie Coogan and Charlie Chaplin, Lord Louis Mountbatten and Edwina Mountbatten, entitled *Nice and Friendly*. It is sometimes shown today. Chaplin told Mountbatten he was a terrible actor, but Chaplin was always joking.

Hollywood, Niagara Falls, the Grand Canyon, Florida, always met by the notable and rich, always royally entertained, publicized, flattered. New York again. A last luncheon given by the New York Press Club. 'Can we in America', asked Hearst columnist and millionaire, Arthur Brisbane, 'produce a young couple of twenty-two and twenty who could possibly be such fine representatives of their country, and do such an excellent job as ambassadors in a foreign country as the Mountbattens have done here in America?'

What answer could there be? Mountbatten's response is not recorded. Perhaps for once he never made one. It was hardly necessary. He and Edwina had responded to the usual warm American hospitality with the unique blend of charm, wit and talent for saying the right yet unstereotyped comments that was to distinguish their style for the two decades between the wars.

The novelist Barbara Cartland, who knew them both particularly well at this time, said of Edwina, 'She was really marvellous. She was like Dickie, she concentrated on you – she put her eyes on you and you knew that you were the one person she wanted to see and talk to. Irresistible.'[20]

And so there ended, on a note of mutual affection and admiration just before Christmas 1922, the first tryst in the long and ardent love affair between the Mountbattens and America. They embarked in their liner loaded with presents which were piled up in their state suite. 'They danced and played and laughed their way across the Atlantic,' wrote one contemporary columnist. No doubt they rested and slept too, and certainly they planned their lives for the following year and where they would live.

Georgie met them at Southampton on 23 December and drove them, with a small nucleus of their luggage, to the Milford Haven home at Southsea where they spent a family Christmas with Nada and the two children, Tatiana and David.

In their absence, the Conservatives had been returned to power with an overwhelming majority. Churchill, who had worked so valiantly for a peaceful solution to the Irish problem, had lost his seat at Dundee and was out of Parliament for the first time in the century. In Ireland the last English troops had left the new Irish Free State, and many people believed that this would mean an end to the murders.

Edwina, as a child, had spent carefree holidays in Ireland with her sister Mary and their Pakenham cousins Joan and Dermot, at a castle in County Sligo in this new Irish Free State. It belonged to her father, but one day she would inherit it, as she had inherited Brook House from her grandfather. It was called Classiebawn. A first visit to the scene of his murder fifty-seven years later was among Mountbatten's plans for 1923.

3
FAMILY AFFAIRS

A VISIT TO the Ashleys at Broadlands in the New Year was followed by a return to London, and to work. At no other time in his life was Mountbatten again to spend so long away from his professional work. He had not for one minute been without occupation during his six months on half-pay. His restless, questing mind was never idle.

The subject to which he had given most thought was his future in the Navy, and what he should specialize in. In the past, he had tinkered with wireless sets, learned the special skills of making movies, renewed his love for fast cars (and he could now afford to indulge himself to the full with these expensive toys), read a great deal, talked tirelessly with everyone he had met, all the way from Wolfsgarten to Beverly Hills. 'Now I was keen to get back to work.

'Marriage to a very rich woman, as my mother had said, posed problems,' said Mountbatten. This was another of the many subjects to which he had given thought during his long honeymoon. 'I then realized forcibly that the only hope of standing on my own legs was to work. I couldn't hope to produce the money that Edwina had. So I had to work very hard in the one profession where money doesn't count. I worked like a beaver to excel.'

Mountbatten had before him at all times the record and example of his father. 'My father worked very hard, too. He was ambitious in the professional sense. He always took on the most interesting and difficult jobs, and it never entered my father's mind nor my mind ever to do a job other than at one's best ability. My father wasn't well off, he couldn't hope to make money in the Navy. My desire to make good was the same as his, except that I had to make good *because* I had a rich wife.'

But this was not the only reason why his standard of hard work was far higher than that of his father, who never worked with the intense, almost manic, zeal of his son, as if pursued by the most dreaded of all spectres – failure.

Like Admiral 'Jackie' Fisher, who had disastrously succeeded Prince Louis as First Sea Lord, Mountbatten liked the occasional aphorism, and could usually produce one for most situations. On hard work it was, 'You can't be any cleverer than God made you, and if you want to get on, that means only one thing – hard work. Apply yourself, and try to succeed. And I did.' It was as simple as that. Or so he thought.

In his determination to excel, Mountbatten suffered under grave handicaps as well as considerable advantages. The first handicap was privilege. When Mountbatten was a boy sitting for his Osborne examinations, his father had lectured him on the advantages and disadvantages of his privileged rank.

'It will affect you in two ways,' he had told Mountbatten. 'When you are young, it will be wholly disadvantageous. You must realize that anyone who appears to be making friends with you has probably got his real eye on the main chance and is just sucking up. *You*,' he went on, 'must make the first step, you must make your own choice. Whenever you join a new ship, you will be under suspicion. Work hard. Be seen to be working hard. If you stick to it, the time will come when people will be prepared to help you. Later in your career, you will find your privileged standing an advantage.'

It turned out just as Prince Louis had predicted, only worse. Ragging at Osborne was one thing. And every midshipman suffered the cruel bullying of the gunroom. But, as a junior officer in his twenties and early thirties, whenever he joined a new ship, or began at a new shore establishment, he suffered a more subtle form of torture. He was, in the eyes of many of them, too good to be true.

You can hear the voices in the wardroom when Mountbatten was known to be joining the ship. 'We'll have to take *him* down a peg or two', 'Be turning up at the dockyard in that Rolls-Royce his wife gave him', and from the Commander, 'I'm not having him flashing his money about the place and talking about dinner at Buckingham Palace.'

'I can't tell you what I went through,' Mountbatten recalled. 'Every time I joined a new ship, I had to start absolutely afresh. I would probably arrive in the wardroom at the same time as a copy of the latest *Tatler* with pictures of me on leave. You could see absolutely the suspicion and the hostility which I then had to break down. I pretended not to notice it.'

It was hard, uphill work before he even began to work hard and show himself willing, and at the same time to conceal the repeated wounds that were inflicted on him. 'Time was the only cure. I just made myself available for any job, and bit by bit I worked myself into a position. But it was very painful and it took time.'

The fact that he nearly always succeeded was witnessed by numerous fellow officers, from his first post-marriage ship to his first command twelve years later. Vice-Admiral Sir Charles Hughes Hallett was a gunnery lieu-tenant in 1923 when he first met Mountbatten. Mountbatten had been with the ship for seven months, and had had a hard time. But now he had settled in, and there were only a few who were still hostile. 'In the service you always ran across a few people who disapproved of Mountbatten – mostly it was from a streak of jealousy, that was all.' Hughes Hallett thought him 'quite obviously a leader. If anything was going on, he would be at the bottom of it, both entertainment and professionally. At guest nights, he always started up the fun and games. He was the natural leader, with comic ideas.'[1]

Hughes Hallett recalled that Mountbatten never had any trouble with the lower deck. 'In those days, it was very different. They were naturally fond of people with a handle to their name. The divisional system was in-troduced about this time, and his forecastle division worshipped him. When we were painting ship, I remember Dickie taking up a chisel and chipping away at the old paint. A seaman would rush up and say "Oh sir, let me do that." So he would hand it over and pick up another. "Oh sir...." It earned the respect of the men and the job was done in half the time.'[2]

Privilege had worked against Mountbatten from another quarter in these early days after World War I. He wanted to get on at once with his long course, which required experience in destroyers. Mountbatten therefore got in touch with an officer called David Joel who had served under his father at the beginning of the century – 'an interesting fellow,' Mountbatten called him, 'who was in command of a destroyer'. Joel later left the Navy, made a for-tune in furniture, and returned for World War II. ' "Yes," said Joel, "a good idea. You must come as my first lieutenant." But the Admiralty said no. They clearly considered that this young fellow had had a hell of a good time with long voyages with the Prince of Wales, and a six-months-long honeymoon with his rich wife. So they sent me to the battleship *Revenge* instead. It was the very last thing I wanted. Not only did I not want a big ship, but the *Revenge* was a part of the International Fleet in the Dardanelles to deal with all the Balkan troubles at the time. And wives were not allowed – too dangerous.'

It was remarkable how closely Mountbatten's naval career followed the pattern of his father's, and how frequently, for both father and son, naval and domestic occasions coincided, partly by design, partly by chance.

When Mountbatten had accompanied the Prince of Wales to India, he was only following the example of his father, who had acted as orderly officer in the *Serapis* to the then Prince of Wales on his tour in 1875–6. Both father and son were twenty-one at the respective times. Mountbatten, before his murder, had arranged to repeat the performance again with the present Prince of Wales in 1979 after returning from Classiebawn.

In 1878, Prince Louis' battleship, the *Sultan*, was one of a squadron sent to the Dardanelles as a deterrent to further trouble in Constantinople. Shortly after his return to London, he began his love affair with Lillie Langtry.

By contrast, Mountbatten came back from Turkey to find his sister Louise in love. Louise was thirty-four, an intelligent, down-to-earth, talkative woman who had spent most of her life at home, with the exception of the war years. 'She was not very pretty,' said her cousin, Princess Alice Countess of Athlone, 'and lacked charm. She was so terribly thin with a little flat face.'[3] According to one of her nieces, she now 'seemed embarrassed, almost annoyed with herself' for being in love.

Louise was in love with Crown Prince Gustaf of Sweden. In 1905 he had married Queen Victoria's grand-daughter, Princess Margaret of Connaught, who had died in 1920, leaving the Swedish prince with five children. He had come over for the English season, a lonely man who was attracted to the woman he had last met in 1914 when she and her mother were returning hastily from Russia through Sweden after the outbreak of war. They became engaged, the wedding was fixed for November, and the Swedish Navy escorted the groom to British waters for the occasion. The *Revenge* was assigned to meet the Swedish squadron, and in this way Mountbatten appropriately met his future brother-in-law at sea.

The wedding on 3 November 1923 was almost as grand, and attended by almost as many royal figures, as the Mountbattens'. The family, and especially Louise's mother, were very relieved at the marriage, although secretly they found the Crown Prince dreadfully serious and boring. The couple later gave the democratic stamp to the Swedish monarchy by bicycling about Stockholm. They visited England every year, except during World War II, until the King's death at the age of ninety-two – visits that continued after Louise's death in 1965 and were accepted with stoic resignation by everyone from the Queen downwards.

By this time, Edwina had completed the reorganization and renovation that would make Brook House less gloomy and less ponderous. There was nothing whatever she could do about the marble, but brighter paint and curtains and carpets helped to relieve the Edwardian mustiness of a millionaire widower's monolithic pile in Park Lane.

Cassel had bought Brook House from Lord Tweedmouth and had given an architect his head, and many hundreds of thousands of pounds, to create from the shell a banker's Buckingham Palace. Unfortunately, when it was finished, everyone called it 'The great lavatory'. It took time. It took a year to quarry the 800 tons of Tuscany marble for the main hall and staircase.

Barbara Cartland visited it after Edwina's conversion, and was amazed at the sight. 'Corinthian pillars, twenty feet high, rose like petrified jets of water in the air,' ran one lyrical description. 'The floors and walls were of marble, with mahogany in the balustrades and wrought metal to enhance the general effect. Rare blue marble was imported from Canada to add to the magnificence of the whole, and the architect, visualizing the possibilities of a *coup d'œil* all marble and glittering lights as a setting for social functions at night, added an effect of rising galleries culminating in a vast skylight dome.'[4]

Just one hundred guests could sit down in Eastern splendour in the dining-room, and they could retire to the Turkish baths after if they wanted to work off the effects of the rich food. That was Brook House in the 1920s.

Edwina was half attracted to the place, half appalled by it. Mountbatten loved it. Nothing could be too enormous and ostentatious for him. Once recovered from the early reservations about being married to the nation's richest woman, he had settled down as one born to it to enjoy her wealth. All his life he possessed this special talent for transmitting to others any pleasure he felt, and this naturally included his delight in having a great deal of money. When Edwina gave him the biggest Hispano-Suiza motor car money could buy, he emphasized its identity and ownership by fitting an 'LM' numberplate and a special mascot, just in case he might not be identified.

The Mountbattens loved showing off Brook House to their friends, and they used it for their London entertaining. Eventually, Edwina would also inherit Broadlands from her father. For the present, the location of their country house must depend on Mountbatten's home port, or where he might be working when ashore.

Mountbatten now made up his mind about the specialist branch to which he would dedicate his naval career. In 1918, when on leave, he had taken private flying lessons. Like his father, he believed strongly in the future of the naval Air Arm, in which, for the present, Britain led the world with the first true aircraft-carriers and torpedo-carrying machines. Then the formidable leader of the RAF, Lord Trenchard, had succeeded in prising from the Royal Navy control of all naval aircraft, leaving the Air Arm as a sort of hermaphrodite for two decades. It was the worst thing that could happen to the Navy, and Mountbatten saw little future in a career in this branch in which he would have to take an RAF commission.

Submarines also intrigued him. They had already proved how formidable they were. But Mountbatten felt with his highly sensitive antennae that the best future for him lay in signals.

While serving in the *Revenge*, he applied for a course at the Signal School at Portsmouth, and was accepted. He then settled down to a long period as a land-based sailor, first at Portsmouth and later at Greenwich. The work was highly demanding, and he never allowed pleasure to interfere with it. On the other hand, his wealth and exceptional energy, as well as an abiding desire for the good things in life, ensured that he also enjoyed himself with a very full and very grand social life.

Those closest to him – even Edwina sometimes – wondered how he did it, and it was indeed an extraordinary performance. At the Signal School at Portsmouth the course was a tough one, and the competition among the officers (most of whom were not well off and led very simple social lives) was intense.

Mountbatten played polo with a string of ponies he had recently bought, went to parties in London, entertained lavishly at Brook House, saw his mother frequently as well as his brother and Nada and their family, dined at Buckingham Palace, and at York House with the Prince of Wales and Mrs Dudley Ward, and found time to include in his daily round an invariable diary entry, 'Amuse Patricia'.

Towards the end of his service at sea, and when the *Revenge* was at Funchal, Madeira, and on St Valentine's Day (again), Edwina had given birth to her first child, a girl. Mountbatten returned to London as quickly as he could. There was a great party at Brook House to celebrate, with the Pickfords among the guests; and Douglas and Mary came to the christening of Patricia Edwina Victoria Mountbatten.

The baby, and professional work, in no way deflected Mountbatten and Edwina's determination to accompany the Prince of Wales to New York in the summer of 1924. They sailed in the liner *Berengaria*, along with a host of their other friends, including Lady Diana Cooper, returning to play her now famed part in *The Miracle* on Broadway. New York was again one long party. So was London, at the height of the season, on their return.

Later, at the end of the Portsmouth signals course, Mountbatten came out with the highest points. He was the winner again. Why? The answer, according to Mountbatten himself, was simple. 'I was born with an ability to concentrate very hard on a job for a long time,' he said, 'and then turn for relaxation to something quite different and work just as hard at that. It has proved remarkably useful in my life. When I was Viceroy of India, for example, and working about eighteen hours a day with a great many difficulties to contend with, I would relax at the end of the day by working on my book *Relationship Tables*.' Anyone who has seen this enormous genealogical masterpiece, which delineates relationships by coded numerals of his family back to the late eighteenth century, will wonder at the concentration and clarity of thought required to compile it.

As a young, ambitious naval officer, this rare talent allowed him to develop exceptional proficiency which nearly always put him at the top, and simultaneously to lead a full and very arduous social life. The trouble was that it was the glitter of his glamorous playboy existence that attracted public attention, and no one outside the service knew how hard he worked to be a winner. But then Mountbatten made no attempt whatever to disabuse the public of their belief that he was a playboy first and last. All that his friends observed from time to time was the old abstracted expression that might creep over his face while dancing the tango at 1 am at the Café Royal, and an unusual drying up of the conversation. Mountbatten was working at a problem related to the conversion of Royal Navy wireless signalling from morse code to voice.

In addition to polo, at which of course he was becoming more proficient than anyone else, Mountbatten and Edwina had taken up sailing, and called their first yacht *Shadow 1*. Mountbatten also amused himself off duty with a ferocious American Garwood Liberty-engined speedboat which could do forty knots.

Now, he considered, it was time to join the Royal Yacht Squadron. This was – and is – a very exclusive club, and membership was strung about with all sorts of conditions, like being well connected, an obvious gentleman, and possessing a yacht of suitable size. For a proposer, Mountbatten thought he should go to the top, and asked the Duke of Sutherland.

The Duke thought that it was a good idea. 'But what is the size of your yacht, Dickie? They can be rather tricky about that.'

It was less than fifty tons, the lower limit. 'Well, I still think it's a good idea, and I'll propose you.'

Later, standing on the lawn outside the club as a guest, Mountbatten saw the dashing pioneer aviator Claude Grahame-White come tearing in in his Garwood Liberty-engined speed boat, spinning round and splashing yachts and people. There were angry protests, and within Mountbatten's earshot one ancient member (no doubt on the committee) said to another, 'There's that bloody young so-and-so Dickie Mountbatten showing off again.'

Mountbatten wanted to say to them, 'But it can't be me – look, I'm here!'

Instead his subsequent blackballing created something of a sensation because the Club depended on royal patronage. 'I'll go and see the King about it – it'll be all right,' said his friend Lord Birkenhead, the Secretary of State for India.

Others were concerned at this snub, including the Club's vice-commodore, Lord Camden. 'Next time I'll get David Beatty to put you up – that'll show the navy approves, and I'll second you.'

This was in 1926. Mountbatten now owned the 66-ton *Shrimp*, well above the lower limit. There were rumours that a retired admiral was lobbying committee members to blackball Mountbatten again. He was identified as Admiral Sir Francis Bridgeman, who had been sacked as First Sea Lord by Churchill and superseded by Mountbatten's father. He was known at the time to be bitterly hostile to Prince Louis, and had sworn vengeance on the family.

The result was a second blackballing, which was almost unprecedented and a real blow to Mountbatten, which he never forgave and never forgot. Many years later, during the war when Mountbatten was Chief of Combined Operations, he found himself at dinner next to the politician-soldier Lord Mottistone, Lord Lieutenant of Hampshire and the Isle of Wight, a keen yachtsman and Royal Yacht Squadron member.

'What are you doing in London?' Mountbatten asked.

'I'm going to see someone at the War Office. Some damn line regiment wants to requisition the squadron's clubhouse. Can't have that.'

Mountbatten told him that by chance he was the one person who could fix it. 'It was for the Guards Brigade, a part of Force J. I'll tell them to find somewhere else.'

'That's really very kind of you,' said Mottistone.

'Kind? Not at all,' Mountbatten protested. 'If I'd been a member (but I was blackballed twice) I would have been horrified at the club's unpatriotic attitude, and disgusted that the squadron should be the only scrimshankers not to play their part in the war. It amuses me to put you in this unfavourable light.'

'Well, I am inclined to agree with you,' Mottistone cravenly agreed, 'I think we should *want* to be taken over. And I do hope you will now join us.'

Mountbatten shook his head. 'Certainly not. If I can't get in by election I am not joining by requisition.'

And that was that. The story, which is undoubtedly true, was one that Mountbatten liked to tell in connection with his yachting days, and is evidence of how deeply he felt the snub. But the anecdote's postscript is equally revealing. 'Some time after this, the King said I really ought to join. I said, "I can't afford the one hundred guineas entrance." And he replied, "Come along, Dickie, be big about it, and show you don't mind." So I did. But the day he died I resigned.'

Part of the trouble had been that Mountbatten's idea of yachting did not altogether match that of the Royal Yacht Squadron's in the 1920s. He soon became impatient with sailing, which depended on unpredictable wind. He really preferred an engine, the more powerful the better, so it was no wonder that he had been mis-identified.

The newspapers frequently reported his racing, nearly always as the winner. But stories like this in the popular Press did not increase his chances of election to that ancient and splendid club: '*Shadow II* at Bournemouth won an exciting race against Claude Grahame-White in *Gee Whiz* over a course of eighteen miles under the auspices of the Royal Motor Yacht Club.'

In common with numerous Royal Navy officers over the years, the Mountbattens acquired a house near Portsmouth for convenience while he completed his signals course. Adsdean, however, was bigger than most of them, and it required eighteen servants to run it satisfactorily, headed by the butler, Frank Randall. It was of stone and flint, and was almost as ugly as Brook House (which required many more servants), although virginia creeper helped to conceal its hideous proportions. Edwina decorated the house throughout in her favourite colours of pink and cream, and there was a good deal of gilt and French walnut about the place, too.

Mountbatten loved it, and incorporated in the grounds a special pit for polo practice, with wire netting to catch the balls and full illumination for night use, a paddock and a golf course. 'We lived there until just before the war,' he said. 'It was ideal. Comfortable and convenient, and I could be into the dockyard in no time.'

The Mountbattens, then, appeared to be settling down to the domestic family life of an affluent, rising young naval officer on a shore appointment. Here Patricia toddled about the terraces and, when old enough, learned to ride.

But Edwina was soon feeling restless. All her life she was impatient with routine, and feared above all else forming a fixed pattern to her life. She loathed the predictable as nature abhors a vacuum. Every so often she felt this need to escape, to discover, to travel, to face challenges and risk her life.

Barbara Cartland was a close friend of Edwina's sister Mary and knew them both very well at this time. (She had just published her first novel, *Jig-Saw*, which was a best-selling revelation of life in Mayfair.) She said, 'Edwina was a complex personality because she had a man's brain in the body of a very beautiful woman. She could be tough when she wanted something because she *always* got her own way, yet she was compassionate in the real sense of that word. She gave the impression that she was really interested in everyone's personal problems. The secret was that she *was* interested and nothing was too small or too unimportant for her to put right.'[5]

Barbara Cartland is unquestionably correct in her summary of her old friend. Edwina was indeed possessed of a complex personality, derived from a blend of Jewish-oriental, interbred English aristocratic and Anglo-Irish blood, combined with a brilliant brain.

Her contemporaries recognized in the bubbling excitement an element of hysteria which took much controlling. She could one moment appear totally selfish and self-indulgent, the next concerned only with the happiness of others. The days of her preoccupation with charitable work and the alleviation of humanity's suffering were still far off, and as a young woman her charity was exclusively personal.

Edwina was a loving mother, but also a severe one with the emphasis on discipline. While she represented female emancipation in her dress and extrovert, extravagant public behaviour, she was Victorian with her children, instilling a sense of high morality while practising a relaxed moral pattern of behaviour herself. She was especially severe with her younger daughter, later keeping her on a modest allowance and insisting that she should go out to work for her living. Her friends mildly remonstrated with her at this, reminding her of her own gay days twenty years earlier, but she brushed aside their protests. Things were different then; now they were living in an age of austerity, and socialist principles decreed that *everyone* should work.

But Pamela had not even been born, and Patricia was still only two, when Edwina suddenly decided to indulge in her new-found lust for travel. Her trip to India in pursuit of Mountbatten had given her a heady taste for exploration, and the money which came to her a few months later removed any barrier to her indulging this taste. So, instead of settling down to the comforts and pleasures of Adsdean and Brook House, Edwina slipped quietly away, at the end of the 1925 season, telling only a few friends.

Mountbatten heard little from her – an occasional letter from Russia, or the South Seas. For four months, Edwina sailed as an ordinary member of the crew of a 50-ton sailing schooner trading for copra among the Polynesian islands. She might never have married, never had a child, never had any responsibilities. She eventually reappeared, in a daze of satisfaction and contentment and in wonderful health, in the early spring of 1926. It was as if she had been through a transcendental experience.

Mountbatten was living at Brook House. He had succeeded in getting on to the prized advance signal course at Greenwich. Now he was longing to get out to the Mediterranean, and before the end of the summer, he heard that, with effect from 14 December 1926, he would be appointed Assistant Fleet Wireless Officer in the battleship *Warspite*, Admiral Sir Roger Keyes' flagship, a plum appointment for a young lieutenant.

The appointment, he was later to learn, almost backfired on him. When Keyes saw a list of names of new officers who were to join him, he put a line through Mountbatten's. 'I don't want a cousin of the King out here on my staff.' He already had Georgie, who was a gunnery commander, in the fleet, and perhaps the hero of the Zeebrugge raid in 1918 thought one King's cousin was enough. So he wrote to the Admiralty. Later, with the letter already London-bound, he relented. 'I was thinking about it,' he told Mountbatten later, 'and I turned up an old file of letters from your father. I realized that he had given me such support as a young man, and shown such confidence in me, that I couldn't do this to his son. So I sent a telegram to the Admiralty cancelling my letter.'

The Mediterranean Fleet was the next stage in the career pattern Mountbatten had traced out to emulate his father's. Prince Louis as a lieutenant had been appointed to the Mediterranean Fleet's flagship exactly fifty years earlier in 1876. His commander-in-chief had been the Queen's second son, Prince Alfred. Fleet gossip at the time told of Court influence. Now Mountbatten had to face similar accusations, hinted at in rumours and gossip columns.

Edwina, as always, listened sympathetically to his complaints that whatever he did and wherever he went he was pursued by tales of patronage originating either in her wealth or his royal connections. She told him to ignore them and just get on with the work. 'Rise above it, darling,' she would say. It was her favourite advice to everyone who appeared to need stiffening.

Shown a letter[6] he had written to one of his closest friends, Andrew Yates, at this time, Mountbatten commented nearly fifty years later that it exactly summed up his feelings of near despair at the way no one ever believed that he worked, and that any special credit was gained by means of special influence.

'I had this special mark after my name in the Navy List,' he said. 'It meant that I had completed the Advance Telegraphy Court at Greenwich. But it is true what I said in this letter to Andrew – that everyone thought I had bribed someone at the Admiralty. It was just the same when I went out to Malta a few months later. I worked like a beaver, but people only saw me on the polo ground. I tried to ignore it and satisfy my own conscience and my superiors.'

Mountbatten succeeded in both quests, but he was never able to shrug off the hints and innuendos that everything that he accomplished was gained by reason of advantages open to no one else. It was a heavy burden to carry through life.

It was why he was inordinately proud of the achievements which could not be ascribed to outside influence. These were his inventions, which no one could deny him, and for this reason they tended to be underrated by those seeking to denigrate him. Here again there is a parallel with his father. Prince Louis was an unflamboyant, modest man, but he, too, took great pride in his inventions like the Course Indicator, which was adopted in large numbers by the Royal Navy and adapted in fire control instruments and bomb sights. It was his and his alone.

Mountbatten's inventions included the Mountbatten Ruler, which was engraved on compass roses and obviated reference to the compass on the chart; a semaphore machine worked on a typewriter board capable of sending forty-five words per minute; a sub-focal signalling shutter, which again was capable of signalling fast, at a much higher speed than by lamp signalling.

Mountbatten's concern about the unjust accusations of favoured treatment in 1926 was compounded by a series of articles, illustrated with photographs, about the Brook House 'cabin'. Mountbatten had taken over a part of the mansion and converted it at vast expense into a facsimile of an admiral's cabin in his flagship. Through the 'windows' could be seen an exact model of Valetta harbour, Malta; the buildings all to scale, the harbour containing the anchored Mediterranean Fleet. Everything, including the ships, was lit up at night, and at a touch of the switch, one man o'war could signal another by morse lamp.

This schoolboy's dream-come-true was widely publicized. 'Lord Louis is so fond of the simplicity of naval life,' wrote one columnist, 'that although he lives in one of the most ornate and decorative mansions in London, he likes to sleep at times in the simple, barely-furnished cabin.' It was neither simple nor barely furnished, but he found it satisfying at the end of a hard day to imagine himself c-in-c Mediterranean Fleet sending orders to his subordinates.

Articles describing the 'cabin', with many accompanying photographs, appeared widely, and not always accurately. Mountbatten was more distressed at the inaccuracies than at the publicity, which he claimed was intended to help the interior decorator and architect who had designed it to get more commissions. But in the end he had to admit that the invitations to the Press were a mistake. 'I agree that it looked like an advertisement for me which is unfortunate,' he wrote to Yates. Then, defiantly, 'If people take it amiss that's there [sic] funeral. Life is far too short to worry about that sort of thing.'[7]

And he never did worry for long. In October he despatched his polo ponies to Malta so that they would be ready for play when he arrived. Neither was the *Shrimp* to be left behind, and her designer and builder, Peter du Cane, accompanied her through the French river and canal system via Paris, with orders to tuck her out of sight somewhere in Malta until Mountbatten's arrival.[8]

The expectation of hard work, regular polo, sailing and a full social life in Malta filled him with delight. In spite of recent discomfitures, Mountbatten was happier than he had ever been before in his life, and perhaps ever would be again. Edwina and Patricia and Edwina's sister Mary would be arriving a few weeks later.

They had nearly rented another 'colossal marble monstrosity', as Mountbatten called the Villa Refalo, but had decided for the time being to take three flats opposite Curzon House in Pieta. A small Fiat and a two-seat Chrysler for Edwina, suitable for getting about Malta, would be awaiting their arrival, as well as a full complement of servants. Everything, then, was extremely well organized as usual, and Edwina was just as excited as her husband at the thought of her first tour of duty-and-pleasure in the Mediterranean.

Edwina and many of her 'bright young things' friends had discovered an enjoyable distraction in the General Strike, which had begun early in May, 1926, soon after Edwina's return from the Pacific. Her friends expected her, as an avowed socialist, to support the strike, and certainly not to cross a picket line. But every day she was driven from Brook House in her Rolls-Royce to the *Daily Express* office in Fleet Street where she and Jean Norton, her close friend, operated the switchboard of their mutual friend Max Aitken, who had been Lloyd George's Minister of Information during the war and been made a baron – Lord Beaverbrook – for his work. In the machine room, Lady Diana Cooper helped with the folding. Lord Beaverbrook caught the spirit of Fleet Street's reaction when he wrote, 'I think everybody enjoyed the strike – on both sides – volunteers and strikers alike. It was treated in a holiday spirit; and the pickets outside the *Daily Express* office were quite as amused as the amateurs working the mechanical side of the newspaper within.'[9]

On a more serious level, Edwina was a witness to the ferocious row that blew up during the strike between Beaverbrook and Winston Churchill, now Chancellor of the Exchequer. Churchill had organized and produced an emergency newspaper called the *British Gazette*, and wanted to requisition the *Daily Express*'s newsprint and delay the publication of regular newspapers when the strike was over. Beaverbrook resisted, and won, at the cost of a broken relationship for nearly fifteen years.

Three years later, Beaverbrook took his two beautiful temporary telephonists to Russia. To Edwina, there seemed to be nothing anachronistic about sailing to Russia, which she admired so ardently for its supposed egalitarianism, in one of the world's most luxurious yachts; nor in helping to break a strike by Britain's workers, whom she regarded as ground-down victims of capitalism.

All this was part of the engaging unpredictability of this restless woman, like the socialist *Daily Herald* left lying about in the house – the only

newspaper allowed – while other papers were reporting her extravagant
parties and dresses, and her appearances at Court. For example, within a
month of the end of the General Strike: 'Some marvellous gowns will be
seen at the 3rd Court of the Season at Buckingham Palace tonight. Distinctive even among such an array will be the "all silver" dress which Lady Louis
Mountbatten will wear. It is composed of nothing else, but silver
sequins – hundreds and hundreds of them.' To many of her friends this
inconsistency was treated lightly – 'Oh, isn't that like darling Edwina!'
Others were puzzled, or outraged.

Six months later, in February 1927, the Mountbattens for the first time
became a married couple serving on a foreign station, just like so many others
in the three services. They were well aware that with their wealth and rank,
their youth and reputation, they had to watch their style of living in Britain's
premier fleet.

Mountbatten, on the C-in-C's staff in the flagship, had heavy responsibilities. His will to succeed, to justify the privileged appointment, was boundless. But he had to face the predictably suspicious attitude of his fellow
officers, with the certain knowledge that he was being watched every minute
of every day.

For the periods when the flagship was at sea leading the fleet on cruises
and manœuvres, Edwina would follow in the *Shrimp*, and if the *Warspite*
anchored at Nice or Naples, Barcelona or Cyprus, the beautiful white
Mountbatten yacht was either already there, or would soon arrive to anchor
close by the flagship, and Mountbatten would proceed on board, usually
with a party of friends. 'Edwina got used to following the fleet around,'
said Mountbatten, 'and the Mediterranean is not a bad place to follow it
in.'

When the fleet was at Malta, Mountbatten spent most of the time ashore,
either lecturing midshipmen in signals, or on routine office work, and living
in their temporary home. Later, and inevitably, they acquired a house quite
as big as the Villa Refalo, 'a charming house called Casa Medina (my
brother's title because we shared the house with him) at the top of a narrow,
winding lane, just wide enough for one car at a time'. Almost every night
there would be some form of entertainment, and the Mountbatten parties
were the most lavish and popular among junior officers, and also of course
the wives of officers.

No one who served in the Mediterranean Fleet in 1927 could be unaware
of the presence of the Mountbatten entourage. The evidence of wealth, the
reputation that preceded them, the sight of this golden couple cruising
among the men o'war in Piraeus or Alexandria, all singled them out. It was

impossible to ignore them, and many retired officers today can recall them clearly, every memory etched in superlatives.

For some, the picture is still marked by resentment, distant echoes of wardroom complaints about the flaunting of their wealth, of seeming slights and echoes of arrogance. For others, it is all admiration for an able, amusing, hard-working young wireless officer, and a hospitable and charming wife.

From those midshipmen who attended his lessons, there is unstinted praise for his enthusiasm and ability to transmit it to his classes. No one could fault him as a teacher. We can see him standing before a blackboard, talking with great lucidity, frequently turning to emphasize a point with a drawing, or restlessly turning a heavy gold signet ring on his little finger as he talked. 'He was enjoying every minute of it, and so were we.' How did a transmitter work? He had built a model from glass tubing, pouring various coloured inks down the tubes to show the current flow, and getting himself covered in the ink in his enthusiasm. No one ever forgot a Mount-batten lesson. A petty officer said, 'The reason we admired him so much was because we were never able to put anything over on him.'[10]

It irritated Mountbatten to see his classes trying to match their note-taking with his own speed, and thus missing much of what he was saying. He decided to ban all notebooks, and instead provided every student with a précis of the day's lecture which they could then work up into notes. These summaries were later compiled into a textbook on wireless telegraphy which was used throughout the Signals Branch of the Navy.

Many of Mountbatten's fellow officers recognized his abilities and enthusiasm, and even the most hostile could not deny him certain qualities nor ignore his style. But few of his contemporaries, or his seniors, judged that he would go very far in the service. 'We always thought of him as having married millions of pounds and being mad on polo and pretty girls, and we thought he was a write-off as far as the Navy went,' recalled Lieutenant-Commander Peter Kemp, who had been a young sub-lieutenant at the time. 'We didn't see why he should *bother* to work. If any of us had had such luck *we* shouldn't have bothered. No, he was becoming the great playboy, and he acted like one. He wasn't going to go far, that's what we said.'[11]

On the manner in which he conducted himself with his great wealth, officers reacted in various ways, but the most intelligent and fair-minded agreed that he stood up well under difficult circumstances. 'It never struck me that Mountbatten had an easy row to hoe as a junior lieutenant,' is Kemp's judgment today. 'He managed things very well, I think. The only mistake that I can remember was a bit later. The C-in-C had to give rather formal and big parties for officers and their wives. By their very nature, they were stiff affairs which we had to attend as a duty.

'Now the Mountbattens lived in great style very near to the c-in-c's
official residence, and one night they held a huge party on the same night
as one of the Admiral's. I suppose we all left the c-in-c's party as early
as decently possible, and walked next door to join a much more hilarious
party. It aroused a lot of talk at the time. Looking back, I think it was
a rather poor show. But being impecunious sub-lieutenants, we enjoyed
ourselves all right. There was something about those Mountbatten
parties....'

Kemp did accept that 'their ruddy great yacht' following the fleet around
got a lot of backs up, particularly the backs of senior officers. Not the lower
deck. In those days, a Lord and Lady in a yacht were not the invariable
target of resentment and envy they were to become later.

Just before he left England, Mountbatten had written to a friend that
he was looking forward to coming out to Malta, doing some real work and
getting some regular polo. To him, the prompt arrival at Valetta of his ponies
was quite as important as the prompt departure of the *Warspite* on a cruise.
For Mountbatten, his polo was less a sport and entertainment than an extra-
curricular activity into which he threw as much energy and to which he
gave as much thought as the development of faster and more efficient
methods of signalling. 'I was never naturally good at it,' Mountbatten said.
'I was not a specially good horseman when I began, and I didn't have a
good eye for ball games. I had to plug away at it to be respectably good.
But I made a point of studying the game.'

From the start, Mountbatten saw a chukka of polo as a close parallel to
a naval battle, with all the needs of leadership, decisiveness, speed, communication, manœuvrability and good fast shooting. As he stood bent over
the table at his house discussing the day's performance with his team, the
'Bluejackets', moving about models, giving orders and uttering rebukes,
spectators were known to liken him to a Prussian cavalry officer after the
Battle of Sedan.

Mountbatten was indeed thinking and talking in terms of war, but exclusively of sea warfare, and of a successful polo player being an exact parallel
to a successful naval commander. This was evident in the language he
employed and the message of his writings. He began first with a duplicated
booklet, which was very elementary, but even this contained such commonsense advice to a polo player or gunnery officer as: 'When knocking about
always aim in a definite direction. Hitting aimlessly may be amusing but
it is a very bad habit.'

Later he wrote a book, which was to become the accepted authority on
the game, and of which he was as proud as his inventions. It was called
Introduction to Polo, and he used the waggish pseudonym 'Marco'. Much

of the advice in this interesting book could be introduced, changing scarcely a word, into a Naval Tactics Manual.

As a destroyer commander in war, Mountbatten followed his own sagacious advice to a polo player a decade earlier: 'The primary factor in a successful attack is speed. Generally speaking, if you are the stronger side you will be the attacking side, and it will be to your advantage to speed up the game. When you are the weaker side, however, you may sometimes feel that your advantage will lie in slowing up the game and making it "choppy". But it will not do you much good to break up your opponent's attack if you do not immediately counter-attack in your turn....'

And these homilies to a polo captain could be translated to any captain on his bridge, in peace or war: 'He should never criticize something that is done, and can't be undone, in the hearing of other people'; or, 'The team should have implicit confidence in his captain's decisions'; or 'Never feel that a piece of criticism or advice is too much trouble to give, or that it is too trivial, or that it exceeds your province.'

The book in every respect provides an interesting summary of some of the qualities that Mountbatten regarded as important to good leadership, and his efforts to spread the popularity of the game throughout the Navy did very much more than improve the sales of his book. Polo is fast, tough, requires quick decisions, initiative, teamwork and, above all, good shooting. He started the Royal Naval Polo Association, persuaded the King to become patron and his sons associate patrons, designed – after months of experiment and study – a new head for the mallet and called it 'The Royal Naval Polo Association Head'.

Mountbatten combined two of his enthusiasms by taking ciné sequences of his team at play, and then screening them in slow motion after practice so that the team could discuss their faults at leisure. He carried in his pocket everywhere a squash ball which he crushed in his hand when it was idle in order to strengthen his wrist muscles – something his nephew Prince Philip imitated when he began four-in-hand riding.

Within months, polo playing at Malta, which had always been a light-hearted game, with the score less important than the fun, had developed a highly professional quality, with a good deal higher standard and rather fewer laughs than before. With Mountbatten, it was the score and only the score that counted, and his 'Bluejackets' – Lieutenant Haywood-Leslie, Captain Neville of the Royal Marines, his great friend Charles Lambe as back, and himself as Captain and number 3 – began to pile up the silver cups.

Mountbatten was promoted lieutenant-commander on 15 April 1928, and was at last given a destroyer appointment. Charles Lambe came with him, and their Captain was M.G.B. Legge. Small, fast ships suited his temperament. Nothing gave him greater pleasure than manœuvring a 35-knot destroyer, making simulated torpedo attacks and retreating under a smoke screen, stalking submarines, or acting with his flotilla as a screen to the battle fleet.

The flotilla leader, *Stuart*, was a very fast 1,600-ton ship which had been launched just before the end of World War I. As flotilla wireless officer, Mountbatten's appointment was a step up but did not carry the same prestige as being on the C-in-C's staff. It was at this time that he sought to improve the speed of visual signalling, a destroyer's wireless being especially vulnerable in combat.

Family life and naval life during the late 1920s ran in close parallel for a period, and then became widely separated, for weeks, perhaps for months. At Malta, or cruising with the fleet, Edwina appeared to have everything she could need for a happy and full life. But her restless mind and her wanderlust were too powerful, and she would leave her family, sometimes at the shortest notice. One of these tours took her to Hollywood again, but her first love was for strange and exotic parts of the world, where she travelled with the most basic luggage – 'shorts, six shirts and a dress', reported the newspapers in September 1932 'is all Lady Louis Mountbatten is taking on her Persian Desert trip' – and living as far as possible with the people.

Mountbatten would have arranged a minute-by-minute itinerary months ahead, with cars to meet him, appointments with notable figures, and sojourns at embassies. This was not Edwina's way. Usually with just one friend – Marjorie Brecknock, Jean Norton or her sister-in-law Nada – she would live rough, in Persia, Egypt, the West Indies, the more obscure regions of Asia and the Far East, returning months later refreshed and usually with treasures from some archaeological dig or a small zoo of wild animals. Once it was a lion cub; Sabi remained a family pet until she became too large for comfort.

'Each journey was an enrichment,' wrote Edwina's biographer, 'yet with each return the urge to wander again became stronger.'[12] Mountbatten was proud of Edwina's travels, her souvenirs and photographs, as he was invariably proud of everything accomplished by his family. His love for her was as strong as ever, and lasted her lifetime in spite of everything, and he missed her badly during these long absences. But he had learnt from his father that a sailor's life entails separations to which you have to learn to reconcile yourself, even if, in Mountbatten's life, it was the wife who left her husband behind.

What he did come to accept with deep regret later was that these long and arduous tours, which took place all through Edwina's child-bearing years, necessarily limited the size of their family, and left him without a male heir. Edwina was physically very tough and treated her body mercilessly. She had now refined her yoga-like sense of detachment from pain and refusal to accept that she was in the least ill when most women would long before have taken to their bed and called the doctor.

Edwina had always been unusually afraid of death, a fear that had grown with the acquisition of everything any heart could desire – wealth, a handsome young royal husband, a position in society and in her married life which enabled her to do exactly what she wanted to do at any time. It is not uncommon for the very wealthy and the very privileged to develop an unnatural fear of death. She never told anyone that she did not expect to live to a great age. But the pace of her life, her impatience to pack in experiences of people and places, to learn and to see, all suggest that she was determined not to waste one minute when she might have only a few years left to her.

Four years passed before she conceived another child. Her rough and restless travels may well have led to miscarriages, and as Mountbatten said, 'Edwina was one of those remarkable women who never show they are about to have a baby.' In December 1928 Edwina was in Egypt studying archaeology. Mountbatten arrived to join her for the more social side of her trip, and then he had to rejoin his ship. They saw one another briefly at the other end of the Mediterranean, and from Gibraltar Mountbatten took time off to accompany Edwina to Morocco. The sea got up so badly before they could return that the regular steamer was cancelled and Mountbatten had to charter a launch to get back on time. Edwina was more than eight months pregnant, but after a night beating about between Africa and Europe, she said that of course she was all right and would drive off at once in order to synchronize with Mountbatten's arrival in his ship at Barcelona.

Edwina drove the 600 miles over very rough roads by herself in her Rolls-Royce. 'I went to meet her at the Ritz Hotel,' said Mountbatten, 'and she was looking very fit and ordinary. "How are you, darling?" I asked her. "Very well. But I think a young Mountbatten is going to appear at any moment." So I got busy on the telephone to find a doctor.' The only doctor available in the city was a throat specialist. 'So I rang my cousin the queen in Madrid. But Ena was away, so I was put through to King Alfonso. "You're having a baby! How exciting! I'll tell nobody." "That's not really the point," I said. "She wants help." I suppose the line was very bad, but I just heard him say, "I'll send the military governor." And so he did.'

Within half an hour the hotel was like a royal palace in a threatened military coup, with guards at every entrance and on every street corner, so that even the throat specialist had difficulty in getting through. However, with his assistance and the help of a nun, Edwina was satisfactorily delivered of a girl.

She was later christened, in the Chapel Royal, Pamela Carmen Louise Mountbatten, with the King of Spain standing as a godfather. The other godparents were the Duchess of Penaranda, her aunt Crown Princess Louise of Sweden and the Duke of Kent.

On her return to England from one of her long tours abroad, Edwina found herself temporarily responsible for a beguiling, bright, fair-haired little boy who, if not quite abandoned by his parents, had so far led an unsettled life marked by long periods of separation from his mother or father, and most often both. He was Mountbatten's young nephew, Prince Philip of Greece.

When Mountbatten's eldest sister, the deaf Alice, Princess Andrew of Greece, had given birth to a fourth daughter, Princess Sophie ('Tiny'), in 1914, he wrote crossly to his mother from Osborne asking why she never had a boy. 'Tiny' married first Prince Christopher of Hesse, who became an ardent Nazi and Luftwaffe pilot, and in the middle of the war recanted and was killed (almost certainly assassinated) in an air crash. She had five children by him. She is now married to Prince George William of Hanover by whom she had had three further children. In appearance, manner of speech and intelligence she is uncannily like her young brother, Prince Philip.

Mountbatten's wish for Alice to have a boy was fulfilled in 1921. Philip was born on Corfu on 10 June while Mountbatten, his future 'Uncle Dickie', was falling in love with Edwina Ashley in England. His father had just received a posting to the front (Greece, as usual, was at war) as an Army corps commander. He had been a professional soldier all his life, and a very good one, though his career had been fraught with exasperation at the corruption and inefficiency that were endemic in the Greek military machine. Like his future son, he did not suffer fools gladly or care much for criticism.

Prince Andrew's father, George, was Danish, his mother, Olga, Russian. He was Greek by adoption, and his elder brother was King, off and on. Prince Philip refers to himself as Danish, and English by adoption. Mountbatten said, 'Prince Philip is the son of a Danish–Greek prince. His mother was a Battenberg, daughter of a naturalized Englishman. He dislikes being referred to as a Hessian.'

All her life Princess Alice was deeply loved by her family (and especially by her younger brother Dickie), and for most of her life was an object of anxiety. Her mother worried first about her seeming backwardness, and, when it was diagnosed, her deafness. When she fell wonderfully in love with the charming, waggish Prince Andrew and married him, they all worried about Andrew's military career in a country that could idolize you as a hero one day and put you up against a wall the next morning.

At one time during World War I, Allied warships had threatened Athens in an attempt to strong-arm Greece on to their side, and one of them had opened fire on the palace, fortunately missing Alice and the nursery wing. After this, the King had to leave, and Prince Andrew and his family with him. They sought asylum in Lausanne, and Mountbatten visited them there, via Paris, immediately the war was over.

'He made the greatest of friends with the children after his first shyness at finding his nieces had grown so big,'[13] Victoria wrote of the meeting between brother and sister. A shy Mountbatten is an improbable figure, but there we are. He also found them, not for the first time, penurious, and Victoria sold some Burmah Oil shares and despatched the proceeds to Switzerland. She wrote, 'I am only sorry I can't see her face when she gets my letter.'

The following year, 1920, the King was returned to power, and Prince Andrew to the Army, now promoted lieutenant-general. He was feeling affluent again, too, and boundlessly optimistic about the future, when he brought his family to England in the summer of 1922 for the Mountbatten wedding, and the recently widowed Victoria had all her children together for the first time for many years. Prince Philip, thirteen months old, did not attend the wedding, but waved cheerfully from a window to his mother and father as they left in the rain, his father in the full dress uniform of a Greek general.

No sooner had Andrew and Alice and their children returned to Greece than there was a counter-revolution, the family sought refuge in a villa, unsuitably named 'Mon Repos', on Corfu, from which Prince Andrew was enticed back and then thrown into prison, charged with treason. Five fellow officers were shot after a token court martial, and Andrew's life was in grave danger, too.

Alice, almost demented with worry, despatched telegrams to the Pope, King Alfonso of Spain, President Poincaré of France, and to her cousin George V of England. At first there was no response from anyone or any government. Then King George, guilt-stricken at the recent assassination of his Russian cousin and all her family, and horrified that he might, by reason of political cowardice, have the blood of another cousin on his hands, acted with the decisiveness of a sailor born and bred. He made use of all his considerable royal influence through the Foreign Office. Prince Andrew must be saved. An emissary had already been secretly despatched to parley with the Greek dictator, Pangalos, and a man o'war ordered to the Piraeus to display her guns. Prince Andrew was smuggled on board at night, and

the warship slipped away with the entire family and put them ashore at
Brindisi on 5 December 1922.

George v was relieved, and ever after proud of the part he had played
in rescuing the family. He did not set eyes on the Prince, who had been
an infant at the time, until he was thirteen years old. Prince Philip remembers
being at Buckingham Palace in 1934 at the time of Princess Marina's marriage to the Duke of Kent, and standing aside for the King. George v paused
beside the fair-haired boy, looked at him thoughtfully, and said, 'You're
Andrew's boy!'

The family settled in that favourite haunt for refugees, St Cloud outside
Paris. They were not at all well off. An uncle paid for Prince Philip's private
education at his first infants' school. Nor did the marriage prosper. Mountbatten, who saw them as often as time allowed, observed some of the characteristics of his late aunt Ella developing in his eldest sister. After her husband had been blown up, Ella had developed a deeply introspective, almost
mystical, religious tendency, combined with a need to succour the poor and
sick. Now Alice was showing the same tendency. She also opened a shop
in Paris and dedicated the profits to Greek refugees even more penurious
than herself.

Prince Andrew left for the gay life of Monte Carlo. He was, like his son,
never very good at playing the solemn rôle, and here 'he easily made new
friends, not exclusively masculine'.[14]

The Princesses were looked after by friends, relatives and governesses,
and quite soon all married. Prince Philip came on one of his visits to England
in 1926, an enchanting, precocious and mischievous boy, much loved by
his grandmother. Alice was not well and was spending long periods in sana-
toria. Prince Andrew was deeply concerned about his son, whom he adored,
but knew that he was ill-equipped to look after him. The family rallied
round. Victoria agreed to act as a mother, and the part of father was jointly
adopted by Mountbatten, his brother Georgie, and by Harold Wernher, an
ex-soldier and now millionaire businessman who had married the sister of
Georgie Milford Haven's wife, Nada.

Prince Philip's boyhood now became more nomadic than ever, and he
found himself in succession in the hands of numerous members of his far-
flung family. He was loved by all, his treatment varying from firm with Victoria to very free-and-easy at Wolfsgarten with the Hessians.

The nearest thing to a home was grandmother Victoria's chambers at
Kensington Palace. 'It was a sort of base, a place where I kept things,' Prince
Philip said. 'She was very helpful and I liked her very much.' Asked if Vic-
toria was a sort of second mother, Prince Philip replied emphatically, 'No.
You see, it was a very large family and there were always plenty of relatives

and places to visit. Dickie was very good at that time, too. I used to see a lot of him, though he was often away for a long time.'[15]

Asked if he felt any sense of deprivation, the answer was another emphatic negative. 'There were just so many people and so much going on. My grandmother was very good with children. Like my own mother, she took the practical approach. Later, it was just the same with my children. They loved being with my mother. She treated them in the right way – the right combination of the rational and the emotional.'

Princess Alice was at this time either in a sanatorium or running her shop, while Prince Andrew continued to live in Monte Carlo. 'People used to think the set-up was more curious than I did, I think,' said Prince Philip of his mother. 'They didn't think it was quite right that she should be selling things in a shop, and I suppose they were really right. I went to see her sometimes, but not very often.'

And how did his mother regard him? 'I think she regarded me as someone, like her husband, who could get on with things – a man, you know. I didn't need much attention. It's difficult to imagine, I suppose, but with a large family one absorbed so much from so many people.'

Others who remember Prince Philip at the time saw Mountbatten's mother very much as a surrogate mother. Among them was the Duchess of York, who, as the Queen Mother today, said, 'She was almost a mother to him, and whenever he could he went to see her.'[16] Certainly she was a very efficient sort of duty movements officer, arranging his journeys from St Cloud to Wolfsgarten, Adsdean (Uncle Dickie) to Lynden Manor (Uncle Georgie) to Holkham (the Leicesters) and back to Kensington Palace ('KP'). Victoria was also responsible for his clothes, and visited him frequently when he went away to boarding school at Cheam.

On her return home from her latest tour, then, Edwina found at Adsdean eight-year-old Prince Philip, who fitted in easily with the routine of life. Mountbatten and the two girls, now one and five, returned from Malta, with the nursemaids.

'Dickie took a great pride in his nephew,' Edwina's biographer noted, 'who was to take the place of the son he would never have. During the holidays the placid and feminine Mountbatten nursery was much enlivened by the appearance of young Master Philip, who, always a tease, imposed his will on Patricia, who soon became his willing slave and imitator.'[17]

Of Prince Philip's upbringing in England, Mountbatten has said, 'We all rallied round but there's no doubt that my mother took the main burden. Andrea [Prince Andrew] was in no position to help, nor was his mother. Andrea was a charming and delightful person, but he lived abroad until he died in Monaco at the end of 1944 – after the invasion. He was a great Anglo-phile and wanted Prince Philip brought up as an English boy. When we asked him about his career and suggested the Navy, he liked the idea – but on no account the Army.

' "I have been driven demented in my career," he told me. "First of all I became a serious soldier – a cavalry soldier – then about 1910 the Greek government said it didn't want a Prince serving in the armed forces, so I was thrown out. Later, I was allowed in again. Then in 1917 I was thrown into exile, came back and thrown out finally. Just look at my life!" he would exclaim. "I was a keen professional soldier, and have been thrown out three times. I don't want that to happen to Philip."

'Apart from my mother,' Mountbatten continued, 'it was my brother and I. We did it to a certain extent together. I looked after him as far as his naval career was concerned, and later did the whole job single-handed.'

Mountbatten saw in Prince Philip all the characteristics he would have liked and expected in a son of his own. There was, from the start, a wonderful compatibility and understanding between the thirty-year-old naval officer and nine-year-old boy. For his part, Prince Philip admired his uncle greatly, but without sycophancy, and was more than ready to shape himself in Mountbatten's likeness.

Mountbatten said, 'From early on, I had no doubt that Prince Philip was abnormally intelligent.' Princess Alice, Countess of Athlone judges him to be more intelligent than Mountbatten – 'and that's saying a lot'.[18] Asked when he first saw signs that his nephew was going to become an exceptional person, Mountbatten replied laconically, after thought, 'Out shooting one day, when he was eight or nine. It was rough. The way he coped told me.

'Prince Philip', continued Mountbatten, 'is an absolute Mountbatten and not a bit Hanoverian, and his children have a degree of intelligence quite lacking in King George V, King George VI or any of those people at all. Prince Charles, too, is an absolute Mountbatten. The real intelligence in the royal family comes through my parents to Prince Philip and the children.

'The Queen, of course, is a marvellous person. Her ministers are always surprised at how well-informed she is. She is extremely sound – not brilliant – and that comes from her mother. There was great worthiness in King George VI, King George V and even Edward VII, but that old Hanoverian line was becoming dimmer and dimmer so that they could not even pass their exams.'

Mountbatten's shaping of Prince Philip the man, and his destiny, is always regarded highly in any estimate of Mountbatten's achievements. Some people think it was the greatest thing he did. Julian Amery regards Mount-batten's 'coaching of Prince Philip' as deserving of his highest credit marks, helping to make him into a personality disassociated from the old establishment, someone acceptable to all shades of political thinking (except the lunatic) and to all classes.[19]

Surprisingly, a modesty about himself and his achievements is something Prince Philip acquired over the years when Mountbatten was such a powerful influence in his life. This writer once wrote of him as 'a remarkable man'. Prince Philip would have none of it. 'Hough refers to me first as "a remarkable man" which is faintly ridiculous as I am only in a remarkable position.' Mountbatten referred this distinction to the Queen, and Mountbatten noted, 'The Queen and I both disagreed with Prince Philip's insistence that he is not a remarkable man, but we both agreed he had a remarkable position.'

Prince Philip's education after Cheam preparatory school was discussed with Prince Andrew. Prince Philip once said on education, 'For some reason it is perfectly respectable to teach history and mathematics, electronics and engineering. But any attempt to develop character, and the whole man, tends to be viewed with the utmost suspicion.'[20] That is a characteristic remark from someone who fell under the spell of the great educationist, Kurt Hahn, and of his two schools, Salem and Gordonstoun. Second to Mountbatten, Hahn had the greatest influence in developing the character of Prince Philip.

Mountbatten had for some time thought that Hahn's school in Schloss Salem near Lake Constance was the right place to develop to the full Prince Philip's evident qualities. Prince Philip's sister Theodora had become, through marriage to Prince Berthold of Baden, the Margravine of Baden. Her father-in-law had been the last Chancellor of Imperial Germany; and here in this castle he had sponsored the birth of Salem school by Dr Hahn. Mountbatten and his brother sent Prince Philip there in 1933. He thrived but didn't like what he saw of the influence of the new Nazi regime, unlike his grandmother who, for a while, thought it was marvellous – deceived by the word 'socialist'. When Hahn escaped to England, and then to Scotland to set up Gordonstoun, Prince Philip followed him there.

It was in Prince Philip's third year at Gordonstoun that two more tragedies struck at the House of Hesse. The Hessian curse had lain dormant for fifteen years. In 1937 and 1938 it was reawakened in the most tragic terms.

The Mountbattens were in London in October for what was expected to be a specially joyous wedding. In February 1931, Prince Philip's prettiest sister Cecile had married George Donatus ('Don'), hereditary Grand-Duke of Hesse. In the next few years they had three children, two boys and a girl.

Early in 1937 Don's younger brother Louis ('Lu') had met and fallen in love with an English girl, the Hon. Margaret ('Peg') Geddes. In September, and before going back to school, Prince Philip and his grandmother stayed as usual at Wolfsgarten, together with Edwina, Mountbatten and Patricia. They all noted that the Grand-Duke was showing signs of his age, and his sister Victoria wrote: 'He is getting very grey and rather deaf.'

A month later the Grand-Duke died, and as a consequence his younger son's marriage to Peg in London was postponed to November. The family took off for the event from Frankfurt on the afternoon of 16 November in a Junkers tri-motor – the hereditary Grand-Duke, his wife, who was expecting another child, the late Grand-Duke's widow, the two boys, their nursemaid, and the best man. Coming in to land at Ostend *en route*, the tri-motor struck a tall chimney concealed by mist, crashed and burst into flames. Everyone on board was killed, and the Hessian family, with its roots back to Charlemagne, was all but wiped out.

Mountbatten recalled that black November evening. 'Lu and Peg had gone out to Croydon to meet the family, and they learned the news while they were waiting. I had sent two cars to collect them all. They came back with just the engaged couple, prostrated with grief. We all went round to Peg's father's house – Lord Geddes – and had a ghastly family meeting. My mother said the wedding ought to go ahead, not in four days' time with all the formality and publicity, but the very next day while they were still in a state of shock. She was absolutely right, of course. I stood in as best man. Then the married couple went to Ostend to the scene of the crash, and on to Darmstadt. What a honeymoon!'

There was a double tragic postscript to the catastrophe. Lu and Peg adopted the surviving infant girl who had been left at home. Eighteen months later she died, 'as if the hand of Hessian fate had signed the cancellation of her reprieve'.

Finally, as the years passed, Lu and Peg found that they could not have children, and the timeless Hessian Darmstadt dynasty was threatened with extinction. Today, the widowed Princess Margaret of Hesse lives alone at Wolfsgarten, though visited by the Queen and Prince Philip and other relatives, as well as (and frequently) by Mountbatten until his murder.

At Gordonstoun, Kurt Hahn broke the news to Prince Philip. Five months later, he had to break the news of another tragedy to his pupil; and this time it was even harder for Prince Philip to bear.

In a family tight-knit with loyalty and affection, there were no ties closer than those between Mountbatten and his elder brother Georgie. People who saw the two of them in the Mediterranean Fleet on a professional level, Mountbatten a signal lieutenant, Georgie a gunnery commander in the *Warspite*, recognized at once the brotherly affection and the contrast: Mountbatten the millionaire playboy, Georgie the diligent professional. 'He was a brilliant chap,' said a sub-lieutenant who served with him. 'We expected great things from him and not much from his younger brother.'[21]

This same officer agreed with Mountbatten that Georgie possessed a marvellous mathematical mind, and that he would have gone to the top. Mountbatten's opinion was that his brother had a conventional naval officer's outlook. 'He had no political *nous* whatever because he was not interested. I had an unconventional outlook which made me do things for which I'm still disliked. In fifty years' time people may think I did quite well.'

'Without trying at all – and his brain was lazy as well as brilliant,' said Mountbatten, 'he would come in first or second in his exams. If he tried at all he always came out top.' Mountbatten always loved to turn the conversation towards his brother, and to hear of others speaking well of him. When this writer spoke of Georgie to the Queen, she recalled an incident which showed his charm and consideration to her when she was a small girl.

'I only once talked to him for any length of time,' she recalled, 'and that was when he – poor man – found himself next to me at the wedding breakfast for the Duke of Kent and Princess Marina. But I don't think I have ever enjoyed a meal so much. He was one of the most intelligent and brilliant of people. He spoke to children just as if they were grown up.'[22] Mountbatten loved to retell this anecdote, and included it in a picture album published just after his death.

Never were Mountbatten and Georgie closer than when they shared as a foursome, with their children, the magnificent Casa Medina in Malta. Edwina and Nada were equally good friends and travelling companions. Then the Milford Havens discovered with a nasty shock that they were living above their income. Much of Nada's money had been lost in the revolution, and although by most naval officers' standards they were well off, Georgie decided that he must make provision for his old age by going into business.

In the winter of 1937–8, Georgie Milford Haven contracted cancer of the bone, and died after much suffering on 8 April. It was a terrible blow to the whole family. 'I was absolutely shattered,' said Mountbatten. And Prince Philip, to whom Mountbatten was more than ever a father, was also heartbroken.

It was one sadness too many for Georgie's mother. Patricia Mountbatten, now thirteen, calling in to say goodnight to her grandmother, found Victoria at her desk attempting to write letters, the tears pouring down her lined cheeks. No one had ever before seen this tough, managing, ever-rational grand-daughter of Queen Victoria crying.

4
SIGNALS OF DANGER

'I CHOSE SIGNALS because I had always been deeply interested in communications,' Mountbatten said. And he meant communications in the widest sense. Signals to Mountbatten meant much more than the first and vital operation of keeping ships in touch with one another. It embraced the narrower but equally important subject of officers keeping in touch with the lower deck, of ships' companies keeping in touch with their families, of sustaining morale by keeping ships' companies entertained and in touch with the news of the day. Signals to Mountbatten was concerned as much with strengthening of morale and ties between ships as strengthening communications in peace and war.

As Fleet Wireless Officer, Mountbatten was in the centre listening post of some seventy men o'war, in touch with every unit wherever it might be in the Mediterranean, in touch with international and domestic news, and with local fleet news, from a leading seaman with a sudden appendicitis in a tug, to preparations for a gunnery practice in a 30,000-ton battleship.

From the day he took up the appointment, Mountbatten began an elaborate programme to increase the efficiency of wireless communications throughout the fleet. From the signal HQ at the Castille in Valetta, he kept the fleet telegraphists tuned day and night to the various frequencies used by the Fleet.

Often he would examine the strips as they came from the machine and despatched comments, favourable or unfavourable, to the telegraphist responsible for the transmission. In this way he at once demonstrated to them his own indefatigable energy and his interest in their work. They warmed to this as anyone warms to attention and care. Over a longer period of time, he even got the telegraphists' status and pay increased, at a time when economies were the order of the day. Higher status, higher pay, an officer in command who took such a keen, critical interest in their work – here was the stuff of leadership and popularity.

On one occasion, Mountbatten organized an elaborate and spectacular demonstration of the efficiency and importance of signals in the big lecture hall in the Castille. It was an electronics pageant extending over three days so that everyone from the Commander-in-Chief to ordinary seamen stokers could attend. They all did too. The show was a sell-out. Like some master-of-ceremonies (which was exactly what he was) he stood before the audience and asked for a message to pass through to the Admiralty. Back would come the reply from London through loudspeakers within seconds.

With war planes circling the island and submarines stationed at the harbour entrance, he would initiate a mock attack – 'Enemy sighted!' 'Commence to attack!' The first naval action in a war was simulated in sound, with the W/T operators working away publicly on the stage like a chorus in a musical. It was the best show in Valetta, and had the audience on the edge of their seats. It did no harm to his own standing, either.

On a more serious level, when the threats to service pay suddenly became real in 1931 as a result of the economic crisis, Mountbatten's rôle as Fleet Wireless Officer proved of importance in helping to prevent the spread of disaffection. On 15 September, the Atlantic Fleet mutinied at Invergordon. It was the first fleet mutiny since the Mutiny at the Nore in 1797, which had resulted in the hanging of twenty-four men. It was almost as if the battle-ships had turned their 15-inch guns on the Treasury in Whitehall.

Mountbatten was the first officer in the fleet to hear the news. The C-in-C was Admiral Ernle Chatfield, Beatty's old flag-captain at the battle of Jutland, his Chief of Staff Sidney Bailey, and Chatfield's flag-captain was Captain Davenport. The fleet was dispersed on its first summer cruise, and the conclusion reached by Mountbatten, and backed by his assistant, Micky Hodges, was that there must be no communication between units of the fleet and that it must remain dispersed.

'The cause of the Invergordon Mutiny, which was a severe cut in pay, would certainly have led to mutiny in the Mediteranean Fleet, too,' said Mountbatten. 'And the reason for that was that most of the officers were in full sympathy. They knew how close to the bone the men's families were living. Davenport said his men would never mutiny – it wasn't possible. I didn't argue. I went straight to Bailey and said there is exactly the same feeling here as in the Atlantic Fleet. I'm stopping all W/T communications, and if you bring the fleet together there'll be a mutiny, I'm warning you.'

Mountbatten was told that, if it was as serious as that, he had better go and see the C-in-C. 'Chatfield was a very remote man. When I saw him, he already had my views through Bailey, and Davenport, who was absolutely furious with me, just as if I was some mutineer myself. Chatfield was upset, too. 'If what you say is true, how is it that I've never been told?"

"Perhaps because they're scared, sir," I said. "Scared? Why should they be scared?"

'So I explained to him that the navy had suffered from promotionitis ever since the post-war cuts when two out of three junior officers were forced to retire. "Nobody can afford to say what they think any more." Then I said something like this: "Imagine, sir, HMS *X*. A mutiny on board is feared. The Officer of the Division, if he knows, is going to pretend to himself that things aren't really that bad and won't say anything to his Commander. If the Commander does suspect it, he won't risk his promotioa by telling the Captain – he'll be too busy sucking up to him. The Captain's in the zone for promotion to Rear-Admiral, so he's not spilling the beans to you because he thinks you may be the next First Sea Lord [Chatfield was!] and he's not going to tell you."

'So Chatfield looked hard at me and said, "This is a terrible condemnation. How is it that you've got the courage to tell me when nobody else has?" "That's very simple, sir. By a pure fluke I was allowed to stay on in the Navy. I had private means. I don't need to buy my promotion by silence. What I do care about is the truth, and that you should know it."

'It may be coincidence that I was promoted next shot. Later, I learned that there were symptoms of mutiny at Malta, and that a few rifles were taken from the half deck of a cruiser and ditched. How did I hear? Through the telegraphists, of course.'

Mountbatten always claimed that he saved the Mediterranean Fleet – the premier fleet – from mutiny in September 1931, which could have had fearful repercussions. As it was, the Invergordon Mutiny brought about a cancellation of the pay cuts, and then directly led, four days later, to a report from the Bank of England that foreign credits were exhausted. With even the Royal Navy unsteady, international confidence in Britain evaporated. On 21 September an act suspending the gold standard was rushed through Parliament, and the pound tumbled.

A year later, Mountbatten was dealing with an altogether more agreeable W/T occasion. The BBC had developed an Empire Broadcasting Service which King George V was due to inaugurate with a talk to his people on Christmas Day 1932. The C-in-C Mediterranean ordered that all fleet personnel should listen to this speech. The only way to do this was to build a new high-frequency receiver high up on the island, linked by a cable to a ship, which, in turn, would re-transmit the broadcast on the medium band used by ships' sets.

The equipment had to be brought from Britain, and the last pieces arrived only on Christmas Eve. In one of the characteristic races-against-time which might have been set up for one of Mountbatten's more flamboyant shows, everything was linked only minutes before the voice of George V came over the ether. It was heard perfectly, with none of the fading associated with long-distance reception at the time. With an elaborate series of street and café loudspeakers also wired up, half the native population of Valetta heard the broadcast, too. The days of satellites and transistors were still decades away. To many who heard the modulated tones of the King-Emperor, in the streets and on shipboard, the achievement seemed like a miracle, which pleased Mountbatten, who liked to perform miracles.

On one of her Hollywood jaunts, Edwina had seen and heard the first of the 'talkies' which had created such an enterainment sensation. Through his earlier sponsorship of movie projectors in the fleet, which developed later into the Royal Naval Film Corporation (Patron HRH The Duke of Kent), Mountbatten had made the Navy film-mad. The early conversion of the projectors to link-up with talkie transmitters was brought about entirely through Mountbatten's ingenuity, and had been the means by which the medium-wave transmission had been picked up for the King's broadcast.

The conversion, according to the company in England that made the equipment, would cost not less than £400. This was a ridiculous figure which the Admiralty would not for one moment countenance. 'I thought the Navy deserved to have the talkies Edwina had told me about as soon as anyone else. Sooner if possible. So I did a very simple thing. I designed a loud-speaker system myself which could be made for £85. Most of the parts could be had as spares from the Fleet Repair Ship anyway. It worked very well. I used to visit ships and help with the installation.'

Late in May 1932, a copy of the Sunday newspaper *The People* for the twentieth of that month arrived in the post at Casa Medina. The Fleet was in harbour, Edwina had been there since the previous August, and the family was complete. Mountbatten had been promoted commander two months earlier, and was awaiting an appointment to his first ship. He was also, more anxiously, awaiting the packet that arrived that morning.

Friends in London had already warned the Mountbattens by telegram that a scandalous article about Edwina had been printed in one of the sensational Sunday newspapers, and they were expecting the worst. They were both hardened to the tittle-tattle of the gossip columnists, a good deal of it malicious, both in England and America. But they had never read anything like this before. This time they were really outraged, and Mountbatten said, 'We'll have to get on to the solicitors.'

'Do you really think it's necessary?' Edwina asked. 'If we sue for libel it'll mean the whole thing coming up again. I'll have to go to London and you'll have to get leave.'

'We'll do what they say,' said Mountbatten, 'But I don't think the paper should be allowed to get away with that.'

'Behind the Scenes' was a gossip column which had run for some time in *The People* under the byline 'The Watcher'. In this issue it was headlined FAMOUS HOSTESS EXILED.

SOCIETY SHAKEN BY TERRIBLE SCANDAL

I am able to reveal today the sequel to a scandal which has shaken Society to the very depths. It concerns one of the leading hostesses in the country, a woman highly connected and immensely rich.

Associations with a coloured man became so marked that they were the talk of the West End. Then one day the couple were caught in compromising circumstances.

The sequel is that the Society woman has been given the hint to clear out of England for a couple of years to let the affair blow over, and the hint comes from a quarter which cannot be ignored.

To almost anyone who followed the gossip columns, 'the woman' could only be Edwina and the 'quarter which could not be ignored' could only be the Palace. To the more knowledgeable, 'the coloured man' was Paul Robeson, whose *Othello* had recently taken the West End by storm.

The Mountbattens were recommended to issue proceedings for libel against Odhams newspapers, the publishers of *The People*, and they both returned to London on 6 July to give evidence. The case came up before the Lord Chief Justice, Lord Hewart; the defendants retained Sir Patrick Hastings; and Norman Birkett, who had until recently been held with a retainer for Odhams, acted for the Mountbattens.

Birkett opened the case strongly: 'It is not too much to say that it is the most monstrous and most atrocious libel of which I myself in all my experience in these courts have ever heard. Your Lordship', he continued, 'may think that the word "scandal" at the top of the article coupled with the words "the hint comes from a quarter which cannot be ignored", puts it beyond all doubt that the writer deliberately intended to defame Lady Louis Mountbatten.'

Later, Birkett asked if 'in the very exceptional circumstances of this case', Lord and Lady Louis Mountbatten might go into the witness box. The judge agreed. Mountbatten was first. He was anxious to clarify at once the real reason why Edwina was living in Malta, and that she had not flown from a scandal in London. He therefore merely made a statement that he was serving in the Mediterranean Fleet, and that his wife and children were, as a consequence, living there and for no other reason.

Edwina followed him into the box. Birkett said, 'The second paragraph in this publication deals with a coloured man. Is there one single word of truth in the allegations there made?'

Edwina replied loudly and firmly, 'Not one single word. In fact, I have never in the whole course of my life met the man referred to.'

'Your friends have named to you the coloured man supposed to be referred to in the paragraph?'

Edwina agreed that they had, although Paul Robeson's name was never mentioned in court. Edwina confirmed again that 'the whole thing is a preposterous story'.

For the defendants, Sir Patrick Hastings made an unqualified apology – 'genuine and deep regrets'. As a point of principle, Edwina refused all damages, which would certainly have been heavy. The case attracted enormous interest and their wiser friends wished they had ignored the article, believing that the whole thing would have been forgotten in a few weeks.

However, no one could deny that Edwina knew the coloured singer Hutch. All West End society loved Hutch, whose sentimental songs and piano-playing enchanted night club audiences. Moreover, Edwina had rather foolishly given him a cigarette case with her name engraved on it.

Edwina did not always sufficiently consider the consequences of her actions, and regarded 'proceeding with care' as only half living. But she cannot be blamed personally for taking out libel proceedings, which brought her name, by association, to people who did not regularly read the sensational Sundays. These included, inevitably, the royal family. It is very doubtful if the attention of King George and Queen Mary would have been drawn to the article, which was only one of numerous column inches of scandal printed every week, if the case had not come up before the Lord Chief Justice and been so widely reported in *The Times* and *Daily Telegraph*.

After the hearing Mountbatten, his mother and Edwina drove to Buckingham Palace for luncheon. This was read by many people as a gesture of sympathy and solidarity by the Crown. But in fact George v and Queen Mary were not at all pleased about the business and there was a noticeable cooling of relations for some time after the case, which Edwina strongly resented.

Later there was a lot of gossip about the Earl of Sefton, who fell in love with Edwina although no one was sure what she felt about him. She and Hugh Sefton would often be seen dining out with 'Poppy' Baring and Prince George (who wanted to marry her) – a steady foursome at a time when dining alone with any man other than your husband was still not acceptable.

Perhaps Mountbatten should have accepted earlier that Edwina – rich, emotional and physically volatile, often alone in London, easily bored and with a range of friends as wide as the Mediterranean – was likely to have affairs. Perhaps he preferred the sailor's licence of the blind eye, even to himself. When he could no longer ignore what was going on, and when everyone knew except Mountbatten, it hit him very hard. 'I was terribly upset, and found it hard to believe,' he said. 'I had never looked at anyone. It was an awful shock.'

In 1919, when he had gone out to Switzerland to see his sister Alice and her children, he had stopped off at Paris, and – encouraged by the future Duke of Gloucester – had visited the usual places in the traditional English gentleman's style. There were no doubt some passing affairs – probably no more than flirtations. But that was all. He was an innocent in love, and in a very English way for a half-German, remained an innocent all his life.

It was also very characteristic of him that women were more important than men in his life. Although he only had serious affairs with women he loved, he could not live without women about him, just as he adored amusing women. He also liked them very feminine, well dressed, with small wrists and high heels.

The sexual act, in itself, and in isolation from the exciting hurly-burly and challenges of professional life, was never of first importance to Mountbatten. He liked to hear about it from others, enjoyed jokes about it, enjoyed learning about the sexual experiences of his men friends and relations. He was a man who enjoyed the sexual act more in theory and anecdote than in fact and practice, and the *voyeur* strain was stronger in him than in most men.

He liked hearing about the infidelities of his friends, and, much later, when he was reconciled to the fact, even liked to hear about Edwina's and was proud of them. Her powerful sexuality fascinated him, no less because he was unable wholly to satisfy it.

Just as Mountbatten preferred to have women about him, and to talk to, than men of his own age, so he was at his best in their company – amusing, teasing, charming, informative. With women there was no sign of the need to dominate which could often be seen in him in masculine company. His competitive element was quite missing with women, and this made him more delightful and agreeable.

Mountbatten knew that he was at his best with pretty women about him, and when he was in a position to do so, always arranged for them to be on his staff. Everyone who worked with him from the time when he became head of Combined Operations remembers them today – 'an absolutely smashing lot!' Their contribution to his success and the outcome of his campaigns was as great as any of his advisers' and staff officers' (and a great deal more than some of them), who tended to joke patronizingly among

themselves about 'Dickie's harem'. They were not there for the reasons most
people assumed. In fact Mountbatten was very moral and sentimental in
an old-fashioned way about women.

He also enjoyed the company of young men, especially when he was older.
They, too, posed no problems of competition, and he enjoyed charming and
flattering them as much as he enjoyed charming and flattering pretty young
women. If he willingly accepted – even preferred – relationships with women
without active sex, any thought of closer relations with men was something
he never even contemplated. 'He wouldn't have risked his career,' his
defenders against accusations of homosexuality have said. Indeed he would
not. But he was by nature, constitution, upbringing, and morality as remote
from irregular relations with other men.

Mountbatten was always equally kind to women as he was, later, to young
men. He could not bear the callous manner in which some of his contemporaries treated their mistresses. He was very much the Sir Galahad
with women, always chivalrous, always kind. His friendship with the Prince
of Wales survived the abdication crisis with ease. It survived only with difficulty the Prince's treatment of Mrs Dudley Ward, who had been his faithful
and discreet mistress for nearly seventeen years. After an anxious period of
nursing her critically ill daughter, she telephoned St James's Palace in the
usual way, only to hear a tearful voice on the switchboard at the other end
announcing the end of the affair in these words: 'I'm terribly sorry, ma'am,
I have orders not to put you through to His Royal Highness.' Behaviour as
cruel as this towards a woman who had herself shown nothing but kindness
was beyond Mountbatten's comprehension.

There were periods in the Mountbatten marriage when both were miserable, and the misery always stemmed from her affairs, until the time of
Edwina's change of life, which hit her very badly. They were, at times, better
apart, and the opportunities for separate lives were always there. 'The real
tragedy was,' said Mountbatten, 'that we were closer than we had ever
been and were getting on marvellously just before she died, and were
looking forward to growing old together because we had everything in
common.'

On the last day of 1932, Mountbatten got his first command. He could ask
for nothing better. It was a destroyer, and a brand new one, the *Daring*,
one of the 'D' class of 1,400 tons, with a speed of 35 knots, and an armament
of four 4.7-inch guns and eight 21-inch torpedo tubes.

'Here I am in my first command – a bit dazed but feeling very grand,'[1]
he wrote to his mother.

Apart from feeling grand – and he was using the word with its old meaning of 'marvellous' – what was it like to command a new destroyer in Britain's premier fleet?

'A captain is God almighty,' he said. 'He can do exactly what he wants with his ship. You can make Easter Sunday into Good Friday. You can shape the spirit of the ship to your own ideas. You can make yourself hated or loved. And for all this, they pay you – pay you for doing the most wonderful job in the world.'

Mountbatten rapidly worked the ship's company up to a high level of efficiency. To perfect anything was a joy to him, and to watch men respond to his style of leadership was an equal pleasure. '*Daring* by name, and daring by nature – that's us,' he told his destroyer's company, and used a quote from Hakluyt as the ship's motto: 'We have made every sea the highway of our daring.'

'Ah, pride before a fall,' he was telling himself only weeks later, and remembered that wonderful letter Nelson wrote to Fanny from the *Vanguard* when he was blockading the French fleet in Toulon and met a disastrous storm: 'I believe firmly that it was the Almighty's goodness, to check my consummate vanity. I hope it has made me a better officer....'

Far from making every sea the *Daring*'s highway, his flotilla was ordered out to Singapore to swap ships with the China Station flotilla, who had old destroyers built in a hurry during World War I. There was much gloom in the flotilla at the prospect of exchanging their new wonder destroyers for the old 'tin cans'.

Mountbatten would have no depression in his ship. It was the sort of situation in which his natural chirpiness and resilience was shown at its best. At Singapore, where they took over the *Wishart*, named after some nonentity of an admiral, he called up all hands, and spoke to his men. 'We have just left behind a ship with a great name. We have now got the only ship in the Royal Navy with an even greater name. Our new ship is named after the Almighty himself, to whom we pray daily, "Our Father wishart in heaven".'

The flotilla sailed back to the Suez Canal and the Mediterranean, through the hot Indian Ocean at ten knots to conserve fuel and the old turbines. To keep the men amused and interested, Mountbatten started a ship's newspaper, and organized a band, competitive games every day and evening entertainments. Rolling through those hot, sulky seas at snail's pace, a ship's company could easily become slack and bored. There was no time for either in the *Wishart*. When they finally arrived in Malta, Mountbatten had a tight, happy ship in which he knew every man by name.

There were flotilla exercises as well, but no opportunity on the voyage for gunnery practice. The Captain (D) was an old shipmate of Mountbatten's father, a gunnery enthusiast, called H.T. Baillie-Grohman. At the beginning, he had taken a bleak view of Mountbatten, and (like Roger Keyes) had to be converted slowly to a pro-Mountbatten way of thinking.

When Mountbatten had first been appointed to the *Daring*, Baillie-Grohman had called Mountbatten to his cabin. 'I told him,' Baillie-Grohman said before he died recently, ' "Look, Dickie, it's all right for you. But please remember in this flotilla that there's hardly one of us with two brass pennies to rub together. So, be a good chap and watch it." He did, too, he really behaved very well and there was no sign of that early extravagance I had seen when he first came out.'[2]

Mountbatten was to brush up against this officer later. He liked Baillie-Grohman but thought he lacked the final polish of a leader. When they arrived at Malta, it was a Friday morning, and Baillie-Grohman had been looking forward to taking the flotilla straight out for target-practice to show his, and the flotilla's, keenness. Instead, he was frustrated by the impossibility of drawing targets before Monday morning. The flotilla leader made a signal to all destroyers which was brought to Mountbatten by his yeoman with a long face. 'I know how anxious you all are to get on with working up,' it ran. 'You share my disappointment that we shall not be able to do so until Monday. Please inform your ship's company.'

Mountbatten read it with dismay. As he had shown earlier with this crew, he believed strongly that disappointing news could always be phrased cheerfully. So, there and then, he rewrote his senior's message to all hands: 'We have just reached our destination after seven weeks at sea. The Captain (D) believes that we have now become experienced seamen quicker than any other destroyer flotilla in peacetime. Although he is now very anxious to start working up, he has very kindly arranged for us to have a full weekend in harbour to rest and recuperate.' The notice was received with cheers, and the liberty boats were soon on their way....

The working up gunnery practice began sharp at dawn on Monday, the flotilla's crews cheerful and enthusiastic after their forty-eight hours' shore leave. Mountbatten had given much thought to destroyer gunnery and had, as often happened, from his father's as well as his own experience, reached an unorthodox conclusion. It had for a long time been the common practice – he called it a fetish – for destroyers to go in for fast shooting with the standard 4.7-inch guns. This is what always impressed the Captain (D), and Baillie-Grohman was of the orthodox school, which was more romantic than practical: the 'Jutland image' of racing at the enemy, then helm hard over, torpedoes away, guns blazing.

Mountbatten held that you would in fact make more hits if the guns were laid with more deliberate care and you fired less frequently. The *Wishart*'s showing at target practice appeared poor, and many of his fellow commanders wondered what had happened to Mountbatten's usually keen and competitive destroyer. Then the results began to come in. The *Wishart* came out top by a wide margin, and had expended less than half the shells of her competitors.

The summer regatta, the most important competitive event of the year, was still three months away, but Mountbatten was already actively preparing for it. Early in June he addressed the ship's company on the subject. 'A ship embarking on the regatta with a will to win', he told them, 'is a ship with a healthy morale bred into her – and the guts needed for winning a pulling race will be invaluable in war.' He told them that the *Wishart* was going to win everything – no question of that. Not just gunnery, but boxing and football, pistol and rifle shooting. And *all* the races. 'I told them that we were going to be Cock of the Fleet. And they believed me,' Mountbatten said.

All through that summer the training continued relentlessly. The summer cruise brought no relief. 'I had a "dry-puller" installed on the forward deck, and every morning I mustered the crew on the fo'c'sle for dry-pulling exercises. Every man would have to pull so many strokes. It was hard going, but it prevented them getting slack at sea.' ('Slack' being a relative word in the *Wishart*.)

Mountbatten had been doing some more calculations. He took the distance between the place where the first oar and the last oar entered the water, and the distance between their seats, recorded the strokes per minute, got out some graph paper.... 'Thirty-eight and a half strokes a minute produced the best results,' he said. 'It was quite simple. But no one had thought of doing the sum before. We kept to that figure for the whaler, and the result?'

The regatta took place on 4 September, the high point of the Mediterranean Fleet's year, with the whole fleet watching, and the wives and families of officers and men who were on the island, and most of the population of Malta, too. The whaler races had all the drama, the knife-edge uncertainty almost to the end, of a Hollywood movie. It might have been scripted by Mountbatten himself. 'If you don't win, I'll derate the lot of you!' he called out to his petty officers.

There was no need. At the end of the long day, his blistered, weary men were the winners. There were ferocious celebrations on board that night. A live cock was lashed to a spar high on the *Wishart*'s mast. A telegram from the King was read out. It was all very stylish.

At the end of the commission, when he said goodbye to the *Wishart*'s company, he said: 'When we arrived at this station, I said we would win every trophy that was to be won. As you all know the *Wishart* triumphed in every game except football, and in football we lost every match. I feel that I was directly responsible for this because I quite forgot to specify which trophy I meant to win, the silver cup for the best team or the wooden spoon for the worst. We won the spoon so I can safely say that I fulfilled my promise.'

This little speech is typical of countless that he made throughout his professional career, right up to his last days as Chief of Defence Staff fourteen years before he died – jokey, flattering, unpatronizing, affectionate, and, you can be sure, with a spontaneous ring to every phrase. Within seconds, Mountbatten could grab the attention of a bunch of cynical newspapermen kept waiting in the cold for too long, as he could a company of demoralized soldiers isolated for weeks in the Burma jungle, weary of canned food, mosquitoes, damp heat, and the ever-present, ever-unseen, danger lurking about them.

Like a trouper who has trod the boards for a living for years, the performance was consistent and never failed. In a moment, the audience was warmed, encouraged, amused, and granted – just like that – new self-respect and new will. It was the show of one of the great actor-leaders, in the same style as Field-Marshal Montgomery, Generals Patton and MacArthur and Winston Churchill in World War II.

As Mountbatten was rowed round the *Wishart* three times and pulled ashore by his officers, with the cheers of his men ringing in his ears, watchers might now say, 'There goes a great leader, and there goes a certain great hero if there is another war.'

Unlike his early Mediterranean Fleet days, it was indeed often said. But there were other voices, and not only – it must be conceded – the voices of the envious, who judged that the success had a brashness that was not altogether attractive, that the success could have been tempered with a measure of modesty. And modesty was as remote, on that summer afternoon, as a cloud in the Mediterranean sky.

Gunnery officers who had trained their crews to a pitch of skilful fast shooting, whaler crews who had worked quite as hard as those of the *Wishart*, knew all about Mountbatten's mathematical calculations and radical departures from accustomed practice. They knew – or most of them did – that the target had been hit, the whalers had crossed the line first, by reason of these calculations. They accepted defeat in the traditional generous spirit, but a certain resentment was raised – was it *really* right, was it *really* quite sporting, quite British? A bit off-side? Of course, Dickie Mountbatten did not even begin to bend the rules. All the same....

Just a touch of humility would have provided the antidote. Why did a man as clever and as sensitive to the feelings of others, who could read the mood of those about him with such speed and accuracy, not apply that antidote? Why did he not recognize that his style of total professionalism, of showy bravado that mixed unevenly with his evident success in all that he did, was not always liked by the British, whose feelings about success and winning are so confused, contradictory, and totally mystifying to many foreigners? Was it because he *was* a half-foreigner that he failed to see what was happening? Would an orthodox public school education, with its force-feeding of a diet of shame at too much success and shame at failure, and a great deal more bullying than at Osborne or Dartmouth – would that have helped?

It might have done. A feminine-dominated semi-royal upbringing is not the best way of acquiring the peculiar British masculine ethic and style of behaviour. Again, one must look at the father, and observe the parallel and similarity. Mountbatten got it more nearly right than Battenberg, but not right enough.

The father had made insufficient effort to cure his German accent and failed to see that regular visits to his German castle and his German naval relations at a time of growing international distrust might be misinterpreted. His son failed to comprehend that a beautiful rich wife, an enormous white yacht and a flash Hispano-Suiza motor car might be misunderstood as the provocative flaunting of wealth and privilege before the less wealthy and less privileged.

The royal connections of both Prince Louis and Mountbatten, and in Mountbatten the great wealth, were slightly discomfiting and obstructive to the forming of friendships. Neither father nor son quite 'fitted into' the Royal Navy, even though both were exceptionally able officers. But just as Prince Louis could have entered the wardroom of a German battleship in 1908 and at once been accepted as a fellow officer, so Mountbatten could have served in a German pocket battleship in 1938. Disregarding politics (which the German Navy largely did), both men would have felt comfortably at home, more comfortably than in their own service, just as their German fellow officers would have felt comfortable with them, and their uninhibited competitive professionalism.

It was this same professionalism which led Mountbatten to take a fresh, un-orthodox view of the navy's *matériel* and equipment. Once again like his father, who served on the committee responsible for the revolutionary battle-ship *Dreadnought* of 1906, Mountbatten for his part did much for destroyer design in the 1930s.

From a curious and trivial incident relating to the improvement of his own comfort in the *Daring*, he came to know A. P. Cole of the Royal Corps of Naval Constructors and a brilliant designer.

Mountbatten, who had never much enjoyed an austere way of life, was disappointed to find the very up-to-date *Daring* had no basin with running hot and cold water in the captain's cabin. 'So I engaged some Maltese dock-yard workmen to fit one,' said Mountbatten. 'They ran the outlet pipe into the waste pipe of the wardroom bathroom on the inboard side of the ship and then through a bulkhead – a non-watertight one of course. In the middle of all this work and while I was ashore, Cole came on board, went to my cabin and saw the men working at what looked like a hole in the ship's bottom.

'The next thing I knew of it, I was summoned to the Vice-Admiral, Malta. Cole was there repeating the charge, in front of me, that I was interfering with the structure of my ship without permission and making a hole in the bottom. I said, "You're a liar. I am doing nothing of the kind, and I think it is amazing that you should snoop about in a captain's cabin without permission, and then report him for something he has not done." I ended by saying rudely, "No wonder constructors are not allowed to wear naval uniform!"

'The Vice-Admiral then kicked him out and ordered him to report and apologize to the CO *Daring*. It was the best thing that ever happened,' Mount-batten concluded. 'We became great buddies after this and I had a powerful ally in the Naval Constructors.'

Mountbatten had been keeping notes all the time in the *Daring* and the *Wishart* for improving destroyer design. He knew that it would be useless to forward recommendations through Captain (D) and then Rear-Admiral (D) and the C-in-C. But by 1936 both Cole and Mountbatten were at the Admiralty, and they arrived just in time to ensure that the new generation of destroyers incorporated a number of improvements. It was Mountbatten and Cole who were jointly responsible for the single-funnel, two-boiler de-sign, and Mountbatten alone who conceived and had installed the all-covered bridge right across the ship, with a deep drop covering the catwalk, a slanting roof and a windscreen, which allowed (for the first time) the bridge personnel to remain dry in any conditions. It marked the end of the era when a destroyer captain was supposed to go into action soaking wet and half-blinded by spume. This was more like driving a car with full visibility, even in a rainstorm.

Before the 'Mountbatten bridge' there was the 'Mountbatten station-keeping device'. Destroyers are nimble, manœuvrable, very fast ships which normally work close together in flotillas. They are not unlike a squad-ron of bombers flying in formation. To keep correct station, therefore, is one of the most difficult and important priorities. Adapting a device he had seen in a French battleship, Mountbatten conceived his 'station-keeping device'.* Its origins were recounted recently by Rear-Admiral J.G. Maclean, a newly-promoted Commander (E) at the Admiralty in 1937 in charge of the design of destroyer machinery. 'One of the papers that came to me was a fat wadge containing approval to fit a "station-keeping device" in the next class of destroyers due to complete building in a year's time. The idea had been invented by Commander Mountbatten,' the officer continued, 'and tried out by him in very embryonic form in the Mediterranean.

'Looking through the papers, I came across many adverse comments on the idea from various members of the department, notably that of the Engineer-in-Chief of the Fleet. It seemed to me, however, that Mountbatten knew more about what went on in the engine rooms of destroyers and other warships than some of the departmental critics of the idea, which in my view would help captains, officers-of-the-watch and especially engine room staff enormously. It would also reduce fuel consumption.'

Approval was one thing, practical development another, an essential element being an infinitely variable gear capable of operating without slip. Maclean called a meeting of the three firms who normally made instruments for engine rooms, and asked Mountbatten if he would come to it. 'It was clear during the meeting that only one member of the three firms could even grasp the underlying idea behind the invention, and he had no suggestion as to how it might be achieved. When the representatives had gone,' Maclean recounted, 'Mountbatten turned to me and said, "Now that Shadrach, Meshack and Abednego have departed, what do we do?" I replied that we would clearly have to abandon them and I would scratch my head.'[3] In fact, by great good fortune, Commander Maclean's assistant had a cousin with a small electrical firm in north London who had the wit and the means, with the result that this invaluable device was fitted to the next and subsequent batches of destroyers.

This was a typical Mountbatten operation. First the recognition of imperfection. Second the ingenuity and the working out of the genesis of an idea. Third the cheek and persuasive power and influence to get it through in spite of hostility. Fourth the overcoming of details like design and manufacture by luck. But would the luck have come his way if the blazing light of enthusiasm had not guided those who could help? The answer is, 'It is very doubtful.'

* A shaft, taken through a differential driven from the two propeller shafts, showed the actual engine revolutions. A timed shaft revolving at the ordered revs entered a second differential which the first shaft also entered. Both shafts turning in opposite directions. The resultant shaft showed no movement if speed was correct, but if the engines made a greater or less number of revs, this deficiency or surplus was shown on a scale in the engine room, on the bridge, and on a correction dial on the after funnel.... This made it possible for the ERA to open up the two engines to keep the pointer at 200. (From *British Destroyers* by E.J. March, Seeley, Service & Co., 1966.)

This station-keeping device, together with its cousin the 'line-of-bearing keeper', which was also Mountbatten's invention, were installed in all classes of destroyers completed on the outbreak of war. As usual, most commanders hated them at first, and later came to rely heavily upon them.

The imminence of two very different looming crises became evident during Mountbatten's time with the *Wishart*. One of them was monarchical, the other international.

The Prince of Wales had dropped Mrs Dudley Ward for Lady Furness, wife of the shipping magnate, Christopher Furness; and then in 1931 had met Wallis Simpson. Mountbatten, as the Prince's confidant in all things, learned soon of his growing affection for the American divorcée, and of the royal family's concern. Mountbatten's mother saw evidence of the strength of the mutual affection at the time of the Silver Jubilee in 1935, and wrote complainingly to Mountbatten of the way Mrs Simpson insisted on showing this publicly.

Before leaving the Mediterranean, Mountbatten and Edwina saw the Prince and Mrs Simpson several times, at Cannes, Monte Carlo and Leghorn, on holiday and apparently inseparable. It was clear that this affair was different from any that had gone before it. There was a new expression of fulfilment and happiness in the face of Mountbatten's friend. He was relaxed and easy with this American woman, who on first acquaintance appeared naive but concealed beneath this façade a clever mind and steely determination.

The two couples made a bright, brittle foursome, watched by curious and envious eyes about the more expensive and exclusive resorts of the Mediterranean and Adriatic, the target of snapshots for the gossip magazines. Edwina intuitively scented serious trouble. Mountbatten was simply pleased to see his old friend happy with a woman who, at last, appeared to give him complete satisfaction. The thought that, with his father's death and succession to the throne, she would press him to marry her, never at this time (1935) crossed his mind.

On 2 October of that year, Mussolini invaded Abyssinia, setting in motion the series of invasions and annexations that led to war four years later. Britain and France at first reacted strongly, and sanctions were imposed on Italy. There was a real likelihood of war, and the Mediterranean Fleet was placed on a war footing and its main base moved from vulnerable Malta to Alexandria.

The *Wishart*'s flotilla, however, was left behind in Grand Harbour to keep the flag flying. The old destroyers were considered expendable, to commit what damage they could if they were attacked. The 'do or die boys', they were called by the other units of the fleet as they sailed east. Edwina, typically, strode up to the wireless station and became the announcer, her voice of optimism bringing cheer to the islanders and the Navy – what was left of it.

Mountbatten liked to speculate on how they would have fared against the full might of Mussolini's fleet. It was a very modern fleet, with many exceptionally fast and well-designed ships. 'We should have put up the best show we could, and have done some damage. Judging by the Italians' performance when war did come, our flotilla would have easily outfought any destroyers we came up against. But a lot of their cruisers were much faster than us.'

With the declaration of war, it was presumed the French would have been allies. Whether they would have been any more effective at sea in 1935 than they were on land in 1940 is doubtful. The nearest French base was Bizerta, and Mountbatten was given the task of liaising with the French admiral there about docking facilities in the event of Malta dockyard being put out of action. 'I knew him quite well,' said Mountbatten, 'and I knew he spoke English. But when I arrived with the *Wishart*, do you know he wouldn't speak a word of English? And he ordered all his staff to talk French, too. Fortunately, I had taken that translators' course and kept my French up. But they were completely unco-operative and extremely rude to us. It was an omen of what we were in for later.'

Mountbatten's return to England approximately and appropriately coincided with the march of the German armies into the demilitarized Rhineland. Mountbatten believed strongly in air power and knew that it was already changing the face of naval strategy and tactics. Three years before World War I, his father as Second Sea Lord had strongly supported the creation of a Naval Air Service, and Churchill had placed him in charge of its development.

Now, in 1936, Mountbatten was given a staff appointment in the Naval Air Service, and the figure of Churchill re-enters the Mountbatten story like a novelist's character planted in Chapter One to add weight to his reappearance as the climax of the plot approaches – in this case the climax of war and great fame and achievement for both men.

In London, at the Admiralty, Mountbatten was in a position to learn the truth of the state of the nation's defences, and by his energy, skill and connections at the highest levels, influence events far beyond those of any other thirty-six-year-old naval commander.

The ominous nature of the year 1936 was also reflected in the lifestyle

of the Mountbattens. This was not the advent of an era of austerity. Both
of them continued to indulge themselves in anything that took their fancy.
Fast cars abounded. The *Shrimp* had been sold – to Puccini's son – but
other boats took her place. Edwina continued her travels to remote corners
of the world – like the mountains of Bolivia.

Edwina had kept Brook House going all through the years of the depression at an annual cost of upkeep of around £20,000. Even by Cassel standards, the lawyers thought this unduly extravagant. So in 1936, amid the
thunder of publicity and falling rubble, it was torn down and a block of
luxury apartments erected in its place – keeping the old name, as can be
seen today. The top two Edwina kept for herself, as a super-duplex and
London's first penthouse. 'It was a glittering film set in which to entertain,
a millionaire's fantasy filled with gadgets to make living easier and faster,'[4]
as Edwina's biographer described it.

From the outside, the two towering floors were quite distinct from the
rest of the building, but to distinguish them further they were floodlit at
night. The penthouse had thirty rooms (five reception rooms could be made
into a single ballroom, or a cinema seating 150); the nursery wing, kitchens
and servants' quarters were all built to the highest standards of comfort and
luxury.

The famous designer Victor Proetz acted as consultant. Mrs Joshua
Cosden, the American decorator and designer and a friend of Edwina's, was
responsible for the interior decoration. A magazine described her work in
the drawing-room: 'The ceiling is overlaid with tarnished silver leaf in a
bold herring-bone pattern that contributes the dull metallic glint of steel
armour and pewter tankards in the glowing velvet of the paintings.'

Here, then, the Mountbattens lived when 'in town' until the outbreak
of the war, Mountbatten every morning descending in his pride and joy
('the non-stop fastest lift in London') for the Admiralty to deal with the
problems brought about by the rapid expansion of the Navy, and with the
problems of air power in particular. Aside from the parties, this new Brook
House was the scene of informal meetings with people of power and influence, including Winston Churchill, who were striving to apply some further
momentum to the rearmament drive and sound the alarum bells for the ears
of a public, as well as a supine Prime Minister and Cabinet, who did not
yet realize how close to catastrophe Europe had already advanced.

The first priority in Mountbatten's appointment brief was, as he put it,
'to bring the Fleet Air Arm back into the Navy'. The RAF's victory after
World War I in retaining joint control over naval flying had been an in-
efficient and untidy arrangement, comparable to the time when the Army
had had control over the Navy's guns in the nineteenth century. In both

cases the Navy came off worst, the other service naturally giving priority to its own equipment, leaving the droppings for the Navy.

Fleet Air Arm pilots were enthusiastic and skilful but were operating with machines fit only for the scrap heap. It was far behind the US Navy; and even more inadequate by contrast with the magnificent Japanese Air Arm, which ironically the Royal Navy had helped to build up at the time of the Anglo-Japanese Treaty of Friendship. One memorandum Mountbatten found on his desk when he came to the Naval Air Division ran:

> Can anyone doubt that if we went to war tomorrow, complete chaos would reign in the Navy's Air Services? Where are the machines? Where is the trained personnel? Where is the up-to-date material? They simply don't exist. There is not a squadron afloat today with aircraft of a type which was not in service three years ago. There is not a squadron with a type whose design is less than ten years old.

Unlike the Prime Minister, Stanley Baldwin, Mountbatten believed (with Churchill) that time was running out, and that unification of the Air Arm had become urgently necessary. Churchill, as co-ordinator of all agitators for strengthening the nation's and empire's defences, was Mountbatten's first ally. Early in 1937, Mountbatten sent Churchill an eleven-page memorandum concisely advancing the case for the Navy's plenary control of the Fleet Air Arm at the earliest opportunity.

Mountbatten had always been prepared – even eagerly willing – to use circuitous routes to reach his desired goal. It was the successful arrival that mattered, he argued, whether it was by way of an out-of-office ambitious genius like Churchill, who had sacked Mountbatten's father but had the security of the nation so close to his heart and so much a part of his endeavours, or through Buckingham Palace. The Fleet Air Arm memorandum brought Mountbatten into that secret club of grey figures who fed Churchill with confidential information that proved the deplorable state of the defences and allowed him to attack the government with facts and authority.

This group of anxious patriots made a disparate lot, ranging from cabinet ministers like Lord Swinton and Anthony Eden to the novelist Sir Philip Gibbs, admirals and generals. Wing-Commander Charles Anderson was probably closer to Churchill than any other airman, and was a steady conveyor of information on RAF defences. Mountbatten concerned himself almost entirely with Fleet Air Arm affairs, in collaboration with the Deputy Director of the Naval Air Division, Captain Cosmo Graham RN, who had commanded a destroyer when Mountbatten's father had been Second Sea Lord and Churchill First Lord twenty-five years earlier.

Mountbatten's victory on behalf of the Navy occurred on 30 July 1937, after some bloody skirmishing with the RAF. A tremendous amount of work remained to be done, and the two years remaining before the outbreak of war were not long enough to complete the changeover, with the result that RAF personnel were still serving in carriers during the early months of hostilities. Little of the modern equipment had come through, no modern fighters were available comparable with the RAF Spitfires, and 150 mph biplanes were the main equipment. As a consequence many defeats were suffered and many lives were unnecessarily lost in the early months of the war. Mountbatten agreed heartily with Churchill who had commented on the government's announcement of the changeover, that 'It is a great pity that this decision was not taken eighteen months ago.... There is really no excuse for it not having been settled earlier.'

The lack of alarm and sense of emergency was still dominant in Whitehall, however, in spite of the efforts of Churchill and his supporters. Mountbatten recalled a conversation with Baldwin, Edward VIII being the host. Mountbatten, well briefed for the occasion, asked the Prime Minister if he knew how many new airfields were being built in north-west Germany, and then told him.

Baldwin asked him how he knew, and Mountbatten told him he worked in the Naval Air Division, where it was believed that they were intended for attacks on Britain. Baldwin did not agree. 'I looked at him in amazement,' Mountbatten said. 'When I asked him why else, he just brushed the subject aside as if it bored him. "Do you think, sir, that Hitler can remain in power without resorting to war?" I asked. "I don't see why not," the Prime Minister replied blandly.

'"I think Hitler's like a bicyclist, sir," I said, rather boldly for a mere Commander RN. "He's got to go on pedalling or he'll fall off."'

Even before Prince Louis' pioneer work to create a Fleet Air Arm, prophets were foretelling the doom of surface fleets by bombing aircraft, and a drawing in *The Sphere* in 1910 showed men o'war at sea being attacked from the air with devastating accuracy. From the beginning, the dive bomber was seen as the main threat, its emotive as well as its material impact being regarded as more accurate and more destructive.

Before and during World War II, the Germans made much fearsome propaganda out of the dive bomber, and especially the Stuka, the JU87 single-engined machine, which, with diving brakes extended and 'terror siren' screaming, became the lead instrument in the chorus of the *blitzkrieg*.

The official British Navy attitude to the bomber was similar to most other navies', including the Japanese and the American. Admiralty opinion in the 1930s was that bombing and torpedo aircraft, like the torpedo boat of the

1890s, were indeed a threat, but one which could be contained by adequate defences.

While at the Admiralty from 1936, Mountbatten formed the strong view that the anti-aircraft defences of RN ships was inadequate, and he was among those who campaigned against powerfully entrenched opinion for improving them.

In January 1937, an expatriate Austrian engineer working for the Oerlikon armament works in Switzerland arrived in London on a sales mission. He had, he claimed, a very fast-firing gun to offer with a very high muzzle velocity which used small 20-mm explosive shells. It was, he said, the answer to the German Stuka. Mountbatten learned of his arrival, liked the sound of the gun, and liked the sound of the man, his own father being Austrian-born, too. 'I had this man Antoine Gazda in my office at the Admiralty all one morning,' said Mountbatten, 'trying to shoot him down. I used every argument against his Oerlikon gun, but he shot me down instead. I was convinced that this was the weapon which could save ships and lives from the low-flying bomber and torpedo-bomber. I arranged for a meeting between Gazda and some of the more important members of the Board, the DNO, the Controller, my own boss, and so on. On the morning, Gazda turned up with his notes and equipment, but no voice, so I took over, doing a quick conversion from the metres in his notes to feet and yards. It went down all right.'

But that was only the beginning of the battle – a battle against entrenched opinion, apathy, conservatism, a belief that the multi-barrel two-pounder pom-pom which had been in service for years could deal with anything flying. The trouble with the pom-pom was that it was too inflexible and too slow to bear on the target. The other trouble was that British gunmakers, and notably Vickers, saw business going abroad.

Delay and procrastination continued for two years, and 1937-9 was not a period when the Royal Navy should have been passing by the most effective defences against air power. In the end, Mountbatten persuaded Oerlikon to proceed with an initial order on the expectation that the converted and enlightened Admiral Sir Roger Backhouse would confirm it when he became First Sea Lord. Backhouse almost immediately died of overwork, and finally Treasury authority was not given for the order until the month war broke out.

It is incalculable how many destroyers and other ships might have survived dive bomber attack at the Dunkirk evacuation and the Norwegian campaign (among others) if Mountbatten's lobbying for the Oerlikon had been successful earlier, nor how many more lives and ships would have been lost if, among all his other tasks and preoccupations, he had not battled so hard and for so long for this deadly cannon when he was at the Admiralty.

The ultimate irony was that, when he got back to sea, though his own ship was one of the first to be equipped with Oerlikons, they failed to save it against a mass onslaught of Stukas.

There is a famous photograph of the entire Mountbatten family in uniform, even if the two girls are dressed for the peaceful pursuit of girl-guiding. But this picture represents an historical marker, staked not just by the Mountbatten family but by all people of responsible opinion in Britain in the late 1930s. The time for play was over. Britain must be prepared. Britain meant business.

'I knew that war was coming, as night follows day, just as my father did by 1912. As a serving officer,' Mountbatten said of this time, 'there was little I could say in public, unlike Winston, who sometimes seemed to be the one voice of sanity. I had two assets, however. I was of German descent and, like my father, understood the German mind. I was well-informed, and thanks to my position and my relationship to the Court, I had the ear of powerful men – others as well as Winston. This was what my father had meant when he had said that at first my privileged position would be to my disadvantage, but later it would be useful.'

Mountbatten recalled a meeting at Broadlands. 'I mentioned again and again to Eden and Salisbury my view of the German situation. Then, at the time Halifax was sent out to double-cross Eden in Rome, I had a call from Eden. Could he and Salisbury come and see me? I suggested Broadlands, being a convenient point for all three of us. We talked at very great length. I remember word for word what I said. I said, "I have been trying to make you English people understand what I as a man of German descent clearly understand, that this situation is unquestionably going to end in war unless this country can make *really* clear the circumstances under which it would fight. As long as Chamberlain is controlling foreign policy, the issue is cloudy and befogged. You must resign, both of you. You must speak in the House supporting each other and denouncing in unequivocal terms the policy Chamberlain is pursuing. You must say you will not be associated with a policy leading to war, explain the alternative policy, and then intelligent people will rally round you.

'"Unless you do this, you'll strangle yourself with your old school tie."

'I know Eden agreed with me. But he never said a word. The rest is history. Hitler never knew, he never understood what the calibre of this country really was, and a bit more than a year later, we had slipped into war again. . . .'

In that same year, Mountbatten attended the Higher Commanders' Course at Aldershot, and there met many of the senior officers of the three services

beside whom he was to fight in the war that was only months away. Seen
now in retrospect, it appeared as if the hands of fate were moulding events
and his career into the shape that would be impelled into a trajectory as
unswerving and spectacular as that of a 16-inch naval shell.

Ten days before war broke out, and now promoted to Captain, Mountbatten took over from the builders the ship that will forever be associated
with his name, HMS *Kelly*. He had been appointed Captain (D) of the Fifth
Destroyer Flotilla – eight men o'war which found themselves (with Mountbatten's connivance) at the centre of the fighting at sea almost from the first
gun blast.

The *Kelly*, of course, was unique. There was no man o'war like her in
any navy. What could possibly be more suitable than that she should be
fitted out in part as a Royal yacht? George VI and Queen Elizabeth had been
due to make a state visit to Belgium in the late summer of 1939, and Mountbatten had arranged that his new destroyer should be their conveyance. The
royal cabin equipment and fittings were, therefore, of the most luxurious
order. And they remained so, to Mountbatten's advantage, when the war
led to the cancellation of the visit. This time, therefore, there was no need
to fit a makeshift, illicit hot and cold water basin in his ship. He had his
own bathroom *en suite*.

Instead of the King and Queen, it was the King's brother and his wife
who enjoyed the royal yacht luxuries of the *Kelly*. One of Mountbatten's
first wartime missions was to bring home the Duke and Duchess of Windsor
from France.

Mountbatten had remained in touch with his cousin and old shipmate
after the abdication, and had even offered to be best man at his wedding,
but had been turned down sharply by the Duke, who still innocently imagined that his wedding could be classed as 'royal', at which, customarily,
there was no best man, only 'supporters', in his case preferably his brothers.

As for the Duchess, Wallis Windsor was never on easy terms with Mountbatten after the abdication. She was jealous of David's old friendships, and
especially jealous of Mountbatten's intimate relations with all the royal
family who had treated her so shabbily. She was suspicious of Mountbatten's
rôle in the abdication crisis, and believed, with reason, that Mountbatten
had opposed the idea of a morganatic marriage, and the abdication.

It was indeed hard for the woman who had once believed that she could
be Queen of England to observe the solidarity of the ranks that closed about
the Court of St James's after she had – in her eyes – been rejected. With
his sharp eye and swift judgment, Mountbatten recognized the compass
courses he should steer through the shoals. He knew that he carried what
the new Queen would call the stigma of close friendship with the man whose

weakness, selfishness and sexual appetite had forced her own beloved husband unwillingly on to the throne.

It was part of the Mountbatten creed to avoid making enemies and to keep friends. In 1937 he accomplished the double act of retaining good relations with the ex-King and developing the already friendly, but not intimate, relations with the new King. In Paris the Duchess of Windsor read with displeasure reports like this:

> By accompanying the Duke and Duchess of Kent to the Westminster [coronation] rehearsal last week, Lord and Lady Louis Mountbatten showed how skilfully they had maintained their position in the new social reign, despite a long-standing friendship with the King who was never crowned.
>
> With the Duke and Duchess of Kent, they had watched the Duke of Gloucester as first Prince of the Royal blood, rehearse his bow before an empty chair. When Lady Louis emerged to public view, she was seen chatting vivaciously to the Duke of Kent, while her husband shared a joke with Duchess Marina of Kent.

'I had been agonized for David at the time of the abdication,' Mountbatten said. 'I know it was terrible for him. Winston was among those who believed he couldn't live without her. I didn't think that, but I know it was a terrible decision for him. I always thought it was his duty to remain King, and told him that he ought to give up Wallis if that was the only alternative. But we remained friends – Edwina and I were too fond of them both for there to be any break.'

There was a break later, after the war, though Mountbatten was never aware of any cooling off, and acted as host to him when he returned to the country with the Duchess in June 1967 for the unveiling of a plaque in memory of the Duke's mother, Queen Mary.

But now, in these early, dark days of the war, the *Kelly* arrived in Cherbourg on 12 September 1939. Churchill, as First Lord again, had not only sent Mountbatten on this errand, but with him his own son Randolph.

The Duke and Duchess were awaiting them, together with their usual mountain of luggage. The Duke greeted his cousin warmly and shook Randolph's hand, glancing down at the spurs he was wearing. Randolph had dressed in the uniform of the 4th Hussars for the occasion, and the Duke pointed out with glee that his spurs were on inside out and upside down – a gaffe that Mountbatten had been the first to notice but had left for the Duke to point out.

The *Kelly* cast off at 4 pm, and set course at high speed for Portsmouth. 'I enjoyed the voyage very much,' said Mountbatten. 'David and Wallis were very impressed with the luxury, and David said, "You're doing yourself very nicely, Dickie." Then he came up on to the bridge with me as it got dark and we approached Portsmouth and we chatted about old days. Of course, the English coast was blacked out, and I remember thinking back to that evening with my father in the Admiralty, with the crowds cheering for the start of the war." ' This time he didn't hear a sound above the *Kelly*'s engines....

5
THE *KELLY* AT WAR

THERE WAS SOMETHING supremely right about the fact that Mountbatten's body still bore the tattered remains of a jersey decorated with the emblem of HMS *Kelly* when it was recovered from the sea. The brief fighting career of this ship, retold time and again, made into a musical, fictionalized in Noël Coward's film *In Which We Serve*, grew into a legend in Mountbatten's own time, and has flourished for forty years. The wonder was that the ill-starred ship survived for as long as she did, for she was seldom out of trouble.

The *Kelly* was one of the 'J' and 'K' class destroyers, which Mountbatten had helped Cole to design, rushed to completion for the outbreak of World War II – modest-sized vessels with a speed of around 34 knots, armed with ten torpedo tubes and six 4.7-inch guns. Unlike the guns of most contemporary foreign destroyers, which were dual-purpose weapons, the *Kelly*'s could elevate to only 40 degrees, and were therefore restricted in their usefulness against high-flying aircraft. Her light anti-aircraft defences were also inadequate, even when later supplemented with Oerlikon cannons.

With her single raked funnel (the configuration to Mountbatten's design), the black band singling her out as flotilla leader, she looked a fine, modern, business-like fighting ship, and Mountbatten was tremendously proud of her. 'Keep On' was the motto he contrived for her; and that seemed to her company to be peculiarly appropriate as they learned from their captain's first speech that they were going to store and ammunition ship in three days instead of the customary three weeks. 'We have a job to do. Let's do it.'

For his officers, Mountbatten selected a number of congenial and highly efficient, experienced destroyer men – 'Egg' Burnett as first lieutenant, Goodenough (torpedo), Alistair Robin (guns) and 'Dusty' Dunsterville as signals officer.

The 'phoney' war period, from September until the German invasion of Denmark and Norway in April 1940, may have been quiet for the Army and

Air Force. At sea it was action from the beginning, with the German Navy recommencing commerce warfare with surface ships and U-boats just as if 11 November 1918 marked only a pause in the relentless duel between the two navies.

The word 'phoney' made the Royal Navy furious. Even before she delivered the Duke and Duchess of Windsor to Portsmouth, the *Kelly* had been in action, an anti-submarine exercise turning into the real thing when the ship's Asdic (submarine detection apparatus) caught a 'ping', and the *Kelly* released a pattern of depth-charges. All that came to the surface were a lot of dead fish and some oil. Mountbatten claimed a 'probable'. Admiralty Intelligence had a good laugh at that, for they knew that the nearest U-boats were many miles away. But they were already doing terrible damage, sinking the liner *Athenia* on the first day of war, and the valuable aircraft-carrier *Courageous* a fortnight later.

The *Kelly* was one of a number of ships that answered the carrier's SOS. Two torpedoes had struck the big ship, sending her to the bottom quickly, with the loss of some five hundred lives. It was cold and rough when the *Kelly* reached the spot in pitch darkness. The stench of oil fuel, the shapeless bundles of the dead wallowing in the waves, the choking cries of those still alive, all the squalid litter of a sunk ship that was to become feared and familiar in the years ahead, could be seen by the light from two neutral ships standing by.

One of the ships was an American liner, and the *Kelly* managed to relieve her of some of the *Courageous*'s men, and they picked up others from the water. At last, after two hours, they hoisted inboard the cutter, and headed for Devonport with their shocked and injured sailors laid out in the sick bay. Among them was the carrier's commander, Mountbatten's old friend and naval equerry to the king, Abel Smith, a future Flag Officer Royal Yachts.

All through October and November 1939, the *Kelly*, joined now by more of her flotilla straight from the builders' yards, operated patrols against the German submarine offensive in the Western Approaches. On 14 October, while escorting a convoy, they got another 'ping', a real one this time. The *Kelly* closed in on the submerged U-boat, and plastered the sea with depth charges. This time there was no doubt. Amid the cauldrons of white foam from the explosions, the smashed U-boat's bows emerged, stood vertically out of the water, remained stationary like a grey gravestone to her own dead, and then slipped to the bottom.

The *Kelly* steamed north a few days later, based on Loch Ewe on the west coast of Ross and Cromarty in Scotland, and then, late in November, to the Tyne. On a foggy, early December day, news of two oil tankers in trouble at the Tyne estuary reached the *Kelly*. She immediately raced down river, in company with another destroyer, and narrowly missing a collision with a big merchantman. Both tankers were sinking. Mountbatten ordered the *Kelly* alongside one that was burning. It was four o'clock in the afternoon and darkness was falling, restricting visibility further.

Almost at once, Mountbatten heard a bumping under the destroyer's bottom. It sounded louder to those below, as if someone was hammering the keel from bows to stern. Then there was a huge explosion, and half the ship's company were thrown to the deck. They had blundered into a minefield, steamed right into the centre of it. The *Kelly*, helped by two tugs, limped back to her old yard at Hebburn where she had been completed in the summer. In dry dock, Mountbatten could see the extent of the damage, and could see how lucky they had been. If the mine had exploded on first impact, the ship could have gone to the bottom. As it was, they had all had an unpleasant fright, a scare that had proved too much for one stoker, who had panicked.

Mountbatten cleared the lower deck and addressed the ship's company. 'Today we have been through one of the most trying experiences which can befall a newly commissioned ship in war,' he began. 'Out of 240 men on board this ship, 239 behaved as they ought to have, and as I expected them to behave, but one was unable to control himself and deserted his post, and incidentally his comrades.' Mountbatten paused. There was no one better in this sort of situation. His eyes flickered over the sea of faces, pausing here and there, exploiting every ounce of drama in the situation. 'I had him brought before me a couple of hours ago, and he himself informed me that he knew the punishment for desertion of his post could be death. You will therefore be surprised to hear that I propose to let him off with a caution. One caution to him, and a second one to myself for having failed in four months to impress my personality and doctrine on each and all of you to prevent such an incident from occurring. From now on, I wish....'

It went down wonderfully. And he followed it with the news that there would be Christmas leave for all. And when the word got about that few of the men had money to pay for their rail fare home, Edwina, who had come to join Mountbatten at the Tyne, was one of the first to hear it. 'I think I'd like to pay for everyone's Christmas leave fare,' she said. 'Very good idea,' said Mountbatten.

The following day, Mountbatten and Edwina travelled down to London. Edwina had joined the St John Ambulance and closed down the Brook House penthouse for the duration. For the present, their only London headquarters was Victoria's suite in Kensington Palace.

Patricia and Pamela had been despatched for safety to New York, sailing in the liner *Washington* from Galway on 14 July, along with Duff Cooper's son, the children of Arthur Christiansen, the newspaper editor, and others who could afford to do so. In later years, Mountbatten was always rather defensive about this decision, anxious that the girls should not be regarded as specially privileged when so many of their contemporaries, including their cousins Princesses Elizabeth and Margaret Rose, had stuck it out at home. 'With their Jewish blood, they would have been the first for the gas ovens if the Germans had invaded,' he would justify their departure.

London was a depressing place on that first December of the war. There were a great many people still against the war, and little of the patriotic fervour of 1914, though none of the hysteria which had driven Mountbatten's father from office, either. Churchill was back at the Admiralty as First Lord, and he was a joy and stimulus as always when they dined at Admiralty House on 5 December. Churchill had an enormous regard and admiration for Edwina, and they always got on marvellously. There was a great deal of torpor and pessimism about the city; and once again the references to the phoney war, and stupid songs like 'We're going to hang out the washing on the Siegfried Line', when nobody was going to do anything of the kind, infuriated Mountbatten.

At lunch, he met Eden with Hore-Belisha, Secretary of State for War. Both politicians were depressed. The Navy, they said, was the only service doing anything, to which Mountbatten concurred, saying that a lot of his friends were being killed and it was not a phoney war at sea.

'What's the Army doing?' he asked Hore-Belisha.

'It's so lucky,' replied the War Minister, 'that the Germans are so busy in Poland and not attacking us, giving us time to build up the Maginot Line, making it completely impregnable.'

That sounded plausible, but Mountbatten was outraged. 'It is an absolute axiom of strategy,' he said, 'that the same course of action cannot be advantageous to both sides. If the Germans are leaving us alone, it is because it suits them to do so. If we go on doing nothing, when the Germans have tidied up Poland, they'll turn round and mop us up.'

Hore-Belisha protested, but Mountbatten persisted in his belief that the British ought to be attacking *now*. 'It is crazy to do nothing. We'll be picked off *in seriatim*. Look, the French army is riddled with communists,' Mountbatten insisted. 'Forty or fifty per cent of those called up are communists and will turn against the government when the Germans attack. The Germans will turn the corner of the Maginot Line and dash through Holland and Belgium, just like last time. Then we'll be finished.'

This plea, Mountbatten said thirty-five years later, made not the slightest impression. Nor were they in the least impressed by his account of the meeting with the French admiral at Bizerta four years earlier. The French were in fine fettle, stalwart allies, both men insisted.

It was a busy time in London for the Mountbattens, both of them pursuing their causes amid the apathy. A few years earlier, they would have been seen, as often as not, throwing themselves heart and soul into parties and following new ideas for diversion and entertainment. Now they were to be seen on other errands, more serious pursuits, uniforms with decorations replacing dinner jackets and evening dresses, but still driven by the same well-known fire. It was a curious and interesting metamorphosis.

On the seventh, at luncheon with the fashionable hostess Sibyl Colefax, Mountbatten's cause was publicity for the Royal Navy, which he felt it sadly lacked. 'The Air Force seemed to bag the whole thing,' he claimed, according to another guest, Harold Nicolson. 'For instance, the other day a merchant ship was arriving in the Firth from the Argentine. . . .' A German plane, it seemed, had raked the bridge with shells and bullets. 'The navigating lieutenant was killed,' according to Mountbatten, 'and the old captain was wounded by thirty bullets. He picked himself up and said to the signaller, "Is Lieutenant Jones dead?" "Yes, Sir." "Then bring me a chair." He sat down and steered the ship in. Later he was found to be dead.'

'Dickie', said Harold Nicolson, 'feels that that story ought to have been written up.' But then Mountbatten never could bear to see a good story wasted.

A day or two later, Mountbatten left London for Portland where he took over the *Kelly*'s sister ship *Kelvin*. There was a letter from Eden awaiting him. The gist of it was that if anyone else but him had been talking about the Western Front Eden wouldn't even have bothered to listen. But after Mountbatten left, he got a careful and up-to-date intelligence report. It is true what Leslie [Hore-Belisha] said. The Maginot Line has been strengthened, the French cannot be turned, you can sleep easy in your bed. . . .

Ten years before this meeting, as a young lieutenant at work on his *Introduction to Polo*, Mountbatten had written: 'Whenever you are doing nothing you are doing wrong.' The same stricture applied to war, he believed. War was *now*, and nothing was being done. 'Now I was really frightened. I had opened their eyes, told them the truth, soundings had been taken, and *still* they couldn't understand. Now I was certain that by the summer of 1940 we should be finished.'

Only Churchill, Mountbatten and a very few hard-core realists recognized the dangers ahead in the winter of 1939. There are two equally remarkable aspects of this true story about Eden and Hore-Belisha. The first is that the British War Minister at the outset of the greatest war of all time, *and* the brilliant and far-sighted politician who had so recently and spectacularly resigned as Foreign Secretary because the government would not acknowledge the dangers of fascist dictatorship, both suffered from the same myopia a mere four months before Hitler's western offensive. The second is that they were prepared to listen seriously to a naval captain, not yet forty years old, with no formal standing in defence or political matters.

So Mountbatten went back to the realities of war, and Edwina returned to her work with the St John Ambulance Brigade.

After more months of strenuous patrols and convoy work in the Western Approaches, Mountbatten got *Kelly* back in time for the great offensive he knew was coming in the spring. Almost at once she was in trouble again. On convoy escort work in the North Sea, she collided lightly with another destroyer, scraping and tearing her side from close to the bows to the stern. She was patched up at Scapa Flow in the Orkneys, and then proceeded slowly down the east coast to London for a complete repair.

It was twenty years ago, at the conclusion of another war, since he had brought the little *P31* up the Thames for inspection by his father and mother and by George V. At the outset of this war, Mountbatten now invited George V's son to visit his destroyer. George VI and Queen Elizabeth, and the Duke and Duchess of Kent, arrived for dinner. It was a very Mountbatten evening, an intimate royal family affair. Mountbatten showed off his new if now rather knocked-about destroyer, and with special pride his new movie projector. Thanks to his old friendship with Charlie Chaplin, Mountbatten had managed to acquire a print of his new film, *The Great Dictator*, which had not yet been shown in London. And so the *Kelly* became the venue for its British premiere.

Mountbatten and the *Kelly* were back at Scapa Flow before the end of April. Norway had been invaded, and had been hard fought over. As a precursor to later events, Royal Navy dive bombers had sunk a German cruiser, the first major man o'war to be destroyed at sea by air power alone. Mountbatten's friend and fellow Captain (D), the brilliant and bold Warburton-Lee, had won a great victory with his destroyers, and had then himself been killed. Narvik had been taken from the German invaders. George VI had written to Churchill as First Lord that he 'would like to congratulate you on the splendid way in which, under your direction, the Navy is countering the German move against Scandinavia'.[2]

Mountbatten was itching to take part in the furious naval actions which were taking place up and down the fjords – bombardments, actions against German aircraft and ship-to-ship skirmishes. His opportunity came at the end of the month, but by this time the Germans were in the ascendancy.

Air power was proving to be the balancing factor in the combined sea–land operations, just as Mountbatten had feared, and the French and British forces were everywhere being pinned down.

Five thousand troops, under the supremely courageous old eccentric, General Carton de Wiart, were gathered at the little Norwegian port of Namsos, awaiting evacuation, and the *Kelly* was among the warships designated to escort the relieving troop transports. They had no air cover and the Luftwaffe bombers and fighters were present in great strength, ranging deep into the North Sea and watching every move on the ground. The convoy's only cover was fog.

'I asked permission for my division of four destroyers to evacuate the first night's contingent under the fog cover,' said Mountbatten. 'It seemed to me to be the only way of ensuring success. The moment permission was granted, I began a mad dash along the seventy or so miles of Norwegian coast to Namsos. It was 5 am. Suddenly the fog cleared, like a curtain pulled aside. A hundred yards ahead was a mass of half-submerged rocks. So it was full astern, and we missed them by yards. It also meant we couldn't continue with our plans, and all that day we played hide-and-seek with the German bombers, in and out of scattered fog banks.

'We tried again at nightfall – or twilight, because that's all you get at this time of the year. We went up the fjord at 26 knots, between the snow-capped peaks and the lush valleys with their wooden farmhouses. It was all incredibly peaceful, and I remember saying to myself, "This can't be war...." But it was!'

The last turn of the fjord revealed Namsos in flames. Every building was burning from a German bombardment. 'It seemed impossible that anyone could be alive, but there was old de Wiart, one eye gleaming defiance.'

'Lord Mountbatten managed to feel his way into the harbour,' the General later wrote, 'and the other ships followed him in. It was a tremendous undertaking to embark the whole force in a night of three short hours, but the Navy did it and earned my undying gratitude.'[3]

'The Germans really missed a trick not putting on a raid while we were taking on board these great numbers of men,' said Mountbatten. 'There were thousands of them lined up on the jetties.'

But at dawn along came the Luftwaffe, and the transports and escort were fiercely bombed all day. The packed French destroyer *Bison* was soon sunk. Most of her wounded survivors were picked up by Philip Vian's big destroyer *Afridi*, and that too was destroyed and nearly all the wounded drowned. The *Kelly*'s gunners claimed one dive bomber and the ship was near-missed time and again.

Carton de Wiart had tried and failed to embark in the *Afridi*. In not being sunk he 'missed a great experience', he later claimed. 'It was the dullest campaign in which I had taken part.'

Mountbatten did not share this detached view of the Namsos affair. This was real war, close-fought, deadly dangerous, clamorous, what he had spent the last twenty-seven years preparing for.

'As we steamed back across the North Sea, out of range at last of the German bombers, I thought about my father, who never saw any action in all his years in the Royal Navy. I hated war as much as he did, but he would have envied me that action off Namsos, just as he had loved to listen to Georgie's descriptions of the naval actions he fought in the North Sea.'

The Namsos evacuation took place on the night of 3–4 May 1940. Five days later, as the German armies opened the offensive that would lead to the collapse of Belgium, Holland and France in a single month, the *Kelly* was at sea again leading the 5th Flotilla – 'the fighting fifth', as they loved to be called – against a suspected German minelaying force believed to be off the Dutch coast.

It was a quiet, still evening, with banks of mist forming and dispersing, making visibility deceptive and ever-changing. It was just after 10 pm, and Mountbatten was on the bridge with the officer of the watch. They both saw the faint shape out of the half-light, travelling very fast.

It was a German motor-torpedo-boat – an E-boat – coming straight at the *Kelly*. The track of its torpedo was like a white towline hurled towards them. Mountbatten remembered thinking, as if he himself were immortal, 'That's going to kill a lot of people!' It did not, though. Someone was shouting, 'Torpedo track port!' A split second later, the dim shape disappeared. The torpedo passed clean under the *Kelly*, dead amidships.

There was no time for relief and self-congratulation. Its companion was hard behind it, and this time there was no escape. The torpedo struck above number 1 boiler room, blasting a fifty-foot-long hole, killing and injuring dozens of men below.

Mountbatten was yelling, 'Take over secondary steering!'

'No answer from the helm, sir.'

They had been steaming at 28 knots. The effect, as she heeled hard over to starboard until the gunwale was almost submerged, was for the seas to pour in with Niagara-like force, tearing at bulkheads, killing, maiming, drowning men in its path. When she was stationary and silent, wallowing uneasily in the swell, no one who had witnessed the explosion and its consequences gave the *Kelly* longer than half an hour.

Mountbatten had trained his men carefully in damage control. It was not a popular exercise in the Royal Navy, in which it was considered a bit 'offside' to assume your ship might be sunk or severely damaged. But on a visit to the American naval base at Pensacola, Mountbatten had made a careful study of their damage control routine under the instruction of Admiral William 'Bull' Halsey USN, and had absorbed the lessons for the benefit of his own flotilla.

Repair parties were at work before the *Kelly* was stationary, rigging emergency lighting, shoring up bulkheads, attending to the wounded. Number 1 boiler room was completely flooded, and water was getting into the second boiler room, too. Weight above the waterline was rapidly disposed of – the ten torpedoes fired safe, the depth-charges and ready ammunition for the guns thrown overboard, along with the ship's boats, except the whaler which was set to tow astern. In accordance with the ship's motto, they were going to 'Keep On', though very few of them thought it would be for long. In the darkness, with the seas already rising, the destroyer *Bulldog* succeeded in getting her in tow and, at a crawl, the *Kelly* headed towards home.

Long after midnight, a curious thing happened. Out of the darkness there came at high speed the shape of an E-boat, like the ghost of their assailant. It was no phantom. It was another German E-boat. Or could it have been the same one? It collided heavily with the *Bulldog*, ricochetted off her hull, then struck the *Kelly*, shedding chunks of her structure, including the steering wheel, which was brought to Mountbatten the next morning and later became a prized trophy. No one ever knew what became of that E-boat after her spectacular act of self-immolation. She must have gone to the bottom almost at once.

It was a long and ardous tow, and the battle was being steadily lost. Deeper and deeper sank the *Kelly*. Mountbatten shed more tons by evacuating almost the entire surviving ship's company – ten tons of them, he calculated. And now there was nothing more to remove.

Then the Luftwaffe arrived, like carrion crows. First a reconnaissance machine, then Stukas following, bombing the *Kelly* and the *Bulldog*, wheeling in low to machine-gun the last boats taking off the *Kelly's* wounded crew.

Mountbatten cursed at himself for ordering the ready ammunition thrown overboard. The remaining nucleus crew managed to bring up some from the half-flooded magazines, and Mountbatten himself manned a .5 calibre machine-gun. 'I felt a great deal better for it, too.'

The weather got worse. The tow parted, was picked up again. The *Kelly's* list increased until she seemed as if she must capsize at any time. Another day ended. Pleas to abandon ship were sharply resisted by Mountbatten. Food and water ran short, and everyone was dead tired. The next day a tug made a welcome appearance and took up the tow. Mountbatten remained awake and on the bridge for more than ninety hours, nursing what was left of his ship back to the yard that had built her.

'As the procession slowly passed into the river mouth,' ran the official history of the *Kelly*, 'a great cheer went up from the people of Tyneside who had come out to welcome their ship back home.... All the ship-yard workers knocked off work with one accord to come and give them a cheer, while at the same time all the ships in the river sounded their sirens.'[4]

But those same 'yardies' wouldn't touch her until she had been cleaned up. One of the *Kelly*'s chief petty officers was in the worst damaged com-partment after she had been dry-docked. 'There were still lots of bodies lying around, and flesh hanging from the pipes and bulkheads. The "Chief" was looking at what had to be-done, and was scarcely able to stop himself being sick, when a voice at his shoulder said quietly, "It's terrible, isn't it, Chief. But there's nothing we can do to help them now. Let's get on with it." It was Mountbatten, who took a broom and worked alongside the CPO until the job was done.'[5]

The bodies, or what was left of them, were buried in Hebburn cemetery, and a plaque in their honour can be seen there today – 'In memory of the 27 men killed in action with E-boats off the German minefields....'

During that ninety-hour tow across the North Sea, history was being made in France and the Low Countries. And in twenty more days, Royal Navy destroyers were bearing the brunt of the German attacks to prevent the evacuation of the British armies, and remnants of the French Army, from Dunkirk.

Once again Mountbatten travelled south to London, leaving his sorely battered ship to be repaired. This time it would take six months. Two double-decker buses could have driven through the hole in her side, she needed an entirely new midships section, a new boiler room and numerous new bulkheads. 'Might as well throw it away and start again,' one 'yardie' was heard to complain.

London was in a state of political turmoil. Chamberlain was on his way out, Churchill was leaving the Admiralty for 10 Downing Street and his long war of near-dictatorial power as Prime Minister – and incidentally re-placing himself with a First Lord of the Admiralty who would do exactly as he was told.

Mountbatten now set up his staff and HQ at the County Hotel at Imm-ingham on the east coast where his flotilla was well placed for the threatened German invasion. During that summer of 1940, the world's attention was concentrated upon the skies of southern England, where the RAF fought off the massed armadas of German bombers and fighters, suffering terrible losses in doing so. It was a public arena, a new form of warfare, and the stakes were as high as Churchill and the free world recognized.

But any invasion had also first to break the Royal Navy, and their battles, witnessed by only a handful of participants or shore observers, were crucial, too. Admiral the Earl St Vincent's old eighteenth-century tag still applied: 'I do not say that they cannot come. All I will say is that they cannot come by sea.'

Mountbatten commanded 'the fighting fifth's' operations from other surviving destroyers, the *Jackal*, *Javelin* or *Jupiter*, his presence on board always honing a special edge to the crew's morale.

E-boats were a formidable and ever-present enemy, especially at night. German destroyers were active, too, as the numbers of massed invasion barges built up in the Channel ports. Enemy minefields had to be swept, British mines laid.

An officer in the *Jupiter*, Lieutenant John Jones, told of one especially testing summer night, with the *Jupiter* and *Javelin* covering a force of four minelayers off the Friesian Islands.

'I was officer-of-the-watch when the disaster happened. The minelayers *Esk* and *Ivanhoe* were themselves mined, *Esk* with her bows blown right off back to the bridge, *Ivanhoe* with her back broken and partly abandoned. Lord Louis had to make a decision either (a) go on to the minefield and get them off and risk losing *Jupiter* and *Javelin*, or (b) leave them there. If (a) failed and the destroyers had been lost he would have been blamed for recklessness. If he decided on (b) he would have faced criticism of an unpleasant nature.'[6]

No one doubted that Mountbatten would choose the first course. 'What a dramatic moment it was for me,' continued Jones, 'as I scuttled away to my station aft to prepare to tow. Going on a minefield to tow a stricken vessel off it is a test for the strongest nerve. We succeeded in getting our $3\frac{1}{2}$-inch towing hawsers out to the quarterdeck of the *Esk* and got her out stern first, and subsequently safely back to the Humber.'

Another of Mountbatten's officers at this time, Allan Noble, remarked crisply of Mountbatten 'that nothing was really worth doing unless it was slightly dangerous'.[7] 'Slightly' is a relative word. Within a few weeks German torpedoes hit the bows *and* the stern of his ship, and the *Javelin* herself had to be towed into Devonport.

By this time – November 1940 – some wag at the Admiralty had coined the phrase that there was no one anyone would sooner be in a tight corner with than Dickie Mountbatten, and no one capable of getting you into one quicker. Mountbatten enjoyed the joke when it soon reached him, and cherished it to the end of his life. Thankfully, he never registered that the phrase had a double edge to it.

Not for one moment did anyone doubt Mountbatten's courage. But there were people in high command – Philip Vian, Dudley Pound, A.B. Cunningham among them – who wished that Mountbatten possessed a less urgent need to make a splash, and a greater sense of ship-preservation. This rushing into minefields, and up fjords with only the sketchiest of radar, was all in the best Elizabethan swashbuckling tradition, but it did lose sorely needed ships at a time when destroyers were like gold.

There was also – and there remains today – another body of opinion that this Francis Drake style was just what was needed at the time, that its value in raising the fighting spirit of the lower deck especially, more than outweighed the risks and damage it occasioned.

This biographer tends towards the second view, while accepting that Mountbatten was, from his earliest days, accident-prone as well as risk-regardless. Many people suffer from an unreasonable number of accidents through their life, from rashness, misjudgment, a poor eye, until – like so many human characteristics – it becomes a habit. For Mountbatten it extended from falls at home and at school, mishaps at Osborne, to accidents all through his naval career, especially on the polo field, of course. It embraced car accidents, even railway accidents – he was very proud of these, one returning from Spain at 70 mph, another in Australia with the Prince of Wales, both serious. The same accident-attraction extended to Mountbatten's ships; and when later he was given the command of a carrier, George VI was heard to utter, with a groan of despair, 'Well, that's the end of the *Illustrious*!'

Late in November 1940, the *Kelly* was ready for re-commissioning. Virtually a new ship, manned by a new crew, facing a new war – a war at sea in which the odds were weighted more heavily than ever in favour of the enemy. Since the fall of France all but a few units of the great French Navy were lost, and the formidable Italian Navy now faced Britain in the Mediterranean. In 1917, when German U-boats had almost throttled Britain to death, their bases were limited. Now, from harbours extending from the northern tip of Norway to southern France, and the Adriatic and North Africa, German U-boats and several of the fastest and most powerful battleships in the world could range the length and breadth of the Atlantic and the Mediterranean. By any statistical calculation, the odds against Allied survival at sea appeared hopeless.

Once again the *Kelly* and her flotilla were drawn to the busiest and most dangerous fighting zones – first to Scapa Flow, then the Clyde and the Western Approaches Striking Forces operating out of Plymouth. Besides numerous U-boats, the German battle-cruisers *Scharnhorst* and *Gneisenau*, and the heavy cruisers *Hipper* and *Prinz Eugen*, were operating from newly acquired French Atlantic bases, raiding the convoy routes.

All these men o'war were as fast as the *Kelly*, and all had a hundred times greater gunpower. But the *Kelly*'s flotilla pursued the battle cruisers into Brest, just missing them, and chased the *Hipper* – or her ghost – as far north as the Faroes. Perhaps it was as well, this time, that her luck was out. Next it was the weather, and not the enemy, that forced the ill-starred ship back into dockyard hands. They all hit the same Irish Sea storm, but it was only the *Kelly* that lost her boats and Carley rafts, her abandon-ship gear and her starboard guardrails.

When she had been refitted and spruced up once more, George VI came to inspect her again, and Mountbatten and his officers dined him in the now more austere wardroom. 'We talked about the war and almost nothing else,' said Mountbatten. 'Like his father, he loved talking Navy – *his* Navy, and always felt comfortable and at home on board one of his ships. The shyness and diffidence seemed to disappear and he was just one of us. Again like his father, he would have loved to come to sea with us and seen some action.'

In honour of his visit, the King gave the ship's company all-night leave. The Luftwaffe chose that night to bomb Plymouth. The watch ashore decided they would have preferred Brest harbour and the German shore batteries. But the *Kelly* was able to add her weight of anti-aircraft fire and was able to use her newly-installed Oerlikons for the first time.

And now Mountbatten took the *Kelly* south. She had been intended for the Mediterranean before the war, and had even been light-painted for that station. But while the war remained fiercest in the north, she had remained in the North Atlantic, the Channel and North Sea. Now the *Kelly* followed the worst of the fighting as a worshipper follows the sun.

Postponing indefinitely the invasion of Britain, Hitler was now hell-bent on turning his armies to the east, and in preparation for the Russian war he determined to neutralize Romania, Greece, Turkey and Egypt to protect his flank for his drive on the Russian Caucasus. The Italian Army and Navy should have carried out these tasks, but Admiral Cunningham had destroyed the Italian battle fleet in Taranto harbour – like some dress rehearsal for Pearl Harbor – and at the Battle of Cape Matapan. The Greeks had contained and then driven back Mussolini's armies, and General Wavell had thrown the Italian armies out of Cyrenaica with a force of one-fifth the Italian weight.

But in the early months of 1941, German Panzers were seen for the first

time in the North African desert, German soldiers stemmed the tide of the
Greeks, and the skies were filled with new and more formidable and more
skilfully flown warplanes: the Luftwaffe dive bomber had come to the Mediterranean, and the Royal Navy, with only the sketchiest air support, began
to suffer savage losses. Once again the price was being paid for an undeveloped and mixed-manned Fleet Air Arm, and inadequate anti-
aircraft weapons.

Nowhere had the new face of sea power shown itself more clearly than
in the Mediterranean. Warships without air cover of any kind were safe only
at night or in fog. The mighty air barrages of 1944 and 1945, when battleships were equipped with two hundred and more anti-aircraft guns, had
not yet been envisaged. Even the Italian Air Force could bomb almost with
impunity from high altitude, though it rarely made a hit.

The German dive bombers had all but closed the western Mediterranean,
and when the 5th Flotilla made Malta safely from Gibraltar, in company
with the new 40-knot minelayer *Abdiel* and cruiser *Dido*, there were thousands on the battlements of Grand Harbour to celebrate their safe arrival.

'Except for our brief brush with the Germans at Namsos, we had not
seen aerial warfare on this scale before,' said Mountbatten. 'The Germans
and Italians bombed Malta night and day. I saw no point in risking the
Kelly's entire company, so I sent half the flotilla's companies ashore to the
shelters every night, and the other manned the guns. I stayed on board every
night. A fine story it would have made if the *Kelly* had been sunk with Captain Mountbatten skulking in an air raid shelter! But in all my life, I've
never been so scared!'

It was a relief to get away from Malta, to cast aside for a while the claustro-
phobia of Grand Harbour, with orders to bombard the enemy-held North
African port of Benghazi. The attack was carried out on the night of 10–
11 May under very difficult conditions. The destroyers succeeded in damaging a merchantman close to the entrance to the harbour, but all the ships
within the breakwater appeared in the uncertain moonlight to be already
damaged or sunk.

Mountbatten ordered his five destroyers to withdraw shortly after midnight, and almost at once they picked up the sound of aircraft. They were
their old enemies, JU87 Stukas, coming in vertically to dive bomb them in
the dark, a bold operation which no one had ever witnessed before. The
destroyers dropped smoke floats, and while these may have confused the
pilots, they also added to the difficulties of the gunners who were unable
to pick out their targets properly until the Stukas opened up with their
machine-guns just before pulling out of their dives.

No losses could be claimed by either side, although the harassing attacks continued until they were far out to sea, and everyone must have been relieved when orders were given to call off the attacks.

Fleet Air Arm reconnaissance and torpedo planes ranged far out to sea from Malta in search of enemy convoys, but during the 5th's brief period at the island none was located.

The final phase in the unhappy career of HMS *Kelly* began in the last days of May 1941. The dust and smoke from the last bombing raid seemed to hang perpetually in the hot air above Valetta. The weather was perfect: hot and dry, with one cloudless day following another. The past weeks had been frustrating for the flotilla, catastrophic for the Allied cause. The war was going badly in Africa, the British had been driven out of Greece after failing to hold the German invasion. The streets of Valetta were blocked by rubble, the people, living underground for much of the time, were demoralized and half-starved.

The German attack on Soviet Russia, which would add new heart to the British cause, still lay a month ahead, and any hope of stemming the German Wehrmacht seemed as distant as the hot Mediterranean sun. In the small world of the *Kelly*, nothing much seemed to have gone right, either.

On the morning of 21 May, Mountbatten was ashore in conference with his commanders for most of the morning. He returned on board after lunch, and ordered the lower deck cleared so that he could, once again, address the ship's company.

'I told them that things weren't going too well in the eastern Mediterranean,' said Mountbatten, 'that the Germans had carried out a large-scale airborne attack – the biggest in history – on Crete the day before, and that our forces there were hard-pressed. I said, "It's our job to go to support them at once. Make no mistake, things are going to be tough, but we have got to stop any reinforcements from getting through. The chief threat, of course, will be from the air. But we've faced quite a bit of bombing already, and I trust that we're about to increase our score." I ended by saying that I knew they would all live up to my expectations.'

Within an hour, the *Kelly* was leading the *Kashmir*, *Kipling*, and *Jackal* out of Grand Harbour – a harbour that held so many memories of regattas and the peaceful to-ing and fro-ing of liberty boats and admirals' barges and whalers and Maltese dghaisos. All through Mountbatten's life, and his father's life before him, this island where they had played polo and attended governors' and admirals' balls and receptions, swum and played tennis and brought up their children, had been the symbol and first bastion of British naval supremacy. For generations, the Navy's finest men o'war from three-decker ships-of-the-line of Nelson's time, to 30,000-ton battleships and aircraft-carriers, had ridden at anchor here, flying the white ensign. Now the harbour was littered with wrecks, enemy mines often closed its entrance, half of Valetta was in ruins, and the life was being squeezed out of the Navy and the people who lived here.

There appeared to be little hope for Malta as the destroyers steamed out for the last time, the watch on deck going about their duties in white shorts and singlets in the heat of the evening, heading for a battle that would be more ferocious than anything they had so far faced. As they steamed east for Crete, no sign of war defaced that first beautiful Mediterranean night, nor much of the next day, which was again hot and clear and calm. A suspected U-boat was depth-charged, a distant enemy reconnaissance plane spotted.

In the evening, as they approached the beleaguered island, high-level bombers were seen by the look-out and fire was opened on them with the 4.7s. Mountbatten was still on the *Kelly*'s bridge, where he had remained throughout the day and night, and he ordered evasive manœuvres. Neither side scored a hit, and he called for his dinner – the usual slice of bread and tin of sardines – still his favourite fish, and, unlike at Osborne, he was allowed more than two now.

Just how fierce the fighting at sea around the island must be was indicated by their first order from Admiral Cunningham: 'Proceed in company with *Kashmir* and *Kipling* to assist *Kandahar* rescue survivors from *Fiji*.' The *Fiji* was a large cruiser; so was the *Gloucester*, also reported sinking from bombing attacks.

The next signal, before they had reached the scene, was even more ominous. The cruisers' survivors must be left to their fate. The destroyers were desperately needed to bombard Maleme airfield, which the Germans were fighting for, and to prevent reinforcements by sea.

Now the *Kipling* suffered a steering fault which would take hours to correct. 'We will go ahead and bombard ourselves,' Mountbatten radioed Cunningham, a signal (from a top signals officer) which later led to some ribbing from the c-in-c. 'Please instruct me how it is done.' Mountbatten was not amused.

That night no one got any sleep. The two destroyers poured a barrage of 4.7-inch shells on to the German positions, then turned their guns on to Greek fishing vessels loaded with supplies and German troops, sinking two of them. Already thousands of German soldiers had been drowned, and it is to the eternal credit of the Royal Navy that – in spite of fearful losses – not one German soldier arrived by sea of the thousands despatched recklessly from the Greek mainland, until the island fell. It was a modern illustra-

tion of the Admiral's waggish eighteenth-century boast referring to Bona-
parte's troops poised to invade England.

But now the invaders did not need to come by sea, though it would have
been infinitely less costly for them to do so. They came by air instead. And
it was air power alone that led to the capture of Crete, and the destruction
of so many fine RN ships – among them, the next morning, the *Kelly* herself.

The date was 23 May 1941. Tomorrow would be his father's birthday, an
anniversary Mountbatten never forgot. Nor would his mother forget it, back
home in Kensington Palace, no doubt worrying about him, and then burying
her worries – as she so often did – in gardening: just seventy-eight years
old and a widow for nearly twenty of them.

Due to a signalling error, Admiral Cunningham had been incorrectly informed that two of his most powerful units, the battleships *Warspite* and
Valiant, were running short of anti-aircraft ammunition. For this reason,
all naval forces were ordered during the night to withdraw from Crete to
refuel and replenish in Egypt. And it was because of the same mistake that
Mountbatten's destroyers were fated to confront alone the full might of Luftwaffe dive bombers while lacking the support of the battleships' gunfire
which would otherwise almost certainly have been available to them. It was
a sad reflection that the one officer who had striven for so many years to
perfect the signalling efficiency of the Mediterranean Fleet should now have
to suffer catastrophe through a signal error.

The first bombers came in at 6 am, out of a cloudless dawn sky. If you
did not actually laugh at high-level bombers in a destroyer, they were not
as terrifying as dive bombers. You could see the bombs fall, and with a
destroyer's manœuvrability, dodge them.

'The Stukas came in at eight, a couple of hours later,' said Mountbatten.
'We knew they would come, as day follows night, but we had hoped there
wouldn't be quite as many. Twenty-four we counted. And they split
up between the two of us, coming down on different bearings to split our
fire.'

The great accuracy of the JU87 Stuka was derived from its near-vertical
angle of dive, the extendable brakes slowing it down and giving the bomb-
aimer time to steady the pilot's aim. But off Namsos a year before, Mountbatten had recognized that this advantage could be turned into a powerful
disadvantage by swift reaction on a destroyer's helm and speed. 'If you can
tempt the pilot into too steep a dive, and then a bit more, by sudden accelera-
tion or deceleration, you may force him beyond the vertical,' he said. 'I was
able to do this twice. The Stukas just went straight in – saving us a lot of
ammunition. But as the Japanese and Americans later discovered in the

Pacific – especially the Americans with the *kamikazes* – there's a limit to the amount of dodging if the numbers are too great.'

Each Stuka carried a single 500-kg bomb under its belly, but after the first ones had dropped, they came in again to confuse the defences, machine-gunning all the way down. For ten minutes of incessant screaming and gun-fire, the bomb sprays spouting up high to break the twisting patterns of the two destroyers' wakes, the *Kelly* and *Kashmir* evaded every bomb. Then the *Kashmir* took one dead amidships. She sank in two minutes, but before she went under Mountbatten saw one of her gunners – he got the CGM for it – continuing to fire as the seas swept over him, destroying a Stuka with his last rounds.

'We got two and probably a third with our guns,' said Mountbatten. 'We were on full starboard rudder when we were hit. I saw the bomb falling from the Stuka's belly, and watched it all the way down. It was just like that torpedo a year earlier, except this time I knew we weren't going to survive. It hit square on x gun deck, killing the 4.7 crew immediately, and exploded just abaft the engine room.

'I gave the order "Midships" when the sound of the explosion had died, and then "Hard a-port". But it was no good, and we listed over more heavily than ever. So I gave the order "Stop engines".'

It was like telling a dead man not to try so hard. In seconds – as before – the doom-laden words were shouted up the voice-pipe by the coxswain: 'Ship won't answer the helm, sir. No reply to the engine room telegraphs.'

The Stukas were still coming in. 'Keep all guns firing!' Mountbatten shouted. He could have saved his voice, which no one could hear anyway for the shattering crackle of the machine-guns, Oerlikons and pom-poms. Then, as the *Kelly* began to roll right over, still travelling at 30 knots, one by one the gun crews were torn from their weapons.

Mountbatten was telling himself, 'I must stay with the ship. Whatever happens, I must stay with her as long as I can – must be the last to leave. . . .'

It was like a great heavy blanket being pulled up over you, bringing suffocating darkness. Mountbatten held on for what seemed a long time, clutching the gyro-compass pedestal, until he was torn from that grip, and, feeling the pressure on his lungs and the desperate need to breathe, put one hand over his mouth, another over his nose.

'I came up in the end,' he said, 'though it seemed an awfully long time. The first thing I saw was the stern of the ship no more than a dozen yards away, travelling fast, propellers still rotating. Lieutenant Butler-Bowden, the navigator, was near me, and I shouted at him "Swim like hell!" A nasty end, being chewed up. The ship just missed us, still travelling fast. When

I paused for breath, and looked around, an oil-stained head popped up beside me. It was a stoker petty-officer, and he said at once, "Funny how the scum always comes to the top, sir...."

'All we had was one Carley raft someone had managed to release in those last seconds, and I shouted at the top of my voice, "Swim to the raft!" Unfortunately, there were quite a lot who couldn't. I realized I was still wearing my tin helmet, and I thought that was crazy. So I took it off and it sank, and the next second the Stukas came in again, machine-gunning us like hell, and I wished I hadn't.'

They put the wounded inside the Carley raft, and the others who had reached it clung on to the side. The Stukas came in again and again. The survivors could see the pilot in his cockpit, goggles up for clearer visibility, and he pressed the button to spray them with bullets. A lot of them were killed, and the worst part was dragging out the dead from the centre of the raft and pushing them into the sea.

'The sea was beautifully warm and dead calm – just the sort of sea people look forward to when they go to the Mediterranean for a holiday. But now we all needed cheering up, so I called for a song or two. We began with "Roll out the Barrel". The *Kelly* wasn't far off, bottom up, but she was going, so I called out "Three cheers for the old ship!" And then down she went.'

In fact, she only turned turtle and remained half awash for some time, true to her motto 'Keep On' to the end.

The *Kipling*'s steering gear trouble indirectly saved their lives. If she had been with her consorts, she would have gone to the bottom, too. But the Stukas never saw her. Commander St Clair Ford, her captain, brought the destroyer alongside the Carley raft, and lowered scrambling nets. Helped by the *Kipling*'s sailors, who eased them out of the water and helped them up on to the deck, the survivors were slowly dragged on board. Then the *Kipling* turned to the *Kashmir*'s survivors. There were more of them, five Carley rafts scattered widely. Then there was a far distant booming sound, increasing in volume. Suddenly it became very loud, and they looked up and saw, high up, a big formation of bombers staining the bright blue sky, peeling off towards them – the ripest target in the whole Mediterranean.

They were big twin-engine JU88s this time, armed with 500-kg bombs and MG 131 and 81 machine-guns, which were used to spray without mercy the men in the rafts and the water, and those who were clambering, oil-soaked and exhausted, up the netting. Rudyard Kipling himself would have been proud of the destroyer that carried his name. For an hour, Commander Ford manœuvred his ship like a speedboat to evade the bombs, and returned in the brief lulls between attacks to collect more survivors.

Every time the sky was temporarily clear of their tormentors, Mountbatten had to make the decision – should they go now, with a better chance of reaching Alexandria, or collect a few more and increase still further the risk to those already on board? Each time they came back to the same oil-stained patch of ocean, with its few remaining struggling figures and many drifting, burned corpses.

Once the *Kipling* grazed the submerged wreck of the *Kelly*. Even in death, the old ship continued to bring bad luck, tearing a hole in the side of her sister ship, releasing oil that was not only precious but that would mark her passage with a trail no plane could miss.

In the long, dramatic ordeal, there were many small tragedies, some of them ironical. One man said, 'I'm all right – I'm fine.' And the next second, or so it seemed, he whispered 'Ave Maria!' and died. A figure floated past, covered in oil all over, sitting in a beer crate like a black baby in its pram. One of the *Kelly*'s officers who had just escaped from drowning was killed in the confusion of lowering the *Kipling*'s motor boat. He was Lord Beresford, a close friend of Mountbatten. His great-uncle had led the attacks against Prince Louis which had driven him from office.

It went on like that to the end. Someone in the *Kipling* logged forty attacks in all from JU88s, and they were still coming in when Mountbatten ordered the ship to leave. There were, it seemed, only corpses and an empty boat left. But she steamed away, with a list and capable of only 20 knots now, several of those on board saw a figure rise from the bottom of this boat, stand at attention and salute. He was still standing when he faded from sight.

The torment was not yet over. It was 400 miles to Egypt, and the bombers came back, time and again. 'She must have had a charmed life,' said Mountbatten. 'But somehow we missed them all. Not that I saw many of the bombs fall. I spent most of the time with my wounded, taking down messages for their next of kin. Some of them couldn't talk and I couldn't recognize their faces. So I had to rely on their identity discs. And for some of them I was too late. We lost a lot of good men from burns and shock in the first hour or two after we sailed.'

The *Kipling* used up the last of her fuel before the Egyptian coast had lifted above the horizon, and for some time she lay wallowing in the swell. It was lucky that they were beyond the range of the bombers now. And before long the 2,900-ton target-tower HMS *Protector* came alongside and replenished the destroyer's tanks.

As they went through the boom defence at Alexandria, there were thousands on shore and lining the rails of the ships in the harbour, caps raised and cheering the battered destroyer with her decks packed with sailors still oil-stained and carrying the scars of their fight.

Mountbatten was wearier than he had even been in his life, his throat still sore from the oil fuel he had swallowed, what was left of his uniform stained and torn. No one had ever seen him come ashore from his ship other than spruce and valeted, least of all his nephew, Philip, who was on the jetty awaiting him.

Midshipman Prince Philip already had much service behind him, including the Battle of Matapan back in March, in which for his part he had been mentioned in despatches. Now he glanced in astonishment at his filthy, battle-weary uncle.

But Mountbatten, though delighted and relieved to see his nephew, for once did not feel that there was much to laugh about. The Royal Navy had been thrashed by the Luftwaffe. There could be no denying it. Many hundreds of British and Commonwealth sailors had died in the seas about Crete. More than half the *Kelly*'s company had been killed outright, or drowned or burned to death, and many more were suffering from appalling wounds. It had been a bad way to celebrate his father's birthday.

At Alexandria, Mountbatten gathered the uninjured survivors of the *Kelly* together for the last time. There were scarcely forty of them. 'I have always tried to crack a joke or two before,' he told them. 'But today I'm afraid I have run out of jokes.' He spoke then of their dead comrades. 'If they had to die, what a grand way to go, for now they lie all together with the ship we loved, and they are in very good company. We have lost her, but they are still with her.'

And now the survivors would be going to other ships. 'And the next time you are in action remember the *Kelly*. As you ram each shell home into the gun, shout "*Kelly!*" and so her spirit will go on inspiring us until victory is won.' Then he concluded with these rousing words, 'I should like to add that there isn't one of you that I wouldn't be proud and honoured to serve with again. Goodbye, good luck, and thank you all from the bottom of my heart.'

It is a measure of the special morale of the *Kelly* that today, forty years since she went to the bottom, the Reunion Association is as active as ever – the only one of its kind run by the survivors of a destroyed ship's company. This is perhaps the greatest tribute of all to Mountbatten's leadership.

A few days later, a Fleet Air Arm airman at a Fleet Requirement Unit outside Alexandria was detailed to fly an officer to Cairo in his Blackburn Skua. The officer arrived, dead on time, dressed in civilian clothes as if he had walked straight out of Savile Row.

The airman at once recognized Mountbatten, whose exploits with the *Kelly* were already legendary throughout the fleet. He was, reported the airman later, off to Cairo to complain about the total lack of air cover during the Crete operations which had cost him his ship and the lives of nine of his officers and 121 of his men. 'When I offered him his parachute harness, he declined to wear it,' reported this airman, 'saying with his usual charm, "I'm sure if anything goes wrong, you will show me what to do." The Skua was not the most reliable of planes and I was somewhat dubious as to what my reactions would have been if put to the test.'[8]

The plane lasted the short journey across the desert; and later another plane flew Mountbatten to London. Within a short time, he was in America, and then out to Pearl Harbor, a guest of the United States Navy, and Admiral Stark, Chief of Naval Staff. As an officer who had witnessed tragically and at first hand the terrible power of the bomber against naval vessels unprotected by fighter aircraft, Mountbatten was appalled at the lack of preparedness at Hawaii.

But when Mountbatten saw Stark again in Washington on his way back to London, and gave him his opinion, the Chief of Naval Staff did not take it as seriously as Mountbatten had hoped. 'I'm afraid putting some of your recommendations into effect is going to make your visit out there an expensive one for the Navy,' he commented with a laugh.

It was just ninety days before the Japanese attack.

6
COMBINED OPERATIONS

WHILE HMS *Kelly* was being completed on the Tyne in the summer of 1939, Mountbatten had been one of the royal party who had visited Dartmouth Naval College in HMY *Victoria and Albert*. The guests, George VI and Queen Elizabeth and the two Princesses, Elizabeth and Margaret Rose, were making an informal visit to join the cadets for morning service. Mountbatten was acting in the capacity of ADC to the King. He was also anxious to see how his nephew was getting on.

Unlike Mountbatten, and to Mountbatten's delight, Prince Philip had revealed no signs of his own early dreaminess and accident-proneness and had shone from the beginning as a cadet, winning the Eardley-Howard-Crockett prize as the best cadet of the year. On this occasion, he had been told to entertain the Princesses, a more prolonged business than had been envisaged as there was a double epidemic of mumps and chicken pox at the college, and it had been decided to omit the service after all.

If ever an occasion has become confused by invention, it is that wet Sunday, 23 July, five weeks before war broke out. Certainly the proceedings of the day are unclear in Prince Philip's mind. Royal reporters, biographers and gossip columnists have, for forty years, pinned down this royal visit as the occasion when romance first sparked between the eighteen-year-old Prince and thirteen-year-old Princess. In fact they had met several times already, as members of the same family do.

George VI's biographer described the meeting as 'of great moment in the history of Britain'.[1] For Prince Philip the day was no more than 'an amusing experience'. 'Well, certainly not at Dartmouth,' he will retort sharply if asked when a decision to marry was made. Another seven years – and the war – were to pass before he and Princess Elizabeth began to talk seriously about marriage. 'I suppose one thing led to another. . . .'[2]

Mountbatten was always equally vague about the date of the birth of romance, and the decision to marry, between his cousin and his nephew.

Like Prince Philip, too, he would say that it was just something that grew. 'When you plant something,' he said, 'you don't keep lifting it up to see how the roots are progressing.' However, Mountbatten would not even accept that he was the gardener who did the planting. 'Of course it was something I had hoped for from quite an early time, when it was clear that Philip was going to settle here and his father said he wanted him to join the Navy. But any sort of match-making is sheer nonsense.'

It did not require an astrologer's crystal ball, nor even a prescient eye, to see that by (say) 1941, a marriage between the heir to the British throne and her cousin, the Danish-Greek-Hessian Prince, was a strong likelihood. If the nation at war had not temporarily lost its abiding obsession with royal tittle-tattle (and incidentally the newsprint to spread it), no doubt the marriage would have been predicted long before 1946.

It was in fact in 1941 that what was probably the first reference to the royal match was made in writing, in diary form and not to be printed for another sixteen years. That able politician and amiable gossip, Sir Henry Channon, was in Greece shortly before the German onslaught, and gravitated towards the royal family. Prince Philip was also present on 21 January, a few weeks before the Battle of Matapan, on leave to see his mother and family – his father had been there two years earlier, the last occasion when the three had been together. 'Chips' Channon chatted to, among others, Princess Nicholas, formerly the Grand Duchess Helen of Russia and the mother of Princess Marina, the Duchess of Kent. Their conversation naturally turned to the handsome young midshipman, not yet twenty years old. Afterwards, Channon recorded in his diary that the Princess had divulged that Prince Philip was 'to be our Prince Consort, and that is why', explained Channon 'he is serving in our Navy. He is charming, but I deplore such a marriage; he and Princess Elizabeth are too inter-related.'[3]

Prince Philip's comment on this prediction, made many years later, was crisply characteristic. 'I mean, after all, if you spend ten minutes thinking about it ... how many obviously eligible young men, other than people living in this country, were available? Inevitably I must have been on the list, so to speak.'[4]

After that, according to Prince Philip, there were occasional theatres, a Christmas or two at Buckingham Palace when he happened to be on leave (not often), the exchange of a few letters. In London, he would stay with grandmother Victoria at Kensington Palace.

Victoria had, in fact, been against his returning to England at the beginning of the war. 'It would have been better if he had stayed in Greece where he belongs,'[5] she wrote to Mountbatten, fearful of having any more relatives at risk in the fighting zone. But, having accepted that, after training for the

Royal Navy, he was going to fight in it, she gave Prince Philip all the support she could offer.

When Mountbatten told Victoria that Prince Philip was likely to marry Princess Elizabeth, she approved but made no comment. In her long life, she had seen so many royal matches, so many unions of dynasties. Besides, engagements in themselves were of no interest to her. 'Like her grandmother [Queen Victoria], love affairs bored her,' recalled Mountbatten's daughter Lady Pamela Hicks. 'She never gossiped and she never discussed love affairs. Either you were married, or not married, and anything in between was a bore.'[6]

If Mountbatten's rôle so far as the match between Philip of Greece and the heir to the throne was mainly passive, the question of his name and title was something close to his heart and genealogical enthusiasm. With the strong sense of family pride, always the mainspring of his energies and achievements, Mountbatten was determined that this surrogate son of his would carry on his own name.

When the suggested, and fairly obvious, name Mountbatten was first put to Prince Philip he was not, as he said, 'madly in favour'. By this time, 1947, his uncle was a world hero in war and peace, and Prince Philip has always attempted to guard his own individuality as strongly as his own achievements. He had no wish to be linked with 'a legend in his own time', no matter how much he loved and admired his uncle.

The general public learned, but did not necessarily believe, that the name Mountbatten had been approved by George VI at the suggestion of the Home Secretary.

'But in the end I was persuaded,' said Prince Philip, 'and anyway I couldn't think of a reasonable alternative.'[7] Royal arrangements, and royal nomenclature, were as usual working out exactly and precisely as Mountbatten wished.

The debate – or even struggle – over the future name of the royal family was not yet over. When Mountbatten had accepted with seeming casualness the loss of his family's name Battenberg in 1917, and the assumption by the King of the name Windsor, he could have had no idea of the dynastic complexities and conflicts that lay just thirty years ahead. When this biographer omitted any reference to the royal surname controversy in the manuscript of his biography of Mountbatten's parents, Mountbatten made an urgent plea for it to be included* and, in the capacity of President of the Society of Genealogists, drafted out a long and complex statement which made it clear that, for the first two months of her reign, the Queen ruled as a Mountbatten, and not as a Windsor at all. Prince Charles and Princess

* It was not.

Anne had the surname Mountbatten. 'Thus the House of Mountbatten ruled for two months.'

The first setback came in April 1952 when the Queen commanded by Order in Council that she had taken the name Windsor for herself and her children. Some seven years later Mountbatten countered by reaching a compromise. Charles and Anne and the Queen's yet-to-be-born children (Prince Andrew and Prince Edward) were given the surname Mountbatten-Windsor. But the legal wording was so ambiguous that the Queen's wishes, claimed Mountbatten, were not clearly established until the marriage of Princess Anne on 14 November 1973 when, in the marriage register, she was described as Anne Mountbatten-Windsor.

Mountbatten seized on this as a great family vindication. Now the four children of this marriage and their descendants would bear the surname 'Mountbatten-Windsor', and 'surely this gives the satisfaction of publicly linking the two family names in the Prince of Wales and his mother and their descendants.'

For those who are not obsessed with genealogy, Mountbatten's part in the marriage of the Queen and Prince Philip and his concern for the perpetuation of his own name in the royal family, may be less important than his work in helping to shape the character, style and bearing first of Prince Philip when he was virtually an orphan, and then of Prince Charles, with whom his relationship was equally close and important.

Midshipman Prince Philip remained briefly in Egypt when Mountbatten flew home at the end of May, and returned more humbly and circuitously by troopship via the Cape, Puerto Rico and Canada, and it was some time before they met one another again.

The Mountbattens had bought a modest house, 15 Chester Street, which was to remain their London headquarters for the rest of the war, the greater part of Broadlands being now converted into a hospital. At their first dinner party, on Mountbatten's return, their old friend Noël Coward was present. Coward had known them both since the early 1920s, and more intimately since his rise to fame in the 1930s, when he was a frequent visitor to the penthouse. Coward had been much concerned with Mountbatten in the formation of the Naval Film Corporation, and Mountbatten had seen to it that his friend and collaborator was offered the honorary rank of Lieutenant-Commander RN. Coward reluctantly turned it down as unwarranted and invidious.

After dinner, Coward extracted from Mountbatten the full story of the sinking of the *Kelly*. 'He told it without apparent emotion, but the emotion was there, poignantly behind every word he uttered,' wrote Coward. He had always been deeply attached to the Navy, and in Mountbatten's account he recognized 'all the true sentiment, the comedy, the tragedy, the casual valiance, the unvaunted heroism, the sadness without tears and the pride without end.'[8] Coward returned to the Savoy Hotel, and on that night was conceived one of the most famous war films, *In Which We Serve* – praised to the skies, and admired so widely that the inevitable mockery of envious 'knockers' reflected adversely only upon themselves.

Another figure from the Mountbattens' past now inevitably re-enters their story. All through the 1920s and 1930s, relations between Lord Beaverbrook and the Mountbattens had remained mainly cordial, but also with some quite violent unevenness. A.J.P. Taylor, Beaverbrook's biographer, has said that 'something about Mountbatten touched Beaverbrook on a raw nerve'.[9] This 'something' was made up of a mixture of irritation and envy. Newspapermen by instinct and training do not care for, and deeply mistrust, anyone or anything that is too good to be true. There must be a chink, a crack that will open up a story, preferably a story with scandalous overtones.

Beaverbrook was frequently exasperated at his failure to find anything wrong with this golden boy of the 1920s. It went against his professional instincts. The two men had much in common. They were both passionately patriotic and pro-Empire and royalist. Even Mountbatten's quirky socialism sparked off something in the Canadian. They both liked power and they both liked to be surrounded by pretty women or men who admired them rather than competed with them. But Beaverbrook had had to work for his riches and privileges and title. For Mountbatten, they had been presented on a plate. They both had unlimited charm and wealth. Mountbatten was extremely handsome, Beaverbrook the reverse. Mountbatten appeared to Beaverbrook (and to many others) as an easy winner. Victories came hard to Beaverbrook.

Taylor has written that 'Beaverbrook's relations with Mountbatten, as with other men, went up and down.' But with no other men did they see-saw so violently. The first deep dip occurred soon after the Mountbatten wedding. In 1923 a close friend of Edwina's was a prominent and extremely attractive debutante. She married and then very quickly fell out with her husband, although there was no separation.

One evening, Edwina arranged a small dinner party which included Beaverbrook and her friend. To the Mountbattens' astonishment, this led to an affair. 'It must have been sheer masochism on her part,' said Mountbatten. But because of Edwina's friendship with Beaverbrook's new mistress, they continued to see a lot of him. 'Then suddenly Max conceived the fantastic notion that I was having an affair with her, too. This was quite crazy and I told him so,' said Mountbatten. 'But he didn't believe me, and we fell out.' This odd non-event was, in due course, forgotten, and Beaver-brook appeared to be on friendly terms when they met during the early months of the war. They were, in Mountbatten's words, 'great buddies'.

Their next disagreement was in no way a personal one. Two days after the Noël Coward dinner on 19 June, Mountbatten had lunch at 10 Downing Street with Churchill and Beaverbrook. Beaverbrook, after doing a much-praised job as Minister of Aircraft Production during and after the Battle of Britain, had recently become fed up with the post. 'We now have more aircraft than the Air Ministry can use,' he had announced with justifiable self-satisfaction. After a certain amount of coquettish side-play, Beaver-brook had now accepted the appointment of Minister of State. 'What that means is anybody's guess,' he and Michael Foot, editor of his *Evening Standard*, wrote in a leading article. In fact it turned out to be considerable, and that is why, a month or so later, he was at number 10 with the Prime Minister and Mountbatten.

Churchill was late, and for a while the two men were alone. 'Max practi-cally kissed me,' said Mountbatten. ' "Here is the hero of the *Kelly* – well, Dickie, it is swell to see you alive...." ' Then Churchill arrived and apolo-gized. 'I bring grave news,' he said. 'We now know that Hitler in about three days will invade Russia. This completely transforms the war. They will suffer a grave defeat.'

Beaverbrook agreed. 'They will be over-run in two or three weeks.'

'No, it will be six or seven weeks,' said Churchill. 'The Americans agree with you, Max, and say it will be three or four weeks. So does the JIC [Joint Intelligence Committee]. My belief is that it will be six or seven.'

At lunch the conversation turned to the purpose of this meeting. 'My dear Dickie,' said Churchill, 'tell us about your experience in Crete and the sinking of the *Kelly*.'

Mountbatten, for the first and last time in his life, brushed aside the sink-ing of the *Kelly*. Instead, he asked if he could express a view about the latest news. 'Max and you are quite wrong,' he said. 'So is the JIC, and the Ameri-cans are crazy. I don't believe that the Germans will be able to fold up the Russians in *any* number of weeks. I think this news is important for quite different reasons. This is the end of the war. The Russians will certainly win.'

Mountbatten's belief was not based upon any military considerations. He had thought about the problem in terms which he understood better than most authorities. In every previous country the Germans had invaded, he argued, there had been a Fifth Column preparing the ground for them. Not in Russia. Any potential Fifth Column had long since been liquidated. The old Tsarist officers were all dead, or had joined the Germans. 'The Russians defeated the Allied intervention in 1919,' said Mountbatten to the politician who had so strongly supported it, 'because they had something to fight for. Their creed and their objective today is much stronger. They have a country to save, as they did in 1812 when they rolled back Napoleon. The German Army will become enmeshed in Russia just like the French Army. Only it will be worse.'

Churchill listened to all this tolerantly, and then said, 'My dear Dickie, it's nice to hear young people speaking their minds.'

Mountbatten replied, 'All right. But do one thing for me. Just remember that I am the only person who has apparently told you this.'

While Mountbatten was being proved wrong (or so it seemed in the summer and early autumn of 1941), and Churchill right, plans for the film *In Which We Serve* went ahead, at first stumblingly and with many obstacles to overcome, and then more swiftly. Coward soon convinced Mountbatten that he had no intention of basing his film 'too exactly' on the career of the *Kelly*, or her commanding officer at all closely on Mountbatten. Coward wrote, 'Mountbatten is definitely one of the most outstanding men of our time. ... My Captain (D) was a simpler character altogether, far less gifted than he, far less complicated, but in no way, I hope, less gallant.'[10]

Once satisfied, he said, that this was to be no personal accolade, Mountbatten got busy cutting through red tape and using all his powerful influence to get total Admiralty co-operation. However convinced Mountbatten himself might be about Coward's motives, there were a number of senior officers who suspected that they were being pushed into helping one friend to present a fat tribute to another, who had received quite a number already. At one point the Ministry of Information threatened to ban the screening of the film outside the country as it was bad propaganda to show one of HM ships being sunk. Coward sent an SOS to Mountbatten, and together they went along to the Ministry of Information, to be received by the Minister himself, Brendan Bracken.

They made their complaint together, and Bracken sent for the official responsible for the threat. 'Dickie went off like a time bomb,' recalled Coward, 'and it was one of the most startling and satisfactory scenes I have ever witnessed. I actually felt a pang of compassion for the wretched official, who wilted under the tirade like a tallow candle before a strong fire.'[11]

The film opened at the Gaumont cinema in September 1942. It is a tarnished milestone in Fleet Street history that it led to another violent see-saw in Mountbatten–Beaverbrook relations, and to a vendetta – no less – that lasted (with only the smallest let-up) until Beaverbrook's death, and caused as much pain to Mountbatten as any other event in his life.

The scene to which Beaverbrook took such violent objection was the one showing in close-up a copy of the *Daily Express* floating in oil-stained water carrying the headline that there would be no war this year. For Beaverbrook, this was an affront to his political responsibility, to his power as a seer and prophet, and to his beloved newspaper.

But if the *Daily Express* had got the story wrong in 1939, this brief shot in Coward's film was less than half the story of the row – a story which will develop as Mountbatten graduated from a lunch guest as Captain RN with the Prime Minister, present to recount his war experiences and with strategic predictions not on the agenda, to a war leader of the highest responsibilities and with the acting rank of Vice-Admiral – all in the time it took Coward, and David Lean as co-director and Tony Havelock-Allan as producer, to make *In Which We Serve*: not much more than a year.

Almost twenty years after they had crossed the Atlantic together on their honeymoon for their first visit to the United States, Mountbatten and Edwina began another tour of that nation. Only if America had already become a fighting ally could the contrast have been greater between that jazzy, lavish celebration of 1922 and the stern, purposeful round of visits of September and October 1941. But the Atlantic Charter had just been signed, Lend-Lease was in full swing, the United States was training RAF personnel as well as supplying the aircraft for them to fly in action. The nation was at peace, but there was an uneasy feeling everywhere that this state of neutrality could not be held for much longer.

In New York, the Mountbattens saw many of their old friends, and then went their separate ways. Edwina's task was to tour the country on behalf of the British Red Cross and St John Ambulance Association to thank those who had contributed over five million pounds during the first two years of war. Before she left, Mountbatten passed on to her the lessons he had himself learned in an intensive course in public speaking in preparation for the responsibilities that must one day be his. He already knew how to speak without notes, or with the barest outline of what he wanted to say on one sheet of card, talking directly and intimately to his audience, skilfully timing the light touches; and transmitting that feeling of certainty that everyone was going to have a good time – and he most of all – which became a hallmark of his speeches.

Mountbatten's own first duties lay at the United States Navy Yard in Norfolk, Virginia. Here the carrier *Illustrious* was undergoing repairs after being hit by six heavy bombs back in January in the Mediterranean, and he was to take over command when she was ready for sea. He also met again Antoine Gazda, who was manufacturing Oerlikons for the American Navy, and had designed a 60-knot E-boat hunter, which aroused Mountbatten's enthusiasm.

Then came the flight to Pearl Harbor, which gave him such concern. It was while he was in Los Angeles on his way back from Honolulu that the call to high command arrived on 10 October 1941. It was in the form of a cable from Churchill: 'We want you home here at once for something which you will find of the highest interest.'

The invitation to stay at the White House on the way home had to be refused – 'We want Mountbatten here for a very active and urgent job', Churchill signalled Harry Hopkins, Roosevelt's adviser – and Mountbatten had time only to give his warning to Stark before taking the clipper across the Atlantic and reporting at once to Downing Street.

Less than two weeks after the evacuation from Dunkirk in June 1940, when in the eyes of the world Britain became a beleaguered island awaiting German invasion, a small group of British troops made a series of raids on the German-held French coast near Boulogne. Two Germans were killed, and a British colonel took a bullet through his ear. The world did not hear about it. But it was the first raid of Combined Operations Command, an organization that was to become associated with some of the most effective and dare-devil operations of the war, and whose work was eventually to culminate in the D-Day landings of 1944, and victory. 'We have got to get out of our minds the idea that the Channel ports and all the country between them are enemy territory,' wrote Churchill in June 1940. 'How wonderful it would be if the Germans could be made to wonder where they were going to be struck next, instead of forcing us to try to wall in the island and roof it over.'[12]

One of the most hazardous and renowned raids of World War I had been made on the German U-boat base of Zeebrugge, on St George's Day, 1918. It had been carried out under the command of Roger Keyes, a vice-admiral with a fine record already behind him, and a straight-talker. Churchill made Keyes chief of this new command, with fifty American 'Tommy guns' and a handful of staff. It developed fast, but not fast enough for the Admiral, who was bursting with ambition and ideas but did not fully comprehend the art of political in-fighting. Time and again he was deprived of promised supplies and support. By the summer of 1941 he was scarcely on speaking terms with Churchill, and later told Mountbatten that 'the Chiefs of Staff are the greatest cowards I have ever met.'

'A new and young figure [at Combined Ops] ... would be in the public interest,' Churchill wrote at this time. And he decided on Mountbatten.

What caused Churchill to single out Mountbatten, a junior captain, age forty-one, from the great wealth of talent available to him to fill this highly important command? Churchill had been attracted to him from the earliest days, even if he did forget his extra sardine at Osborne. He had admired and worked well with his father, had recognized Mountbatten's special qualities when he was at Cambridge. His admiration for Edwina has already been mentioned. He judged her mind to be at least the equal of Mountbatten's own, and – more important – saw that she kept her husband's wits fine-edged.

Churchill regarded them, as a couple, among the most brilliant in the land. Martin Gilbert, Churchill's biographer, considers Edwina's emotional appeal to Churchill as being very strong, and has published Churchill's moving letter to her on the death of her grandfather. Gilbert has also written of Churchill's dislike of what he used to call the 'instinct for the negative', which he recognized in leaders like Admirals Jellicoe and Dudley North and General Auchinleck, as opposed to the 'instinct for the positive' which he saw so clearly in men like Beatty, Montgomery and Mountbatten.[13]

Brains and positivism, then, were the two qualities which led to Mountbatten's selection, and to the crucial turning point in his career. And, once again, the royal connection was no handicap either. From this time, Edwina and those who knew him well recognized a new authority in Mountbatten's stance and style. 'Dickie much grown in stature since he took up his highly important, indeed vital, command,'[14] noted the observant 'Chips' Channon. The sixty-eight-year-old Admiral of the Fleet Lord Keyes handed over his command to the officer twenty-seven years his junior, whom he had once refused to have in his flagship, and then come to admire. 'He was very friendly about the turnover,' Mountbatten said.

' "The trouble is that the British have lost the will to fight," Keyes said. I could see *he* hadn't but I didn't agree with him. Winston had told me what he wanted, and now it was up to me to carry it out.'

Beaverbrook ordered his editors to condemn the appointment in the strongest terms. Mountbatten's mother, remembering how Press attacks had so wounded her husband, wrote reassuringly to him that 'Luckily the general public is not much perturbed by the *Daily Express*'s outcries and scandal-sniffing.'[15]

'It was a two-fold job,' Mountbatten defined his task. 'The first was to continue the raids, so splendidly begun by Keyes, in order to keep the offensive spirit boiling and harass the enemy. Second, to prepare for the invasion of Europe, without which we could never win the war. "I want you", Winston had added, "to turn the south coast of England from a bastion of defence into a springboard of attack." '

Britain and the Commonwealth and their Allies were no longer fighting

Above: Edwina, age 27.

Above right: Goodwood Races, July 1926. On Mountbatten's left is his sister-in-law, Nada, Marchioness of Milford Haven.

Right: Mountbatten, Edwina and her sister Mary at the Highland Gathering, 1923.

Mountbatten with his
first Rolls-Royce, a
'Silver Ghost' model,
with 'signalman'
mascot, Edwina's
wedding present to
him.

Above left: Douglas Fairbanks, Patricia, age 7 (today Countess Mountbatten of Burma),
Edwina, and her father, Colonel Wilfred Ashley.

Above right: Discussing tactics with the Duke of Gloucester before a chukka, June
1937.

The Royal Navy Polo Team in 1937. (l to r) Lieutenant-Commander E.G. Heywood-Lonsdale, Commander C.E. Lambe, Mountbatten, and Commander E.W.B. Sim.

Pranks at Balmoral Castle, August 1936. Mountbatten and King Edward VIII (dressed as a peasant) on the left, Wallis Simpson and Edwina on the right.

The Penthouse, Park Lane, in 1937, with furniture by David Joel and a scattering of books, including *Treasure Island*, *Memoirs of a Fox-Hunting Man*, *In Search of History* and a biography of Mountbatten's relative, Kaiser Wilhelm II. The model is of his first ship, HMS *Daring*.

Above: The destroyer commander, Full Speed Ahead. Captain Lord Louis Mountbatten on the *Kelly's* bridge, 1940.

Left: Mountbatten (2nd left front row) and his senior officers of 5th Destroyer flotilla in jovial mood.

Below: The *Kelly*, torpedoed and listing, off the Dutch coast, 1940.

Above: General 'Vinegar Joe' Stilwell and Mountbatten at Kandy, 1944.

Left: Mountbatten, General R.A. 'Specs' Wheeler and the Chiang Kai-sheks, 1944.

alone. But the Russian armies were falling back all along their enormous front, the German armies had taken one after another the major Russian cities and were almost in the suburbs of Moscow. It had been a terrible year in the Mediterranean and North Africa, the Japanese were becoming more and more threatening in the Far East. It took enormous courage and optimism to talk in the autumn of 1941 about a springboard for the destruction of Germany, especially when the dire predictions of June about the fate of the Russian armies seemed about to be fulfilled.

But after the attack on Pearl Harbor, when Mountbatten's own pessimistic predictions were fulfilled all too fearsomely, Churchill was able to note: 'So we have won after all!'

For Mountbatten it was now the end of his fighting war. And it was the beginning of his command war. He had inherited an uneasy and unloved organization that was neither fish, nor flesh, nor fowl, and it was distasteful to lovers of all three. If the Combined Ops dish had not yet gone bad, it was widely regarded as 'going off'.

A command that is widely regarded as a *corps d'élite* by its nature and comparatively small numbers always attracts enemies among the majority, who fear they will lose their best to it and, at once, a degree of their own status. (Bomber Command later had the same trouble in creating 'Pathfinders'.) For example, the proposal that the new Commandos should be distinguished by special berets at first aroused the fiercest hostility, and was turned down. Applications for special equipment met every obstruction. The regular HQ mind hates irregular and non-uniform organizations and activities. The old, straight-talking Keyes had made numerous enemies. Bernard Fergusson has written of the 'formidable inheritance of feuds'[16] Mountbatten had to cope with the moment he entered the Combined Operations HQ situated on a single floor in Richmond Terrace, Whitehall, London.

The staff, including messengers and typists, numbered around twenty, and most of the officers were superannuated. Mountbatten was appalled, and amazed that anything had so far been accomplished. He inspected this set-up and its establishments for a single whirlwind month and reported back to the Chiefs of Staff. His suggestions were accepted without question, and he began his appointments, expansion and reorganization.

Judgments on Mountbatten's powers of administration and organization are as mixed as they are on everything else about the man. The reason for this is simple. He was brilliantly good at some things, and less good, even quite bad, at others. Some of his appointments were masterly, others were weak. Some of the good appointments lasted too short a time, some of the poor ones lasted far too long.

Mountbatten in high command needed, looked for and nearly always found great brains and smart, dedicated organizers who could prepare the briefs he needed. But he also needed charmers and sycophants with a ready sense of humour like the fun-lovers of the days of peace, who could be relied upon to say what Mountbatten wanted to hear; as one of his senior staff put it, 'handsome social chaps who could always be relied upon to say, "The champagne's over here, Dickie."' The second were mostly recruited from his own service, and one or two admirals with 'not much on top' lasted to the end of Mountbatten's serving career. But their presence made Mountbatten comfortable, they tended to be good on the public relations side, and for this reason alone their contribution cannot be entirely written off.

Captain 'Jock' Hughes Hallett, who became the Naval Force Commander on Combined Ops' biggest raid, had a fine, original mind and was utterly courageous. His brother Charles could be indirectly classed as one of Mountbatten's 'brains' since his Division in the Admiralty was responsible for dealing with Combined Operations' day-to-day naval needs. This division was also responsible for the strategic disposition of landing craft. 'It was the Admiralty that mostly staffed him in those early days,' he said, 'and some of the people they put in were not first class. And Mountbatten did not realize how bad some of them were.'[17]

Mickey Hodges, an old friend who had served with him in the Mediterranean, became Mountbatten's Chief Signals Officer. Halsey was made his personal assistant, his 'winger'. Captain 'Ronnie' Brockman was later lured from the First Sea Lord's office and remained at Mountbatten's elbow, or just behind it, for twenty-two years as his secretary.

If Mountbatten enjoyed simple 'salts' who charmed and admired him, and made him chuckle, this was balanced by an admiration for eccentrics. The Hessian tradition of open-mindedness and liking for sharp and unorthodox brains, inherited so strongly by Mountbatten, was one of his greatest assets, and it showed most brightly at this difficult time when his pitiably small organization had, in the broadest and most literal sense, to prepare to beat Germany in Europe. The German armies could be beaten only by a successful preliminary invasion of the mainland. And this was what Combined Ops was ultimately preparing for, its final *raison d'être*.

Mountbatten needed planners and visionaries with minds as broad as the Channel that would one day have to be crossed in force. In the end he obtained three, all men who, in some degree, resembled the popular idea of a mad inventor, but whose genius mercifully stopped far short of insanity. It is a reasonable assumption that a scouring of the free world at that time could not have turned up a more valuable trio than Geoffrey Pyke, a discovery of Leo Amery, Secretary of State for India; Professor J.D. Bernal of London University, sponsored by the eminent scientist Sir Henry Tizard; and Professor Solly Zuckerman, then an anatomist and authority on apes, and soon known throughout Combined Ops as 'the monkey man', and by Mountbatten as 'my witch doctor'. All were to do brilliant work. Zuckerman became Mountbatten's lifelong friend whose contribution to his achievements to the end of his serving life, and beyond, was immeasurable in its weight and extent; the absolute antithesis of the simple naval flatterers whose function was to play games and arouse laughter.

One more figure among so many recruited during these early months was his relative Sir Harold Wernher, the ex-soldier and immensely successful businessman – a sort of latter-day Sir Ernest Cassel – who had special talents as liaison and co-ordinating officer. When Mountbatten grabbed him, Churchill (not a slouch at nepotism himself) raised an eyebrow. 'Some relation of yours?' he is said to have asked bleakly. Sharp as that new invention, the Sten gun, Mountbatten retorted, 'Not as close a one as Duncan Sandys!' – Churchill's son-in-law, recently catapulted to Financial Secretary to the War Office.

If, by the end of 1941, Mountbatten's Combined Ops team was a mixed one, it was complete, its comparatively small number of really brilliant appointments more than outweighed the larger number of weak appointments, and above all it was established and stabilized and recognized. This was entirely due to Mountbatten's energy, charm and ruthlessness; and to a factor which a few shrewd brains had recognized from the beginning: he had the priceless asset of access. He could talk on equal terms to George VI *and* his Prime Minister *and* his Foreign Secretary. He had the ear of anyone whom he wished to complain to, acquire something from, or praise.

The First Sea Lord, the crusty, able (and already sick) Admiral Sir Dudley Pound, had some grave reservations about Mountbatten's style and character. 'He was always suspicious of Mountbatten', said Admiral Hughes Hallett, 'for not being in the general run of people at the Admiralty.'[18] But Mountbatten was the only officer below flag rank who could raise the telephone (as he often did) and speak to him personally at any time. Poor old Keyes had scarcely been on speaking terms with anybody at the Admiralty.

This reformed and enlarged Command could now begin its creative work and plan and carry out its first raids under the new regime, with the few landing craft it had now acquired, with the Commandos it had now trained, under the Force Commanders who now appreciated and possessed the powers to carry out the functions Combined Ops HQ had defined. There were to be ten raids of varying sizes in the first six months of 1942.

The first of note, but on a very small scale, was on a cliff-top in northern

France. A reconnaissance plane had photographed an unusual radar station which Allied scientists clearly wished to examine. Combined Ops laid on a brilliantly conceived and executed raid on the night of 27 February 1942, with paratroopers dropping behind the site at Bruneval and Commandos with a radio mechanic landing on a nearby beach. In the face of intensive fire, the necessary vital parts of the radar set were dismantled and brought safely home. The findings were of immeasurable importance, especially to the future air offensive.

A second raid a month later was of equal value to the Royal Navy. One of Germany's mighty battleships, larger and more formidable than any possessed by Britain, had been sunk in May 1941 after a dramatic chase and at the cost of the Royal Navy's biggest man o'war.

The *Bismarck*'s sister ship, *Tirpitz*, was now complete and such a threat to the Atlantic supply lines that she was distorting the whole structure of Allied naval strategy. However, her destructive powers could be greatly reduced if she could be deprived of the only dockyard on the French Atlantic seaboard big enough to accommodate her.

This was at St Nazaire. The idea of destroying this dock was broached to Mountbatten by one of his oldest naval friends and contemporaries, Captain Charles Lambe, Director of Plans. The operation, which led to the award of no fewer than five VCs, was carried out with complete success on the night of 27–28 March 1942, and involved the ramming of the lock gates by an old and expendable ex-US Navy destroyer, with delayed charges on board.

This second triumph by Combined Ops confirmed Churchill in the wisdom of his choice of leader, and ensured once and for all that Mountbatten was henceforth to take his part at the very top for the remainder of the war. A few days later, Churchill wrote to Roosevelt:

> Dickie's show at St Nazaire, though small in scale, was very bracing. For your personal and secret eye, I made him Vice-Admiral, Lieutenant-General, and Air Marshal some few weeks ago, and have put him on the Chiefs of Staff Committee as Chief of Combined Operations. He is an equal member, attending whenever either his own affairs or the general conduct of the war are under consideration. He will be in the centre of what you mention about the joint attack on Europe.[19]

'I was now an Admiral at forty-one, two years younger than Nelson,' Mountbatten said, 'and with the other honorary ranks, I was the first serving officer to hold all three ranks in all three services. To save Keyes' feelings, my official position up until then had been Chief Adviser to Combined Operations, although of course I was still the boss. Now Winston felt able to call me the boss properly, and I was one of only four members of the British Chiefs of Staff Committee.

'But all that was nothing compared with the fact that I now had the power to get what I wanted,' Mountbatten continued, as if he had up until then been deprived of the means of getting anything. 'There were still a lot of people about who saw nothing virtuous in combining the work of the three services. They were no use to me, but they had been a pain in the neck in the past. Now, not only did I not have to use them, I could over-rule them. And did so. The people I was working with now were the heads of the services, all of them a lot senior to me in age of course. The one nearest to me in age was Peter Portal [Air Chief Marshal Sir Charles Portal, Chief of Air Staff] – he was only about seven years older. And I got on specially well with him and we became great friends.

'Dudley Pound was now much more helpful, too. He had been pretty sticky sometimes in the past, and he explained to me why he had not always been helpful towards Combined Ops. It was, he said, because the Navy had to give all its attention to winning the Battle of the Atlantic. If we lost that, we lost the war.'

Increasingly during 1942, 'Combined Operations' came to mean not only combined services but combined Anglo-American. America's entry into the war, with the agreed commitment that the first priority was to defeat Germany, the second to defeat Japan, led to immediate and close liaison and constant Atlantic traffic as American participation rapidly increased, and the miracle of American war production altered the strategic and tactical concepts on every front.

In April 1942 Roosevelt sent his personal adviser, Harry Hopkins, and his Chief of Staff, General George Marshall, to London to formulate plans, long-term and short-term. One of their first visits was to Combined Ops HQ. Whatever conflicts and abrasive relationships there may have been – and were, sometimes serious – between British and American commands, none of these occurred when Mountbatten was involved, or were soon smoothed over. Mountbatten's love for America, added to his natural tact and charm, created valuable harmony in war.

'The most important man in the American military machine throughout the war was George Marshall,' Mountbatten believed, and at the same time claimed his friendship. 'We got on marvellously from the start. He was a terrific personality. There was absolutely no nonsense about him, and you always knew where you were with him. When he came to Richmond Terrace he was amazed to see the three services working side by side as if there were no barriers – as there weren't of course. Marshall said, "This is amazing – it's inspiring. How did you do it?"

'I said, "It's quite simple, sir. They all speak English, you see." He didn't
understand what I was getting at at first, then he laughed, and I took advantage of the moment and made a suggestion. "General, I believe you speak
English, too, in America. So why don't you send over some soldiers and
airmen and sailors and join us here at headquarters?"

'And so, quite early on, we got the first integrated Allied Headquarters
operating in London.'

This worked like a dream. Not only staff officers, but the equivalent of
British Commandos – American Rangers – were soon training alongside
British and Commonwealth troops. And on the next big raid, Rangers served
in strength and suffered heavily. This was real partnership fighting, literally
elbow to elbow under fire.

Fundamental political attitudes were more difficult to resolve. In the
simplest definition, American high command believed that they discerned
in the British attitude to the war a certain caution and weariness, pessimism
even. The Americans possessed all the fresh eagerness for battle, but did
not yet possess the hard statistics nor the hard experience. 'Snob and snub'
summed up the view of some officials in Washington of their British counter-
parts.

For their part, the British attitude to American enthusiasm could be
patronizing and condescending, like that of the professional veteran's lofty
or humorous view of the amateur. There was a very serious conflict of temperament and character between those who had been fighting alone, vastly
outnumbered, for the greater part of two and a quarter years, taking all the
hard initial punches, and the newcomers to the battlefield, all eagerness,
inexperience, smart uniforms, and medals before they had even begun, or
so it seemed. In the lower echelons, the mutual wisecracking was not always
comradely, and the British definition of American troops in England as
'overpaid, oversexed and over here' had an edge to it.

Only the bigger minds could lift above these conflicting attitudes and see
that co-operation was all-essential and conflict destructive. One of Mountbatten's greatest contributions to victory was to help to bring about a fundamental reform of attitude on the part of the two great Allies. A visit to
Washington in the early summer of 1942 by Mountbatten was notable in
the history of Anglo-American relations during the war.

The most serious conflict arose about the date of 'the return to Europe'
– the invasion, the liberation of the enslaved nations. The American Chiefs
of Staff in early 1942 believed that an invasion of France was possible later
in that year (Operation Round-Up); and if not, then certainly in 1943
(Operation Sledgehammer).

'The British Chiefs of Staff paid me the compliment of suggesting that

I was the only person capable of convincing them that Round-Up was quite impractical,' said Mountbatten. 'My task in Washington was probably the most important job I had to do in the war. I had to persuade Roosevelt and his advisers that American strategy and expectations needed re-thinking.'

'Dickie will explain to you the difficulties of 1942,' Churchill told Roosevelt on 28 May. Mountbatten arrived to begin this formidable task on 3 June. On that same day was fought the Battle of Midway, the Pacific naval engagement that proved to be the turning point in the war against Japan. The Americans were jubilant, and rightly, for they had sunk four carriers, destroyed 250 enemy planes, and broken the back of the Japanese Air Arm which had everywhere been triumphant.

In a sense, this worked against Mountbatten, especially as the war in North Africa was going badly and Tobruk was soon to fall to the Germans. American senior officers of all services saw these events as confirmation of American strength and superiority, and British weakness and defeatism.

No one could have won round some of the hard-core prejudiced senior service officers in Washington. It was a measure of the success of Mountbatten's mission that he brought round to the British view a number of men of power and influence. He left behind him an impression of resolution and goodwill, and a President, according to Bernard Fergusson, 'who was fast coming to share the British conviction that Sledgehammer was impossible, and Round-Up in 1943 rash'.

For his part, Mountbatten brought away with him one of the most able American admirals, H. Kent Hewitt, who was commander of the newly formed American 'AmphibLant' in Norfolk, Virginia. He had been selected by Admiral E.J. 'Ernie' King, Chief of Naval Operations, to be an observer at Combined Ops HQ in London for a period.

Churchill flew off to Washington a few days after Mountbatten had reported on his meetings and conclusions. It was an appropriate time for Admiral Hewitt to be in London. He had no idea that Churchill would be discussing with the President the subject code-named 'Tube Alloys' – the atomic bomb – but he was well aware that a fundamental switch in strategy and priorities was on the agenda for the White House talks, and that preparations for an imminent landing in France were likely to be altered to preparations for a landing in French North Africa that year. He was therefore a witness to the planning operations in Richmond Terrace for 'Torch'; and another, much smaller operation, though the biggest of all raids, which was even more imminent.

A great deal has been written about the Dieppe raid of 19 August 1942, and a great deal of it is rubbish. The most lunatic judgment on it was (not surprisingly) provided by the enemy. The Germans, for propaganda purposes, put it about that the raid was a full-scale invasion, which they had easily and bloodily repulsed. They then, like most liars, began to believe their own lie, which did their cause considerable damage.

Dieppe was, in the simplest definition, a raid in unusual strength to test German defences, absorb lessons for the real invasion nearly two years later, capture some troops and invasion barges in the harbour, give the Russians an earnest of our intentions, at the same time prove British resolution to doubters at home and across the Atlantic, and lift the flagging morale of the idle Canadian troops in England, who were to be the chief participants. Its motive, then, was about four-fifths political, one-fifth military.

Dieppe is particularly fascinating in the context of Mountbatten's life and war record because it was widely regarded as ill-conceived, poorly and expensively carried out, dubious in its lessons, and very much Mountbatten's 'show'. To the end of his life, 'Dieppe' was engraved upon Mountbatten's heart, and the name would always raise an instant defensive response, almost as if he were protesting too much.

It was while Hopkins and Marshall were in Britain that the first plans were formulated for a major raid on Hitler's 'Atlantic Wall'. The most suitable target was clearly Dieppe, and Jock Hughes Hallett and his team devised a scheme for a pincer attack from the east and west, avoiding a head-on assault. The town, port and airfield would be held briefly, and the force re-embarked on the same day.

There were certain objections to this plan and factors in favour of the frontal approach. Mountbatten remained convinced throughout that the pincer plan was better. Then came his Washington visit in June 1942. In his absence, General Bernard Montgomery, c-in-c South-Eastern Command, pressed for the frontal assault, after a heavy bombardment. Churchill refused to allow bombers to carry this out because of the French casualties and anti-British feeling this would cause. Dudley Pound had already refused to allow battleships to be used for a bombardment in case they, in turn, might be bombed by the Germans. A staff assessment at Combined Ops showed that any sort of bombardment would fill the streets with so much rubble that the tanks would be stalled and become sitting ducks.

The problem was still unresolved when Montgomery conveniently departed for North Africa to win his spurs at Alamein. No one knows to this day whether anyone tried to explain the problem to him before he left. But everyone agreed later that there was a lack of communication between Southern Command and Combined Ops HQ, and for this Mountbatten must finally be held responsible.

Another officer who departed before the raid was Baillie-Grohman, Mountbatten's old Captain (D) in the Mediterranean before the war. He was in command of the naval forces, but Mountbatten, who had never held him in the highest regard, replaced him at the last moment. Most of Combined Ops' staff agreed that this was the right thing to do.

The date of the attack, conditioned by moon and tides, was postponed twice, and in spite of security risks, was finally fixed for the night of 18–19 August. By this time, Mountbatten had been back at HQ for weeks, knew that the operation was to be conducted in quite a different manner from that devised by his own planning staff and approved by him, but did nothing to halt it. 'He should have cancelled or bombarded,'[20] is Charles Hughes Hallett's view today.

As the world learned very quickly, the assault was a bloody fiasco. There were local successes, examples of great heroism, and further valuable radar secrets were unearthed, but in all its prime military objectives the raid failed, and the frontal assault was repulsed on the beach and promenades of the town.

The statistics of losses, when they first came in, appeared alarming. Of the 5,000 Canadians engaged, nearly 1,000 were killed, 2,000 captured (many of them wounded), and of the 2,000 who got back, 25 per cent were wounded. A destroyer and 33 landing craft were sunk, 106 RAF aircraft shot down in the biggest fighter air battle of the war. There were over 1,000 further casualties above the Canadians' figure. The Germans suffered 591 casualties, and won a considerable propaganda victory.

Aside from those who, even today, call out 'Disaster!', there are still many historians who consider that the lessons of Dieppe could have been learned less expensively. They may be right, or simply wise after the event. In the count of war, one dead soldier can be defined as a disaster. But the Dieppe casualties must be seen in terms of 1941–2, when, say, many more sailors were killed in HMS *Hood* by a shell or two than all the soldiers at Dieppe; when the RAF were losing many times that number every month; when a small-scale raid on a quiet afternoon outside Stalingrad could result in ten times as many casualties; when the Japanese would not bother to count 1,000 dead defending a minor beach-head on a Pacific island.

The scale of casualties at Dieppe in terms of World War II were tragic and infinitesimal. Yet they were large enough for their shock to have a salutary effect and for the lessons learned to be taken much more seriously than if the operation had been a walk-over.

The price paid, the benefit gained, from loss of life in war, is as incalculable as the numerical reckoning. But to talk of Canadian lives being 'thrown away' on the beaches of Dieppe, which has often been heard, is remote from the truth. Never were more life-saving lessons learned on one operation than at Dieppe.

Among them was that an attack on a defended coast required many times more powerful bombardment than that provided by destroyers. From this stemmed the multiple-rocket (a thousand at a time) bombardment ship, with what Bernard Fergusson referred to as its drenching fire 'reducing the defenders to a state of gibbering'. It was also realized that tank obstacles must be breached before tanks are landed; that landing craft needed very skilful piloting; that a higher degree of training was required for beach assault parties.

Above all, Dieppe provided beyond doubt the confirmation that an assault on a port must result in the total destruction of that port. Therefore, invaders must either capture them intact, *or bring their own harbours with them.*

Mountbatten afterwards claimed that he had already reached this conclusion. He also claimed that Churchill took all the credit for Mulberry, the famous floating artificial harbour of the 1944 French invasion. He would imitate Churchill's voice – 'You must have great piers that rise and fall with the tide. ...' raising and lowering his hands as he did so, and with a mischievous smile on his lips.

'The truth is this,' Mountbatten added. 'I knew we would have to make artificial harbours. I knew we would have to bombard any port to such an extent that it would destroy the facilities. We had to have them because of the weather and the vast supplies we would have to put ashore immediately. No one person invented Mulberry. The knowledge that we had to have this floating harbour slowly *grew*. But no one outside Combined Ops believed in it. So I went to Winston and asked him to write a minute to show that he liked the idea, and he said yes. And he wrote it and it was very powerful, and it is now used as evidence that he thought the whole thing up.

'I am not complaining for myself,' Mountbatten continued. 'I couldn't care less. But Winston long ago (it was the same in my father's time) got this habit of picking up people's ideas without their permission. His claim later that he thought of ideas that really belonged to others was the price you had to pay to get them through.'

In fact, Churchill in his war memoirs makes no such claim. The prime originator of Mulberry, which made a successful invasion possible, was Jock Hughes Hallett, according to Churchill.

Zuckerman, Pyke and the other 'boffins' (the slang name for scientists was then much in vogue) busied themselves with finding answers to the lessons of Dieppe during the autumn and winter of 1942. Things were never quiet at Richmond Terrace; they were never more productive and tumultuous than during these months.

Dieppe post mortems continued far beyond this time, and for long after the war was won. When Mountbatten was Fourth Sea Lord in 1951, he was shown the draft of the Confidential Staff History covering the Dieppe raid. The whole operation had been examined in immense detail, and it came up with the conclusion that it failed operationally because of the last-minute interference of General Montgomery, who insisted on the frontal assault. No direct cause of failure was ascribed to Mountbatten.

Yet when the draft reached Mountbatten's desk he telephoned Lieutenant-Commander Peter Kemp, the head of the branch responsible for Staff Histories. 'He wanted it withdrawn,' recalls Kemp, who said that this was hardly possible. ' "Well can you rewrite this bit saying it was an operational failure?" he asked. And I replied, "Frankly, sir, no. We are merely repeating what the official records say." He walked up and down his office. He seemed more hurt than cross. Then he said, "Now, about these figures of casualties. I'm sure they're exaggerated." "No, sir, we have seen all the returns, the prisoner-of-war lists, and so on. They are as written." In the end he persuaded us to do a little tinkering, dividing the casualties into those wounded, taken prisoner, and dead, which was fair enough.' Kemp concluded his account: 'But it is quite interesting because it shows how badly he felt about Dieppe.'[21]

Dieppe was a recurring sore for Mountbatten because it was seen by some as *his* failure. It was not a failure because the price was high. It was not a failure at all, by some interpretations.

One of the strongest reasons that Mountbatten gave for not permitting an authorized biography to be written in his lifetime was that he believed he had never made a single mistake in his life. 'It is a curious thing, but a fact, that I have been right in everything I have done and said in my life,' Mountbatten said many times. 'No one would believe a biographer who made this claim while I was still alive because readers would conclude that I had caused it to be written, that I was leaning over the author's shoulder.'

It was, then, to be left to posterity. Posterity would correct the record. Posthumously, the public was more likely to recognize the truth that his official biographer was certain to write: the truth that he had never made a single mistake in his life.

Dieppe was a threat to this clean record; and there was one man who never allowed him to forget it: Lord Beaverbrook, who had not yet seen *In Which We Serve*. 'In spite of his violent attacks on me later, Max Beaverbrook always claimed that I was made head of Combined Ops and then promoted and made one of the four running the war on the Chiefs of Staff Committee on his advice to Winston,' said Mountbatten. ' "This is a very important position I've got for you," Max would say. "Preparing for the invasion."

'Max had been using his newspapers for some time for agitating for an invasion – "Second Front Now!" It was one of his great wartime campaigns. He really believed that we could successfully invade Europe long before we had the men and the arms and equipment – just like some of the Americans.

'Now, having – as he tried to convince me – got me on to the Chiefs of Staff Committee and made a Vice-Admiral, he expected me to support *his* cause. He saw me as the young man who would make Winston change his mind about the date of the invasion. It was a sort of exchange arrangement. "The Chiefs of Staff will need my help, and you as a young man can let me know what you hear." Several times he said, "Stick to me!" Of course I could do nothing of the kind, and told Max so. And – well, "Hell hath no fury. . . ."'

Then two events occurred in quick succession, which between them set the seal on a most notorious public vendetta. First Dieppe. Not only was this not the invasion for which Beaverbrook had been agitating, it was an ill-judged gamble in which Mountbatten had laid down the chips – and the chips were thousands of Beaverbrook's countrymen. They were lost, squandered. They were wasted by military folly. Just to prove the hollowness of Beaverbrook's campaign for a full invasion *now*. Then came the premiere of *In Which We Serve*, a month later on 17 September 1942, the work, in Beaverbrook's judgment, of an effete 'pansy' and war slacker. Noël Coward had often been the target of the Beaverbrook newspapers in the past. Now he had produced a film which made a mockery of the *Daily Express*, purported to show Coward as a naval hero, when the whole world knew that it was Mountbatten – Mountbatten, who had broken his trust with the man who really put him into a position of power, and then thrown away Canadian lives in a futile exercise. . . .

The extent of Beaverbrook's anger, which might have warned Mountbatten that this time it would be a lifelong vendetta, became evident a short time later, on 21 October 1942. It was Trafalgar Day, and Averill Harriman gave a large dinner party to celebrate the occasion.

'Max was there, and he got very drunk,' said Mountbatten. 'Afterwards, he came up to me and said very loudly, "You and I were once good friends, but now I'm through with you." Suddenly there was great attention concentrated on us, but Max went on, "You attacked me in that film of yours – you changed the real events to attack me. *You're* responsible for linking that film with me. That was a very unfriendly thing to do, Dickie." He hadn't finished yet. I was stunned. "And then what about Dieppe? You murdered my countrymen. So, you look out – your career's finished." I tried to soothe him down and make the peace, but it was no good – he was beside himself and much too drunk.'

The next operation for which Mountbatten's HQ prepared all the plans put the controversial Dieppe raid in its right perspective as a small but important signpost pointing towards victory over Germany: Operation Torch, the invasion of North Africa, to be followed by the invasion of Italy. 'So much of my time when I was serving in the Mediterranean had been spent in preparing for war against Italy,' said Mountbatten, 'that it was a particular satisfaction for me that my HQ prepared the plans for its defeat.'

Mountbatten's term as Chief of Combined Operations was nearing its end. Soon he was to be called to even higher responsibilities. But it is appropriate to mention two occasions which show the variety and weight of his activity during this time; and add two personal impressions from far down the line of command which show the extent of his effect on the men he led.

New weapons and instruments of war of all kinds, from rocket-launching bombardment craft to giant floating platforms made from a frozen compound (Pykerete, after its inventor) of seawater and sawdust, were one of the chief preoccupations of Combined Ops HQ. Mountbatten, with his ingenious, curious, technical, inventive and ever-open mind, followed all proposals and experiments with enthusiasm. Nothing was beyond consideration; it was a characteristic that he shared with Churchill, and a factor in Churchill's decision to give him this job.

At one stage, new underwater craft were high on the agenda at HQ, and Mountbatten turned up at a joint Chiefs of Staff meeting somewhat damp and dishevelled from an examination of a new craft. Churchill looked at him in dismay. He had never seen Mountbatten improperly turned out. 'What have you been up to, Dickie?' he asked.

'I have been trying out a new one-man submarine,' Mountbatten replied.

'What on earth for?'

'Well, I think it might be useful for Commando raids, or fixing limpet mines and that sort of thing.'

Churchill glanced up and down at the figure again. 'How did you get so wet?'

'I tried it.'

Churchill, aghast, demanded, 'You don't mean to say you went down by yourself?'

'It's a one-man submarine, so only one man can go down in it.'

Churchill bellowed at him like a sergeant-major on the parade ground. 'This is the most irresponsible thing I've ever heard. I give you an important job in the conduct of the war and you go and try and kill yourself. If you do it again I shall fire you.'

At about this time, August 1942, there came another gentler rocket, from another quarter. The Duke of Kent, serving in the RAF, was killed in a flying accident, along with all the crew. He and Mountbatten had been good friends as well as cousins, and Mountbatten was deeply shocked. Shortly after the news came through, he went to see the King at Buckingham Palace. George VI was heartbroken. 'I'm also very proud, Dickie,' he said, 'that one of the family has given his life. I know David took many risks in the Great War, but this is the first member of the British Royal Family to lose his life in a war for a very long time.'

The question of the funeral and other matters were discussed, among them the fact that there were no brothers left who were available to take over from Kent the voluntary societies of which he had been grand president, etc. 'I'd like you to take them on, Dickie,' George VI said.

Mountbatten replied that he was greatly flattered at the suggestion but that he did in fact have a pretty full-time job on his hands already.

'But there's no one to take over the Royal Societies', the King persisted. 'Surely you could manage them. You only need to keep formal contact until after the war.'

Mountbatten reluctantly agreed, and that was why, from this time, increasing numbers of lines in *Who's Who* were given up to his presidency and patronage of Royal Societies and others. It was not until the last years of his life that he began to shed some of these responsibilities.

Throughout his period at Combined Ops, just as if he were still in command of a mere destroyer and a couple of hundred men, Mountbatten insisted on keeping in direct touch with the men, rightly confident in his belief that his presence could directly lift their morale and fill them with greater vigour and courage. At the end of an inspection, and talks to many of the individuals present, he would give a general talk.

The routine was invariable, and became known to tens of thousands of men during the remainder of the war. He would call for a box – anything to stand on, which always happened to be immediately available. Then he would get up on it, and if an over-assiduous officer had provided his stand with a pulpit-like rest, he would have the stand reversed, or more often turn it round himself so that there was nothing between him and his audience. He was usually without his hat, and if it was warm, he would be without his jacket, too, informality being the essence of his style.

Often, Mountbatten would start off with a crack appropriate to the men's circumstances. Before a raid, he would often tell the assembled Commandos, weary from training, 'Well you have done it here, now you've got to do it over there. It reminds me of a sailor who had a girl friend at home and then was posted overseas. He wrote to her for a while, then stopped. Her letters remained unanswered. Eventually, in desperation she wrote, "I am sure you have found another girl, but I can't understand what she has got that I haven't!" To this he replied, "She hasn't got anything that you haven't got. You've got everything that she's got, but she's got it here!"'

It never failed, any more than the inspection that preceded it could fail. 'We were lined up,' wrote one lieutenant RNVR preparing crews for tank landing craft, 'and each member of the Staff was presented to him. I shall never forget the manner in which he looked at me – I have never been looked at so "squarely in the face" in my life – his eyes seemed to be reading my thoughts! It was a wonderful experience and, by his questions, he obviously had a great knowledge of the work we were doing. He spoke to each of the officers in turn, and all of us were astounded by those penetrating eyes. He ended with an encouraging remark, and a smile. It was an experience of a lifetime.'[22]

It also, inevitably, became known as 'the Mountbatten touch'. It was a style of leadership practised by few Allied leaders. Air Chief Marshal Sir Arthur Harris, C-in-C RAF Bomber Command, for instance, rarely visited an RAF bomber station during a four-year-long offensive, when crews with a lower expectation of survival than subalterns in the trenches in World War I could have benefited from personal encouragement of the Mountbatten kind.

By the summer of 1943, with Africa cleared of the enemy, Italy vanquished (though not yet liberated) and the plans and men and weapons and equipment for the invasion of France almost complete, Mountbatten felt that he had done all that he could for his Command. Like his father, the longer an appointment rooted him ashore, so did his longing to return to sea increase. He did not care how many temporary ranks he dropped: he wanted to feel the throb of turbines beneath steel decks, and the salt air in his face.

He got both, but not as he expected or wished. The ship in which he sailed down the River Clyde on 4 August 1943, twenty-nine years to the day since he had dined with his father in Mall House on the night the country went to war, was the *Queen Mary*. He was a mere passenger. His fellow passengers included his boss, Winston Churchill, his fellow Chiefs of Staff, almost two hundred more staff officers and advisers in every field of warfare, including General Orde Wingate and the bomber 'king' Guy Gibson, VC, DSO, DFC. It was a pleasent enough voyage, with much interesting talk and the usual amount of heavy drinking in Churchill's cabin. Mountbatten remained restless, however. Here, on board this liner and lacking the distractions of Whitehall, was the time and place to cultivate the First Sea Lord, the one man who could 'fix' a sea appointment for him.

'I followed him like a shadow,' Mountbatten said, 'pacing the decks for exercise, or up on the bridge. He always seemed to be talking to someone. It never occurred to me that he might be avoiding me. Then one day I did catch Pound alone. '"I've about finished my work at Combined Operations," I said, "and I think it's about time I went back to sea." He did not seem to take any interest at all. "Look, sir," I persisted, "I'd very much like to go back to the *Illustrious*."

'"Yes, yes," he said – or I thought he said. But it was more a mumble, and then someone came and interrupted us.'

A few days later, Mountbatten discovered why the First Sea Lord was even more uncommunicative than usual.

7
'SUPREMO' I

THE *Queen Mary* docked at Halifax five days after clearing the Clyde, a voyage completed in the usual impeccable style of this great liner, whether in peaceful seas or an Atlantic Ocean infested with U-boats. Even Churchill the gourmet commented that the menu was up to peacetime standards. He had been looking forward to a short period of rest; instead, every waking minute had been fully occupied, so unrelenting was the pressure of conducting the war.

Shortly before leaving London, Churchill had discussed the possible creation of a new command in South-East Asia, where the land war had grown stale and unsatisfactory, and the morale of the troops was known to be low: 'This lethargic and stagnant Indian scene', as he defined it. He had asked Clement Attlee, the Deputy Prime Minister, and the Foreign Secretary, for their views, and on his suggested candidate for the job of running the command. Churchill referred to this matter again in the first report he telegraphed to George VI, for the first time mentioning Mountbatten by name. 'I am increasingly inclined to suggest this solution to the [American] President,'[1] he added.

In fact, the die was cast, regardless of the views of anyone. Churchill knew that the King would welcome the new and dramatic promotion of his cousin, and that Roosevelt, already an ardent admirer, would also approve of his choice. Among those of his fellow passengers on the voyage with whom Churchill discussed the appointment were Dudley Pound, his Senior Assistant Secretary of the War Cabinet, General Leslie Hollis, and Ian Jacob.

Jacob recalled later that Churchill had teased them by asking who they thought would make a good Supreme Commander. 'It was rather an important question, but we suggested some names,' said Jacob. 'Then he, with a look like a naughty schoolboy, produced Mountbatten's name and asked what we thought of that. I said I thought it a splendid idea, and one which would appeal to the Americans.'[2]

The Quebec Conference of August 1943 took place in the Citadel – 'in every way delightful, and ideally suited to the purpose,' as Churchill pronounced it, and made a special point of thanking the King for arranging ramps for the mobile convenience of the crippled American President. On the agenda for discussion were such items as the invasion of Italy, now that the island of Sicily as well as the Italian dictator had fallen; and Operation Overlord, the invasion of France in the following spring.

But, according to Churchill, 'The greater part of it concerned operations in Burma and the Indian Ocean....'[3] No discussion could take place until the choice of Supreme Commander had been approved by all concerned, and Mountbatten remained in ignorance of his nomination until several days after their arrival in Quebec.

'Winston asked me to take a walk along the battlements overlooking the Heights of Abraham,' Mountbatten recalled. 'He asked me about my health, as he knew that I had been badly overworking and had been feeling the strain. I said I thought it was pretty good, and he asked me next, "Do you feel up to anything?" and I said "Yes".

'Then he asked me what I thought of the situation in South-East Asia. "It's a pretty good mess," I said, and he said – rather surprisingly – "Do you think you could put it right?"

'I thought about this for a moment. It would mean a lot of paper work and I had a lot on my hands already without another assessment for the Chiefs of Staff. "Isn't that a thing for 'Pug' Ismay?" I said. [He was referring to Churchill's Chief of Staff, General Hastings Ismay.]

'"Pug Ismay?" Winston exclaimed. "You don't understand what I'm offering you. I am offering you to go out there and do the job!"

'I still didn't understand. I thought he meant that I should make a trip out there before doing my assessment.

'"A trip!" This time it was an explosion. "I'm offering you the job of Supreme Allied Commander of South-East Asia. What do you think of that?"'

Mountbatten said, after a pause to digest this astonishing proposal, that he would like twenty-four hours to think it over. Churchill provocatively asked him if he was afraid he couldn't do the job.

'Not at all,' said Mountbatten. "I have a congenital weakness for feeling certain I can do anything, but I do want to ask the British and US Chiefs of Staff to satisfy myself that they agree with your choice wholeheartedly and will back me to the full.'

Churchill assured him that he had the support of the President. 'He's as keen as I am, but you can talk to the Chiefs.'

Mountbatten always claimed that he satisfied himself in his own unique way and with his usual destroyer-like speed, starting with Field-Marshal Sir Alan 'Brookie' Brooke, who assured him that all the Chiefs thought he was the right man for the job. 'If I don't like your Generals out there, can I sack them?' Mountbatten asked.

'We can consider it,' said Brooke.

'That's not the point,' Mountbatten insisted. 'Do you trust me enough – can I send you a signal saying I am sending so and so home?'

Brooke agreed; and Mountbatten next pinned down the Chief of the Air Staff. Portal not only agreed at once but added, 'If you like we can go through the list and shift some of them around now.'

A day or two earlier, by chance Mountbatten had literally saved the First Sea Lord's life, when he had stumbled on the edge of a ravine during a sightseeing trip – further confirmation that Dudley Pound's health was failing. There had been no further opportunity of discussing a sea-going appointment. Now the old Admiral enthusiastically welcomed Mountbatten's appointment. 'This is absolutely splendid, Dickie, to have the Navy getting this job. Now you understand why I couldn't let you talk about going back to sea.'

Mountbatten thanked him, and followed up smartly with the question, 'Can I sack anybody – including James Somerville?' Somerville was C-in-C of the Eastern Fleet and was already a post-captain when Mountbatten had been a sub-lieutenant, twenty-three years his junior. Nor was he an easy man to work with.

Pound replied, 'Well, no, Dickie, obviously you can't. We can't have a young chap like you going out and sacking all the admirals.'

At once Mountbatten said, 'Thank you very much, sir. I don't want the job. You know I want to go back to sea, and this lets me out.'

Pound said he did not understand, and Mountbatten continued, 'You don't think I'd go out there with the authority to sack generals and air marshals and not officers of my own service?'

'Have you really had this permission from the others?'

Mountbatten confirmed that he indeed had, and Pound reluctantly agreed. 'Well, yes, I suppose so. But you mustn't abuse it.'

'No,' said Mountbatten, 'I won't abuse it, but I shall certainly hold you to that.'

Mountbatten recounted this episode many times, and it has frequently been printed. But, at best, it is an over-simplified account of what happened at Quebec. Field-Marshal Lord Alanbrooke and Marshal of the RAF Lord Portal, when questioned about it after the war,[4] both denied that Mountbatten had been given this authority. And Dudley Pound's successor as First Sea Lord confirmed that only Churchill, or the Minister concerned, had the power to sack a C-in-C, so that these Chiefs of Staff were not even in a position to grant Mountbatten the power he insisted they gave him as a condition of his acceptance of the appointment.

No doubt Mountbatten sought, and was granted, unusually strong independent power to appoint and sack without reference to his Chiefs, but certainly not the dictatorial power he claimed. But this story of his, like so many others, is more self-glorifying and the better for being without qualification.

Having now, as he claimed, 'cleared the British team', Mountbatten said that he set about the American Chiefs of Staff. There was, it seems, no serious trouble with any of them. George Marshall said, 'Sure – sack anyone you like so long as the President confirms you have the authority.' General H.H. 'Hap' Arnold said the same thing, and Ernie King (now an old friend) not only agreed but offered Mountbatten one of his biggest aircraft-carriers, the *Saratoga*. As Britain had flatly refused to lend the US Navy a carrier in the desperate post-Pearl Harbor days, this was particularly magnanimous.

'After that, I went to see the President,' said Mountbatten. 'And he gave me a little lecture. He said, "Now don't forget that you're an *Allied* commander. Ike [General Dwight D. Eisenhower] is loyal to your King and you've got to be loyal to me. It's a matter of trust. I trust you to act not from the point of view of your country but from the point of view of the war effort – the Allied cause."

'I agreed with all that and asked, "Can I fire your generals if I think it's essential?"

'And Roosevelt replied, "With pleasure. But don't fire them directly. Send me a personal telegram saying PLEASE REMOVE THIS OFFICER. It can be Stilwell [Lieutenant-General J.W. 'Vinegar Joe' Stilwell, already in China, and Mountbatten's nominated Deputy]. But don't say 'You're fired!' I'll do that."

'I said, "Thank you very much," and went back to Winston. "All right," I said. "All six say yes, and the President agrees, so I'm prepared to go."'

Mountbatten returned to his quarters in the Château Frontenac. 'I drew up a chair, sat down, took a blank sheet of paper and began to write down all the things I would have to do. Before I had even finished, there was a knock on the door. It was Bill Donovan, Head of the OSS. "Let me be the first to congratulate you on being appointed Supreme Allied Commander South-East Asia."

'I was appalled. It was still white-hot secret. "I don't know what you're talking about. Why do you come barging in here talking complete nonsense? Anyway, I'm much too young – half-way down the captains' list."

'"You can't fool me," he said. "Why do you think we're here? I've got spies everywhere. I know that the PM and the President have offered you the job."

' "Well, supposing you're right, why do you come and worry me about it?"

'Quick as a shot, Bill replied, "Because I want your permission to operate in South-East Asia."

'I told him that Joe Stilwell was already there so why didn't he ask him. "That bastard won't let me operate with him. He's a prejudiced old son-of-a-bitch. But you've been working with SIS and SOE so you know what we're all about."

' "Are you any good?" I asked him.

' "You bet we're good."

' "Then I'm going to test you." The test was to get me two best seats for *Oklahoma* when I was due to stay in New York for a couple of nights with my flag-lieutenant.

'He nearly exploded. "Goddamn it, that's impossible. There are absolutely *no* seats for six months. How do you expect me ... ?"

' "No seats for *Oklahoma*, no operations in South-East Asia." Then I threw him out.

'A few days later, he met us in New York. He had two best seats and two of the prettiest girls in New York for the evening for Arthur Leveson and me. After the show, we all went to a night club. On the way out, there were a couple of photographers in the foyer. By this time, Bill thought he was in. But I said, "If those photographs are published, not only are you out, but I'll probably be out, too." And in a flash, two toughs suddenly appeared and marched off with the photographers.'

Immediately after receiving Mountbatten's agreement, Churchill sent telegrams to all those closely concerned with the most important outcome of the Quebec Conference. To the Viceroy of India, Lord Linlithgow, who would be most affected by the decision, Churchill wrote:

We have now formed and set up the South-East Asia Command, separate from the command in India.... We have had some discussions with the Americans in the weeks that have passed upon the person of the commander. After a great deal of consideration I decided to propose Lord Louis Mountbatten for this very important post. Mountbatten has unique qualifications, in that he is intimately acquainted with all three branches of the Services, and also with amphibious operations. He ... knows the whole of our war story from the centre. I regard this as of great importance on account of the extremely varied character of the South-East Asia front by land and sea. Mountbatten is a fine organizer and a man of great energy and daring.[5]

On the following day, 25 August 1943, the appointment was made public officially. And that was the reason why Mountbatten was being hounded, even more than usual, by photographers.

Had those night club pictures been published, they would have been accompanied by a story, and this story would, most likely, have been critical of Mountbatten's appointment. Many Americans, and a number of powerful politicians, were incensed when they learned that this new Command was to be led by a British officer – and a young, recently elevated, naval officer at that. It was one thing to be popular as a royal playboy in peacetime, and the hero of the *Kelly* (and *In Which We Serve*) in wartime. But this appointment was seen as a snub to General MacArthur. 'It would be a tragic thing,' wrote one columnist, 'if MacArthur were to be shorn of his authority while a London glamour boy is elevated.'[6]

The anti-Mountbatten lobby in the American Senate was led by H. Styles Bridges, a Republican from New Hampshire and a member of the Senate's military affairs committee. Letters were 'planted' in newspapers all over the USA. 'A wave of anger will sweep this nation,' ran one, if it should turn out that 'America's No 1 hero MacArthur is to play a subordinate role to ex-playboy Mountbatten....'

In the end, Churchill protested to Roosevelt. Mountbatten, he told the President, 'has been affected by accounts telegraphed here describing him as "the British princeling and glamour boy who has ousted the proved veteran...."'[7]

The campaign simmered, died down in the press of events, was briefly revived, and then finally ended some eight months later.

In the last weeks of 1941 and the early months of 1942, the free world had watched in wonder and fear the spread of Japanese power across the globe. Few observers had recognized the eventual disaster that must overwhelm Japan as a result of the attack on the American Fleet at Pearl Harbor; and only a few far-sighted members of the Japanese High Command recognized that if Japan did not force America to agree to surrender terms swiftly, the Imperial Japanese Empire must eventually be doomed.

At one time American defeat seemed very close, when the Japanese Navy controlled most of the Pacific and Indian Oceans, and the Japanese armies were at the doors of India, had conquered huge areas of French, British and Dutch territory, the Philippines and vast numbers of Pacific islands, and had penetrated deep into China. The tide had been turned at Midway by a handful of US Navy fliers, but the Japanese were even more tenacious on the defensive than they had been swift and successful on the offensive. The war was clearly going to be long and arduous.

In August 1943 Japanese arms were opposed by hundreds of millions of Chinese, a great part of the rapidly growing American military machine, a substantial Indian Army, and British, Commonwealth, French, Dutch, Burmese, Gurkha and East and West African troops. This ring about Japan comprised four commands – those of Admiral Chester W. Nimitz in the Central Pacific; General Douglas MacArthur in the South-West Pacific; Generalissimo Chiang Kai-shek in China; and now, despite widespread American antipathy, Mountbatten in South-East Asia. Of these, the two American commands were doing best. Chiang Kai-shek was fighting a desperate battle, relying for supplies on the Americans. The British command was in a sorry mess.

It was this deplorable and humiliating situation that was to occupy all the creative energies, the inspiration, tact and diplomacy which Mountbatten could muster for the next two years – twenty-four epochal months of unprecedented strain and achievement in a life of eighty years.

After his two nights in New York, Mountbatten proceeded to Washington to pay what he called his 'official respects' to the President and the Chiefs of Staff. 'They couldn't have been better or kinder,' he said. 'I was wearing a khaki uniform, and I called on Ernie King for the last time. We chatted for a while and then I said – eyeing his uniform – "Admiral, I have a very great favour to ask you. I want to ask you for something of yours which must be very precious to you."

'He looked at me doubtfully. "Carriers?" he asked. "More carriers?"

'"No, not carriers. I just want one of your buttons. Will you cut that button from your coat and give it to me?"

'"What in hell's name ... ?"

'"Look, Ernie," I said, "I'm going to have a button of yours, and one from George Marshall, one from Hap Arnold – Brookie's going to give me one, and so is Peter Portal. Just five buttons, that's all I ask."

'Ernie laughed for a long time, then took a pair of scissors and cut it off. I got all the others, too, and had them sewn on to a coat. I still wear it sometimes.'

When Mountbatten left the American continent at the end of August, it was as if he were following that old appeal of Kipling, whom he so admired, and in careful truth and steadfastness was taking over 'the yoke in youth'. For Dudley Pound was dying at the time when his young protégé, representing his beloved Royal Navy, took up his new command. He was looking very ill when Mountbatten had last seen him, and suffered the first of several strokes on his arrival in Washington. Pound eventually made it back to England, dying on 21 October – Trafalgar Day – 1943.

Churchill, suddenly in poor health himself and increasingly concerned about his First Sea Lord, was now worried about the decision that most of what he called his 'war machine' was returning to England by air without him. Without the navigational aids and the engine reliability we take for granted today, these long-distance flights posed many natural hazards in addition to the very real risk of interception by the enemy. The Duke of Kent, Admiral Yamamoto, General Gott (en route to take over the 8th Army), Air Marshal Leigh-Mallory, the bandleader Glenn Miller, were only a few of the many who were killed flying on wartime duties.

Alan Brooke, Eden, Portal, Jacob, Mountbatten and others were due to take off in a flying boat from the St Lawrence River below Quebec on the morning of 28 August for the direct flight home.

'Splashing about in his bath,' as Eden described him shortly before their departure, and agreeing to take a long rest, Churchill in maudlin mood told him, 'I don't know what I should do if I lost you all. I'd have to cut my throat. It isn't just love, though there is much of that in it, but that you are my war machine. Brookie, Portal, you and Dickie. I simply couldn't replace you.'[8]

By any reasonable law of averages, a man with an accident-prone record, who had experienced two serious train crashes, should have had at least one serious – if not fatal – air crash in the course of his wartime flying, hundreds of thousands of miles of it. In his new Command Mountbatten flew in single-engine 'spotter' machines of doubtful reliability, bombers of all kinds, countless C47 Dakotas (very reliable, unlike the weather conditions and landing strips) and flying boats.

In the course of his morale-boosting tours, he once flew 600 miles southwest of Ceylon to Addu Atoll. On arrival, he told his audience, 'I am the Supremo and as such I have come to see you all. As I am "important" many precautions are taken for my safety, so the Navy despatched several ships on the route here in case my aircraft ditched. Additionally, the RAF sent a Sunderland flying boat out ahead in case it was needed to rescue me. I flew here in an American Mitchell B25 bomber fitted with extra tanks. On the way the radio operator sitting next to me stubbed out his cigarette on a metal can, so I said, "What's inside?" and he said, "Gas!" So much for saving the Supremo.'[9]

On take-off for the return flight, the pilot left the autopilot on 'engaged' and the Mitchell nearly crashed. So Mountbatten returned in the reserve Sunderland. The pilot warned, 'It'll mean a night flight and I haven't flown one of these at night for a year or so.' It was not only pitch-dark but a thunderstorm was raging when they reached Ceylon. The great flying boat got down all right, however, and the pilot said, 'My passenger was completely calm throughout. He even left me a note thanking me for the trip.'[10]

It was another flying boat, a 'Clipper', in which Churchill's 'war machine' returned, before Mountbatten took up his command eighteen months earlier. The nineteen-hour flight went off without a hitch, and the great Boeing touched down in Poole harbour, Dorset, to the utmost relief of the British War Cabinet as well as the White House staff. Mountbatten hastened with the others to London. Edwina and George VI were among the first people who greeted him.

Mountbatten had just one month to prepare himself and his staff and to learn all that he could about the state of the war with Japan and those fighting it. From that single sheet of paper which he had begun to fill in at the Château Frontenac, he swiftly built up the structure of his command.

'I chose Al Wedemeyer as Deputy Chief of Staff – an American, one of Marshall's smartest staff officers – a tricky customer but very loyal to me. As Chief of Staff, I chose an Englishman, Pownall, a very good mediator. Marshall had recommended to me "Specs" Wheeler, who was already out there, and I took him on as Allied Principal Administrative Officer.* Winston had told me he wanted me to take on Wingate, for what he was worth. He was a great hero, and Winston liked heroes. Wingate's Chindits were famous for their deep penetrations behind the Japanese lines, but they suffered dreadful casualties, mainly due to lack of air support of their own. I got them this, through Hap Arnold, and we called it "No. 1 Air Commando". I hoped now that there would be no more of this leaving behind of the wounded with a revolver, six shots and some rations, which I thought was very bad.'

The set-up Mountbatten was inheriting consisted, on the ground, of Eastern Army under General Sir George Giffard; an Eastern Fleet consisting of a single ancient battleship, an escort carrier, seven cruisers and a handful of destroyers, submarines and auxiliary craft under Somerville; and a relatively much more modern and numerous Air Force, Eastern Air Command, under Air Chief Marshal Sir Richard Peirse.

Mountbatten's relations with all three commanders lacked mutual trust from the start. With Somerville the difficulties were compounded by a daft directive that Mountbatten had no control of his fleet when it was operating in the western end of its area of responsibility. In his characteristic way, Mountbatten wasted no time complaining about this and other anomalies, pitfalls and hazards. His business was to get on with things.

Before he had been rudely interrupted by Bill Donovan, Mountbatten

* General Raymond A. Wheeler. Others mentioned here are General Albert C. Wedemeyer and Lieutenant-General Sir Henry Pownall, c-in-c Persia–Iraq.

had got as far as putting down his own initial 'M' three times on his piece of paper. He already knew a good deal about what was going on in Burma, for Combined Ops must eventually be involved on every fighting front, and about the only way of defeating the Japanese finally in that terrible terrain of jungle, swamp and mountains was by landing along the coast in amphibious operations, just as the landing at Salerno (a week after Mountbatten returned from Quebec) was intended to cut off the Germans in Italy.

Now Mountbatten completed in London the private exercise he had begun in Quebec, and under the first 'M' he put 'Morale'. 'It hardly existed,' he said. 'It had sunk so low because defeatism was rampant and so many of the troops were being cut off by the Japs. I put down three means of correcting this state of low morale. First, I'd try and pick the right Generals. Second, I'd go round stumping on a soap box, much as I had done at Combined Ops. Third, I'd start a paper, call it *SEAC*, and I thought of two men at once who should be involved – one was Charles Eade of *The Sunday Dispatch*, another was Frank Owen, who had edited the *Evening Standard* so brilliantly for Max before the war, and among the others was Ian Coster. I wanted this paper to be closely linked with the British Press so that the families at home would feel proud of their chaps out there – who had absolutely no chance of home leave for years on end – and they would feel in touch with what was happening at home.'

The second 'M' that Mountbatten put down, firmly and irrevocably, was 'Monsoon'. He had learned to his astonishment that for five months in every year the British Army did not fight, due to the monsoon. It was just like the British Grand Fleet in World War I which did not fight at night because it had not practised, which was one reason why the German Fleet escaped at Jutland. 'I saw no reason why we shouldn't fight right through the monsoon. It would obviously give us a tremendous advantage to do so.'

Then there was 'M' for 'Malaria'. 'I can't remember the exact figures which I had put down in Quebec, but as far as I recall 130 per cent of the Eastern Army got malaria every year. That is, on average, everyone got it once, and a third of them for a second time. Scrub typhus was another menace, and the ratio of battle casualties to disease casualties was something like one to a hundred. For a start, I persuaded Winston to let me have a Medical Adviser in Chief to head a Medical Advisory Division. With the help of that old German invention, DDT, Paludrine and other drugs, mosquito-repellent, orders to wear long sleeves and long trousers, the ratio soon started to tumble, until we seriously considered making malaria a disciplinary offence. We never did, but COs were told that if they reported more than two or three cases, they'd be sacked. This gave us a huge advantage because the Japs had been suffering as badly as us and went on doing so, fighting nature instead of us.'

Finally, 'M' for 'Movement' – an additional item. No longer must units be surrounded and cut off from supplies, their morale slumping to zero so that everything seemed to confirm that the Japs were unbeatable. There must be mobility on the ground at all times, and where necessary, supplies must be flown in. Constant movement on the ground and in the air and at sea to keep the Japs on the run, never knowing where the next attack would come from.

To fly in supplies, as the Chinese were now being supplied exclusively, meant aircraft in great numbers; and that brought Mountbatten up against the hard fact that as far as war materials was concerned his new command might have been the most important item on the Quebec agenda, but was at the bottom when it came to priorities. 'We were worse than at the bottom,' said Mountbatten, 'because we often had to send back stuff that we had managed to squeeze out of the Chiefs of Staff – like some 5.5-inch ammunition, for example, a calibre of shell that was the only answer to the Japanese foxhole. And landing craft. . . .'

Under the 'Morale' heading, sub-heading 'Sense of Identity', one of the decisions that could be made in the few weeks remaining in London was the design of a badge for Mountbatten's new army. Mountbatten's abiding interest in heraldry and genealogy gave him a head start when it came to design, and he rather fancied himself as a designer and letterer. Shortly before his death, he recast for the publisher the jacket design of his parents' dual biography, much to its advantage, in about one minute flat. By 1943 Mountbatten had already designed the insignia for Edwina's St John Ambulance uniform, and the flash for Combined Ops, which consisted of RAF wings, an infantryman's rifle and a naval anchor, all in blue and gold.

For his new Command, Mountbatten sketched out a circle of red on white, representing the enemy, with a blue sword cutting a slice. It was warmly approved all round, and an order for a million was despatched to America. Then, by chance, it was seen by an Oriental authority at the Foreign Office who, in horror, protested that any prisoner wearing this blatant insult to the sacred emblem of Japan would certainly be tortured to death instantly.

So that was scrapped, to Mountbatten's chagrin, and later someone came up with the idea of a phoenix, which became, as one wag put it, 'the burning question of the day'. Someone else, who happened to have a first edition of *Lady Chatterley's Lover*, recommended the phoenix used as a device on all D.H. Lawrence's books. 'Lady Chatterley's Plover!' was Mountbatten's disgusted comment; and got to work himself again.

'I was still working on it during my last night in England,' Mountbatten said. He was very proud of his phoenix. When one of his staff was asked what it meant, he explained that: 'It represents the transition from the futile fumblings of the past into the flaming fantasy of the future.' But the facetious comment was not made within the hearing of Mountbatten, who took this sort of thing seriously.

Mountbatten took off with his staff on 4 October 1943 in a Douglas C47 lent to him by Churchill and named by Mountbatten *Marco Polo*, signalling both his enthusiasm for that game and that he was going out East. Like all his subsequent planes, it was fitted with every luxury Mountbatten could lay his hands on, and among his considerable luggage was a box of chocolates for the eight-year-old King of Iraq, to be presented *en route*.

His arrival in New Delhi was received with mixed feelings. There was plenty of the old hostility and suspicion which had greeted him in the past when he came on board a new ship. There was also a deep sense of relief among many of the senior officers of all services. In spite of Dieppe, still regarded as a black mark by most people, his work at Combined Ops could not be denied him; and the glittering image of the rich playboy, spoilt by wealth and royal connections, had faded into the dark reality of four years of war.

General Giffard entertained the gravest doubts and thought Mountbatten far too young and inexperienced. The Air Force usually tended to be more sympathetic than the Army to Mountbatten: a youthful service's fellow feeling for youth perhaps, for he rarely had any trouble with airmen. The outgoing Viceroy, Lord Linlithgow, was to be replaced within a few days by Mountbatten's old friend, Field-Marshal Archibald Wavell, who referred to Mountbatten as 'the boy champion' and was not the only one to predict that he was in for some rude shocks and a shattering of his optimism.

SEAC did not formally come into being, and Acting (now full) Admiral Lord Louis Mountbatten become its Supreme Commander, until midnight 15–16 November 1943. But he was in action at once, expressing a wish to continue his flight, with scarcely a pause, to Chungking to see Chiang Kai-shek.

Mountbatten sensed that the Generalissimo was going to be his own equivalent of Churchill's de Gaulle – the worst cross he had to bear, the Cross of Lorraine; and he was absolutely right. Mountbatten wanted to leave at once, with only one or two of his staff, mostly Americans, to make contact with the Generalissimo and Stilwell and his party. At the last minute he was warned that it would be a more than usually dangerous trip.

'I was almost ready to take-off', said Mountbatten, 'when the Chinese Foreign Minister, who was also the Generalissimo's brother-in-law T.V.

Soong, arrived on the scene. "Please don't fly out now," he pleaded with me urgently. "The Japs are lying in wait for you on the Hump, they know you are coming and will shoot you down."

'This was just an occupational risk which I had to take, and I told him I had to disregard the warning. Then Soong tried another tack. "I must be there before you. The Generalissimo wants to talk to me before you come."

'This was confirmed by the American General Bill Somerville, who had been sent out by Roosevelt to explain to Chiang Kai-shek about the new SEAC. So I put off my flight.

'But the Japs had a complete sweep and shot down a record number of sixteen aircraft on the day I was to fly. When I did get over the Hump and arrived in Chungking, the reception was sticky all round. In fact there wasn't any from the Generalissimo. I didn't see him for three days.'

General 'Vinegar Joe' Stilwell was a man of complex character in an almost impossibly complicated position. He was already Chief-of-Staff to Chiang Kai-shek and Commander of the Americans in the China theatre, when he was given the additional task of Mountbatten's Deputy in his new Command. He was therefore now responsible through Mountbatten to the Allied Combined Chiefs of Staff, through General Marshall to the American Joint Chiefs of Staff, and to the Generalissimo himself.

Stilwell shared the general American view that the British were fighting for the sole purpose of recovering the large chunks of their colonial empire the Japanese had taken from them, all the way to Singapore and Hong Kong. Stilwell's political officer, John Paton Davies Jnr, had already explained all this to his master, also declaring that the American presence in India and Burma was for this reason only an embarrassment to the British; but, if there was to be a partnership, the British were determined to dominate it. Thus Mountbatten's appointment as Supreme Commander.

Stilwell, always receptive to anything anti-British, agreed vehemently and was set to give Mountbatten almost as unwelcoming a reception as those Japanese Zero fighters had intended for him. But then a curious thing happened which had quite unintended repercussions. Before Mountbatten's plane landed, Chiang Kai-shek sacked Stilwell, just like that. If Mountbatten had been puzzled by Soong's concern for his safety, and his own need to reach Chungking first, all was now clear. Soong brought with him Roosevelt's approval of Stilwell's dismissal – if the Generalissimo insisted.

Chiang Kai-shek did insist. The Generalissimo had lost face as a result of Stilwell's efforts to reform the corrupt and reluctant Chinese Army. He had had enough of the American's criticisms.

Mountbatten learned of the loss of his Deputy as soon as he landed. 'It

was a disaster. Stilwell was a fine fighting soldier and he was the only man
who could get the Chinese to behave,' said Mountbatten. 'I went straight
to his HQ and he confirmed that he had been thrown out. I took him by
the arm and led him outside where there were a lot of photographers and
reporters waiting to record our meeting.'

Stilwell appeared uncharacteristically reluctant to meet them. 'Don't be
seen shaking hands with me,' he told Mountbatten, 'or you'll be finished,
too.' Mountbatten insisted, however, and the two men shook hands and
smiled at one another.

Then Mountbatten said, 'Do you want this job back?'

Stilwell said, 'You bet.'

'Well, I'll give it back to you.'

'You can't,' said Stilwell. 'He's made his decision, it's a matter of "face".'

'I can give it back very easily. You see.'

Mountbatten went to Soong. 'Tell the Generalissimo that I've no Chinese
armies. Not one Chinese soldier will be moved one yard nearer to the enemy
on the orders of General Stilwell. They can rot as far as I'm concerned.
You tell him that. And if he doesn't believe me, he's making the biggest
mistake of his life. Tell him I'm one of those curious people who mean what
they say. Tell him his ruddy Chinese are right out of the fighting from now
on.'

As Mountbatten controlled every plane supplying Chiang Kai-shek and
transporting every one of his soldiers, the Generalissimo either had to re-
instate the American or accept the greater loss of face in taking no part in
the new SEAC's future campaigns. Stilwell got his job back.

According to 'Vinegar Joe's' biographer, Stilwell's first reaction to
Mountbatten's defence of his office was to say that Mountbatten was only
'burned up because he'll have to work with a new man. Wants me to wait
over and break him in.'[11] But later Mountbatten's straight manner, ease,
authority and tact made its usual impression. Mountbatten, Stilwell decided,
had not only saved his job at a tricky time; he was 'a good egg, energetic
and willing to do anything to make it go'.

From this time, the two men got on brilliantly. 'He thought I was wonderful,' said Mountbatten. 'So wonderful that he came to stay with me in Delhi
and we became great personal friends. But just to show how difficult he
could be, and how well we got on, he once made the unanswerable remark,
"Admiral, I like working with you. You're the only Limey I've known that
wants to fight." A very curious fellow. He hated the British, was rude and
prejudiced, didn't like staff work. But he could train the Chinese and could
lead them in battle. And that made him pricelessly valuable.'

Even Chiang Kai-shek succumbed to the Mountbatten touch, and when the two men parted they had developed a working relationship. 'But he was always a problem,' said Mountbatten. 'He didn't speak a word of English and didn't want to. He didn't care twopence for our problems or the logistics of getting supplies to him. He just wanted more and more of everything. He was also extremely rude and didn't think much of our fighting capacity. He was really my worst headache.'

An old acquaintance from the Norwegian campaign, a man whose life Mountbatten had probably saved at Namsos, now did a very great deal to ease relations between Mountbatten's SEAC and its giant, difficult neighbour across the mountains, casting his single beady eye in turn on the Supremo and the Generalissimo, willing them to remain on speaking terms. General Carton de Wiart had succeeded in remaining in the fighting line after Norway, had been captured, and had successfully escaped from his Italian prisoner-of-war camp. Churchill decreed that he should have a quieter time for a while, and sent him out East as his personal liaison officer to Chiang Kai-Shek. It was a curious choice as the General was noted first for his fighting prowess, but it worked very well, and he became Mountbatten's ambassador, too.

The other prominent and effective ambassador at Chungking was another General, the Frenchman Petchkoff, who became a great friend with de Wiart. As they both had one arm, one eye, and a great number of medals, the Chinese may have gained a curious conception of the qualifications in the West for a diplomatic career.

Although de Wiart always referred to Mountbatten behind his back as 'Archduke Charles', he had a high regard for him, and later recounted this anecdote:

> Dickie Mountbatten is a curious mixture of royal democracy; he can mix equally well on a high or low level and be exactly right in each. He was inspecting some American posts, and it was obvious that the Americans had been well primed beforehand as to their behaviour. All went swimmingly until Mountbatten came up to a certain sentry who immediately stretched out his hand and said: 'I'm Brown from Texas.' Mountbatten, not the least taken aback, shook the outstretched hand and answered: 'There are a lot of you Texans out here.' Whereupon the soldier replied: 'Yes, that's why the war's going so well.'[12]

Among multi-national, multi-racial Allies, this quick adaptability was a priceless asset, and worth hundreds of guns. One of Mountbatten's shrewdest choices for his staff was John Keswick as political officer. De Wiart had a great deal to do with him and regarded him highly, too. 'He was very knowledgeable and gave me much valuable advice. He seemed to have a different attitude from that of the others who knew China intimately, for they all appeared to shrug their shoulders, content to explain that "East is East and West is West...."[13]

He was also 'very struck with Wedemeyer; he was a charming man, tall, well-built, with a young face and white hair, and he was a perfect staff officer with quick wits and sound judgment.'[14]

During the early months of his command, Mountbatten's first offensive had to be directed against apathy, defeatism, and morale as deep as the Chindwin River. Moreover, it had to be fought at every level, and a new spirit, a new philosophy of fighting, an entirely new attitude of mind, instilled.

It was easiest to effect this revolution of will and mind with the troops, and Mountbatten was always at his best with them. He made so many morale-boosting visits to so many units – a mere platoon sometimes within grenade distance of the enemy, or a massed battalion on a barrack square – that he worked out an act as carefully scripted and timed as any put on by the ENSA professional performers whom he was, at the same time, persuading to come out to entertain the Forces.

In the early days the script, delivered as always from the conveniently available box, invariably began, 'Gather round so you can all hear me.... Right, now I understand people think you're the Forgotten Army. I understand you all talk about yourselves as the Forgotten Army on the Forgotten Front. I've come here to tell you you're quite wrong. You're not the Forgotten Army on the Forgotten Front. No, make no mistake about it. Nobody's ever *heard* of you!'

This always caught their attention. He had his audience with him, and he went on from there. 'Now the picture's changing. People are hearing about us, and they're going to hear more. From now on they'll be hearing about our victories. If the Japs try their old dodge of infiltrating behind you and cutting your lines of supplies and communications, you're going to stay put. There's going to be no more retreating, and you'll be supplied from the air, and that's my job.' Then he would talk about the enemy. 'Who started this story of the Jap superman? I've seen them at work in Japan. Most of them are unintelligent slum people, with no factory laws, no freedom, no trades unions. They've got nothing that we take for granted – nothing at all except an ignorant, fanatical idea that their Emperor is God....'

Short, sharp, confidently delivered, confidence-inspiring, so gripping and memorable that, nearly forty years later, many of those who listened then can remember every word today. Sikhs, West Africans, Americans, Hindu and Moslem Indians, French and Dutch, and Burmese, an English corporal from Tyneside who hadn't heard from his wife for three months, a Belfast Irishman with septic blisters, and a Glaswegian sergeant still hoarse from morning drill – all of them in their khaki drill, upturned faces shining with sweat, listened and felt comfort and inspiration.

Major R. A. Cooper, MC, in command of B Company, 9th Battalion Border Regiment, remembered him when he was in the Chin Hills, 9,000 feet up. Mountbatten had driven two hundred miles over mud tracks in his jeep with just two members of his staff. He had come to make himself known to widely scattered companies, including these twenty men, to give them encouragement in a very trying, very dangerous outpost. The major, with an injured hand, had just returned from an arduous patrol on which he had successfully ambushed a Japanese column.

'He stood on his well-known soap box, dressed in a bush jacket like us, and began talking, telling us our position absolutely straight, without frills. He seemed to have a complete understanding of what we were up to, and how we felt. It was a marvellous tonic. We could feel our spirits revive as he talked, and felt we had some place in the general scheme of things. Then he enquired about our needs and promised to get what he could for us. . . .'[15]

Mountbatten worked out a quite different technique to deal with officers at big-scale inspections. 'I would get an ADC to write down every officer's name above the rank of Captain [Army] upwards, adding anything special about them, professionally or domestically, any special awards and so on,' said Mountbatten. 'You could call it calculated, but it worked.' Then he would have the officers fallen in at double intervals to allow privacy, for he had the same two questions for every one and did not want to be overheard.

'How long have you been out here . . .?' And, 'Where do you come from?' In most cases, he knew the place and talked about it briefly before moving on.

The sergeants came next, and the same formula would be followed, before he called them to gather round for his speech, at the end of which he would usually introduce some topic or future event that he gave the impression was confidential, although it was really nothing of the kind, but certainly encouraged further a sense of solidarity and sympathy.

Meanwhile, the senior officers' names were all noted and filed, and the office system was organized so that if anything important happened to them, or they were killed or got a bravery award, a letter would automatically be typed out and would land on Mountbatten's desk. 'Dear Major so-and-so, I congratulate you on your well deserved MC. I well remember discussing Bodiam Castle near your home on. . . .' Or, 'Dear Mrs so-and-so. Your loss, I fear, is a terrible one, and I would like you to accept my condolences. . . . When I last talked to your husband. . . . He was a very brave officer, and it was a privilege. . . .' He signed them by the score without even glancing at them. A grandson of one of Queen Mary's old ladies-in-waiting received one of these letters after he had been wounded. 'Queen Mary asked me after the war how I had time, with all that was going on, to keep in personal touch with him? "He was your slave for life!" she told me....'

Two interesting things, which reflected the new and the old spirit of fighting the Burma war, happened at one of Mountbatten's earliest visits. It was at Calcutta on the way back to Delhi from Chungking, at the HQ of the 3rd Tactical Air Force. Air Marshal Sir John Baldwin was the Commander. 'A great man,' said Mountbatten. 'I was asked if I'd like to meet the senior officers, and I said yes. They were all lined up, over a hundred of them, colonels American and British, group captains and the rest. I said my usual piece, fighting through the monsoon, fighting tropical diseases, and so on.

'Afterwards, a chap came up to me, a brigadier of about my age. I'd played polo with him before the war. And he said "Dickie, why don't you take a tip from an old friend? What you've just been telling us, it won't wash you know – all this march on, fly on, fight on. You don't yet know what it's like out here. And for God's sake, don't put the troops in these disease-ridden places – they'll die like flies." I listened but didn't say anything. He had plenty more to say, all about competing with the terrain, which is what I had told them we had to do. He ended up by saying, and he was very friendly about it, "I'm afraid your speech went down rather badly, Dickie." So I said, "Oh, I'm sorry about that." I really was surprised because I thought it had gone down rather well.

'But something else, more important and more encouraging than this, happened too. I met the 15th Corps Commander,' said Mountbatten. 'He was called Bill Slim and he was very tough looking. I took the most violent liking to him at once, and I said, "Would you like to be the Army C-in-C?" He said he would. He also said, "Let's change this ghastly name Eastern Army. Let's just get a number."' And that was how one of the most effective partnerships of the war was sealed; and the 14th Army got its name.

George Giffard was, according to Mountbatten, 'a dear old fellow, and as obstinate as hell'. He represented everything non-Japanese that Mountbatten had come out to fight. He was reactionary, defeatist, inflexible. He was also, unfortunately, a sort of living caricature of Stilwell's idea of a British general. It was not surprising that they could not get along at all and 'Vinegar Joe' refused to serve under him.

Mountbatten recounted a skirmish with Giffard at a staff meeting some time after his arrival at HQ.

'I want some divisions to fight in the monsoon,' Mountbatten demanded.

'I've none to spare,' parried the C-in-C.

'All right, then I'll have to ask you for a list of all the Divisions in South-

East Asia and India, what they're doing and which, in order of priority, can't be spared.'

Later, Giffard approached Mountbatten and said, 'Supremo as I understand it, your job is to tell me to produce the troops, and I then produce the troops. Is that right?'

Mountbatten confirmed that that was so.

'I tell you, Supremo, there are no troops available. Can't you spare the time to come and check for yourself? Then you'll see I'm telling the truth.'

'If I don't get the troops from you then there'll be no fighting during the monsoon.'

Giffard pounced on that. 'That's just what we shouldn't be doing.'

Mountbatten then told him that it was the Supreme Commander's decision whether or not there was to be fighting during the monsoon, and he had decided that there was to be.

Giffard said, 'If I don't make any troops available, does that mean you've lost confidence in me?'

'If you don't help me – then, yes.'

Later, Mountbatten had to ask Pownall to demand a relief. The moment it was known he was going, Giffard let him have as many troops as he wanted. 'I'm no longer responsible,' he said in explanation of this sudden change.

The early days at Delhi were chaotic. If he had been starting from scratch, it would have been comparatively simple. Mountbatten was trying to put together an entirely new Command out of the sorry, disillusioned mess of an old Command that had become discredited in its own eyes, and was made up of numerous nationalities, many of them in full-scale departmental war with one another. No one trusted anyone else, and *everything* was in short, sometimes desperately short, supply – transport, weapons, clothes, medicines, ammunition, fuel. . . .

'There were just a few of us to get things started, and we worked from day to day, supported by the certain truth that every day things *must* get better if only because they couldn't get worse,' said Mountbatten. 'The first thing was to make contact, make friends. It wasn't the men who were wrong – Slim had been there for a long time, after all – it was the leadership and the spirit.

'It's quite a big thing to set up an Allied HQ to deal with a war and over a million men with nothing to start with and no one willing to help. If Chiang Kai-shek was my first difficulty in China, Auchinleck was my first difficulty at home. He had had a very rough going over from Winston, been kicked out of North Africa by him and was c-in-c Indian Army. He was supposed to be training my troops, and my HQ was actually in his area. So that was very tricky. He was touchy as hell and it took me about six weeks to break him down. However, things gradually began to get into shape.'

Nor was there much time. A high-level conference was due to take place at Cairo at the end of November, at which the Allied chiefs were due to sort out their priorities and difficulties before 'The Big Three' (Roosevelt, Churchill and Stalin) met at Teheran later in the month. Mountbatten was due to present his plans for the defeat of Japan in South-East Asia, and Chiang K ai-shek and Stilwell would be among those flying in from the East.

It was a reassuring and enjoyable get-together for friends and those who understood one another, especially Churchill and Roosevelt, and Marshall, Mountbatten and Brooke. But there was a great deal of fighting, too; much of it so fierce that the word 'Allies' took on a new reversed meaning. At one moment Brooke (supercilious) and King (straight talkin') were almost reduced to fisticuffs, according to some who were present.

Amid searchlight beams of curiosity, the Chinese delegation made its first appearance, Chiang Kai-shek taking offence straight away, even at the airport, because his arrival was top secret and there could be no one of equal standing to receive him.

From then on, the Generalissimo and Madame Chiang made every meeting they attended hell and chaos by their implacable insistence on having everything they wanted, by their deafness to any sort of reason, and by frequently going back on what they had earlier agreed. Churchill could not understand why Roosevelt was so sympathetic to the Chinese cause, and Mountbatten was brought in to use his charm and powers of simple explanation to the Chinese. It worked, as always, but, like a winter tan, quickly faded in its effect.

The Americans thought the British were ducking out of 'Overlord', the invasion of northern France, and that Churchill was still preoccupied with an attack on Europe from the south, the 'soft underbelly', the soft option.

Through all this unseemly international bickering, Mountbatten presented his promised plan. An amphibious fleet was to assault and conquer the Andaman Islands off the coast of Burma, Operation Buccaneer. At the same time, on land there were to be assaults down the Arakan and across the Chindwin; and to the north there were to be three related thrusts to open up a direct route to China, and a major attack by Wingate's Long-Range Penetration Force: seven offensives in all.

Churchill's orders to Mountbatten on his appointment to his new command had included this clear-cut directive: 'Your first duty is to engage the enemy as closely and continuously as possible, so that his forces may be worn down and consumed by attrition, and to establish our superiority to the extent of forcing a diversion of his forces from the Pacific theatre.'

Mountbatten's plan, which had been prepared during the first hectic weeks at Delhi, was expressly designed to meet these requirements. It certainly went some way towards easing Chinese and American doubts about British willingness to fight at all in South-East Asia. Churchill's reception of the proposal was cool. But worse was to come.

Mountbatten returned to Delhi with his staff, leaving the leaders (minus Chiang Kai-shek) to join Stalin at Teheran. He was in buoyant mood. His great offensive was due to open in March. He had the necessary equipment, or it was promised to him, detailed plans for the land campaigns were well advanced, training for the amphibious landings was going ahead speedily. At this time, Mountbatten was utterly confident that he could break the Japanese in Burma and be in occupation of Rangoon, the capital, by the middle of 1944 at the latest.

Within a week or two of Mountbatten's return to Delhi, Churchill and Roosevelt were jointly drawing up a message to Stalin which was to dash all hopes of launching SEAC's great offensive. At Teheran, Stalin – truculent, resentful, censorious and implacably demanding – had got his way with the Americans and British.

Roosevelt, in his innocence, had come to Teheran in the dual role of a solid ally to Britain and a peacemaker between Stalin and Churchill who – from the other side of the Atlantic – appeared to be at loggerheads over almost everything. Roosevelt assumed, at best, the white mantle of prophet and arbitrator; at worst, a Western toady bent on encouraging a Russian view that the USSR and USA were the two great powers with so much in common – forward-looking, egalitarian and above all anti-colonialist. The implication of Operation 'Grovel' (as some cynical observer named it) was that the arch-Imperialist Churchill must, by joint effort, be gently nursed into accepting the right priorities.

In spite of every protestation by Churchill and Brooke, the Americans and Russians both believed that the British were still stalling on the invasion of France, from the north and south. Stalin also strongly opposed Churchill's eastern Mediterranean 'soft under-belly' plans, which might thwart Russian well-laid ambitions on Romania, Greece, Bulgaria, Hungary, Yugoslavia, Albania, etc.

Not all the American generals considered their remarks very carefully, the exception being Marshall. Eisenhower, for instance, at one point suggested that the Italian campaign, where Britain was heavily committed and the American contribution had not been wholly successful, should be run down in favour of the southern French invasion. Stalin thought this a wonderful idea, Churchill thought it madness, and got his way.

As to the East, Stalin refused to come into the war against Japan until Germany was defeated. He had no interest in Chiang Kai-Shek's war; and as for Burma, this was a side-show, a skirmish unworthy of comment had it not been for SEAC's ambitious amphibious plans for 1944, which involved a great number of landing craft. To Stalin, landing craft meant only one thing: the means for an earlier invasion of France by his allies, which would draw off German troops from the Russian front and allow the Russian armies to storm into eastern Europe – Prague, Budapest, Berlin. . . .

Roosevelt and Churchill returned to Cairo to unravel, as compatibly and neatly as possible, the criss-cross pattern of national demands that would shape the post-war world; and despatched their message to Stalin with their conclusions. It included this paragraph: 'We have reduced the scale of operations scheduled for March in the Bay of Bengal to permit the reinforcement of amphibious craft for the operation against southern France.'[16] The consequences for Mountbatten and SEAC were much more fundamental than this reassurance to Stalin suggested. Churchill had, in fact, persuaded Roosevelt very reluctantly to accept that the whole Buccaneer operation should be abandoned, and that virtually all the landing craft assigned to it and prepared by Mountbatten for the amphibious operations should be returned. Roosevelt was in favour of the invasion of the south of France but strongly against letting down Chiang Kai-shek and Mountbatten.

On 9 December 1943 Churchill confirmed to Mountbatten that Buccaneer was off. 'This arises from the decisions at Teheran to concentrate everything on Overlord and a simultaneous operation against the south of France.' He then did a very characteristic thing, showing that the schoolboy in him was never far beneath the skin, while his eye on history's verdict upon himself was as keen as in the time of Mountbatten's father. Anticipating the justifiable protests, he drowned them with a great shout of abuse. 'Everyone here', he continued, 'has been unpleasantly affected by your request to use 50,000 British and Imperial troops . . . against 5,000 Japanese. I was astounded to hear of such a requirement, and I cannot feel sure you are getting competent military advice . . . while such standards as those you have accepted for the Andamans prevail there is not much hope of making any form of amphibious war.'[17] Mountbatten was outraged as much at the loss of his landing craft as the accusation that he had been extravagant and poorly advised militarily. It was the greatest rebuke of his active career, and he never forgot it.

Mountbatten regarded Churchill's jealousy and vanity as only marginally less than Max Beaverbrook's, and his eye on posterity infinitely keener. Churchill had sent Mountbatten out to South-East Asia to win the war against the Japanese in that theatre. But Mountbatten harboured the gravest suspicions that the speed of his preparations had taken Churchill by surprise and that he did not want the thunder of the invasion in the West to be stolen by victory drumbeats in the East: drums beaten by the handsome, royal hero who could so easily and truthfully claim that he had, first, laid the foundations for the successful invasion of Europe, and then gone East to avenge the greatest humiliations the British Empire had ever suffered. It was just too much.

No one adored a hero more than Churchill. But megalomania had seized him in a tight grip, as Mountbatten saw it, and he could not allow the stature of anyone to overshadow his own. For ever after, Mountbatten suspected that Churchill feared for his own exclusive position in the annals of history as the man who had saved the free world, and had 'put him down' by cancelling Buccaneer and making it impossible to implement, for a long time, the original instructions he had given Mountbatten only seven weeks earlier. Churchill had written of 'amphibious descents' with the 'necessary transports, assault ships and landing craft' made available to him. Now, he had taken them away. Churchill had also instructed Mountbatten to make his superiority tell and force 'the Japanese enemy to divert his forces from the Pacific theatre'. Instead, Mountbatten had been deprived of that superiority so that the German enemy would be forced to divert his forces from the Russian front. It was an odd turn-about. As Mountbatten saw it, Churchill at a stroke had done more by this deed to appease Stalin than all Roosevelt's petty flirtations had succeeded in achieving.

'I was completely horrified by this sudden cancellation,' said Mountbatten. 'It was unjust and unwarranted. We weren't asking for a thing. We had everything for the operations, our men were training hard, our morale was rocketing. Winston had sent me out primarily to conduct amphibious operations to beat the Japs quickly. And now we seemed fated to slog our way through the Burmese jungle and the worst terrain in the world.

'As to the accusations of extravagance, this was absolute rot and Winston knew it, and the rap over the knuckles was purely political. The Americans, with all their experience and terrific resources in the Pacific were using a six-to-one superiority when air cover was only from carriers – which was always much riskier and more limited than from land-based planes.' Allowing for the fact that a third of Mountbatten's force was non-combatant, the ratio of superiority for Buccaneer had been no higher.

Mountbatten feared that the repercussions in Chungking would be disastrous, and he was right. 'The Generalissimo broke entirely with us, and wouldn't make his armies available under any circumstances.' Only Mountbatten's innermost circle learned of the depth of his bitterness and disappointment at Churchill's policy reversal and what he called 'the complete lack of support of the Combined Chiefs of Staff'. At no time during the war did Mountbatten's youthful resilience prove more valuable. 'Well,' he said, 'the Japs were still there, the war was still going on, and we had to adapt ourselves and keep our peckers up. Frankie Festing [Major-General F.W. Festing commanding 36 Division] and George Giffard said that the news would be disastrous for morale and we would never be able to do anything again. The whole of 33 Corps had been trained for the amphibious landing, and somebody had to tell them.

' "I'm not going to do that," they both said.

' "You mean you want me to do it?" I asked. "Don't you mind my coming and doing your work?"

'They both said, no, they didn't. So I went down and spent three nights with each Divisional Corps. I knew I had to follow my old principle of turning bad news to good, but this was going to be tough. What I did say was something like this:

' "I've come down here personally to bring you some very exciting news. You all know that you'll not be able to get home to see your wives and families until the war is over – and that means when Germany is beaten as well as Japan. Now, when I left England the war against Germany was going very slowly. But things are better now. I've just heard some highly confidential news. The invasion of Europe will take place sooner than we all expected – in fact this very spring. I know this because they have taken away for the time being our landing craft. Now this is splendid because it means that the Germans will soon be crushed, we'll get all and more of our landing craft back, and we'll have a very quick victory."

'This was received with loud cheers.'

Mountbatten always retained the firm conviction that fate was on his side and setbacks merely temporary. A month before his aborted operations were due to begin, the Japanese opened a major offensive against two divisions of xv Corps, relying on the past experience that the British would retreat, leaving behind them, as before, massive supplies on which the Japanese would sustain themselves. This time it did not work out like that. Under Brigadier Geoffrey Evans, the troops did not retreat. It was as if Mountbatten's spirit had infused them with a special grit and sense of pride and purpose – just like the *Kelly*'s company and the Commandos who had gone out with blackened faces and knives on those earlier raids. They held on for eighteen days, and when it seemed as if their supplies must be exhausted, the planes came in as Mountbatten had promised, and then the relief columns arrived, and the Japanese were forced to retreat. They lost half their men – and their record of unbroken victory.

It was called 'The Battle of the Admin. Box' by Slim, who considered it the turning point of the war in Burma. Meanwhile, Wingate's long-range penetrations had some spectacular successes – again thanks to supplies from the air. During these early months of 1944, the Burma war became the first major campaign in history to be supplied almost exclusively from the air.

A month later, the Japanese struck again at Imphal, and the toughest battle of the campaign began. The Japanese infantryman was a superb jungle fighter, but his first asset was his relentless determination and disregard for setbacks and the desperate rigours of living and fighting in the jungle.

At one time Imphal and Kohima were surrounded by Japanese forces and it appeared as if both towns must fall. High fighting morale and the tireless courage of the transport aircrews turned the tide. Against express instructions from Roosevelt, Mountbatten borrowed large numbers of American machines flying supplies to China over the Hump. He like to relate this incident as if it were one of great daring, with apologies afterwards to the President, who was so forbearing because he was such a 'big' man and understood Mountbatten and the nature of the emergency. But in fact the thirty C47s were taken off the China run with Churchill's encouragement and a guarantee that he would square things with F.D.R. if there were any trouble.

Another story of this time, on a lighter level, which Mountbatten enjoyed concerned Major-General F.W. Messervy, who commanded the 7th Indian Division when it was over-run by the Japanese, half his force being outside the Admin. Box. To keep open some form of communication was as essential as the burning of all code books. All the General retained to keep in touch with the part of his force from which he was separated was one radio telephone.

'Messervy recognized that it was of the utmost importance,' Mountbatten recounted, 'that the Japs, who were known to be listening in on their wavelength, shouldn't be able to understand the messages. An absolutely unbreakable new code was required. The General had an inspiration. At each end of the line he put an ex-public school English subaltern and they were instructed to talk only French. Not even the French knew what they were saying, and the French-talking Japanese thought it was gibberish.'

Now at last things really did seem to be going better. Churchill, in more benign mood, signalled, 'I am so glad this measure of success has attended [the fighting]. It is a sign of the new spirit in your forces, and will, I trust, urge everyone to keep closer to the enemy.'[18] (Churchill loved the Nelsonian phrase 'keep close to the enemy' and used it frequently.)

The three 'Ms' were proving their worth, contradicting every pessimistic prediction by those who 'knew'. The 14th Army held the Japanese, who hoped now to build up supplies during the monsoon before another, final onslaught which would lead them to India. Instead, to their amazement, the British and their Allies continued to fight – through drenching rain, through cloying mud; and the planes, at high risk and with considerable losses, continued to fly, thanks to the indefatigable work of the ground crews, and the unflinching courage of the aircrews.

Once again, Mountbatten's early choice of Signals (in the broadest sense) as a specialist branch proved its value. From the beginning as Supreme Commander, Mountbatten had taken a special interest in Signals Intelligence. Ultra, the cryptoanalysis machine, was already established at the Wireless Experimental Centre, analysing Japanese Army and Air Force formations.

'Our unit was just beginning to produce useful short-term inferences on Japanese intentions and reactions,' wrote an Indian Army officer in Signals Intelligence. 'Japanese security was in some respects very lax and our very well trained intercept-operators, British, Indian and African, laid the foundations for the extraction of much accurate and timely intelligence from the Japanese networks.

'I recalled that Mountbatten, having found his own "baby" flourishing in the unexpected environment of the Indian Army, overspent his time in his inspection of our sub-unit. He met everyone involved and went through the minutest details of their work with them. We were intrigued to have a Supreme Commander who had an intimate grasp of the technical details of the work. Later I heard that Mountbatten had made it a high priority to ascertain that Signals Intelligence was in good working order in his Command. His relaxed and confident manner and his assessment of the value of our team were very great morale-raisers.'

Backed by greatly superior Intelligence, the 14th Army was fighting through the monsoon, malaria was comparatively negligible, morale was high – and the Army was continuing to move. Only just sometimes, with 2 mph a good average for a motorized convoy. But it moved. The Japanese, stricken with fever, did not. And, the c47 Dakotas roared overhead – over the most dangerous terrain and through the most dangerous weather in the world. This sturdy, twin-engined American transport, mainly American-crewed, was the jungle war's real winning weapon.

By the end of the monsoon, the 14th Army had by no means won the war and driven the Japanese out of Burma. But it had broken the spell of Japanese invincibility, gained valuable ground, shaken the Japanese High Command, and was bursting with pride and self-confidence. 'The Forgotten Army' was ready for the last offensive, and was feeling that it might be remembered after all.

At the height of the battle for the Imphal plain, Mountbatten was struck down by one of those silly mishaps to which he had always been so prone.

Although highly competent drivers were, of course, always available, he often chose to drive himself. On 7 March 1944 he was driving his own jeep, fast and leaning out over the left side, when a bamboo stump, over which he had just driven, sprang up and struck him hard in the eye. He was rushed, in great pain, to the nearest field hospital, an American one. For a time, the doctors feared for his sight. Here he remained for a week, with both eyes bandaged. The accident could not have happened at a worse time. The Japanese had attacked strongly on 8 March and were within an ace of cutting off IV Corps. The military situation was fluid and dangerous. With Pownall's aid, Mountbatten kept in touch with Slim and with the day-to-day situation.

On the fourteenth Mountbatten persuaded the doctors to unbandage his eye and discharge him, and he flew straight back to Delhi for consultations with Slim and Baldwin. Ten weeks later, with his eye now completely recovered and the battles for Imphal and Kohima now transformed into a pursuit of the enemy, Mountbatten was further cheered by a message from the Joint Chiefs of Staff.

'It was dated 10 June, and was about the nicest telegram I ever received during the war,' said Mountbatten. 'The invasion of northern France had occurred four days earlier, and I had already had news that the Allied armies had secured a toehold on the Normandy coast and that things were going pretty well. I learned later that Marshall had composed the message to me while at dinner with Brookie, Winston, Ernie King, Smuts and Hap Arnold. He had handed it to the others, and they had all signed in turn:

> Today we visited the British and American armies on the soil of France. We sailed through vast fleets of ships, with landing craft of many types pouring more and more men, vehicles and stores ashore. ... We wish to tell you at this moment in your arduous campaign that we realize that much of this remarkable technique, and therefore the success of the venture, has its origin in developments effected by you and your staff of Combined Operations.

The most willing signatory to this message of recognition was Field-Marshal Jan Smuts, the South African statesman, whose judgment was so sought after by the British War Cabinet, and by Churchill himself. Smuts had a very high regard for Mountbatten, and told Churchill (27 September 1944) that he thought he had had 'a raw deal'[19] over Operation Buccaneer, and was glad that he would 'get his chance in Burma and Malaya'. The far-seeing Smuts was referring to the amphibious operations that must clear out, and finally defeat, the Japanese in South-East Asia. These would be on a scale that would make Buccaneer appear like a minor skirmish. The landings on the Malaysian peninsula in 1945 would be Mountbatten's own Overlord, the relief of Singapore the equivalent to the Allied liberation of Paris, the final vengeance for Japanese infamy and British humiliation.

8
'SUPREMO' II

THE SITUATION IN China remained unsettled and unsatisfactory, the only predictable factor being its complexity. It was becoming increasingly clear that the Generalissimo was as concerned with his future war with the powerful communist elements in his own country as with the occupying Japanese. The Allies, and more particularly the Americans, were investing vast sums in supplying and supporting the Generalissimo's armies, constructing air bases for bombing the Japanese mainland, and building a road from Burma (a million dollars a mile, and up to heights of 16,000 feet).

Chiang Kai-shek procrastinated, lied, dodged decisions, issued orders behind his generals' backs. The War Lords in the south-east were on the point of revolt; the communists in the north-west refused to accept orders from Chungking while they laid plans for the civil war they would one day win. Mountbatten viewed the picture with an anxious and increasingly cynical eye. Roosevelt again sent a personal representative, Major-General P.J. Hurley, and at the same time promoted Stilwell full general to increase his prestige in the Generalissimo's eyes. But the end, deferred by Mountbatten in 1943, was near for 'Vinegar Joe', and the one general who had attempted to lend direction and will to the Chinese for so long had to be recalled by Roosevelt at Chiang Kai-shek's insistence on 18 October 1944.

With Mountbatten's agreement, the American Chiefs of Staff took Wedemeyer from SEAC to replace Stilwell and divided the American China–Burma–India theatre into two, with General D.L. Sultan commanding the Burma portion and Wedemeyer the China portion, while also acting as the Generalissimo's Chief of Staff. It was hoped at Mountbatten's HQ that Wedemeyer would behave at Chungking with the needs of his old command in mind. Not a bit of it. Within weeks, the Japanese were overwhelming one Chinese American air base after another, and even threatening Chungking and the vital Hump air terminal – an advance of 300 miles. With China out of the war, some four million Japanese troops could be released for operations in defence of their homeland.

Wedemeyer promptly advised his new master that he should demand the withdrawal from Mountbatten's Burma front of two American-trained Chinese divisions and five cargo- and troop-carrying squadrons of planes. Mountbatten, hoping to forestall even greater demands, complied. But he felt extremely bitter about it, and the man he had once admired for his loyalty, for it meant a further postponement of his plans. Now it seemed that commitments were being broken from East as well as West.

'Wedemeyer did a terribly naughty thing,' said Mountbatten. 'He at once started appreciating the situation in South-East Asia from his now out-of-date knowledge acquired from the privileged position as my deputy Chief of Staff.'

Mountbatten had decided some time earlier to move his HQ from Delhi, where the heat was as stifling as the in-fighting, and set up a base well removed from the intrigue and politicking of the capital – a place he could call his own and from which he could more suitably control the final stages of the war in Burma and the eventual invasion of the Malaysian peninsula.

To the surprise of everyone but his closest staff, and the disapproval of the Delhi 'brass' he left thankfully behind, Mountbatten chose Peredynia, a little place high in the mountains of Ceylon and near the town of Kandy. Here the climate was healthy, the scenery exotically beautiful, the gardens paradisical. A royal residence had been built here many years earlier for Mountbatten's godmother in the event of Queen Victoria's visiting the island. She never had, and this palace-like building in its lovely gardens had been used instead as a summer residence for the Governor. It now housed Mountbatten in the very considerable splendour he always relished.

'Supremo's palace' was surrounded by informally laid out buildings linked by roads named Fleet Street and Ludgate Circus, Times Square and Broadway, to give a home-from-home as well as an Anglo-American style to the HQ. The various messes and clubhouses, thatched living quarters and canteens, were situated on the banks of a river.

On first arrival, men and women who had become hardened to soul-less barrack life imagined they were dreaming. Surely the war was over and they were trespassing on some country club! But if Kandy came closer to Mountbatten's Valhalla than any HQ he ever created, including almost all the very prettiest servicewomen in their trim uniforms, it was also very Mountbatten in its odd mix of weak and strong, experienced and inexperienced. He had been sent or had chosen some first-rate brains and brilliant soldiers. For instance, General Frederick 'Boy' Browning, fresh from the Arnhem battle,

arrived to replace Pownall as Chief of Staff and was immensely inspiring
and capable.

But the amount of 'dead wood' at Kandy, recognizable within a few days
of arrival by an experienced eye, was also considerable and revealed that
Mountbatten was as often undiscerning in his selection of staff as he was
occasionally brilliant. The instinct was never reliable. All that you could
be sure of was that the numbers would rapidly grow like any self-multiplying
bureaucracy that is not run with a tight rein. The numbers at Kandy eventually grew to over seven thousand, which appalled Churchill and a great many
others in London when they heard.

One brigadier recalls being given the task of arranging for cut-up landing
craft to be flown into Burma, and finding that this was technically impossible
with the aircraft available. At every stage up the hierarchy, his case was either
shrugged off or he was told of the dire consequences for himself if he ever
reached the top. At length he got to Kandy, forced his way higher, to Browning, who then passed him on to Mountbatten himself. The brigadier spread
out his drawings which proved his case. Mountbatten understood at once,
pushed aside the papers, shrugged his shoulders and with a sigh said, 'Why
doesn't my staff *tell* me these things?'[1]

On the other hand, Kandy's cumbersome, overstaffed machine could also
work very speedily and efficiently, thanks to the driving force of the
'Supremo' and the ablest of his lieutenants. Mountbatten would claim that
Kandy was unsurpassedly efficient in every respect, and that this was partly
because of the creature comforts provided and not in spite of them; just
as, long before, the *Daring* had hot and cold water for the commander, and
the *Kelly* had a covered bridge.

Before Stilwell was relieved of his command, and while Mountbatten was
briefly absent in London, the American General took over at Kandy. It was
like putting John Wayne's sheriff's office in the Palace of Versailles. He used
Mountbatten's magnificent Cadillac to send his cook out for the groceries,
drove about in a scruffy jeep himself, and was completely at sea in the
Supreme Commander's daily meetings, which he soon cancelled. He never
could bear conferences.

For reasons which many thought at the time to be reasonable, Giffard
and Peirse both refused point-blank to move their HQ to Kandy, which they
regarded as too remote from the Burma fighting areas. Both were relieved
of their command in October and November 1944.

It is no reflection on these Commanders that the Burma campaign
prospered after their departure. The build-up of reinforcements and of
supplies, the growing experience and winning spirit, were all playing their
part in the 14th Army. In continuous and intense fighting, the once-

forgotten army increasingly got the measure of the enemy – and its share of the headlines at last.

The great Irrawaddy River was crossed by means of giant teak barges, made on the spot and powered by small marine engines flown in. Slim, by a series of feints and bluffs as cunning as anything the Japanese could have contrived, completely outwitted his opposing generals – one of whom later described them as 'the master-stroke of Allied Strategy'. Mandalay fell on 9 March 1945; Rangoon itself, after a combined amphibious and land attack, capitulated two months later, just as the monsoon broke.

'Heartfelt congratulations' arrived from Churchill, regretting that Mountbatten had been deprived of landing craft and shipping which 'had to be retained in the decisive European theatre'. 'In spite of this diminution and disappointment you and your men have done all and more than your directive required,' Churchill continued. 'Pray convey to everyone under your command or associated with you the sense of admiration and gratitude felt by all at home at the splendid close of the Burma campaign.'[2]

So perhaps Mountbatten had been getting 'competent military advice' after all. Certainly this message served to offset the damaging earlier one concerning Buccaneer.

Churchill concluded by telling Mountbatten that George VI had commanded that a special decoration, the Burma Star, should be struck. The ribbons would be flown out shortly. No campaign ribbon was worn with greater pride than this Star, by the men who had fought through swamp and jungle, in suffocating monsoon rain and heat, over precipitous mountains, across raging torrents, against a ruthless and formidable enemy.

'Looking back now,' said Mountbatten nearly thirty years later, 'there seemed to have been more events in the spring and summer of 1945 than in all the inter-war years together. Certainly, I had to make more important decisions than at any other time in my life.'

The saddest event in April was the death of Roosevelt. 'Every time I had met him it had been a thrill, and I had a terrific admiration for him – long before the war. I thought his New Deal was a master-stroke. He was a compassionate as well as a very brave man. Like Churchill and everyone else in Britain, I was thankful for his moral and material support when we were alone. We became personal friends in 1942 when I stayed at the White House. And later, when I was offered South-East Asia, I had promised him I would be a good American. "You stand in a very special relationship with me, Dickie," he had said. And that was one of the nicest things anyone said to me. When he died, I knew that I had lost a very good friend. He knew that victory was just ahead, but it would have been nice if he had seen it, for it was the war that killed him, of course.'

One of the arguments that Roosevelt had used against placing SEAC under MacArthur during the period of American sniping at Mountbatten was that the two commands were thousands of miles apart. But now, every day that passed and the four-pronged pincers squeezed Japan tighter, this distance diminished as the need to formulate joint policies increased.

A month before the fall of Rangoon, MacArthur's forces had stormed the island of Okinawa, and already Mountbatten was preparing Operation Zipper, the amphibious assault on Malaysia.

'I thought I ought to go and see MacArthur at Manila, and flew off,' said Mountbatten. 'I had heard much about his presence and his powers, that he was an outstanding figure. When we met, I wasn't disappointed. He was a terrific man. He simply oozed personality. He was also – unlike me – a complete autocrat. We got on marvellously, and our talks were terribly useful. I would have liked to stay longer, but I was needed back in England.'

The reason for this had now become a commonplace in Mountbatten's Command. During his last night at dinner with MacArthur two things had been agreed. The first was that the boundaries of SEAC should be further expanded in order that MacArthur would be able to concentrate his resources more fully on the eventual invasion of the Japanese mainland. The Dutch East Indies, French Indo-China, Portuguese Timor and Borneo would all come within Mountbatten's scope – another few million people, another few thousand square miles!

The other point of agreement between the two Commanders was that Mountbatten had had a raw deal in the line-up for supplies. 'I didn't raise the subject,' said Mountbatten. 'It was MacArthur. It was at the end of dinner. He was smoking that pipe of his, looking like a caricature of himself, and he had given me a very good cigar. Suddenly he said, "I am the best person in the world to judge how difficult it is to run a Command when you are low in the priority scale. I have had a terrible time, while Ike got everything he asked for. I also know that you have had an even worse time. Some time in the future, history will prove what a wonderful job you have done, all without priorities." I thanked him. It was a nice thing to say, and I gave him some compliments, too. It was a very satisfactory meeting. But with these huge new responsibilities. I knew I should have to go to London to get some reinforcements – and this time without any double-crossing.'

Mountbatten had decided to stop off at Paris to pay his respects to de Gaulle in his newly liberated capital. He got no farther than Cairo. During the refuelling stop there, an urgent telegram arrived from Churchill. The

'Big Three' – the new American President, Stalin and Churchill – were meeting in the ruins of Berlin, at Potsdam. And Mountbatten was summoned to join them.

Everyone was in buoyant mood. Mountbatten dined privately with Churchill the first evening. Even before the first drink, Winston – after checking the doors and windows – told Mountbatten in a low voice, ' "I have something highly confidential and very important to tell you. You are going to have to revise your plans." I thought, "Oh no – not again – not more cuts – I've had enough ... !" But before I could speak, Winston said, "The war with Japan will be over in less than a month. We are going to use a new bomb, an atomic bomb, against the cities of Japan, and the Emperor will be forced to capitulate. Of course, you are not to mention this to a soul. You'll have to tell your people without explaining how or why...." How could I? It was an impossible situation.'

The next day, at lunch with the Chiefs of Staff, Brooke looked around the room cautiously before saying in a hushed voice, 'Dickie, I have something highly....'

Then he had words with the new American President. 'I liked Truman very much. He was very precise and business-like. After a while, it was *his* turn. "I have something highly confidential...." The funny thing is he never told MacArthur, so I was a lap ahead of him there.'

Then there was Stalin, this almost fabulous figure, this dictator, the most powerful man on earth, who had smashed Hitler's dreams and the most efficient military machine ever conceived. It was more than thirty years since Mountbatten had confronted a ruler of Russia. Then he had been the Tsar, his own kindly uncle, and Mountbatten had been met by a laugh, an exclamation of wonder at his cadet's uniform and how he had grown, and an embrace, with Uncle Nicky's beard tickling his face, just as his father's always had.

In those far-away pre-revolutionary days, one passed between lines of Cossacks, and the surroundings were the most glittering and extravagant of any monarch in the world. Now, in this desolate, tragic city, filled with the smell of death and dust, Mountbatten, in the uniform of full admiral, was escorted swiftly through ring after ring of ferocious-looking sentries and secret police to Stalin's presence, with his brilliant interpreter, Pavlov, beside him.

'He was in a very benign mood,' said Mountbatten, 'as well he might be. His face was just like his caricatures, but I was struck by his clothes – a white doeskin tunic with nothing but a hammer and sickle in red on each shoulder, and dark blue trousers tucked into calf-length boots. He didn't repeat yet again the "confidential" news. He assumed I knew already and agreed that the war with Japan would very soon be over. He was very polite and correct.'

Frontiers and areas of influence and areas of control, armaments and priorities and a thousand other things that have affected the world ever since, were discussed and decided at Potsdam. On South-East Asia, the new areas of control for SEAC agreed at Manila with MacArthur were confirmed, and even more territory allotted to Mountbatten's Command.

'There was a very interesting consequence to this,' said Mountbatten (at the height of the Vietnam War). 'Roosevelt had had this mad desire to suck up to Chiang Kai-shek and I'm sure he had transmitted this to Truman. Truman also knew that there was a lot of jealousy and worry about the Generalissimo losing face in Chungking. But after I left it was decided that I should have only the south part. The Generalissimo was to take over the north. I asked how far north? "At the 16th parallel," I was ordered. "You're to clear things up south of the 16th parallel and then hand over to the French." I was forbidden to send a soldier, a plane or a ship north of that line.

'The Chinese sent in a second-rate lot under a second-rate Commander and they were swallowed up in Hanoi. I went in and rounded up the Japs, looked after and then got rid of the internees and prisoners-of-war, and got some sort of civil organization going. Much later, the French gave me a procession up the Champs Elysées for this, and a Médaille Militaire and Légion d'Honneur.

'After things were going, I took away our troops and General Le Clerc came in. Later, I handed over to Admiral Dargenlieu – everything south of the 16th parallel – and I remember him saying to me, "Thank you very much, but I wish you could have given me everything because without the North there's always going to be trouble in the South."

'So that's one of the results of Potsdam.'

In the midst of this epochal international meeting in Berlin, Churchill left with his daughter Mary to hear the result of the British general election, a remarkable event in the eyes of Stalin. To the surprise of the Americans, but not of the British, the Russian was also displeased when Churchill as Prime Minister was replaced by Attlee, who picked up the ferry boat in mid-stream and just carried on, with Bevin as the new Foreign Secretary but the rest of the crew as before.

'I had had a lot to do with Attlee and liked him very much,' said Mountbatten. 'Nor was I surprised that he had won the election. I had seen plenty of signs among the troops out East of a likely turn against the Conservatives. I had meetings with him in London and told him how I proposed to deal with the liberated territories, and was delighted that I had his full backing.'

Mountbatten had always believed that the Japanese had to be defeated in the field – demonstrably defeated – and was appalled at the nation being given a chance to surrender before this happened. They had to lose 'face'. Now, threatened with unprecedented bombing, the destruction of all their cities and the loss of millions of lives, they were offered unconditional surrender, and at once refused.

'My feelings about the dropping of the atomic bomb were mixed ones. On the one hand I was afraid that this would mean the end of the war *without* the defeat of their armies in the field, just as the Germans had claimed in 1918. Against this was the colossal saving of human lives. As many Japanese had been killed defending the small island of Okinawa as at Hiroshima. Imagine what the invasion of the Japanese mainland in 1946 would have led to! You didn't count Japanese casualties – you counted their *dead*. They would blow themselves up rather than surrender. Millions would have been killed – civilians and soldiers.'

For Mountbatten, after his return from London, the last act remained to be played out: Operation Zipper, his own 'Overlord'. The attempt to set up this invasion of the Malay peninsula had been as slow and obstacle-strewn and disheartening, as every major offensive Mountbatten had attempted. Until the successful invasion and liberation of France, it was the European operations which had, time and again, deprived Mountbatten of resources. Now it was the invasion of Japan that demanded all the priorities. On 6 April 1945, the American Chiefs of Staff flatly rejected Zipper for this reason.

It was no use Mountbatten arguing that the greater the delay the stronger would be the enemy build-up, especially in Singapore, and the greater the suffering and mortality among civilian detainees and prisoners-of-war. Later, there was an easing of the American attitude. Zipper could go ahead, but Mountbatten could not have the light fleet carriers he had already been promised. He would have to make do with much less suitable escort carriers.

At every stage, both in London and Washington, Zipper continued to be regarded as something of a side-show. With the war over in Europe, the Far East seemed farther away than ever. The lights were on in London again. In Washington, where they had never been turned off, everyone's eyes were on Nimitz and MacArthur, and the cataclysmic closing stages of the Pacific war.

It is a measure of Mountbatten's dogged determination and implacability that he managed to assemble a very considerable force for his own final act. A preliminary bombardment would be provided by heavy bombers from the Cocos Islands and south Burma, and two battleships, cruisers, destroyers and landing craft. He had managed to rustle up nine carriers whose planes would provide air cover until landing strips ashore were completed within a week of the invasion. In the first seven weeks from D-Day it was planned to put ashore 182,000 men, nearly 18,000 vehicles and a quarter of a million tons of stores.

Mountbatten reluctantly postponed the date until 9 September, but by June all seemed set for SEAC's final effort, its first major assault, when the Command was struck a new and completely unexpected blow. The British involvement in the war in the East, already nearly six years long, had led to troops being separated from their families for unacceptably long periods – four years was common. An operation code-named Python had therefore been instituted which permitted very-long-serving men to return. This had been allowed for in all SEAC plans. Now, with an election approaching, the Churchill government sought votes by announcing a radical reduction in this period, without any reference to Mountbatten or his staff.

'This wasn't just bad manners,' said Mountbatten. 'It was military insanity. Suddenly we faced having to recast all our plans, and even postpone Zipper yet again.' He protested in the strongest terms. The Chiefs of Staff replied, in effect, that they were sorry he had been inconvenienced, but he should go ahead anyway, 'with a weakened force of six divisions on the agreed date, regardless of the risk of failure should the opposition prove greater than estimated.'

Zipper was launched on schedule. The great fleet put to sea and headed for its beach-heads on the Malaysian coast. Meanwhile, Hiroshima and Nagasaki were both devastated by atomic bombs, and on 14 August 1945 Japan at last submitted to unconditional surrender.

'So our landings, when they took place, would meet no resistance,' said Mountbatten. 'The war was over. But we had to press on, of course. And then came the bombshell. MacArthur suddenly issued orders that no Japanese-held territory was to be reoccupied and there were to be no individual surrenders, until the big formal surrender in Tokyo Bay. This was all very well, but it left us in a difficult situation.' Mountbatten was concerned on two counts. First, many of his landing craft were already at sea and they could not turn back because they were not designed to head into a south-west monsoon and could easily sink. Most of them took shelter under the lee of the Nicobars, where they were refuelled and provisioned.

Then what about all the starving prisoners? For many of them, further delay could mean death. And the delay was almost three weeks.

Singapore was relieved on 5 September, and a week later the Council

Chamber of the Municipal Buildings of Singapore City provided the scene of the formal surrender of the Japanese in South-East Asia. The ceremonial, the little touches, all were pure Mountbatten. With his American Deputy, 'Specs' Wheeler, at his side, Mountbatten was driven in an open limousine by a recently released prisoner-of-war through streets lined by sailors and Royal Marines, and was received at the Municipal Buildings by his C-in-CS. Four guards of honour, mounted by the Royal Navy, RAF, Australian paratroops and the Indian Army were lined up for inspection. Massed bands played 'Rule Britannia', and a seventeen-gun salute was fired.

In the chamber two long tables, six feet apart, had been drawn up for the delegates of the victors and the vanquished. A large painting of the King and Queen, hidden during the occupation, had been reinstated on the wall. But internationalism was everywhere evident: armed guards standing at the pillars represented every country which had suffered under brutal Japanese occupation: French and Australians, Dutch and Chinese, Americans and Indians and British; and at the table sat the senior officers of these nations and the top brass of Mountbatten's staff, from old one-eyed de Wiart, who had won his VC in another war, to little Major-General Feng Yee from Chungking, who had been fighting the Japanese for longer than anyone else present.

At the table facing them sat the seven Japanese admirals and generals, balding, impassive, expressionless, bespectacled. Behind them was a crowd of some four hundred, many of them released detainees and prisoners-of-war, pale, thin and hollow-cheeked from their years of suffering.

Mountbatten, sublimely resplendent in admiral's white tropical uniform, and looking thirty rather than forty-five, marched in, feet characteristically splayed wide. His expression, as always on ceremonial occasions of great moment, was one of solemn exaltation. He stared straight in front, heading for the raised dais with its microphones and the throne-like chair. Behind him trailed four ADCs; and the whole assembly arose in silence.

'I have come here today to receive the formal surrender of all the Japanese forces within the South-East Asia Command. . . .' The voice already familiar to so many thousands within his command, consciously authoritative, patrician, slurred at the end of each sentence.

The Japanese Field-Marshal had sent a message of regret at his absence. He was indisposed. Mountbatten said that he had sent a doctor to confirm this claim: '. . . but I have warned the Field-Marshal that I shall expect him to make his personal surrender to me as soon as he is fit enough.' (He did, too, two and a half months later, surrendering his two swords, one sixteenth-century, the other thirteenth-century. Mountbatten gave one to George VI and kept the older sword for himself.)

Mountbatten also made clear that this was no negotiated surrender. 'The Japanese are submitting to superior force, now massed here.' A large fleet, 100,000 men already ashore....

So all the massive planning and execution of Zipper had not quite gone to waste, not become quite dissolved in the mushroom cloud of Hiroshima. Zipper had brought Admiral Mountbatten to this dais before this international crowd of spectators, the world's Press, the movie cameras, the flash-bulbs.

The enemy was there, before him, General Itagaki of the 7th Area Army, placing his signature on the Instrument of Surrender. But afterwards, outside at the head of the steps reading out the Order of the Day, a Union Jack (concealed all these years in the notorious Changi jail) breaking out on the flagstaff, there remained one absent note in the grand chorus of triumph on that day.

No one had fought more bravely against more fearful odds than the 14th Army, no airmen in any theatre of war had flown more intrepidly in such dreadful conditions; and between them they had cleared the enemy from Myitkyina and Mandalay, Meiktila, Imphal, Rangoon, and the whole of that mountain-and-jungle-wracked land of Burma. But there had been no great decisive and final battle, no Utah or Juno beach, no Falaise Gap and pursuit to the Rhine, no Guadalcanal or Okinawa – no Agincourt for Mountbatten to be told by his herald, 'The day is yours.' At first forgotten and later denied supplies, right to the last wickedly ironical denial while it was already at sea for its own D-Day, Mountbatten's Command was also deprived of its climactic last triumph.

The war in the East had been ended by two explosions of awesome power and destructiveness. But for SEAC it had been an atomic anti-climax. Even the unopposed landings had been bogged down on unexpectedly difficult beaches, with dozens of vehicles sunk without trace, and hundreds more stranded in the unforeseen drainage ditches inland.

Julian Amery, the distinguished diplomat and politician, was on de Wiart's staff, and witnessed this grandiose yet unfulfilled conclusion to a hard campaign. 'It was', he says, 'a tragedy that the atomic bomb saw to it that Mountbatten never had a chance to show himself as a great Commander.'[3]

Among those on the balcony of the Municipal Building during the sur-render-signing in Singapore was Edwina, who found the ceremony 'quite the most impressive and moving I have ever seen'. Following in the train of the liberating armies in Europe, she had already accomplished a great deal in visiting the sick and wounded, and comforting released prisoners-of-war. Edwina was a tireless and practical administrator, and it was not her wealth nor her name that had taken her to the rank of Superintendent-in-Chief of the St John Ambulance organization. No one could discover the real state of a hospital or rest camp as speedily and relentlessly as she could. She talked to everyone and missed nothing. Then she ruthlessly used her influence to correct faults and make good shortages of everything from bedpans to VAD nurses. She was formidable but fair.

Edwina had already made one quick and effective tour of the SEAC area early in 1945, visiting Chungking as well on behalf of the Red Cross. With the end of the war in August, Mountbatten signalled an appeal for her to come out again.

The moment she arrived in Kandy, looking svelte yet business-like in her khaki uniform, eager as always for work, Mountbatten gave her a letter of authorization to go where she wished and apply for any help she needed in locating prisoners-of-war and internment camps and doing what she could for the inmates. The work was gruelling and harrowing, with travel that was primitive, or – in the air – hazardous. The Surrender Ceremony was only a brief interlude in her hectic round, from Borneo to Hong-Kong, Sumatra to Malaysia, from one camp to another, organizing relief, giving what comfort she could to the dying.

Edwina travelled 33,000 miles, making countless calls in sixteen countries, sustained by her will to give relief and her remarkable endurance and ability to go without sleep. When she next saw her husband, she told him of the almost unbelievable tortures prisoners had suffered – sadistic beatings were low on the horror list – of hospitals full of dying women and children. 'Conditions indescribable' was all she could write on one report sheet after another, from Kranji to Adam Park, from Kakom Nayok (she found a young Cassel cousin here, his hair white) to Nakom Pathom.

Mountbatten had seen many terrible sights, too, but it was Edwina's first-hand accounts of bayoneted corpses, of men and women hung up by their feet for the amusement of the guards while urine was poured down their nostrils, of one more evidence of horror after another. Auschwitz and Belsen were mere kindergartens by contrast with some of the Japanese camps in Sumatra and Malaysia.

When time allowed, Mountbatten visited camps, too. An officer who had been one of six survivors of a party of twenty-six working on the notorious railway told of Mountbatten's arrival, greeted by the usual antagonism and suspicion, of how he broke through by talking to them naturally, man to man, about the closing stages of the war and what would have happened if they had not pushed the Japanese back. He never uttered a single word of sympathy. At the end, they were all ready to do anything he asked, 'even to going back to do a personal act of daring against the Japs'.

The measure of what the Mountbattens did for the spirits and physical wellbeing of these starved, neglected and maltreated sufferers from Japanese cruelty was incalculable. This, their first contribution to the new era of peace, was certainly the greatest. But there was no trace of charity or forgiveness towards the Japanese in their personal reactions. Mountbatten especially was deeply and permanently affected by what he had seen, and the accounts given to him by Edwina.

'I had not liked the Japs when I had visited Japan in 1921. They seemed to me to be hard people with hard eyes,' said Mountbatten. 'Now I knew just how horrible they were after seeing such terrible things in Singapore and in the camps. It was the one thing during the war that seared my mind. There were no extenuating circumstances, and I could find no compassion for them at all. I loathed them. That was why I didn't go to the Tokyo Bay surrender – I just couldn't have stood the sight of them all there. My own ceremony at Singapore – well, duty obliged me to be there. But I didn't like it.'

The Japanese people was almost the only subject Mountbatten could find nothing to laugh about. No funny stories, no jokes, ever crossed his lips. When describing the sinking of the *Kelly* and the aftermath, the smile and the jokes might be grim. But he harboured no bitterness against the Germans for machine-gunning them in the sea. 'It was war – all part of the war,' he would say with a shrug of his shoulders. When the Japanese Emperor came over on a state visit to London in October 1971, Mountbatten at first refused to meet him. In the end the Queen commanded him – very gently – and he had to go to the Palace but refused the official banquet invitation. The Japanese, alone among the great nations, were pointedly omitted from the invitation list for the funeral which Mountbatten had so elaborately and meticulously prepared before his death. They were deeply wounded.

Mountbatten's unforgivingness towards his ex-enemy contrasted sharply with his humanity and compassion – over and above his realism – in his treatment of the Indian, Burmese and Siamese nationalists who had fought with the Japanese under the illusion that they were also fighting to free themselves from the yoke of colonialism. So long as they behaved themselves, Mountbatten refused to allow any reprisals against them.

In India, he made himself exceedingly unpopular with many people, especially the old colonial administrators and the bureaucrats of Delhi, but his liberal upbringing as well as his commonsense told him that the old Imperial age had passed with the four years of war in the East, and whatever evil the Japanese brought to the lands they conquered, they had also encouraged the growth of the demand for independence. In this he was strongly supported by Clement Attlee. 'He impressed me greatly,'[4] was the socialist Prime Minister's typically economical way of describing Mountbatten.

Over the following months, there were appalling difficulties to overcome in Indonesia and Singapore, Siam and Indo-China. 'This was something for which I had no previous experience,' said Mountbatten. 'Suddenly I was responsible for one-and-a-half million square miles of territory and 128 million people, many of them starving, many more in some degree of political unrest. I had three-quarters of a million Japanese prisoners-of-war to house and feed and employ until I could get them home, and 123,000 of *our* ex-prisoners-of-war and internees to house and feed and get home. And there was the world's worst-ever shortage of shipping.'

Steadily, surely, progress was made to reconstruct the machinery of government and civil order. During these months of recovery and reorganization, Mountbatten met many of the future leaders of the liberated countries. One meeting especially was to prove of supreme importance. In March 1946 Jawarharlal Nehru, the most important politician in the Indian interim government, came to Singapore, Mountbatten's HQ since the surrender. Against the strong wishes of the local authorities, who wanted to pretend he was not there, Mountbatten had him to dinner and lent him a car for his tour through the streets, to be greeted by the thousands of Indians and Indian troops in the city. Mountbatten prevailed upon Nehru not to lay a wreath at the Army Memorial to the Indian Nationals who had fought (not very effectively) with the Japanese. That was pushing things too far, Mountbatten judged. But both he and Edwina forged a close friendship with the brilliant, good-looking, highly articulate future Indian leader. And it was a relationship that was to pay heavy dividends little more than a year hence.

As soon as Pandit Nehru had left, the Mountbattens flew off to New Zealand and Australia, playing much the same part that the Prince of Wales had played after World War 1 – making a small gesture of gratitude to the Dominions for all the great achievements and sacrifices their people had made in the Allied cause during the war. Mountbatten had always got on well with Australians. One newspaper headlined Mountbatten's life story: 'Australia Welcomes Mountbatten – Prince, Playboy and Paradox.' And that was difficult to improve upon as a definition in four words.

Then, at last, it was home to Chester Street and Broadlands. First the honours, then the rest, and a happy family occasion. In June 1946 the Victory Parade, and, later, a special Parade, too, for Edwina and himself, with an open carriage drive through the City of London, to be presented with a

Sword of Honour and the Freedom of the City. A Viscountcy was bestowed on him, and other Freedoms and degrees and foreign decorations, for which his appetite, as always, was insatiable.

Both the Mountbatten daughters had long since returned from their refuge in the USA. Patricia had served on her father's staff in Kandy during the last months of the war, but Pamela was still too young for war service. It was a great time for family reunions and the Mountbattens' was as happy as any. Whatever difficulties there may have been in the past between the parents – and they were numerous – the family always presented a united front.

Mountbatten enjoyed a special relationship with Patricia. He loved them both but he saw more of himself in her than in Pamela, whom he loved for her tenderness, understanding and creative abilities in the arts. Many years earlier, Victoria Milford Haven had likened the two girls to their cousins and friends, Princess Elizabeth and Princess Margaret Rose, and it was an interesting parallel. A sense of duty, industry and steadiness was to be seen in the elder girl of both families, while the younger tended towards the artistic, haphazard and forgetful.

Patricia – today the Countess Mountbatten of Burma – sits on numerous committees and is full of good works. Her father never failed to add JP after her name when writing it. Pamela, with her dreaminess and restlessness and lack of organization, irritated both her parents, and in his widowhood and her middle age she continued to exasperate Mountbatten with her failure to keep appointments, or write letters, or confirm arrangements. For example, as recently as 1974, when both daughters and sons-in-law accompanied Mountbatten to China, Pamela's seeming failure to pack and prepare, and near-failure to arrive at rendezvous, drove Mountbatten near to distraction. He never could understand how one of *his* children could be so disorganized.

Patricia never gave any cause for anxiety, let alone exasperation. She grew up to be tidy and orderly and organized, like Princess Elizabeth, and both girls went into the services and, of course, performed their duties diligently.

In due course, Patricia met, in Kandy, John Ulick Knatchbull, 7th Baron Brabourne, and her father's ADC, and agreed to marry him. The groom's father had once been Governor of Bombay and Bengal, and temporary Viceroy of India in 1938. It was as satisfactory a match as Mountbatten could hope for.

Broadlands had been restored to its former domestic state, and from here, in October 1946, Patricia left with her father to be married in Romsey Abbey – where Mountbatten was to be buried thirty-three years later after he was blown up – along with the bride and groom, the groom's mother and two of his grandchildren.

It was a very grand, very Mountbatten, social event as well as a wedding. As at Mountbatten's own wedding, the King and Queen were there. For the first time, Prince Philip and Princess Elizabeth were photographed in each other's company publicly. The King was in the original photograph, too, but most of the newspapers printed only the young couple.

As the very satisfactory year of 1946 drew to a close, Mountbatten had one last wish to be fulfilled. He wanted to get back to sea again, and to set a steady compass course towards the real culmination of his career, the office of First Sea Lord.

9
VICEROY

NOT LONG BEFORE he died, Mountbatten said, 'You can divide my life into two. During the first part of my life I was an ordinary conventional naval officer, trying not to be different in the sense of being royal, trying not to show myself off as being rich and ostentatious – like always using a small car to drive to the dockyard instead of my Rolls-Royce.* Then we come to the period when I was pulled out and pushed one generation up. Dudley Pound, for instance, was twenty-four years older and was a post-captain while I was a two-striper. From that time everything was new for me, and most of it for the first time for anyone.

'But my mother had prepared me for it. From the time we began liberating Burma and after the atomic bomb was dropped, I was out on a limb. None of my staff had anything to offer me except conventional nonsense about putting the clock back, suppressing national freedom movements, shooting traitors and all that. I decided not to go along with them and I put the brake on – I didn't want things to go too quickly – and I think history proved me right. But this unconventional decision was largely due to my mother, who was always prepared to look at things unconventionally.

'I was the first inter-service officer, with a rank in each service. I was the only man who had ever been that. When I was Chief of Combined Operations, I was entirely inter-service. In South-East Asia I was not only inter-service, I was inter-Allied. I was right out of the ordinary run from a military point of view. Then the war ended and I was the Supreme Commander with direct control over 128 million people. I had to get them food, give them health, see to law and order, give them information, a broadcasting service. I had to offer them a policy, and I went ahead and did exactly what I thought was right. And in this connection, I always tried to imagine what these decisions would look like in history.

'My mother said, "Don't worry what people think now. Don't ever work

* Not at first. This was something he learned, painfully.

for popularity. Above all, don't care what the newspapers say. What is important is that your decisions should be clear and stand up to history. So all you've got to think about is whether your children and grandchildren will think you've done well."

'On that basis, I made my decisions about Burma, French Indo-China, etc. I was the first person in the world (and I mean this because MacArthur knew damn all about it and Eisenhower was merely going into highly civilized countries) to deal with former colonies where the Japs had been driven out.

'A lot of people today still think I gave away India, but. . . .'

Mountbatten was forty-six and still looked ridiculously youthful. And now he was going back to his first love, in the more orthodox substantive rank of captain. But no, he was not. The Lords Commissioners decreed that he must remain an admiral. Mountbatten was furious. 'It was the same old story. Already, straight away, I was being put again in a false position. My promotion was not due for months, but they insisted that I should carry the rank of rear-admiral immediately.'

Mountbatten could see the progression of his service life clearly. He wanted to return to the Mediterranean, to command the 1st Cruiser Squadron, the closest parallel to his father's appointment as Rear-Admiral Commanding the 2nd Cruiser Squadron in 1905. Then he would be appointed Commander-in-Chief Mediterranean, the 1919 appointment of which his father had been robbed. Next he would come to the Admiralty as his father had done, and work his way up to First Sea Lord. Then, and only then, would his naval and family ambitions be fulfilled, and pride and order restored in the annals of Battenberg–Mountbatten achievement and duty.

As a start, and a refresher after his years of absence from the common round of naval practice, he went on a Senior Officers' Technical Course at Portsmouth. His attendance was brief. One morning, he was interrupted with a message from Downing Street. Please come and see me – signed Clement Attlee. It was not the first of its kind. Recently, his advice had been sought over Burma and about 'the mess caused there by the Governor', as Mountbatten himself expressed it. 'I recommended General Rance as Military Administrator.'

This time India was the main item on the agenda. With Attlee was Sir Stafford Cripps, an expert on the subject, who had recently led a mission to Delhi which had very nearly pulled off an agreement for the transfer of power. 'I had kept in touch with what was going on,' said Mountbatten, 'and I was able to produce reasonably intelligent answers. Suddenly I began to have suspicions. We were talking about Wavell, who was having a very difficult time. I said, "You're not by any chance talking about me relieving him?" Attlee said, "Yes", and I said, "Not on your life. And I'll give you my reasons. First, Wavell is a very honourable man. He may be taciturn but he's first class and if he can't succeed, no one can."

'This, and all other reasons were swept away, so I started making conditions. I must choose my own staff, and there'd be a lot of them, and I'd want Wavell's too, and everyone must be allowed cars and to bring their wives. I wanted "Pug" Ismay. I wanted complete control of the Honours List at the end, with no queries. I wanted my old York aircraft back, fitted out just as I liked it. I wanted....'

Was Mountbatten teasing them? Did he know that all the conditions he was likely to ask would be met? We can assume that he did. Then he tried two tough ones. First, he demanded that he could have his present appointment to the 1st Cruiser Squadron back again when he had finished in India as Viceroy, the highest appointment any British citizen could hold. Attlee said yes. But Mountbatten insisted on Admiralty approval, now. So the First Lord (Lord Hall) and the First Sea Lord (Admiral Sir John Cunningham) were called to Number 10.

Hall agreed at once. 'Hey, not so fast!' said the Admiral. 'We had the gravest doubts about Dickie coming back after running SEAC, where he commanded fleets. It was only allowed after a lot of hesitation. But to come back after being Viceroy of India – absolutely out of the question.'

There was a brief pause. Then Attlee spoke in his dry, sharp, even-toned voice. 'I am not asking for your comments,' he said to Cunningham. 'I am giving you an order.'

After they left, there was another pause before Cripps spoke: he would gladly go as Mountbatten's Chief of Staff if that would help. Mountbatten thought this a terrible idea, and that it would be read by the Indians as confirmation that Mountbatten was a mere regal figurehead. 'It's very good of you, sir. But that is too great an honour,' said Mountbatten.

Years later, Mountbatten insisted that he was being relentlessly cornered. 'I went on fighting.' Next he brought up the King's name. He would have to discuss it with him. Attlee said he had already squared George VI, and that he thought it was a marvellous idea. But, argued Mountbatten, the King had not yet heard his arguments against his appointment. The meeting broke up with nothing decided except that Mountbatten would see the King at once.

Mountbatten reminded George VI that there were hundreds of princely and native states. The Government had treaty relations with them, the King had a special responsibility towards them. Then, if there was civil war, terrible massacres, the royal family would be directly associated, perhaps even held responsible for them, through himself, even if he was only a minor member of the royal family.

Mountbatten reported George VI as saying that it was precisely because of his rank that he approved, that the royal family still had a cachet in India, that Mountbatten should take a personal message from him to the princes.

Mountbatten: 'You do know that the job is almost impossible?'

George VI: 'It *can* be done.'

Mountbatten: 'Only by a miracle. And look how bad it will be for you and the family if I fail.'

George VI: 'Ah, but look how good if you succeed!'

'And that was that!' said Mountbatten. 'I went back to Attlee and said I thought the King was quite wrong, and produced my trump card. I asked innocently if the Secretary of State for India was above the Viceroy, and was told yes, but that he was only a spokesman for the Cabinet.

'You mean I am going to have the Cabinet sitting on top of me all the time? This is ridiculous. The decisions must be mine and mine alone, on the spot.'

Attlee replied, aghast, 'But anything else would mean giving you plenipotentiary powers. We cannot possibly consider that.'

Mountbatten claimed that at this point he rose from his chair. 'For this relief much thanks,' he said, smiling.

'You don't mean you're going, Dickie?'

'I'm going all right. I'm going back to the Navy.'

With hardly a second's pause, Attlee said, 'All right, you can have plenipotentiary powers.'

A week after Mountbatten arrived in India, with a time limit of just fourteen months to hand over power, Nehru asked if by any chance Mountbatten had managed to get some special dispensation. Mountbatten said, 'Yes, as a matter of fact I did. Why do you ask?' Nehru said, 'Because you act entirely differently to any other Viceroy. You talk as if *you* are making the decisions.'

Between the time when the news of the appointment was made public and Mountbatten's departure, his enemies were inclined to say he had taken on the task for its grandeur and pomp, ceremonial and uniforms, and for the historical record: the great-grandson of Queen Victoria, proclaimed first Empress of India, giving away 'the brightest jewel', a 'socialist' viscount behaving traitorously to his class.

His friends and relatives were concerned for quite different reasons. At the best, he would be presiding over a great retreat. The man who had fought so hard to liberate and recover for the Crown vast areas of the Empire was

now forced to hand back the sub-continent. At the worst, he would go down
in history as just one more whose reputation had been lost in the jungle
of Indian politics.

A naval captain, R.C. Todhunter, who had been Mountbatten's Director
of Combined Operations Material, invited him round to lunch shortly before
he left. 'Why on earth', the host asked, 'did you agree to take on such an
absolutely impossible job when you were happily back at sea – where your
heart has always been?'

'The whole thing appals me,' said Mountbatten. 'If I could have turned
it down, I would have done so. But what do you do if you are asked to do
a job, first by the Prime Minister, and then by the King? How can you
refuse?'[1]

Mountbatten's mother was horrified when she heard the news. She saw
at once that her son was being made a scapegoat for the government's
timorousness. He was going to soil his hands in politics – and look what
the politicians had done to her Louis! It would be the end of her Dickie's
career, too.

'Politicians are incorrigible!' she exclaimed to him. He would be playing
with fire. She was very passionate and almost incoherent with rage – not
at him but at Attlee. 'Damn! Damn! Damn!' was all she could say; and
when her son apologized, that made it worse. They finally parted lovingly
as ever, but Victoria's heart remained full of anxiety.

Attlee remained anxious, too, about the Mountbatten appointment, even
though he was responsible for it (and was very proud of it), until he knew
that it would be seen as approved by both parties. This would be revealed
in the House of Commons debate on Indian policy in March, which would
precede Mountbatten's departure.

Lord Butler recalls being summoned to the presence of the Prime
Minister, and finding him characteristically 'sunk in the bottom of his chair'.
He was asked by Attlee if he would test the opposition Conservative Party
to see if it would support or oppose the Bill. 'I don't speak to Winston on
India,' Attlee said. 'I don't trust him. I would be glad if you would take
some soundings over the next twenty-four hours and let me know.'[2]

Butler agreed to do so. He had been Under-Secretary of State at the India
Office for five years, and was a considerable expert on India. He was able
to reassure Attlee. Butler had the gravest reservations about Churchill's
India policy anyway. 'Winston's initial mistake over India', he says today,
'was to lock up Nehru for the greater part of the war. Nehru was very
pro-English, he was almost more English than the English, educated here,
and called to the Bar, and so on. All he had to say to Nehru was, "Japan
is the great danger, you must see that. If they invade and conquer, they

Above: The new Viceroy and Vicereine arrive at Delhi airport, 22 March 1947. Field Marshal and Lady Wavell left the next day.

Below left: 1947: the last Viceroy and Vicereine.

Below right: In full rig, India 1947.

Above left: With Edwina, Princess Anne and Prince Charles, Malta, April 1954.

Above right: The ultimate ambition fulfilled. Mountbatten as First Sea Lord, 1955, with Edwina at Broadlands.

Edwina at her last London home, Wilton Crescent. The portrait is of the late Duke of Kent and the photograph of Princess Elizabeth and Prince Philip shows their arrival in Malta in 1949.

Edwina's bedroom at Wilton Crescent. The portraits are of her children.

Mountbatten's study at Wilton Crescent.

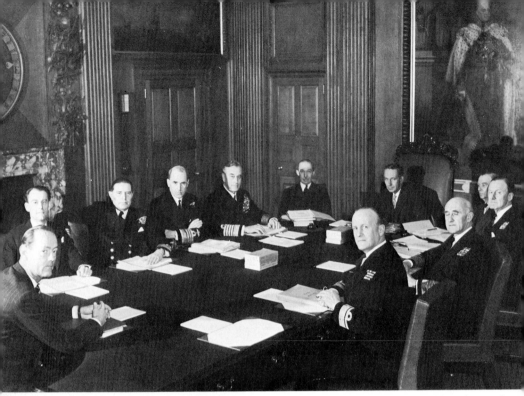

Above: The Board of Admiralty, February 1959, with Mountbatten as First Sea Lord (centre) and the Earl of Selkirk as First Lord in the chair. The Admirals round the table are (l to r) Sir Manley Power, Deputy Chief of Naval Staff, Sir Caspar John, Vice-Chief of Naval Staff, D.E. Holland-Martin, Second Sea Lord, Sir Peter Reid, Third Sea Lord and Controller, and N.A. Copeman, Fourth Sea Lord. Sir John Lang, Secretary, sits between Lord Selkirk and Admiral Holland-Martin. The portrait is of King William IV. Above the fireplace is the wind dial dating from the sailing navy.

Left: The Suez Crisis, 1956. An anxious Mountbatten arrives at 10 Downing Street. He had already warned Eden in writing and by telephone that the operation would certainly lead to disaster.

won't give you your freedom. But you know that we are only searching for ways to transfer power to you peacefully." '

There was much criticism of Attlee's policy in the long debate, even though the Conservative Party did not vote against the Bill. Butler himself, when he spoke, had some grave reservations – but not about Mountbatten. 'It is true that Blake [Civil War colonel] became an admiral after the age of forty, and it is said that one of his commands to his ships was "Right wheel," ' said Butler. 'It is also said that this command, nevertheless, won a battle, and, so, it may well be that the distinguished admiral ... although his methods may be as unorthodox as Blake's, may yet be as successful in meeting the unsatisfactory complicated constitutional problems with which he will have to deal.'[3]

One of Mountbatten's favourite stories about his Viceroyalty was that he had nearly been appointed four years earlier instead of being given the South-East Asia Command. Churchill had asked Leo Amery, Secretary of State for India, for a list of names for a successor to Lord Linlithgow, shortly to retire. Four names were produced, those of Eden, 'Rab' Butler, Lord Salisbury and Mountbatten. Churchill favoured Eden, but the King turned him down because, for safety reasons, he had to have Churchill's successor at home. Butler was out, according to Lord Butler today, because, as Minister of Education, he was too busy and his work too important.

According to Mountbatten's story, that brought his own name to the top of the list. According to Leo Amery, he had put his name in as 'an outsider', and at the bottom of the list. Churchill laughed at the suggestion. 'No, no, much too young!'[4] he said. But Mountbatten maintained that he had not been given the job, and had been given SEAC instead, because Churchill feared he might be too swift and too successful in India.

Churchill certainly feared that Mountbatten would be too swift four years later in the debate in the House of Commons before his departure as last Viceroy. 'Everyone knows that the fourteen months' time limit is fatal to any orderly transference of power,' said Churchill, 'and I am bound to say that the whole thing wears the aspect of an attempt by the Government to make use of brilliant war figures in order to cover up a melancholy and disastrous transaction.'[5]

It could well be disastrous, according to Mountbatten, too. But the adjective 'melancholy' was never spoken in Mountbatten's hearing and was never heard to cross his lips. The job of transferring power in India did, however, carry strong emotional overtones, and was one that would lay him open to criticism from all parties in India with whom he would have to negotiate.

The statistics were truly alarming. Mountbatten was charged with securing the political freedom within a unified state of some 400 million people (one in five of the earth's population), 250 million Hindus, 90 million Moslems, 6 million Sikhs, and the rest made up of numerous sects and Buddhists and Christians and over 500 independent princes and maharajahs. They spoke 23 languages and 200 dialects, and were divided into some 3,000 castes, originating in racial, tribal, occupational and territorial differences. In the past few years, millions had died of hunger and tens of thousands as a result of internecine riot. Some had fought against the Allies, many more had formed the main strength of Mountbatten's armies. Many princes and maharajahs did not welcome the end of British rule. The giant Congress Party, led by Nehru, wanted a united India within the Commonwealth. The Moslem leader, Mohammed Ali Jinnah, called out from the Moslem League for a separate Pakistan. The Moslems had been mainly loyal to Britain during the war, and had provided by far the greater number of troops. Congress helped to widen the division by opposing the war, and Nehru, Gandhi and some 60,000 of their followers were arrested. Nothing much seemed to have changed since 1921.

Mountbatten was taking on the political commitment of a socialist Prime Minister, and would be recognized everywhere as the King's cousin and representative. Attlee himself 'thought the odds were about six to four against success'. Mountbatten's estimate of a thousand to one against seemed more realistic. It was a task that appeared even more difficult than that of liberating South-East Asia and bringing law and order, food and housing, to that ethnic stew of creeds and colours of millions.

The record of past Viceroys was not encouraging. Wavell, a great soldier and with the best will in the world, had in Attlee's judgment, been a disaster as Viceroy in the rapidly changing circumstances and the urgent need for a transfer of power. 'He was a soldier and a singlularly silent soldier,' was Attlee's comment. 'A great man in many ways, you know, but a curiously silent bird, and I don't think silent people get on very well with Indians, who are very loquacious. His mind wasn't supple enough.'[6] Lord Linlithgow, and those before him, had also struggled unsuccessfully with the intractable problem.

There must be a time limit for the transfer of power. Mountbatten claimed it was his idea. This was not true. It was Cripps', and Wavell had already agreed that this was essential. But 'Wavell was frankly defeatist by then,' said Attlee; and 'suddenly I had what I now think was an inspiration. I thought of Mountbatten.'[7]

When all the official records, and Mountbatten's own records in the Broad-

lands Archives, are made available, they will add little to the story of the
transfer of power in India to what has already been written, and especially
in *Freedom at Midnight* by Larry Collins and Dominique Lapierre (1975),
for which Mountbatten provided considerable documentation and as much
of his time and as many of his memories as the authors desired.

It is not proposed here to recount yet again the full sequence of this remarkable contest of wits, of devious negotiation, of dashed hopes and final
agreement thrashed and beaten out of the contestants for power in the two
nations that emerged. All that we will do is to observe the manner and style
employed by Mountbatten *and his wife* in these negotiations, set against the
main outline of events, and judge whether the high claims made for Mountbatten's achievements were justified.

The last days before the departure from London were marked by two
massive social events, an evening reception at India House given by the High
Commissioner, at which the Press was quite uncontrolled and Mountbatten
('We live and learn') was driven nearly demented by Indian and British
reporters and cameramen; and his own farewell party at the Royal Auto-
mobile Club, of which he was President. Members of the royal family, the
Prime Minister and many senior politicians (mostly socialist), and many
theatrical celebrities were there.

Noël Coward was among those who were very indignant about the corner
into which his old friend had been forced. 'The position having become
impossible, they call on Dickie,' he said. And when one of the few Tory
MPs present inveighed against Attlee's government, Noël Coward turned
on him and told him, 'You're no better. Nicer manners perhaps, but no
more talent.'[8]

There were 700 guests altogether, and there can be no doubt that few
of them gave Mountbatten much of a chance.

Mountbatten's York aircraft took off from Northolt airport in north-west
London at first light on 20 March 1947. Besides Rear-Admiral the Viscount
and Viscountess Mountbatten and their daughter Pamela, there were on
board their personal servants, Mountbatten's senior ADC Lieutenant-
Commander Peter Howes, who did so much of the hard work, and Captain
'Ronnie' Brockman, his private secretary and for so many years before, and
after, sharer of private jokes, whom Mountbatten always found congenial
company for lighter moments.

As usual when Mountbatten travelled, the luggage was prodigious in
volume and quantity, and even Edwina, normally the lightest of light travel-
lers, was obliged as Vicereine to bring a wide range of possessions and
clothes. As on her honeymoon (and this year marked their silver wedding),
she brought with her much of her jewellery as well as a diamond tiara for

the proclamation in Delhi. Then there were all the documents, and the two-page definition of the terms of Mountbatten's mission, signed by the Prime Minister.

Mountbatten had laid down a gruelling timetable for the flight, which set the tempo he was evidently intending to sustain throughout the mission, like the destroyer commander he was. Most of the rest of his staff had left the previous day at Ismay's insistence, preferring a more relaxed flight, like the good (no, exceptional*) Army staff officer he was.

Wavell, the outgoing Viceroy, invited Mountbatten's staff to lunch after their arrival. This straightforward, courageous military man who enjoyed history and poetry and had struggled so long and patiently to bring about a settlement that would be acceptable to all parties (and was much admired by all Indians for his honesty and integrity) had accepted dismissal with the same dignity as he had responded to Churchill's telegram of dismissal at the height of the North African war. 'I suppose they are right,' he muttered as he had opened the letter from Attlee. But after talking to Mountbatten's staff, he wrote without bitterness in his journal, and quite truthfully, 'They do not seem really to know very much about it [India] or to have any very new or definite policy.'[9]

Mountbatten's plane, because of its tight timetable, arrived only a few hours later, and the sixty-three-year-old Field Marshal greeted his forty-six-year-old naval successor. Their characters and styles were opposite in almost every respect, but the two men had always got on well. Wavell also knew all about Mountbatten's enjoyment of ritual and ceremonial. On his arrival, wrote Wavell, 'the Bodyguard in full dress looked well and he was very pleased with them.'[10]

The two men then settled down to a two-and-a-half-hour talk. It was a mixed success. With uncharacteristic lack of tact, Mountbatten let it be known that he had been asked to take on the job while Wavell was actually in London and while Wavell was being told by Attlee that all was well, 'So that Attlee's assurances at that time and subsequent letters were completely insincere,' wrote the Field Marshal, now with unmistakable bitterness. 'I am glad that I have finished with politics,'[11] he added as he flew out of Delhi.

'Wavell was very helpful,' said Mountbatten, 'but I saw very little of him. He was anxious to quit as soon as possible so as not to be in the way and

---

* Mountbatten used to say that, during the war, without Ismay, Churchill would have been thrown out and have never been credited with winning the war, such was the power of restraint the Chief of Staff exerted over his boss. 'For thanks, he was left out of Winston's Honours List. He gave him nothing because if he had plied him with honours it might detract in some way from his own reputation for winning the war single-handed. Luckily, Attlee stepped in and put things right when he became PM.'

an embarrassment. We had dinner with him that first evening, and we talked a lot of politics but there was not very much new above what I knew already or had learned in London. I told him that I hoped to bring Gandhi and Jinnah together and he looked at me rather inscrutably. He was probably thinking, "Here comes the new smart boy who thinks he knows everything, but just let him wait!" '

The next morning, Mountbatten and Edwina saw off the Wavells from the airport, an unusual and appreciated gesture, and returned to work. On 24 March, two years after Mountbatten had taken Mandalay, he and Edwina were sworn in as Viceroy and Vicereine, a function as grand as any Swearing-In Ceremony, but for this last time with the single purpose of granting political freedom to 400 million people instead of ruling them.

It was the nearest thing to a coronation, though mercifully briefer: trumpets sounding the prelude, the ADCs leading the Mountbattens, he solemn and noble in the pale blue robe of the Grand Master of the Star of India over the full dress admiral's uniform and wearing the dark blue ribbon of the Garter above the dazzling array of Grand Crosses, orders and decorations; Edwina in gold brocade, with her splendid tiara and more modest display of decorations. They moved to their thrones, cunningly lit red and gold with scarlet velvet hangings, and Sir Patrick Spens, the Lord Chief Justice of India, administered the oath ... 'I, Louis Francis Albert Victor Nicholas Mountbatten....'

Then, with the prior knowledge of only a few members of his staff, Mountbatten delivered a brief address, an unprecedented step. 'This is not a normal Viceroyalty on which I am embarking,' Mountbatten began. 'His Majesty's government are resolved to transfer power by June 1948.... I am under no illusion about the difficulty of my task, I shall need the greatest goodwill of the greatest possible number, and I am asking India today for that goodwill....'

June 1948 – fourteen months. For thirty years a means acceptable to all parties had been searched for. And now this young admiral told them the transfer would take place in fourteen months. The shock when the Indians had first heard could only have been more electric if he had added now that he had promised his family that he would be home in a year. But even his staff did not know that.

He had spoken of goodwill, and it was the search for that goodwill that occupied Mountbatten's earliest days. 'Everything, absolutely everything, was going to depend on personal relationships,' said Mountbatten. 'This I had known from the beginning. I knew Nehru, and there was plenty of goodwill there. We liked one another and Nehru had always been one for rank and titles – a great snob and pro-English even if the English had put him in jail so often. He was marvellous to look at – wonderful eyes, very tall and handsome. Above all, he and Edwina got on marvellously, too. That was a great help.'

In a country not at that time noted for the political influence of its women, the wives of those involved in the transfer negotiations played a strong part; and the leading role was, of course, played by Edwina herself, her leading man Jawaharlal Nehru, now widowed and lonely and needing a woman in his life.

Edwina charmed all the Indian leaders – and every Indian she met, for that matter, and they numbered thousands. Her blend of grace and authority, transparent kindness and interest in everyone she spoke to, her evident love of India and her people, played quite as big a part in the negotiations as Mountbatten himself in one formal and informal meeting after another.

Whether in some riot-and-strife-torn town, the bodies lying rotting in the streets among smashed glass and wrecked rickshaws and the litter of looting, with the temperature in the 110s and her hair soaking with sweat as she grieved or gave comfort; or in Viceroy House, surrounded by the glitter and riches of Imperial power, two hundred servants at her bidding, acting with ease and charm as hostess to her guests, the Vicereine was indeed the graceful empress of the last months of British power. Nothing was too much trouble for her, her patience and energy inexhaustible, whether at home or at the numerous social occasions, from maharajahs' banquets to minor luncheon parties, to which they would fly to all parts of India.

At one of these, in South India, British residents – almost all tea planters – assembled with their wives. The host, who had served in the 14th Army, received the Mountbattens and Pamela. 'Lady Mountbatten, as usual, had done her homework,' the host remembers, 'in respect to the people she was to meet and, on being introduced to my wife, expressed her appreciation of the good work she had done.'

The host felt that a short speech of encouragement to the planters, all of whom had understandable misgiving about the future, was essential, but Mountbatten flatly refused on the grounds that it was an unofficial occasion and he might be reported in the Press. Reassured that there were no reporters and the hall would be cleared of servants, Mountbatten still refused and continued to eat ('and no one enjoyed the meal more than the ex-Supremo himself!').

The host then appealed to Edwina, telling her how disappointed everyone would be. 'Lady Mountbatten immediately got the point and, cupping her hands, leaned over to her husband and earnestly spoke to him.' Mountbatten at once nodded, and indicated that he would make a speech. And, of course, it was superbly done, and had exactly the right tonic effect – 'a clear case', noted this now satisfied host in a grave understatement, 'that behind every successful man is a woman!'[12]

This is a good example of Mountbatten's already fast-developing over-reaction to the Press, which transmitted itself to Prince Philip, the difference between uncle and nephew being that while Mountbatten loved being reported but was so often misreported that he hated to be taken by surprise, Prince Philip would have been happy to go through his official and private life without any reporting at all. Once bitten, twice shy – but Edwina could always apply the soothing antidote.

But on his way back to Delhi (from Nilgiris in this case), on landing at Palam Mountbatten revealed another element in his style of leadership. A signals officer in the control tower recalls how the viceregal Rolls-Royce, waiting in the shade, would speed out to meet the viceregal plane as it taxied in. The Chiefs of Staff, or their deputies, would line up. 'His Excellency would greet the representatives as though he was about to miss the last train, but before entering his Rolls, he never failed to stop, turn round, raise his hat and wave to our little group on the balcony. I never once saw him fail to do this, no matter how hot, tired or harassed he might be. How we loved him for this small courtesy!'[13]

Edwina's action in 'saving' that tea planters' lunch was noted by all the wives. It says a great deal for the quality of mind and tolerance of the British women in India (contrary to common belief) that they accepted and admired Edwina's style as Vicereine, especially as she was widely known as a socialist and had – to say the least – a very liberal manner with the humblest servants.

The fact that a strong affair developed between her and Nehru, and so many people knew or suspected it, in no way diminished her standing. Rather the reverse; and the relationship that developed between the beautiful forty-five-year-old Englishwoman of such notable wealth and aristocracy, with a good stiffening of Jewish blood in her veins, and the English-educated Hindu barrister from Allahabad, leader of the Congress Party and thirteen years older than Edwina, had the most profound effect on the negotiations for the transfer of power.

Gandhi, too fell under Edwina's spell, and was soon calling her 'my dear friend', although the nature of his love for her was utterly different from Nehru's. Gandhi was the first target of Mountbatten's 'search for goodwill'. With the Mahatma on his side, he would, as he defined it, 'be half-way home'.

'We didn't talk any business at all at our first meeting,' said Mountbatten. 'It was just a personal chat. He was fascinated when I told him about my efforts to bring about a meeting between him and the Prince of Wales, when he was in prison in 1921. He talked about his early life, the development of his political beliefs and the non-violent independence movement. We were together alone for two hours, and when we came out, the waiting reporters thought we must have been solving the difficulties of the transfer. Actually, we hadn't mentioned them!'

In fact, politically, Gandhi now carried little weight, but it was of the utmost importance that Mountbatten should have a close understanding and friendship with India's beloved prophet, and this he succeeded in achieving. The other major politicians and statesmen in turn warmed to the aura of affection and goodwill and at the same time recognized Mountbatten's genuine love for their people.

But the one man who could drive home the bolt and secure the lock of a united India was Jinnah. 'Jinnah *was* the Moslem League,' said Mountbatten. 'He held the future of India in his hands. I tried the same technique with him, but it was almost impossible to warm him. He had only one dream, and that was a separate Moslem state.' Jinnah was cold ('My God, he was cold!' Mountbatten would exclaim), arrogant, vain, inflexible – all the characteristics that make negotiation virtually impossible.

Before a word could be said, his appearance was sufficient to depress anyone attempting to negotiate with him. He was as thin as a reed from the Ganges, narrow in face, his brown skin dry even in the hottest weather, his eyes bright and alert, missing nothing. He was a terrific dandy and displayed a wide range of perfectly cut suits, and a monocle completed the picture of some suntanned eccentric from a Michael Arlen novel.

At morning meetings of Mountbatten's staff – 'the Dickie birds' – the subject of Jinnah was more often on the agenda than anyone else. In the end Mountbatten claimed to have thawed him. But everyone knew that the temperature change was that of one man's breath on a frosty dawn. Jinnah was seventy, in poor health, and destined to live little longer than a year.

'It was Jinnah, and the Moslem riots and massacres, that convinced me of two things soon after my arrival,' Mountbatten said. 'The first was that we had to be quick to find a solution. The second, that it was more important to be quick than to have an undivided India. Government was losing control. I decided that we had to be out not in fourteen months but in five months.'

It was as if the sub-continent had been sown with politico-racial time-fused mines. As fast as Mountbatten and Edwina sped about the country defusing them, others were laid in their place. One of the worst problem areas was the North-West Frontier Province. On 28 April, the Mountbattens flew to Peshawar. They were told that a crowd of Moslems, numbering around 75,000, was about to march on Government House, and that their mood was violent.

Mountbatten agreed to meet and show himself to the demonstrators. At the last minute, Edwina insisted on joining him in the car. The sound of chanting, rising to crescendos, could be heard from a distance. The crowd were in a large park and its surrounding fields, stretching far into the distance. They were crying 'Pakistan Zindabad!' over and over again, and waving the illegal green flags of Pakistan. Their imminent march was also illegal and certain to lead to violence.

The Mountbattens climbed up on to a railway embankment, both of them looking informal in khaki bush shirts, and waved to the nearest people in the crowd. The word of their presence spread like a tidal wave. Children were held up to see them, and the cries soon changed to 'Mountbatten Zindabad!' No speech was possible. But their presence was enough. For nearly half an hour, they exchanged waves and smiles before leaving for lunch with the Governor. They learned later that the entire crowd had dispersed peacefully and were returning to their homes.

Edwina made a journey alone to the Punjab where communal rioting was bloodiest, and thousands had already met deaths almost as horrible as those in the Japanese camps two years earlier. It was a harrowing experience, emotionally as well as physically, with temperatures up to 114 degrees in the shade.

She could do little to ease the misery directly. The indirect influence of her dangerous and exhausting work was profound, however. As soon as she returned, grieved and distraught by what she had seen, Mountbatten sent her to recount her experiences to Nehru. Together, the leader of the Congress Party and the most powerful man in India, and the exhausted Vicereine, grieved for Mother India. Then Mountbatten himself worked on Nehru, socialist Viceroy and admiral and socialist barrister and politician, friends with so much in common, and certainly no jealousy on Mountbatten's side of Nehru's relationship with Edwina. On the contrary, he was proud of her rôle.

With every show of reluctance, Nehru agreed that the only way to communal peace and freedom for his country was to divide it.

Whatever other conclusions can be reached about this stage in Indian history, however the figures of the massacred before and after the transfer of power are read, there can be no denying that if freedom for India was to be granted in months and not years and partition was absolutely inevitable, then the Mountbattens between them did a marvellous dual job in putting together the new dual structures of power in India.

Never in Mountbatten's career had Edwina's influence been more openly evident. Only Mountbatten himself fully appreciated the extent of her support through a quarter-century of marriage, guiding him through the tricky channels of those early days in the Mediterranean, from healing the injured pride of fellow officers to charming captains and C-in-Cs; supporting him in those months at Combined Ops, dealing first with the affronted Keyes, the eccentric specialists and wild men that this HQ attracted and the hard men of the services who disapproved of Mountbatten and all his works; above all impressing Churchill with the depth and glitter of her mind so that the war leader always saw Mountbatten as one half of an unique team.

Nehru had capitulated. A great deal of choppy water lay ahead but they had clawed their way off the lee shore of catastrophe. 'So there we were,' said Mountbatten. 'We had all had dreams of a united India, handing over to a single government. Within weeks they were shattered, and we had to make do with second best. But that was better than what I knew to be the alternative.'

By 3 June all seemed clear sailing. There had been last-minute hell from Jinnah and other problems. But now the Mountbatten Plan had been agreed; and on the same day that the leaders met, Attlee announced what he claimed as complete success to the House of Commons.

Four months earlier to the day, commenting on Mountbatten's appointment, the London *Times* predicted that if he brought with him no new initiative, no solution, it 'may reinforce the determination of the Congress Party and the Moslem League to make no concessions to each other'. And then, under the threat of complete breakdown, there would be a decision 'in favour of the claims of one side or the other'. And now it had worked out exactly like that. India was to be partitioned and Jinnah had his Pakistan.

Hindu India formed the great central area of the sub-continent, and because of the approximate lines of religious population distribution, Pakistan was divided, East and West, without any linking corridor – the one concession Jinnah was forced to make.

This was the broad outline, but there were many ragged ends, such as the provinces of Punjab and Bengal, and Kashmir. The legislative assemblies would deal with their future. The representatives of the Moslem districts and the others would vote separately in favour of partition or against it, a simple majority being decisive. If the vote favoured partition, then a boundary commission would set up the frontier line. The North-West Frontier, Sind and British Baluchistan would have a referendum on whether or not to join the Constituent Assembly or form their own.

This was the essence of the Mountbatten Plan. For all but a handful of veteran authorities on Indian politics, races, religions, frontiers, hates and loves, objectors were certain to be blinded by the complexity of the whole business. That, and the speed and decisiveness with which agreement had been reached, were its chief strength. Its weaknesses were to manifest themselves over decades and generations to come.

But, for the present, there were few dissenting voices. Not only Attlee proclaimed that this was a success. Millions of Hindus and Moslems regarded it as a triumph, and outside India some informed opinion and nearly all uninformed opinion considered that the Mountbatten Plan was 'a good thing'. But, of necessity because of the self-imposed time factor, the surgeon had no opportunity of sharpening his knife and the incisions of partition were coarse, leaving millions on the wrong side of boundary lines, and leaving the nawabs and rajahs, khans and maharajahs, many ruling vast areas, in what Mountbatten truthfully described as 'a pathetic situation'.

They still had to be dealt with. 'I knew some of them well, had played polo with them, and they were my friends,' said Mountbatten. 'But these were only a few out of five hundred, some of them rulers of only a small town or a few square miles, others of vast wealth controlling huge and rich areas. I saw some of them separately, and then summoned a full-scale meeting of the Chamber of Princes and told them they had until 15 August to make up their minds whether they would remain independent or throw in their lot with one or other of the two new States.' Some Mountbatten bullied, with others he used more subtle methods. 'He could', commented one observer, 'not only talk the hind leg off a donkey but also the throne from under a prince.'

A tremendous amount of other work remained to be done. Mountbatten had a much-photographed calendar in his office with a ring round 15 August, and every day a date would be deleted as a further emphasis of the urgency.

Friday 15 August 1947 was the most memorable day in Indian history, and one of the most significant in the mid-twentieth century. The world's greatest Imperial power was handing over voluntarily and (with some exceptions) gladly, a great sub-continent, and one in five of the world's population would now control its own destiny. All over Pakistan and the new India, the speeches rang out and the new flags were unfurled. If anyone should question the goodwill that accompanied the exercise, an Indian or a Briton could point to the figure of the first Governor-General, for Mountbatten had been asked to stay on in this role in free India, and had agreed, though for a few months only. (He had hoped to be Governor-General of Pakistan, too, but Jinnah, who had been granted almost everything for which he had worked, would not have that).

The installation of Mountbatten as Governor-General, and now created an Earl, was as elaborate and stately as his installation as Viceroy barely

five months earlier. Messages of goodwill from the world's rulers were read
out, Mountbatten made a speech of friendship and gratitude, followed by
that of Dr Rajendra Prasad, in Hindi and then in English: 'Let us grate-
fully acknowledge, while our achievement is in no small measure due to our
own sufferings and sacrifices, it is also the result of world forces and events,
and last though not least it is the consummation and fulfilment of the historic
tradition and democratic ideals of the British race.' That seemed to say it
all.

Many more ceremonies and celebrations remained, and nothing, it
seemed, could tarnish the glitter and douse the happiness of that day – only
perhaps the thought that 'at this moment the man who had done more than
all of them put together to win India her freedom' felt no call to rejoice,
rather to mourn. 'It was true that the country was free. But more important,
it was also torn asunder and bleeding. For Mahatma Gandhi, there was only
one place to be at this moment – in a noisome slum where he could bring
a little peace and comfort, where he could fast for his people's sins, and
where he could mourn the India, united as well as free, for which he had
worked and prayed and schemed and dreamed.'[14]

'No power in history', ran one Indian newspaper comment on these stirring
days, 'but Great Britain would have conceded independence with such
grace, and no power but India would have so gracefully acknowledged the
debt.'

But there were other debts to be paid – the anguish and sufferings of some
twelve million people forced to uproot themselves for fear of the future.
Communal strife and frenzy on a scale never known before even in this great
suffering land. No one has calculated accurately the number who were shot,
burned, hacked, battered and tortured to death. Perhaps one million, perhaps two million died in the months following partition – certainly many
more than British and Imperial (including Indian) troops killed in World
War I.

With fear and death, there inevitably came famine. Edwina set up a United
Council for Relief and Welfare. At one time, with the hysteria of mass
murder now sweeping in to Delhi itself, many of her Moslem staff were
murdered and Edwina was seen, a mask over her face, helping to move the
corpses to the mortuary, and then touring the hospitals, tending the
wounded and attempting to allay their fears. Delhi resembled a city of the
dead, with no transport entering or leaving. Somehow, Gandhi appeared
on the scene of horror, a frail little spindle-legged saint whom Churchill
had once called a seditious Middle Temple lawyer now posing as a half-
naked fakir.

In a few days it was his seventy-eighth birthday. 'Send me only condolences,' he said. 'There is nothing but anguish in my heart. I cannot live
while hatred and killing mar the atmosphere.' He spoke, too, of the sufferings
of the refugees. 'I have heard that a convoy of Hindus and Sikhs fifty-seven
miles long is pouring into the Indian Union from West Punjab. It makes
my brain reel to think how this can be. Such a happening is unparalleled
in the history of the world and it makes me hang my head in shame.'[15] In
the midst of these scenes of anarchy and death across the sub-continent,
with Edwina working as desperately and effectively as she had during the
liberation of South-East Asia, Mountbatten insisted that they should both
go home.

Nine months earlier, on 25 January 1947, the Mountbattens had given a
dinner party at Chester Street for the royal family, a farewell celebration before
their departure on a tour of South Africa. It was also in the nature of a
pre-engagement party for Princess Elizabeth and Prince Philip. The King
and Queen had finally given their approval to the marriage of their elder
daughter to her cousin. The couple were clearly in love, and everybody was
delighted. The official engagement announcement would not be made until
July. Until then, the news remained highly confidential. But now their health
was drunk in champagne in the house still used by the Mountbattens as
their London base, a comfortable enough residence, but a far cry from the
marble ostentation of Brook House in the old days.

Among the subjects they discussed was Prince Philip's name, and the process of naturalization. The naturalization business was a mere formality. He
would just come up in some list in the near future, along with a lot of others,
probably mostly German-Jewish refugees.

The name, of course, would be Mountbatten. He would have a surname
for the first time. But Prince Philip's uncle, and the King and Queen and
his future wife, were all anxious that none of the dirt of the Beaverbrook
vendetta would brush off against Mountbatten's nephew with the taking
of this name, let alone against the heir to the throne whom he was shortly
to marry.

This was especially important because the campaign would hot up as
Mountbatten took over as Viceroy, and would inevitably be attacked more
fiercely than ever by Beaverbrook's pro-Imperial newspapers for being a
traitor to his country and giving away the Empire. 'I told the King and Queen
that I would talk to the Beaverbrook chairman on the subject,' said Mountbatten. 'When they asked if that wasn't putting my head in the lion's mouth,
I said I thought I would survive. So I telephoned the chairman of Beaverbrook newspapers, not Max, and asked him if he would come along with

his editors Arthur Christiansen of the *Daily Express* and John Gordon of the *Sunday Express* for a drink. He was very surprised and obviously couldn't imagine what it was all about, but said they would come.

'Prince Philip was there when they turned up, but after the introductions he kept out of the picture and didn't say anything. I said, "I've asked you along because I would value your advice. Prince Philip is applying for naturalization and if he is successful, he will assume the family name Mount-batten. You must know as much as anyone in the country about public opinion, and how the public will react to this. What do you think?"

'They all agreed in turn that they thought that it was an excellent idea – difficult to say anything else with him there – and that the British public would warmly approve. So I said, "That's awfully reassuring and very good of you to come along and let me ask you frankly like this," and so on. "Have another drink?"

'Of course, when Max heard how three such hard men of the world had been outmanoeuvred, he was amazed, and when the official announcement was made they were forced to say what a wonderful thing.'

Shortly after this the *London Gazette* published the names of 817 newly naturalized citizens. Under 'M' was 'Mountbatten, Philip; Greece; serving officer in His Majesty's forces; 16 Chester Street, London, sw1. 28 February 1947.' This new Englishman would, it added, be known as Lieutenant Philip Mountbatten, RN.

The wedding was to be on November 20. In the post-war era of gloom and austerity, it would be the greatest, most glittering royal occasion since the coronation of 1937. For Mountbatten it was a great deal more. The seal-ing of ties between the British monarchy and his own family was at once a triumph and the natural culmination (as he saw it) of his family's ascent from the dynastic depression into which it had fallen when his great-grand-father had married a commoner and the *Almanach de Gotha* had gone so far as to derate the Battenbergs.

Prince Louis' enthusiasm for the Royal Navy, his naturalization, his pro-motion in the service, Queen Victoria's affection and admiration for him, his young brother's marriage to the Queen's last daughter. Then the growing family ties with the royal family, Mountbatten's father's position at the very top of the Royal Navy, the birth of his sister's son Philip in the year of his father's death, like the passing on of some great seal of office – and now this boy's marriage to the future Queen.

The stage-by-stage progression seemed now to have a sublime inevitability to it, and a tidiness and content of everything he loved and admired which warmed Mountbatten's heart as no other family event could equal. If only his father could have been there to see it! How he would have approved, and loved this enchanting young couple! (His mother approved, too, but was being predictably matter-of-fact about the business.)

The November royal wedding was in Mountbatten's mind when he had cut the period allowed for the transfer of power, already far too short in the eyes of Indian government officials, the Indian Civil Service, the Indian Army, the India Office and the Foreign Office in London as well as numerous senior politicians, all of whom conceded that self-government was eventually inevitable. A second consideration was his urgent wish to get back to the Navy, in order to continue his climb up the ratlines to the crow's nest of the First Sea Lord's office.

Well, the Mountbatten destroyer had proved it could still make 35 knots, and by mid-August it looked as if he would be able to conform to his own compressed timetable. And then came the riots, on a scale and of a degree of horror no one had predicted. And there was no sign of any improvement in the situation throughout the whole sub-continent. Could he and Edwina leave for the wedding under these circumstances, with his office working day and night, and Edwina racing from one scene of riot to a hospital and on to a refugee camp, day after day? With military and civil decisions of a most crucial and life-and-death nature to be made daily?

If there was any struggle of conscience, it was a brief one. Edwina was deeply concerned about leaving her work, and the unfortunate interpretation that would be put upon their departure; and for the captain of the *Kelly* who had not gone down with his destroyer, talk of rats and sinking ships was considered in the worst taste. His public relations officer, of great experience, loyally reassured Edwina that of course she must go. To cancel now would only add to the sense of crisis in the public mind. Mountbatten, independently, told the same officer that he was far from happy about leaving, right up to the last moment, and was similarly reassured, as he knew he would be.

They set off for their brief return home early on Sunday morning, 9 November, following their usual breathless schedule, and landed at Northolt. The arrival was in character, too, both Mountbattens throwing themselves into a whirlwind of telephoning, letter-writing, parties and arrangements. Edwina sped to Broadlands, lovely in its autumn colours, the cool River Test and the chill weather in such sharp contrast with Delhi. Here she completed arrangements for the honeymoon stay of the royal couple, a parallel of their own twenty-five years earlier.

Mountbatten reported to Attlee, and got a warmer reception than Wavell. Then on to lunch with the King, then to unveil a portrait of Nehru at India House, and back to Buckingham Palace for dinner.

Then the christening of their first grandchild, Norton Louis Philip

Knatchbull, by the Archbishop of Canterbury, and everybody attended that, of course. An eve-of-wedding cocktail party, with Edwina as hostess, and Mountbatten rushing off to Prince Philip's bachelor party. And so to the Abbey on the twentieth....

The Mountbattens were in India again a week later. Edwina went straight back to her relief work. Over and above the deaths by violence, thousands were dying from exposure in the November winds in refugee camps in the Punjab.

Two events followed in swift succession, each marking symbolically the extremes under which the masses in India suffered. The first was the Silver Jubilee of the Maharajah of Jaipur, as grand and glitteringly ostentatious and extravagant an affair as ever occurred in the days of the British Raj. In this land of extremes, the scene in Jaipur contrasted grotesquely with those of riot, pillage, rape and murder that stalked the nation.

In one more desperate attempt to stem the flow of violence and bloodshed, in the New Year, Gandhi began a fast, a fast unto death, and was soon so weak that he had to be carried to prayer meetings. Mountbatten visited him anxiously. Mahatma was just able to whisper. Roguishly, he said, 'It takes a fast to bring the mountain to Mahomet.'

Then, on the afternoon of 30 January 1948, Mountbatten returned to Delhi from a visit to Madras. He arrived to receive, first, the grave news that two men had been found with grenades in a crowd being addressed by Nehru, and that they were certainly intended for the Prime Minister. A few minutes later, the news came over the car's radio that shots had been fired at Gandhi, and that he had been hit three times. Before a doctor could arrive, Mahatma had died, muttering, '*Hey Rama!*' – Oh God.

'To say that I was appalled conveys nothing,' said Mountbatten. 'I was numbed and utterly terrified. His little pinched face looked serene in death when I went to his house, where a great crowd had already gathered.

'Someone in the crowd shouted, "It was a Moslem that did it!" I immediately shouted back, "You're a fool. You know nothing. It was a Hindu."

'I had no idea, of course. How could I? But if it had been a Moslem, then civil war was inevitable and the carnage terrible. Luckily I was right. It was a Hindu fanatic.'

Four months later, the term of Mountbatten's office expired, and he and his family prepared to leave India. It was a parting of two friends, and warm were the words, glittering the ceremonies, generous the gift on both sides. Edwina in particular had forged a deeply loving relationship with the people to whom she had given so much of her time and energy and compassion.

Mountbatten was seen in the simple terms of a great and royal figure who had given them their freedom. The love for him endured all his life. In Britain, when he was murdered thirty-two years later there was a day of mourning. In India, mourning was ordered for two weeks, and the feeling ran even deeper among all classes, including those who had grown up since the last days of the British Raj.

Many judgments representing all shades of political opinion have been passed on Mountbatten's mission of 1947, from the one extreme of Churchill and numerous pro-Imperial politicians and Lord Beaverbrook, for whom it was one more act of criminal folly by the Earl he loathed; to the extreme left view that it had come too late to save the massacres.

Today, elder statesmen hold widely divergent views on the transfer of power. 'Whatever one thought of the instructions he was given as Viceroy, he was only doing his duty as a public servant in carrying them out. His judgment over Kashmir may have been good or bad,' says Lord Hailsham. 'I am in no position to say. But I think the Conservative Party treated him ungenerously considering that he was only carrying out his instructions. Certainly he was a very good selection as Viceroy, and it was a great strength for him to have the royal connection.'[16]

Sir Harold Wilson says that his party was surprised at the bad reception Mountbatten got on the completion of his Viceroyalty. 'I think everyone in the party agreed with what he had done,' he said, 'except perhaps a few diehards like Reggie Paget.'[17]

Lord Butler, who really knew the Indian scene and was Under-Secretary of State at the India Office for five years in the 1930s, thought that Mountbatten's great mistake was in underestimating Jinnah, 'an inflexible, tough and ruthless man, a terrifying chap'. Butler thought that 'we all underestimated the strength of Jinnah's jealousy of Mountbatten's relations with Gandhi and Nehru. Then Edwina was dynamic with Gandhi and Nehru, especially Nehru,' said Butler, 'but she was not dynamic with Jinnah. All the same, partition could not have been avoided even though the Cripps Mission had got so close to agreeing a formula which would have avoided it. By 1947 and with Jinnah so jealous, it was too late. It was also inevitable that Jinnah would become Governor-General of Pakistan, in spite of all Mountbatten's efforts to become super-Governor-General of both countries.'

Lord Butler thought that Mountbatten deserved but actually escaped the full impact of the odium for the massacres, adding a lighter footnote to this dark page in history: 'Monty [Field Marshal Earl Montgomery of Alamein] came out to give his opinion on the massacres. "All you want is three divisions!" he said in that clipped Army voice of his.'[18]

Mountbatten's public relations officer described the acceptance by all parties of the Plan as Mountbatten's 'moment of personal triumph'.[19] It was no such thing, alas. Given the time that the British government had calculated was needed, the Mountbatten mission might have pulled off what Sir Stafford Cripps had come within an ace of doing a year earlier. Wavell, given time (Julian Amery believes he wanted ten years) might have pulled it off, for, however hard he played the part of 'the strong, silent man', he was greatly respected by everyone for his honesty and truthfulness. Even Jinnah respected him, and he was the key figure always. And Wavell had been sturdily neutral.

But the destroyer captain rang down 'Full Speed Ahead' from the moment he put to sea on Operation Transfer, and Nehru and Congress were battered into accepting Partition with the gunfire still echoing in their ears. No one really had time to think, except Jinnah who got 90 per cent of what he wanted. He certainly did not think that he owed any thanks. This old, sick, prickly Moslem had indeed seen Edwina being 'dynamic with Nehru', seen the warmth of Mountbatten's relations with Nehru, too. Nothing in Jinnah's mind called for gratitude.

Historians will go on arguing for ever about Mountbatten's mission, and its degree of failure or success. Mountbatten himself knew, as always, that he had done the right thing, and in this case, the only thing. But even he did not regard it as the triumph claimed for him by his public relations chief.

It is the easiest defence in the world to claim that speed was essential. It can never be disproved. No one can ever prove that more, or fewer, lives would have been lost if there had been a greater show of patience and less need to finish the job in a rush, and then go tearing off to his nephew's wedding, and return for the assassination of Gandhi.

Three months after Mountbatten's death, on the day that the statue to Lord Attlee was unveiled in the House of Commons, the political commentator, Alan Watkins, wrote in the London *Daily Telegraph*:

> Indian independence, we can now see, was inevitable. But under Attlee a lot of people – the precise number is still disputed – were massacred. Perhaps the carnage would have been even greater if independence had not come at the time and in the way it did. We do not know. But it seems excessive, to say the least, to hail an act which directly led to the sanguinary deaths of millions of people as one of prudent and enlightened statesmanship.

Attlee's self-defined 'inspiration' in selecting Mountbatten stemmed from his recognition that India, as a deep barb in the new Labour government's flesh when there were so many other massive solutions to be sought and resolved, had to be extracted quickly, the flow of blood staunched.

The choice of Mountbatten was anything but an inspiration. Given that the transfer of power must be accomplished swiftly and with the least possible regard for the long-term consequences for India and every regard for the short-term benefits for a harassed and near-bankrupt nation committed to an unparalleled volume of legislation, there was *no one* but Mountbatten available who could do the job, even without Edwina.

The job needed youthful energy, a lust for speed, authority, charm and ruthlessness. Edwina was the bonus, and the most subtle and percipient minister could never have predicted the unusual role, with Nehru as partner, that she would play. Attlee knew from wartime experience that Mountbatten possessed a sense of duty 'deeper than did ever plummet sound', and also an urgent need to resume his career. Wavell would go on patiently negotiating, seeking justice for all, for years. But that was not good enough for Attlee. And so the soldier who had saved Egypt and defeated an army five times the weight of his own, at a time when Britain stood alone and with nothing else to cheer or hope for, was thrown out.

Attlee did not even have the courage to sack him to his face, but let him leave the country ignorant of the fact that his successor was already appointed. And at the end there was precious little gratitude shown to one of the greatest and certainly the most decent of all Britain's great soldiers for his attempt to carry out a difficult task. On his return, he had reported to Attlee, who after a brief conversation, in Wavell's words, 'bowed me out without one single word of thanks or commiseration'.[20] Wavell did not rule out partition as the final solution but he never wavered in his belief that the transfer could be made to a united India. But there must, as he told Attlee at this last unhappy parting in March 1947, be 'detailed arrangements so as to avoid confusion when we leave'.

Alas, no such detailed arrangements were ever made. There was no time. Churchill's prediction that 'a fourteen-month time interval is fatal to an orderly transference of power' was proved tragically true. In the Delhi files was a contingency paper written by Lieutenant-General Sir Francis Tuker, GOC Eastern Command in India in March 1946, detailing the preparations that should be made if it should come to the division of India. And partition was inevitable, judged this soldier, if the negotiations for the transfer were rushed. Mountbatten never saw it, and of course no such contingency planning was made in the period of Mountbatten's Viceroyalty. There was no time, for a decision in favour of Partition was made within fourteen days of his arrival.

The result was the worst horrors India had ever known, and inter-racial outrages on a terrible scale. It led to the disembowelling of tens of thousands of pregnant women, the cutting off of breasts, the rape of girls – all before being bludgeoned to death or hacked to pieces; to the indescribable tortures carried out on countless Sikhs and Moslems and Hindus; to tens of thousands dead from exposure and starvation.

Attlee believed, for the comfort of his conscience, that it could have been worse, that India would remain divided only temporarily, and persuaded Mountbatten that this would be the case. Instead, more than thirty years later, the sub-continent, after several wars and the threat of wars, remains as divided as ever, with incalculable consequences for both nations, and on the defence of the world against revolutionary Marxism.

When Mountbatten's mother deplored his acceptance of the thankless task, she believed that, whatever happened, he could not win. If he became involved in politics, some of the dirt was bound to rub off. When Noël Coward called the job 'hopeless', he did not mean that Mountbatten was incapable of accomplishing it. He meant much the same thing. Whatever the outcome, he would be vilified. Both these wise people were right.

Mountbatten should never have been given the job, which for reasons of duty he inevitably accepted. His German mind and naval upbringing made him constitutionally ill-equipped for the slow, patient negotiations with the Oriental mind, navigating amid the intricacies of political and inter-religious, inter-racial shoals and currents.

Having completed the task, he should have tempered his judgment on the results of his mission with a touch of modesty. In view of the terrible suffering caused to this great land following independence and partition, no matter to what degree it was caused by haste, he should not have looked upon Independence Day 'with completely undiluted pleasure',[21] as he described it. A touch of humility and even shame was perhaps called for; and, over the subsequent years, less readiness to recall with pride and vainglory his regal, busy days as 'The Last Viceroy'.

So much of what he accomplished in his life he could be justly proud of. But not of those months in India. Churchill's word 'scuttle' for the transfer of power was journalese and an exaggeration. But not much of an exaggeration.

10
FIRST SEA LORD:
THE SUMMIT

WITH APPEALING self-perception, Mountbatten once said, 'One of the reasons I was so keen to get back to sea and rattled that I had been frustrated was that I was sure I was becoming a megalomaniac. I had seen it happen to Winston, I saw it happen to Roosevelt, and I knew I was getting the disease, too.

'At the beginning you think it is going to be OK, that you won't fall for this self-obsession. Then you begin to think you're doing the right thing, and you turn out right. Then everybody says you're right, and you begin to think how right they are to think you're always right. You get very pleased with yourself. I was getting very pleased with myself and I knew this was very bad for me. It means one can't do one's job properly.

'All this was a very important reason for getting back to sea where you can never afford to get too pleased with yourself. And it was another reason why I wanted to get back to my proper substantive rank, and so furious when they wouldn't let me.'

On the Mountbattens' return to England in June 1948, after elaborate celebrations and an emotional farewell (compounded for Edwina by having to put down her beloved twelve-year-old dog whom she feared would not survive six months of quarantine), there was wide speculation on Mountbatten's future. Most ex-Viceroys were so old that they were put out to grass with a load of honours and decorations. Mountbatten had just about every decoration, and the idea of his retiring at forty-eight was ludicrous. Nor did anyone who was not privy to Attlee's bargain believe that he could return to the Royal Navy, where he would have to serve under senior admirals who had recently been subordinate to him.

'A lot of posts were offered to me at around this time,' said Mountbatten. 'The Duke of Gloucester had already offered to hand over his governor-generalship of Australia, and I had politely turned it down. He was rather put out when I went to India instead. I was also offered the governorship of Malta, and rather rudely in this case turned it down, pointing out that there are more towns and villages in India than there are people in Malta.

'At a Government dinner just after we got back, I found myself talking to dear old Ernie Bevin [Foreign Secretary in the Attlee government] and he said, "You ought to be our man in Russia. If you were offered the post of ambassador, 'ow would you feel about it?" I said, "I don't think I would be very popular there even though I'm supposed to be a socialist." " 'ow's that?" he asked. And I said, "Well, the Bolsheviks murdered my father's first cousin, two of my aunts on my mother's side, and five of my first cousins."

'Bevin looked shocked and puzzled. "Who were *they?*" he asked. So I said, "The Tsar and Tsarina, their five children and the Grand Duchess Serge." I don't think he actually said "Gaw blimey!" but it was something like that.'

Not long after this, in 1949, Lord Jowett flew out to Malta to invite Mountbatten to become Minister of Defence. There were numerous other offers, political and diplomatic, including ambassador in Washington. 'But everyone was wasting his time,' said Mountbatten. 'I was going to the Mediterranean again, and I was going to command the 1st Cruiser Squadron, and that was that.'

Before leaving for the Mediterranean, there were official and domestic duties to attend to. Broadlands, which had been in Edwina's possession for some ten years, had never seen them for more than a few weeks at a time. There was much to be done here, and at Classiebawn Castle, where they spent a few days with Pamela and Patricia and her family, and where the lobsters were better than ever. Classiebawn became for Mountbatten's grandchildren the summer holiday centre, the rendezvous for the families, just as Heiligenberg had once been for Mountbatten.

A few more days in Canada to open the Canadian National Exhibition in Toronto, and then to the south of France to see a retired family retainer, and the Duke and Duchess of Windsor ('He was looking marvellous, and they had both thrived on the war'), but not Winston Churchill: he had refused to speak to Mountbatten since his 'sell-out' of India.

A last visit to Broadlands, this time with a surprise guest. Nehru had arrived in England for the Dominion Conference, and Edwina insisted that he should come and spend a night at Broadlands, where she taught him Racing Demon. He remained a close family friend and they met whenever they could. He outlived her by four years.

It was more than ten years since Mountbatten had served in the Mediterranean, and Edwina had been a service wife in Malta. 'It was an odd experience to go back again,' said Mountbatten. 'So much was the same and so much was different. I had seen once before Britain's defences run down, and now it was happening again, though nothing like to the extent they have been today [1973]. We still had quite a strong surface fleet, we had battle-ships still serving in the Navy, and my cruiser squadron was still powerful by the standards of that time. I found myself slotting back into the old life, and enjoying it.' Asked if there was any problem about his rank, he answered brusquely, 'Certainly not.'

Casa Medina had somehow survived the holocaust, but was now con-verted into flats. The wounds of the George Cross Island were to be seen everywhere, and Edwina and Pamela wondered how anyone had survived the years of bombing. They stayed at a hotel while Edwina searched for a house, and at length (for there was a severe shortage) discovered a derelict ruin.

The ex-Vicereine who had managed two hundred servants moved excitedly into one room and bullied workmen to prepare the rest of the house for occupation. The Villa Guardamangia made a modest but comfortable home for the Mountbattens, and they began entertaining again as in the old days, but – like everything else – on a diminished scale.

In October 1949 Prince Philip arrived on the island to take up his appointment as First Lieutenant in the destroyer HMS *Chequers*. This was the happiest and most fulfilled period for uncle and nephew. What more could they ask for? They were serving on Britain's premier station, loved their work, and their off-duty recreations – polo especially, and a new dis-covery for Mountbatten, aqualung skin-diving, a hobby he enjoyed for years. Princess Elizabeth joined them, and for a while the party was complete, enjoying the most relaxed and carefree time in their lives, sunbathing, swim-ming and playing games in privacy and with few of the weighty responsibili-ties they were soon to bear.

In 1950, Mountbatten was recalled to the Admiralty and appointed Fourth Sea Lord. It was a rung on the ladder, if a modest one. He was a vice-admiral now – a real, substantive one, and with only one ring fewer than seven years earlier. The anomaly of his position was easier to manage at sea than in a shore appointment. Senior admirals were inclined either to 'pull' their rank or act in an ingratiating manner towards him.

Sir John Lang, who had joined the Admiralty only days after Prince Louis had resigned as First Sea Lord and is more knowledgeable about the inner workings of the Royal Navy than anyone alive today, was Secretary of the Admiralty at this time and remembers a subdued Mountbatten, anxious not to be seen to be throwing his weight about. 'He was relatively piano as Fourth Sea Lord,' Lang recalls. 'Dealing with the nuts and bolts, stores, victualling, seeing about oil supplies, transport, that sort of thing. He didn't attempt to interfere with anything outside his own department. He just got up and spoke his part on his subject and no more.'[1]

But after a time he could not resist giving his opinion on other subjects, and began to show some of his irrepressible spirit. As First Lord of the Admiralty, Lord Longford found that the other members of the Board could find Mountbatten a handful. Admiral of the Fleet Bruce Fraser, a great war hero, was First Sea Lord, and successor to Somerville in the Far East when Mountbatten finally succeeded in having the latter removed. Not so long ago, therefore, Mountbatten had been his superior.

Lord Longford recalls a brief exchange, typical of many at meetings of the Board. Mountbatten had intervened again outside his department. 'You leave me, young fellow me lad, to run my department, and I'll leave you to run yours.' Mountbatten responded at once in proper quarterdeck manner, 'Well, sir, if that's how you put it, I must bow to your superior stripes.' Fraser, much chastened, replied, 'No, no, my dear boy. We are all equal on the Board of Admiralty.'

It was not a very comfortable time.

Mountbatten's first period on the Board coincided with a severe family loss. 'My mother decided that she wouldn't die until she saw me safely back in the Royal Navy and on my way to the top. She never doubted for a minute that I should get there. She didn't care twopence about me being Viceroy, in fact she hated it. All she wanted was for me to be First Sea Lord, and that was because she understood how I felt.

'She was taken ill in the early autumn of 1950. She was at Broadlands at the time. When I went to see her she said, "I must get back to London, Dickie. It's much better to die at home. I shan't be coming back here." There was no point in arguing with her on something like this, though I argued with her about almost everything under the sun.'

The doctor called at Kensington Palace. 'He was a very nice chap,' Mountbatten recalled, 'and he came in and said, "Your heart's giving out, but I think we can pull you round though you're in a very bad way." And my mother replied at once, "Oh, that's good because I want to go quickly. I don't want you to interfere with this. I am eighty-seven and have decided that the time has come for me to die. Thank you so much for all you have done. Goodbye and please don't call again." Next day he did call and my mother said, "What are you doing here? I told you I didn't want to see you again. Can't you let me die quietly?" Then she turned to me when he had gone and asked, "Why do doctors always think they've got some sort of ghastly duty to keep one alive. I've come to the end of my useful life and that's that." She wouldn't have any nurses either, but she allowed some nuns to come and help.'

But the Dowager Marchioness of Milford Haven, Queen Victoria's favourite grand-daughter, did not die as quickly as she wished. She would wake up very cross. 'Why am I still here?' she would demand. Her grandchildren had to come and see her to say goodbye twice, and this was contrary to her sense of order and tidiness. She was even more furious when she heard that Prince Philip and Princess Elizabeth had put off an important engagement on her behalf.

This very remarkable old woman died at last, without pain, on 24 September 1950. When the present Queen was a young girl, she saw little of her, but when she was eighteen, Victoria came to stay at Windsor Castle with the King and Queen to rest from the flying bomb attacks on London which were wearing even her down.

'She was dressed and shaped very much as old ladies were at that time,' the Queen recalls. 'She always wore large black hats, she said grey depressed her. Her voice was very loud and rather guttural, and she seemed so masculine in many ways – she used to walk with heavy masculine strides. I don't think she liked children very much, and she thought we were rather a nuisance. But she talked *all* the time, coughing and smoking, with our instruction in mind. I remember her as having a man's mind, and she was very formidable and rather frightening. We certainly never teased her, any more than I would have teased my grandmother. We used to take her for walks to help look after her. Formidable, frightening, with a brilliant man's brain, that's how I would sum her up. A quite extraordinary woman.'[2]

Queen Elizabeth the Queen Mother also spoke of Victoria Milford Haven's 'practical man's mind', and recalled her long memory and her fund of stories going back to the German and Russian royal families. 'What a great reader she was! She would read everything she could lay her hands on, and especially history. She was a very concise person, and she knew exactly what she wanted to say without any hesitation,' she said. 'She always got on well with the King, who enjoyed her company.'[3]

Princess Alice, Countess of Athlone, also a grand-daughter of Queen Victoria, remembers her today as 'a very fascinating person'. This Princess, now ninety-seven, can remember her as quite a young woman with a growing family, and ascribed her deep sense of responsibility to the early death of her mother. 'Everyone who knew her liked her very much,' she said, 'but she was not the kind of person you loved greatly. She always used to say that Prince Philip had a better brain than Dickie, and that is saying a lot.'[4]

Prince Philip, for his part, remembers his grandmother's 'remarkable mind'.[5] And there is no doubt that this astute, analytical, incisive brain

which Mountbatten inherited also had a tremendous influence upon his development. To have a mother of the calibre of Victoria Milford Haven for
fifty years of your life, a wife of the calibre of Edwina for thirty-eight years,
with a nimble brain yourself and the privileges of wealth and royal birth,
is bounty for any man.

Many women had a great influence over Mountbatten, as we have seen,
and they continued to wield it to the end. But with the loss of his mother,
who had taught him from his earliest years and had always been so close,
emotionally and cerebrally, a gap, wider than that caused by the death of
his father, made itself felt to Mountbatten. 'I missed her terribly,' he said,
'and would have loved her to know for certain that I would be First Sea
Lord. Perhaps she did in her heart.'

If she did, she showed brave confidence in her son, for many obstructions
still lay between Mountbatten as Fourth Sea Lord and his ultimate ambition.
First, at his own request, he went to sea again, his last active seagoing command, the one to which his father had aspired. In May 1952 he was appointed
c-in-c Mediterranean, his old Brook House model cabin reality at last.

It was a very different fleet, in its strength and the nature of its *matériel*,
from the Mediterranean Fleet of 1907 when Prince Louis was second-in-
command. By no stretch of statistics could Britannia be said to rule the
waves. The United States Navy was immeasurably more powerful, and the
Soviet Navy was growing fast, too – so fast and so threateningly that a
North Atlantic Treaty Organization had been set up to deter any further
excesses of Russian aggrandizement. In the 1870s Prince Louis had taken
part in the naval moves in the Mediterranean to contain Russian expansion-
ism. Now, in 1952, Mountbatten was appointed NATO Supreme Commander
Allied Forces, Mediterranean. Once again, father and son strode through
the ever-repeating cycle of history, separated by no more than a few steps.

'By now I had had some experience of dealing with a multi-national force,
some of whom had been our enemies, some our friends, others neutral in
the last war,' said Mountbatten. 'Of them all, the only ones with whom I
had much difficulty were the French. They remember for a long time, and
many of them still had not forgiven us for destroying their fleet at Oran.

'I made use of the same formula I had always believed in – I made friends
with the commanders and persuaded them to work together. It wasn't easy
at first, but we slowly thrashed it out, and then we began training – just
as we had in SEAC back in 1943–4.'

This, without doubt, was Mountbatten at his best: at sea, but with great
responsibilities that could be sustained only by his special qualities of firm-
ness and charm. At the lower level, he was loved and admired by almost all
he came across, just as he had been in the little *P31* thirty-five years earlier.

'He attended to the everyday affairs of the ship as if his promotion depended on it,' wrote the chaplain of his flagship. 'Also he was on the easiest of terms with the sailors and never failed to jump up on a bollard and address the ship's company about a forthcoming cruise or exercise. The closeness to every man in the cruiser [HMS *Glasgow*] showed that the man had not changed. He had the rare virtue of being able to communicate with all from top to bottom.'[6]

That he had succeeded with the top, too, was emphasized at the end of his tour of duty in December 1954 when six admirals representing the Allied Commanders-in-Chief under him formed a crew, and rowed him – all grinning broadly – to his flagship. No one could have devised a nicer and more symbolically appropriate conclusion to his last service at sea.

Shortly before he left the Mediterranean Fleet for the last time, there took place what seemed at the time to be a rapprochement with Churchill. Late in 1954 Churchill celebrated his eightieth birthday. He was still Prime Minister, the Conservatives having returned to power in 1951, but long past his best and due for retirement.

He was staying in Beaverbrook's villa at Cap d'Ail when Mountbatten's despatch vessel, HMS *Surprise*, which the Mountbatten family used as a sort of glorified yacht, anchored at Villefranche. 'A message arrived,' Mountbatten said, 'inviting us for dinner. So Edwina and I went and Clemmie was there, but no one else. We had a very good dinner, and when Winston and I were alone with some good brandy and cigars, he said (and there were tears in his eyes), "Dickie, I have always loved you, and I am glad we are friends again. I can even forgive you for the terrible things you did in India."

'So the next day I invited him on board the *Surprise* and he said he'd like to see a submarine so I fixed that. He was very interested in everything, and there were flashes of the old Winston, but he was very doddery. A few nights later the Préfet of the Alpes Maritimes gave us both a dinner. He made a long, flowery speech full of *entente cordiale*, and I replied, and Edwina and Clemmie bullied Winston into making one, too, all in his usual terrible accent.'

So it seemed that the two men were friends again after the years of silence, and that when the vacancy for First Sea Lord came up in 1955, Churchill would give his full support to Mountbatten's appointment, just as he had to his father forty-three years earlier.

Within the Admiralty, there was a lot of opposition to Mountbatten's appointment. 'There were many brilliant men who had made great names for themselves in the war,' Lieutenant-Commander Kemp recalls, 'men who had mostly followed the classic path upwards, with a big staff appointment, then a sea appointment, and another staff appointment, and so on up the ladder the traditional way. These were the people who were the candidates for First Sea Lord, and there was very strong prejudice against Mountbatten by hard core professionals like Bruce Fraser.'[7] It was all a long way from the admiring fraternity of the NATO admirals.

Another opponent, long since retired but, as an Admiral of the Fleet and wise old bird, certain to be canvassed was 'A.B.C.', Admiral Lord Cunningham of Hyndhope, who had succeeded Dudley Pound in 1943. 'A.B.C.' had, in Mountbatten's eyes, been the first culprit in depriving him of ships for his last big operations in SEAC in 1945. And a senior officer at the Admiralty at the time recalls Cunningham, after receiving a further request for carriers, declaring firmly, 'I don't give a damn, I'm not going to send any more ships to that bugger Mountbatten.'[8]

Relations between the two admirals had been cool ever since, and when Mountbatten's candidature for First Sea Lord came up and Cunningham was asked for his opinion, he gave an emphatic 'no'. But Cunningham was always prepared to listen, and to change his mind if he was convinced he was wrong: it was one of his great qualities. It happened that Mountbatten's Chief-of-Staff in the Mediterranean was Rear-Admiral Sir Manley 'Lofty' Power, who had formed a very high opinion of his C-in-C, and at a suitable opportunity passed this opinion on to Cunningham. Mountbatten was, said Power, exactly the right man for the job of First Sea Lord. Cunningham accepted Power's judgment and passed his reversal of view on Mountbatten through Admiral Sir Rhoderick McGrigor, the retiring First Sea Lord, the First Lord, J.P.L. Thomas (later 1st Viscount Cilcennin), and thence to the Prime Minister, Churchill. And there it stuck.

Vice-Admiral Sir Arthur Pedder says today that 'Winston wouldn't have him because he "had given away the British Empire".'[9] Mountbatten himself believed additionally that Churchill struck his name out because he had lost all belief in the Navy in the context of the nation's future defences – 'a few fast gun vessels and submarines – that's all' – and wanted to run it right down in favour of the RAF. The aged statesman and great romantic admirer of the Royal Navy since early childhood now sought to prove that there was no place for it in the modern world. 'He made a long speech in Cabinet,' said Mountbatten. 'Three-quarters of an hour long and full of the most brilliant invective. Sir Norman Brooke, the Secretary, economically recorded it thus: "The Prime Minister then passed a few observations concerning the Navy." But with me in the Admiralty he knew he wouldn't get away with it,' said Mountbatten.

Undiscouraged, and as determined as ever, Mountbatten continued to lobby through his friends. A particularly useful one at this time happened to be passing through the Mediterranean – the Emperor of Abyssinia, Haile

Selassie. Mountbatten entertained him on board his flagship at Malta on 7 October 1954 and asked him, when a suitable moment arrived, to work on Churchill on his behalf.

Mountbatten's luck was in. Soon after his arrival in England, Haile Selassie was guest at a reception in his honour in the long picture gallery at Buckingham Palace. The aged Emperor cornered the aged Premier and told him of Mountbatten's hospitality. 'He will no doubt be the next First Sea Lord,' said the Emperor as if it was a *fait accompli*. By further happy chance, Prince Philip was nearby, and his ears pricked up at the subject of the conversation, knowing all too well his uncle's ultimate ambition.

No doubt Churchill knew that he must finally bow to the inevitable, that Mountbatten's cause must prevail. What better time than now to concede defeat and make it appear a victory and please the royal family all at once, something he always enjoyed? Turning to Prince Philip, Churchill said, 'Sir, I want you to be the first to know that your uncle is to be the new First Sea Lord.'

'What excellent news! I'm delighted,' replied the Prince.

To Mountbatten's amusement, one of the first to congratulate him on his appointment was Churchill himself. 'He had done everything to stop it, and now this,' said Mountbatten. 'He really could be a very naughty boy.'

It was some days before the Admiralty was informed. Perhaps Churchill forgot his decision (he was by now forgetting a great deal), and only remembered later. To many of those in the Admiralty hierarchy, the news came as a rude and unwelcome shock. Others had seen the writing on the wall for some time, including the wise old Sir John Lang. 'Winston may well have reflected on the repetition in history and been guided by it.'[10] Or it may have been the intervention of an aged Emperor.

On 18 April 1955, Mountbatten entered the First Sea Lord's office at the Admiralty for the first time as professional head of the service to which he had committed his life. He was fifty-four years old, still extremely spritely, his hair only just beginning to turn grey in places. His father had been four years older in years, a great deal older in appearance and general wear-and-tear.

For Mountbatten, it was a highly emotional day, charged with memories, filled with ambition and zest for work. As always on momentous occasions, the scene had long since been set with care. He had arranged to use his father's old office, his father's old desk, with a portrait of his father behind him above the fireplace, and a bust of his father standing on a pedestal outside the door.

Suggestions from his staff that he might prefer the present First Sea

Lord's office, because the old one had been empty for so many years and was considered unusable, were brushed aside. Mountbatten was to have Admiral Prince Louis of Battenberg's old office, no matter that the magnificent view across the sweep of Horse Guards' Parade had been cut off with the war, and a solid concrete blockhouse wall replaced it at a distance of a few feet.

A further irritation was the frustration of his order that a colour portrait of himself should be placed in every office. He was told, with every show of regret, that the Treasury provided no funds for this sort of thing.

By 1955 there had been further massive cutbacks in the strength of the Royal Navy, as severe as those after World War I, but this time they had been applied to ships and *matériel* rather than personnel and committees. The Navy was top-heavy, slack and with only indifferent morale. With the acceptance of the need for an independent nuclear deterrent, defence costs had gone sky-high, and not at all in parallel with the growth of the economy. If Mountbatten was to save the service from the fate Churchill had decreed for it, there would have to be urgent and drastic pruning.

Lord Cilcennin was First Lord, and Mountbatten said that he went straight to his office and gave him a friendly speech.

'I have come in to reorganize the Admiralty prior to reorganizing the Services,' he said. 'The Admiralty is an absolute mess because it never streamlined itself after the war. It requires a proper committee to investigate it. I suggest that it should consist of myself in the chair, the Sea Lords as deputies, with junior ministers in attendance, and of course John Lang. But not you,' he continued firmly. 'With you it would make it the Board of Admiralty. Ours will be a sub-board, with members making up working parties, thinking up reforms, doing all the briefing.

'When the sub-board passes a resolution, then everything will come before the Board of Admiralty, with you in the chair, and you will pass our proposals. They will be Board decisions, and the whole thing will be done in ten minutes.

'Jim [Cilcennin] said he'd think about it, and I said, "No, don't do that. Now is the time for decision. You can either go down in history as the First Lord under whom the Admiralty stagnated, or you can go down in history as the First Lord under whose wise direction the Admiralty entirely reformed itself."'

Cilcennin said he would back Mountbatten, and the work began in earnest. 'My Way Ahead committee, as I called it, succeeded in cutting 7,000 uniformed personnel and 23,000 civilians in short order,' said Mountbatten, 'and we were saving £15 million a year without losing a single ship from the seagoing fleet.'

Sir John Lang, while not allowing himself to be bullied, observed a new Mountbatten from the admiral who had been Fourth Sea Lord in 1951. 'We all recognized that this was a new era of a very emphatic person,' Lang recalls, 'although he was never overpowering with me. Mountbatten's term of office was a period of fundamental difficulty for the Admiralty. Duncan Sandys [now Lord Duncan Sandys, Minister of Defence January 1957–October 1959] had no time for the Navy and, like Churchill, would have done away with it altogether if he had had his way, but Mountbatten withstood the onslaught very well. He recognized areas in which cuts could be made, and entered into economies in a spirit of willingness. The Way Ahead committee worked well, and Mountbatten sought economies in less hurtful areas, while keeping our strength of defence where it most mattered.'

But Lang's judgment on Mountbatten at this time was not without criticism, and he picked on an aspect of his character and style of later years that many others observed. 'He expected everything to be crisp,' says Lang, 'but Dickie himself was very verbose. He didn't seem able to stop talking and bubbling over. My impression is that he became more verbose the higher up the ladder he climbed. Unlike Edwina, he had no sense of time. If he had ten minutes to inspect something, he would get caught up with someone and become completely involved. When he wanted to know something, it had to be everything.

'Now Edwina had an inbuilt clock. If she was inspecting a hospital, it was ten minutes here, five minutes there. She never had to look at her watch or needed anyone to remind her. This was quite unlike Dickie.'[11]

The Mountbattens had a house in Wilton Crescent now, a town house in the Regency style. Broadlands was back to its old perfection, with the additional benefit of modernization. As in the last years before the war, they went there for weekends from London, and for entertaining and shooting.

They had both been deeply affected by the death of George VI, and moved by the Proclamation of Queen Elizabeth II on 8 February 1952. 'The King had great strength,' said Mountbatten, 'and a great sense of duty and determination. He saved the monarchy by taking over reluctantly from his brother, and did a marvellous, unrewarding job. I knew him well, and we had a tremendous amount in common, especially the Navy, of course. He always loved to talk about the Navy and took a great interest in it. But I felt even closer to our new Queen and her family. I had known her since she was a baby, and she and Princess Margaret were great friends with Patricia and Pammie. I became her personal ADC the following year, and always adored being with her. She is a marvellous person.'

The Mountbatten family grew at a great rate in the late 1950s and early 1960s. A third grandchild was born in the year Mountbatten became First Sea Lord, and Patricia had four more children, including twin boys in 1964, one of whom was to die with his grandfather. Pamela had married an interior decorator and designer, David Hicks, in 1960, and they had three children. The pilgrimage to Classiebawn Castle in August became a ritual that was rarely broken.

At Classiebawn, Mountbatten's children and grandchildren saw a completely new figure, far from the responsibilities of office, recharging his giant batteries for another year of swift endeavour. He set about being on holiday with the same practical purposefulness he applied to everything he did in life. He rode, climbed, fished, swam, spear-fished with his aqualung, played games, ate his usual huge meals (his capacity almost equalled his father's), and played tirelessly with the children. Classiebawn was synonymous with peace, family relaxation, and the happiness of children, right up to the fatal summer of 1979.

Mountbatten would have made a good primary schoolteacher. He treated children completely naturally, talked to them as if they were adults, listened to them with a patience that would have amazed his staff at the Admiralty, told them funny stories, played with them, swam with them, took them for walks, holding their hands and chatting away. His own enjoyment in their company was transmitted to them, and they loved him for it.

A special relationship developed with Prince Charles, whom he saw as frequently as his own grandchildren. Throughout his boyhood, and later when at Cambridge and in the Navy, Prince Charles found a marvellously relaxed and amusing alternative at Wilton Crescent and Broadlands to the predictable rituals of Buckingham Palace, Windsor, Sandringham and Balmoral.

The age gap meant nothing to either of them, from the time when Mountbatten used to bath him as a small boy, until the end. If, during his naval instruction, he was on a course at Portsmouth, he would drive over in his drophead Aston Martin to Broadlands for dinner and the night. Prince Charles could remember Mountbatten when he used to play polo, and he took up the game himself, instructed all the way by Mountbatten as well as by his father.

Nothing showed more clearly that age meant as little to Mountbatten as creed and colour, than to be with him, first, when he was with his nephew, then on another occasion with his great-nephew. As always, the generations melted away, whether they were arguing about some fine point on a polo match, a technical matter connected with some new device of Mountbatten's

Above: Another family occasion. The wedding of the Mountbattens' second daughter, Pamela, in January 1960, to David Hicks. Among those present (standing) are Patricia (Lady Brabourne), Mountbatten, The Duke of Edinburgh, Edwina (who was to die a few weeks later) and Lord Brabourne; Princess Margaret, the Queen Mother, the Queen of Sweden (Mountbatten's sister Louise), the Duchess of Kent and Princess Alexandra. Princess Anne and Prince Charles are in the front row, right.

Right: Mountbatten kisses, then casts into the sea, a wreath of lilies after the burial of Edwina. Behind him is his eldest sister, Alice, Princess Andrew of Greece, Prince Philip's mother. Behind Prince Philip are Lord and Lady Brabourne.

Above: Retirement job: Mountbatten at Wormwood Scrubs during his ill-starred prison security inquiry.

Left: With Princess Anne in Vienna. The bride he holds is Princess Michael of Kent.

Old friends since the 1920s: with Noël Coward.

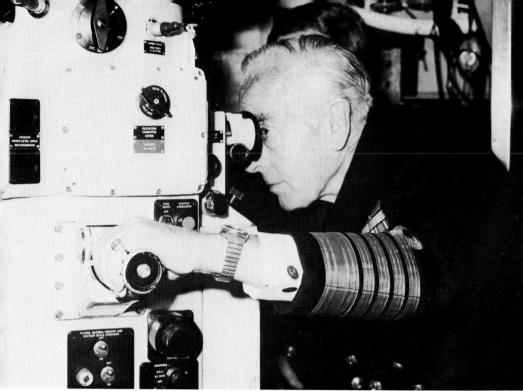

On 30 May 1979
Mountbatten paid his last
visit to one of HM ships,
the submarine *Superb*.

TO MY H.G.F. AND G.U. FROM HIS

LOVING AND DEVOTED H.G.S. AND G.N.

CHARLES

Left: From Prince Charles, godson and great-nephew, who felt Mountbatten's loss so sorely.

Below: Mountbatten wanted his funeral to be 'a jolly occasion', but the sight of Dolly, with rider's boots reversed, caused more tears than the coffin she led.

(and there seemed to be no end to these), or recounting the details of some journey, whom they had met, what had been said.

Two elements were invariable: as in Mountbatten's boyhood, with his family, or surrounded by his clever non-stop-talking German relatives, there was always argument. It would be certain to break out at some point, and it would often be heated. After a tour of remote Easter Island in the Pacific to study the unique archaeology, once re-embarked in the royal yacht the argument on the likely origins of the statues was long and ardent. But not content with that predictable subject under the circumstances, when this was exhausted an argument then broke out concerning the number and breed of wild horses on the island. It was prolonged and acrimonious – full of fascinating information. The second certainty was that any discussion, any argument, almost invariably (as in this case) ended in laughter, the deep rumble of Mountbatten's laughter matching that of Prince Philip with its higher pitch.

If, on that occasion, Prince Charles had been present instead of his father, the argument, the questioning, the evident appetite for controversy and knowledge in equal measure, would have been similar. The only differences would have been Prince Charles's more intellectual approach and greater earnestness, and the curious fact that his laughter would be pitched deeper than his father's and at the same tone as Mountbatten's.

The evident enjoyment of all three men of three generations – thirty-one, fifty-eight and seventy-nine years at the end – in one another's company, the matching minds and opinions, the speed of thought, the repartee (Mountbatten much the swiftest and funniest), together with the intermittent but frequent breaks into laughter, made a marvellous impression of mutual compatibility and happiness.

But of the three, the eldest and youngest were closest, sharing a deep emotional bond. There is no question that Prince Charles suffered the worst blow of anyone in the family with Mountbatten's murder, and that he grieves for him and misses him more than anyone else.

In Whitehall, in 1955, Mountbatten continued to make many allies and many enemies, and many reforms. 'The Royal Navy loves rows,' Harold Macmillan commented on Mountbatten's period at the Admiralty. 'They always have done – Charlie Beresford and all that lot.' And Mountbatten himself spoke of the spikyness of many naval officers. 'It's quite unlike the Army,' he said. 'In the Navy you've got perhaps only a few fellows locked up in a small ship for weeks on end. There are bound to be rows and clashes of temperament. There always have been. It's better in bigger ships, but not much better.'[12]

'Jackie' Fisher, the arch-reformer of the Navy at the turn of the century, had been ruthless and made numerous enemies; in fact he prided himself on his 'three RS', on being 'ruthless, relentless and remorseless'. Mountbatten's reforms, and his methods of bringing them about, made enemies, too.

He claimed to have worked well with his First Lords, but only because (like Cilcennin) he tamed them. Given the smallest lead, he would launch himself into a series of stories to prove this point. There was the First Lord who, after a mere ten days in office, went off for the weekend at a highly critical period without informing anyone. ('I thought that was a bit offside!') Mountbatten claimed to have called up Scotland Yard, and had him brought back by the police. 'I had no more trouble with him.'

According to Mountbatten's stories, First Lords who tried to interfere with appointments – for example, that of his own successor in the Mediterranean (his old buddy, Charles Lambe), and others were 'hit for six'.

'The First Lords amounted to nothing in my time. None of them knew Christmas from Easter,' Mountbatten boasted. 'When they fought me, I defeated them quickly, and when they didn't fight me they had to go along with me. Churchill in his time appeared to run the Admiralty but he didn't.'

Why did Mountbatten have to open fire with a full broadside every time the relationship between the civil and professional branches of the Admiralty was mentioned? Why all this bombast? His father and Churchill worked in admirable harmony and did great things together, but when the necessity arose, it was Churchill who told him he had to go. Churchill was in command, finally. From all accounts, the same applied to Mountbatten, and he worked in good harness with his First Lords under the Ministry of Defence, and great things were accomplished.

What is even more curious is that these stories were either grossly inaccurate as to date and the people involved (one of them was about Lord Longford who had been briefly First Lord over four years before Mountbatten became First Sea Lord) or complete fabrications and capable of being proved false very easily. Nor could they be accounted for as the wanderings of an ageing mind because his mind remained sharp to the end, and these stories were being recounted many years earlier. Moreover, no one was a greater stickler for accuracy, and his memory was normally marvellously reliable.

Only the irresistible need for self-glorification can account for this astonishing contradiction. But, then, why did a man so glorified by the nation and loved by his family have to brag so much and so often?

There are a number of reasons, but the most important was the same old insecurity, which led to the over-reaction and over-competitiveness, which hounded him all through his life.

Speaking of Mountbatten's seeming arrogance, Lord Butler said, 'I had a funny feeling about Mountbatten. One was a little defensive with him. He so liked an argument, and then it all came back in your face. I think he felt that he had missed something important in life, that it had been one-sided, that whatever else he had achieved, he had missed the academic and intellectual side. He felt he had been left out of that world, and he resented it.'[13]

Lord Longford also referred to Mountbatten's intellectual insecurity, and remembers him saying once, 'You know I am much more intelligent than you think.'

Sir Harold Wilson believes that his insecurity stemmed from his being uncertain of what he was, royal or non-royal. He also cited the same story as Lord Butler, both of whom have been appointed Knights of the Garter, the highest of all honours. Before the service in the Royal Chapel, one goes to be robed in a special room. There one meets old friends, a handful only, for it is also a very rare honour. But Mountbatten was absent, and people were asking, 'Where is Dickie?' 'Dickie's not here.' And of course he always attended as he loved the pomp and ceremony of it all. And then at last he emerged, but from the entrance reserved for the sovereign and members of the royal family, the royal entrance, with an expression of great solemnity upon his face. 'He was only a half-royal,' added Sir Harold, 'but he made up for it by becoming the shop steward of European royalty.'[14]

'Why did he never speak in the House of Lords?' asked Lord Longford. 'You would think he would have done so often. But he never did. Was it that he feared people might think he was not really royal?'[15]

In fact, he very nearly did once, at a critical time when he was trying to save the Navy. He refrained at the last moment, he said, out of deference to the royal family. In view of their special relations with the Royal Navy one would have thought they would have been delighted.

Lord Hailsham confirmed again that he had excellent relations with Mountbatten, even though 'he was highly emotional about Suez'.[16] This is no overstatement. In June 1956, fourteen months after Mountbatten took office as First Sea Lord, the Egyptian leader Colonel Nasser nationalized the Suez Canal. The Israelis invaded Sinai, and on 5 November French and British forces attacked Port Said, instigating a world crisis.

Mountbatten disapproved of the operation at every level, humanitarian, diplomatic, moral and military. 'A complete disaster,' was his summing-up, although he always defended the performance of the three services once the operation got going. 'It was the reverse of everything I had tried to do in South-East Asia and India immediately after the war, so of course I hated it.'

Anthony Eden had succeeded to the premiership a few days before Mountbatten became First Sea Lord; and as inevitable hostilities approached, his attitude towards Mountbatten was half patronizing and half censorious. His remark to Edwina at a 10 Downing Street party about a week before the operation reflected Eden's feelings towards his First Sea Lord. 'Dickie is being splendid,' he said. 'He disapproves of everything I am doing but is taking every step to get the Navy ready.'

'The only one who showed any guts was Eden,' said Mountbatten, 'and he was completely and utterly wrong in everything he did. Monckton had one outburst and then disappeared and wouldn't resign. He seemed to think that he could control the ministers better by staying in the Cabinet. Then Hailsham took over from Cilcennin, and that made more sense. But Eden, you'll notice, doesn't mention him by name, or me, in his account, which was kind of him and I told him so later, because if he had said anything he could only have blasted me.

'I had told Eden from the beginning that Nasser would be certain to block the canal as a counter-measure, and it would take three months to clear it. As night follows day, when the fiasco was all over, Macmillan – who had taken over from Eden who was ill – approached me at a diplomatic party at Buckingham Palace. The Queen was putting a brave face on the whole terrible thing, and that was more than Macmillan could do when I answered his question: "How long will it take to clear the canal?"

'I said, "All steps have been taken to mobilize salvage vessels and experts, and I can assure you it will take no longer than three months." Macmillan was horrified. "Three months! The country'll be bankrupt in that time with the long haul round the Cape.... It must be quicker." I told him, "I said from the beginning it would take three months. I have spoken out clearly all along, so don't complain now because the Navy can't get you out of your mess." Then I turned on my heel and walked off.

'But it is a great credit to Macmillan that he loved me enough not to sack me when he became PM. I thought he would.'

No man was to have a greater influence on Mountbatten's last professional years than Macmillan. He had been Minister of Defence for seven months immediately prior to Mountbatten's arrival at the Admiralty, and had at that time attempted to bring about a reform of the services.

'The Norwegian campaign in 1940 was the first lesson in the need for combining the services,' Macmillan says today. 'The top men simply didn't know what was going on. This led to the creation of the Chiefs of Staff, and Dickie Mountbatten's own Combined Operations. Then ten years after the end, came Suez, and that showed again the need for unifying the services at the top. I tried to do something about this when I was at Defence but the opposition was too strong. The Prime Minister [Churchill] was not interested, and diehards like Boyle [Marshal of the RAF Sir Dermot Boyle, Chief of Air Staff 1956–9] would have none of it.'[17]

Under the premiership of Macmillan, and with Sandys as Minister of Defence, the economies and streamlining of administration completed, Mountbatten set about reshaping the Navy for the future – in spite of Sandys' doubts and initial lack of support. It was a very different service, fined-down, fast and twice as professional, when Mountbatten's term of office expired in 1958, with nuclear power, missiles, computers and commando carriers all in use or on order. The age of technology was firmly established, space programmes were all the rage, battleships were for museums, the Americans were already launching nuclear-powered aircraft-carriers and nuclear-powered ballistic missile submarines. Mountbatten revelled in it, and loved to quote the comedian who had satirized him saying, 'Actually, I invented technology.'

Far from the fascinating fields of technology, Mountbatten in 1957 was able to perform an important service for justice and an old friend. Admiral Sir Dudley North, Mountbatten had always believed, had been made the scapegoat for the Dakar fiasco in 1940, when Vichy French cruisers had escaped through the Strait of Gibraltar and caused the failure of an expedition to capture the French African base.

The ties between North and Mountbatten had always been close in the service. North served alongside Mountbatten's brother Georgie in the *New Zealand* in World War I, and had been with Mountbatten as an extra equerry to the Prince of Wales afterwards on the world tours. They had met frequently between the wars, when North had served in the Admiralty and been Flag Officer Royal Yachts. He was an able, amiable, not outstandingly gifted officer, who did not deserve the rough charge of neglect of duty thrown at him by Dudley Pound and Churchill. He had, ever since, unsuccessfully pressed for a court martial. There had been a number of abortive attempts to clear his name, but always politicians – and most notably Churchill – had brushed them aside. A sensational book defending North reopened the affair and there was talk about another Dreyfus case.

'I knew that this time something had to be done, not only for Dudley but also for the good reputation of the Navy,' said Mountbatten. 'So I went along and saw Macmillan and told him so. He completely agreed but said there couldn't be a court of enquiry or court martial. "But we have a number of Admirals of the Fleet," he said. "They're all on the active list. Why not get them together to thrash the thing out?"

'Macmillan was always a fast mover, and he sent messages and cars, and all these old boys got together – all except Chatfield who was ill. The upshot was that they all said Winston behaved disgracefully and the Admiralty had behaved disgracefully. So we drafted out a statement exonerating Dudley, but not actually accusing Winston, who was still just alive.'

This signed statement gave Dudley North great satisfaction and relief. Macmillan provides a postscript to this *cause célèbre* today. 'All those old Admirals who had been First Sea Lord at some time were against any action beyond this statement, and those who hadn't, like old Lord Cork and Orrery, were dead set on doing more.'

In no area was Mountbatten's sense of justice more aroused than towards individuals who had been harshly treated while in search of freedom. Gandhi's incarceration when Mountbatten had been in India with the Prince of Wales as a young man outraged him as much as that of Makarios at the height of the Cyprus crisis many years later. 'I remember a Staff Meeting at the time of his banishment to the Seychelles, and a Colonial Office official came in and asked me if they could have a frigate to take him there. I said, "Certainly. But would you be good enough to ask the Colonial Secretary how long the frigate would be needed?" The official replied that it could leave again at once. So I replied, "I think we'll keep her at the Seychelles to save fuel." "How do you mean, sir?" "Presumably you want to keep the negotiations going, and as they can't move one inch without Makarios, the frigate had better be ready to bring him back again."

'This didn't go down very well with everybody. Afterwards General Templer said, "I hate you, Dickie, you're anti-British – you're just yellow!" So you see how I was always getting into trouble.'

Lieutenant-Commander Peter Kemp, who was still at the Admiralty in the spring of 1958, and remembered Mountbatten in the early days in the Mediterranean, recalls a lunch he gave at the United Services Club. 'Hugh Hanning was there, and John Terraine, and one or two officers. We were talking about Mountbatten, and I made the rash prediction, "Well he's obviously going on now, and will be our new Chief of Defence Staff." I remember everyone threw up his hands and said "Not in a thousand years," or "Never a hope." To me it was certain.'[18]

It was to Mountbatten, too. He never had the slightest doubt that he was next in line for the highest defence post. Moreover, he always claimed he knew exactly and precisely what he was going to do in his term of office, which began in July 1958. He was going to reorganize the whole defence structure of the country, and integrate the three services into one. 'I really started this on a small scale with Combined Operations Command, then developed it further in SEAC, and later in peacetime when I headed NATO in the Mediterranean.'

In fact, Mountbatten knew that Macmillan as Minister of Defence had conceived the shape of the new integrated defence structure and attempted to bring it to life. 'Dickie always claimed the credit for it, of course, but I didn't care twopence,' Macmillan recalls. 'That was all right. Dickie was a great extrovert. My only care was that it should come off.'

Suez had shown the need more than ever for this reorganization, and it was much more difficult for the earlier opponents to sustain their case again. 'I could have done it without Dickie, of course,' says Macmillan. 'But he was a great help, and he did his part very well. Surprisingly enough, he was quiet and restrained about it, and of course very loyal. He was especially good at handling the difficult people. He always somehow made the opposition feel small.'[19]

There are plenty of people today, including Macmillan's son-in-law, Julian Amery, who think it was all a mistake. 'I am one of those who believe the English operate best in small units, like public school houses, clubs, and so on. I was therefore against combining the three services. With the services combined, the sense of corporate loyalty disappears. It's a typical German conception, and reduces opportunities of access. For anyone to get to the Minister now, it is a long and difficult process. Peter Carrington, Hugh Fraser and I fought against it but were defeated.'[20]

'This hostility had almost gone when I became Prime Minister in 1964,' said Sir Harold Wilson, 'and the job was almost complete. Certainly Mountbatten was happy with the outcome for the Royal Navy, which had been so threatened. Mountbatten was the first Chief of Defence Staff in the strategic sense to recognize the impact, and have an understanding of, the importance of technology.'

Sir Harold recalled Defence Committee meetings when he was in the chair. 'If Mountbatten thought anything might go wrong, he always came to see me privately beforehand, and I always found him extremely stimulating. Solly was very useful then on the scientific side, and he used to report to Winston for old times' sake.'[21]

Solly Zuckerman had re-entered the Mountbatten orbit with his appointment as Scientific Adviser to the Ministry of Defence in 1959; and 'Ronnie' Brockman, now a rear-admiral, was among those who rejoined the old Mountbatten team and made up the heart of it – the 'brains', and what the staff often referred to as 'the social chap'.

'Solly was Mountbatten's brains,' a senior member of Mountbatten's staff said. 'The sheer speed of Solly's mind was amazing. They stimulated one another, although in brainpower Solly was vastly superior.'

As for Brockman, this same officer was told by Mountbatten at his first interview, '"Now, if you are ever in any doubt what goes on in my mind, go and see Ronnie Brockman." The first time this arose, I quickly discovered that the one person who did not know what was going on in Mountbatten's mind was the admiral. But he was very charming, very nice, very good-looking and very ordinary – and absolutely terrified of Mountbatten.'

The reaction of many young officers coming to the Ministry for the first time was one of amazement that Mountbatten was there at all. It was nearly twenty years since the end of the war, and in most minds Mountbatten was connected with the war. 'My first thought,' said one officer, 'was "Is he still alive?" He was such a distant figure connected with the war. But one soon learnt that he was alive all right. I was amazed to find out what an enormous influence he was in Whitehall, dominating it completely. And inside, you suddenly found that when dealing with lieutenant-generals or air marshals, there was a gap a mile wide between them and the Mountbatten retinue. It was like the difference between the Duke and the dustman.

'I also soon learned that he loved the young, and didn't like the old at all. Once he told me that everyone was finished when they had reached two stars.

'Another curious thing – when I was told I was joining his staff, chaps said, "Oh you're going to be a spy – one of Mountbatten's spies." And I laughed. But I soon found out that it was true. The first thing I found on my desk was a confidential office memorandum: "Do you know, have you ever met, Chapman Pincher? [chief defence correspondent of Beaverbrook newspapers]. Write me the answer please."

'I answered this truthfully in the negative, and when I went to see him, he said, "Your job is to get into the Whitehall machine and find out what is going on and report to me." And that's what it was all about, because he always had to be a jump ahead of everybody. The chaps he was two jumps ahead of were those who thought he was an old has-been. They failed to recognize the danger. The Foreign Office was crammed with these people, and Mountbatten always out-manœuvred them.'

It was not a restful life at the Ministry of Defence in those days. As Sir John Lang said of him at the Admiralty, "There was no question of a seven- or eight-hour day. You were lucky if you got a seven- or eight-hour night.'[22]

'He was always creating crises,' was the comment of one of his Staff. 'It was as if he had this need for constant achievement, and terror of showing that he might not be wanted.'

Mountbatten by now had his own Comet jetliner, fitted out with every conceivable gadget and comfort, a bevy of the most beautiful Wrens, and, often, his current black labrador, who refused to walk on and had to be carried. The dictation started before take-off, 'Memoranda, papers, etc. copies to Washington, copies to everybody. And sometimes at the end of it all, I realized that we actually hadn't done a bloody thing!'

One of his Wren secretaries describes a flight out to the Far East, quoting from her diary: 'January 23rd 1964. Chris Warren [my other half-leading Wren] woke me at 5 am. After breakfast went to Wilton Crescent. Mountbatten had loads of luggage. Took off for Bahrein 0800. The Army polo team came with us, and Lady Brabourne and the Brockmans....' Then it was dictating briefs and letters and papers non-stop; and on the tour: 'I had to go down to CDS in the middle of breakfast. He was having a massage. Most embarrassing. He often dictated while getting ready for an official function.... I sat outside the bathroom door while he splashed and shouted reports at me....'[23]

To those in his entourage, from Wren secretaries to his senior staff, the pace seemed unremitting. And then, at the end of a particularly heavy day, he might come into the office of one of his hard-pressed secretaries before leaving for some function, sit on the edge of the desk for a few minutes, deplore how hard he worked his girls and fish out a box of chocolates as a reward. They loved it and so did he; and he would probably have one or two chocolates before he paced out of the room.

The little touches were frequent, well-timed and always appreciated. One of his pilots recalls how he would always have a chat before take-off: 'Good morning, how delighted I am to see you again. ...'* then he would enter the Comet briskly, stretch out on his special seat that was more like a chaise-longue, and instantly begin dictating thank you letters for the recent reception or hospitality, however trivial.

A glimpse at a typical working day at the height of his period as Chief of Defence Staff reveals several aspects of his personality and working methods. There is a staff meeting in the afternoon, and from the beginning the day revolves round this.

His secret is briefing and preparation. Everything is worked out at preliminary meetings with his staff, what so-and-so is going to say about this item, what will Admiral x say he is going to do about that. The morning is employed in a full-dress rehearsal of the afternoon's meeting. This

* This pilot, Wing-Commander G.P.B. Bailey, RAF (Retd) remembers how amused he and his fellow pilots were with Mountbatten the sailor's preoccupation with the winds. 'When he flew he was always more concerned with the "*Winds*" than any other problem an airman would be concerned with: i.e. cloud, fog, icing, diversions. "What are the *winds* like?" would be his invariable question before take-off.' Perhaps he feared delay, and disruption of his ever-tight schedule.

leads to great speed and efficiency at the main event, and hardly ever a surprise.

At the end of the morning meeting, he says – not for the first time – 'I want to finish off on some high strategic note, some really statesmanlike "above-it-all" remark.' Then he turns to one of his staff: 'Let me have something, will you?'

At one minute to three he comes straight out of the lift after lunch, quite probably at the Palace, walks in, feet wide-splayed, sits down, and looks around the table.

'Well, gentlemen, the first item is ... I gather Admiral x has some views on this....' With a bored expression on his face, his eyes cast round the table, stopping at the Admiral. He knows exactly what he is going to say, and what the next speaker is going to say, and what the decision will be on every item on the long agenda.

Tea is brought in, his eyes light up until he wills the waitress with the best plate of biscuits to put them in front of him. She does, and he takes a handful and eats them all before his tea and before anyone else has started.

The meeting lasts until just after 6 pm. Mountbatten is due for a glass of sherry with a visiting potentate at Wilton Crescent, then a dinner party which will keep him from bed until 2 am. He has left behind an immense amount of work for everyone. But before he leaves, he looks in at one or two of the offices. 'Is everything all right? Did that meeting go well? Yes? Good.'

He is the only person any of the staff and their minions have known to work them so hard *and* do this, and the difference it makes – like the wave to the airfield control tower balcony – is immeasurable.

A mid-rank, young officer on his staff at this time, who had known Field Marshals Alexander, Montgomery and Templar, claims that 'to work with Mountbatten was the most exhilarating experience I've ever had. I've never known his like,' he continued. 'He really was a most outstanding man, and marvellous to work with, not least because you never knew where you stood. He was an enormous man, in the Alexander the Great class, who, in a different age and setting could have conquered the world.'

But with the higher echelons he was less popular, and with many highly unpopular as well as feared. When angry or in low spirits, he had often been heard to say, 'They *all* hate me, you know.' But the young were like the women in his life: he loved them all for what they were and because they presented him with no competition. Not everyone was as tolerant of his boasting as was Harold Macmillan. Julian Amery found his name-dropping and assumption of social superiority distasteful. So did many others. 'He was grand in his position, and grand in his conceit of himself,' said Amery, who was at the War Office in 1957–8. Nor did Amery care for his social manners at times, particularly at receptions, when Mountbatten would suddenly break off in the middle of a conversation 'as if you had had your apportionment'.

Amery also recounted how Mountbatten had once told him that George VI had 'expressed the view to me that he hoped that one day I would continue in the parallel ranks I was given during the war. I am now an Admiral of the Fleet,' he continued, as if the world did not know it, 'and I would also like to be a Marshal of the Royal Air Force and a Field Marshal.' Amery expressed the view that he did not think that this was a good idea, but he would follow it up for Mountbatten. But before he could do anything about it, he was asked to come to Mountbatten's office with John Profumo, who was Secretary of State for War for three years from July 1960, in order to press the matter again. They said, 'We will discuss it, but frankly it would be better if you did not press the matter because we may get a negative answer.' Fearing this above anything, Mountbatten nodded, and no more was heard of the matter.

Julian Amery, who knew Mountbatten so well, does however give him one great credit mark, besides his coaching of Prince Philip. This was his usefulness in remaining politically neutral yet royal. 'During the catastrophic period when the middle Labour party was destroying all our institutions, Mountbatten as always continued to be acceptable to them and was a firm hand on the reins. For example – and to his eternal credit – at one weekend at Chequers, when the independent British nuclear deterrent was at risk at the hands of Denis Healey, Mountbatten talked him into keeping it. And his Court connections, knowing people of importance socially, his rapport with Macmillan, all gave him an edge on anyone else.'[24]

We have, then, a very mixed judgment on Mountbatten as defence chief in the early 1960s. Harold Wilson, who saw him through his last months as CDS, is full of praise for his performance. 'While having confidence in those serving under him, he was also a long way ahead in his job, and in technology,' he said.

Among Americans of this period, there were almost no reservations about him. Mountbatten described with relish a visit he made to Washington when he was Chairman of the Military Committee of NATO, and met President Kennedy.

'The first meeting of the Committee wasn't much use,' he said. 'That was in Paris. Then we went to the USA for the next one, and we made it much smaller and easier-running, with no records kept except just one copy. Kennedy came with Lemnitzer [General Lyman L. Lemnitzer, Chairman Joint Chiefs of Staff 1960–2], and afterwards I was asked to call at the

White House as a NATO official. The meeting was supposed to last fifteen minutes, but it ran to fifty, and we went through the whole world situation.

'I hadn't been very pro-Kennedy before, but I was now. I found him very intelligent, with clear views, well-briefed and with a fresh approach. He knew about every subject we raised except Berlin, and at that time the NATO allies were not in step.

'Kennedy said that we must be firm and strong with the Russians, and Lemnitzer said that General Norstad's plans were complete on Berlin. These consisted of a small probe, followed by a battalion, and finally a divisional force, if there was any further trouble.

'I told the President that I thought this made no military sense at all. What would happen to a battalion on the autobahn? The Russians would blow up a bridge in front, a bridge behind, and then sell seats for people to come and laugh. And if that was a farce, a division would be a tragedy. It would require a front of thirty miles to keep moving – fifteen miles each side of the autobahn, and it would be seen as an invasion of East Germany, and that would lead to all-out war.

'Lemnitzer disagreed, and Kennedy listened and believed me when I said that another airlift would be the only answer. If we went down the autobahn with a battalion or a division, we would be the aggressors. If we used planes again, they would have to shoot them down, and the Russians would be the aggressors. Kennedy smiled and said, "I'll look into that."

'Then I said to him, "It's the same old story, we British are being accused of being yellow and against military operations. All we are doing is giving military advice. If we invade with a division, then it would certainly be war. If we supplied Berlin and kept the city alive by air as before, kept alert, militarily ready and making it clear we would go to war if there was inter-ference, then we are in a stronger not weaker position."

'I said, "It is brave not yellow to show you are ready to go to war. And this is a time of great danger."'

The degree of danger to the free world was emphasized by Mountbatten in the speeches he made around the world during his last years as Chief of Defence Staff. He would speak about 'the fast-changing world', with science advancing at an exponential rate, with weapon systems developing so fast and at such costs that the aphorism 'If it works it's obsolete' was a reality. He saw NATO as a stabilizing force, he recognized the continuous need to reassess defence philosophy, and the need to keep defence spending down.

In these speeches he constantly made the point that Russia had no inten-tion of risking a nuclear war, that the damage caused by a nuclear war would be irreparable, that very soon we should have reached a point of nuclear sufficiency. He believed that the monopoly of the United States had long since gone and could never be recovered, and that the First Strike Option which had been open to the USA no longer applied. The real danger, he would say, lay in the technical accident which might escalate into a general nuclear war.

As for Britain's part, in 1965 he believed that Britain still had a significant part to play in 'holding the flanks', in dealing with the unforeseen, and in providing an important maritime airborne strategy, with a powerful Transport Command and the means to charter aircraft at short notice for troop transportation.

The speeches were delivered with all the verve and inspiration of his speeches during the war, and those who had considered him a has-been when he came to the Ministry seven years earlier were forced to change their minds.

The deaths of two of the most important people in Mountbatten's life occurred while he was at the Ministry of Defence, and within four years of one another: his wife; and the man who had helped to make and break his father, and who had been his own sparring partner, sentimental friend and implacable enemy, guide and mentor, admirer and critical observer, Nestor to Mountbatten's Achilles.

Edwina Mountbatten, after the flighty, fun-loving years of her youth and early married life, had steadied on her course in the late 1930s when, like so many of her contemporaries, she came face to face with the evil of fascism. From an Agatha Runcible in Evelyn Waugh's novel *Vile Bodies*, restlessly searching for new and ever more outrageous distractions, she became converted to the faith of good works.

The relief of suffering began to absorb her and claim her time and passionate attention during the vulnerable years around forty. She worked quite as hard as her husband all through the war. Just as she and Mountbatten had been identified together in the noisy vanguard of the bright young things in the 1920s and 30s, so the two of them were recognized as a pair, still colourful, still glamorous, but in the context of South-East Asia and India and their suffering millions, instead of Mayfair and night clubs, royal occasions and chukkas of polo of the earlier decades.

It was a remarkable metamorphosis for both of them, but especially for Edwina, whose only work until shortly before the war was the running of large houses and organizing of large parties. When the St John Ambulance claimed her, she gave them with all the massive generosity she possessed, her talents, charm, influence and organizing abilities. It is, for once, no exaggeration to say that she did the work of ten. Her charitable work became first a way of life, then a drug. She seemed unable to stop herself, any more than once she could not restrain herself from wandering dangerously in far-away places. Long after the war, when the need had greatly diminished, she continued to work and travel as Superintendent-in-Chief of St John Ambulance Brigade.

Edwina Mountbatten overstressed herself year after year, like a fine-tuned engine racing at high revs. She was only fifty-eight when she left on one more whirlwind tour of the Far East on behalf of her charities. A few months earlier, one of her grandchildren had contracted chicken pox, and Edwina picked it up from her in a particularly virulent form – or perhaps it seemed so only because she was in such poor physical shape. She had had some angina pain recently, too, and she was not sleeping and was taking barbiturates.

It was February, Pamela had just married, and Edwina, in spite of the poor state of her health, had been especially radiant and admired at the wedding. No one could have suspected how near to breaking point she was. Her timetable was typical: utterly demanding and only just capable of fulfilment, if she went flat out.

'She was in Borneo,' said Mountbatten of one of the great tragedies in his life. 'I found out later that she had done a tremendous day's work, and had to attend an official party in the evening. She had to be half-carried to it, but once there, she pushed aside her supporters and put on her usual show, sparkling, charming and talking to everyone. After it she went to bed and never woke up. We had never been happier together, and I felt utterly pole-axed when the telephone rang at three o'clock in the morning with the news.'

Her heart had ceased beating while she was asleep. She had expressed a wish to be buried at sea, and after her funeral at Romsey Abbey, where six weeks earlier her younger daughter had been married, her body was taken on board a frigate. She was 'commited to the deep' off Portsmouth, within a few miles of Adsdean where they had lived for so many years when they were the toast of 'the bright young things'.

The last years of Winston Churchill could not have been in stronger contrast with Edwina's, and filled Mountbatten with a dread of drug-supported old age. The relationship between these two remarkable men was compounded of passion and mutual admiration, suspicion and mutual understanding, a canny, unspoken comprehension of one another's strengths and weaknesses. The word avuncular is too mellow to describe Mountbatten's regard for his patron. Yet the relationship was like that between a famous, talented, jealous and proud uncle keen to show off his clever nephew, so long as the limelight was not too bright – and, alas, it often was.

Churchill, who all his life worried about money, envied 'the golden boy's' wealth. And Churchill, the deep-dyed aristocrat with insatiable ambition, envied Mountbatten's easy access to the royal family and the palaces of Europe.

Churchill's admiration for Edwina has already been mentioned. He adored her, loved to flirt with her and to please her. Together with his own Clemmie, they made a marvellous foursome of wit and mischief and wisdom, with so much in common and their blend of American, English, Jewish and German blood making up a potent brew.

Churchill also enjoyed teasing Mountbatten, but there could be a schoolboy's sharp edge of jocular provocation to it. This was a one-sided game. Mountbatten only teased women, the young and those who were no threat in the never-ending competition that was his propellant charge.

There is a true story of lunch at Hyde Park Gate soon after Churchill's belated resignation as Prime Minister in 1955. Mountbatten, Julian Amery, Harold Macmillan and two or three others were present. Mountbatten had recently become First Sea Lord, to Churchill's chagrin. Churchill was grumpy through the meal, and they were all trying to cheer him up. Towards the end, Mountbatten arose to leave early. The dining-room at Hyde Park Gate was curiously constructed, with stairs leading up to a half-landing below the door. On this landing Mountbatten paused and turned to address his audience below. 'I'm so sorry,' he announced, 'but I have to go to a Chiefs of Staff meeting.' This completed Churchill's cure, and when Mountbatten had gone he was grinning as he asked the others, 'Who is that man? Ought I to know him?'[25]

Churchill felt great admiration for Mountbatten, and great regard for his abilities and his power to attract the affection and loyalty of the common man. It was for this reason that he made him Supreme Commander in SEAC. Only a genius of Churchill's calibre could have recognized in the young captain RN the ability to convert the morale and fighting spirit of a distant jungle army. But there was not much love there. Churchill found faintly distasteful Mountbatten's German characteristics, what he saw as his preoccupation with his lineage, his medals and decorations, his seeming pomposity on parade, his name-dropping and stories proving how clever he was.

For his part, Mountbatten's admiration for Churchill was boundless, even though he never trusted him and often thought he behaved 'a bit naughtily'. Mountbatten once said, 'Winston did a lot of naughty and a lot of silly things in the Second World War. But none of this detracts from the fact that if it had not been for him, we should have lost the war. It's as simple as that. He had this quality of leadership, this vision, this drive, and the courage. These are what his reputation rests on. Not on individual acts, many of which were appallingly stupid, like Dakar and his disgraceful behaviour over Dudley North, and his idiotic behaviour over the *Repulse* and *Prince of Wales*.

'We could see Winston behaving disgracefully. But history will say that he saved us from defeat single-handed and won the war. And that's enough.'

On the day before Churchill's funeral in January 1965, Mountbatten told one of his staff, 'When Winston goes tomorrow, I'll be the only one of his original pallbearers on parade. I am the only one left. You'll see all sorts of Admirals and Air Marshals and so on, but I am the only original. Winston laid it down in 1940 who was to carry his body and I was included,' he ended proudly.

A few minutes later, he was studying the seat-placing for the funeral, his keen eyes scanning the board like an admiral before a Royal Fleet Review. There was a sudden, indignant shout. 'Where are the Poles?' He turned round and called out to the world at large, as if exposing some national sin, 'You haven't made any provision for the Poles at Winston's funeral. This is terrible.'

It was exactly the small omitted detail of protocol and justice that he was sure to spot. He not only saw to it that a contingent of Poles, the first to fight the Germans, and so bravely, on their own soil, were provided for in the seating. He saw that they were in the front. And left it to others to dig them out in twelve hours – some of them chefs in remote restaurants – and see that they came.

After the funeral, and there was not to be another like it until Mountbatten's, the whole world watched as a special steam train took Churchill's body to the little village of Bladon close to Blenheim Palace where he was to be buried. Tens of thousands of people flocked to walk past the grave. A police officer helping to control the crowd observed a bare-headed figure, without overcoat, standing watching the slow-moving line. The policeman had last seen Mountbatten in a jungle clearing standing on a box addressing members of the 25th Indian Division on the Arakan front. He recognized him at once, and noticed that he could not see the grave from where he was standing and was making no attempt to break into the queue.

The officer said, 'I know you, my Lord, would you care to come to see the grave?' The ex-Supremo and the ex-soldier did so, standing silently side by side. Then he led Mountbatten back to his car, telling him that he had once served under him. 'In "The Ace of Spades", sir.' 'Ah, the 25th Indian Division.' They talked as old friends, of the war, and the greatness of the man just buried. 'Then he shook my hand warmly and thanked me.'[26]

The great statesman had come into Mountbatten's life during his first months in the Royal Navy as a cadet. He had failed to give him the promised extra Saturday sardine. Forty-two years later he did his best to deprive

Mountbatten of the appointment he had sought all his naval life. Yet in between there had developed a rich, quixotic, fascinating and fruitful relationship. Six months after Churchill's funeral, Mountbatten finally retired as Chief of the Defence Staff, all that he had sought to accomplish now fulfilled.

The year 1965, then, marked the death of Churchill and the end of Mountbatten's professional life as a sailor. So closely were their lives spliced together that it was appropriate that the hawser that bound the 'former naval person', as Churchill liked to describe himself to Roosevelt, and the Admiral of the Fleet who had saved the Navy when it was most threatened, should be severed so cleanly.

11
RETIREMENT

~~~

IN MANY WAYS, Mountbatten faced the same problems as any widowed sixty-five-year-old man in retirement. The Military Order of Merit and other decorations, his appointment as Colonel of the Life Guards, Life Commandant of the Royal Marines, Governor of the Isle of Wight, were retirement gifts just as a retiring company director might be presented with a gold fountain pen.

'I suppose you can say I became an odd-job man,' he said. 'A Mr Fix-it. I had 2,000 acres to farm at Broadlands, and I had already formed an Estate Committee to help with this. I had also founded the National Electronics Research Council a year earlier, and in 1966 I became President of the British Computer Society.'

In the mid-1960s Mountbatten was associated, often as president or chairman, with no fewer than two hundred organizations, ranging from the Variety Club of Great Britain and the Inner Magic Circle, to the Swedish Naval Society. He headed an Immigration Mission for the Prime Minister, Harold Wilson, and volunteered to lead an enquiry into prison security. He loved anything to do with the *Kelly* Reunion Association, of which he was very proud, the British Commonwealth ex-Services League, King George's Fund for Sailors, and of course the Burma Star Association.

Under the inspiration of Kurt Hahn, the founder of Salem and Gordonstoun schools, an Atlantic College was set up in South Wales to promote international education. Mountbatten became the first President, and did his utmost to spread the principle and reality of United World Colleges (as they came to be known) in all five continents. For years this responsibility took up the greater part of his time.

Mountbatten espoused dozens of causes a year, small ones that grew in size, like the Atlantic Colleges, to individual acts of assistance or the correction of an injustice. For example, in 1970 the former Commander of the Sierra Leone Army, Brigadier David Lansana, was sentenced to death for

treason. Lansana had known Mountbatten when he was Chief of Defence
Staff, and when his case came to Mountbatten's notice, he wrote letters,
spoke to people of influence, appealed personally to the High Commissioner
and the President of Sierra Leone. He at last got the unjust conviction
quashed. When the authorities went back on their word, hanged the Brigadier, and publicly exposed his body, Mountbatten was heartbroken.[1]

This was a rare example of defeat. He usually completed his odd jobs
successfully, although the outcome of the prison security investigations and
recommendations was also unsatisfactory in his eyes.

Mountbatten always became uneasy with time on his hands for reflection,
especially since the death of Edwina, whom he continued to miss painfully.
He read very little, for example, like most members of the royal family. He
either skimmed printed matter swiftly, like a publisher's reader, acquiring
the essence; or slowly, his lips moving with the words, even with a finger
following them across the page.

This uneasiness was one cause of his taking on so much. Other motives
were kindness and a sense of duty. Both the first and last of these reasons
were behind his agreement to meet the newspaper magnate Cecil King at
his London house in May 1968. The nation was in the depths of depression
and anxiety about the future. In Cecil King's judgment the Prime Minister,
Harold Wilson, was destroying the country, which faced anarchy and civil
war. King envisaged the temporary end of parliamentary democracy, and
believed that the country would be forced to turn to 'somebody like Lord
Mountbatten as the titular head of a new administration, somebody
renowned as a leader of men who would be capable of restoring public
confidence....'

Hugh (later Lord) Cudlipp, a friend of Mountbatten, brought about a
meeting and was himself present. Mountbatten telephoned earlier in
the day to indicate that Solly (now Lord) Zuckerman would also be there.
Cecil King said his piece about civil disorder and machine-guns at the
street corners, and ended by asking Mountbatten if he would head a new
administration.

Mountbatten remained silent. Then he turned to Zuckerman, who said
firmly that he would have nothing to do with it, that it was rank treachery,
adding 'Nor should you, Dickie.'[2]

And that was that. But what would have been the outcome if Mountbatten
had not had his adviser at his side? Would the British people, at their lowest
ebb, have welcomed this royal neo-dictator?

The answers are less important than the fact that Mountbatten had insisted on bringing Zuckerman and unhesitatingly followed his lead. Zuckerman has written that: 'It did not take more than a few minutes for Dickie

to realize the madness of the idea'. Those minutes (or seconds) were filled with Zuckerman's advice.

As First Sea Lord, Mountbatten was the strongest proponent of the nuclear deterrent and was more responsible than anyone for the construction of the nuclear-powered Polaris submarines with their immense nuclear destructive ability. But as an old man in retirement, Mountbatten was beguiled into believing that he had been quite wrong, that we were 'rushing headlong towards a precipice' with our nuclear weapons. In one of his last speeches, to the Stockholm International Peace Research Institute in 1979, Mountbatten spoke about his sadness at the little that had been achieved in the way of disarmament between the great powers, especially nuclear disarmament.

Disarmament had become the leading cause of the last years of his life. This is a very different Mountbatten from the man who had been held back only by his naval and royal rank from proclaiming loudly to the nation the need to rearm against the anti-democratic powers of the 1930s, and was one of Churchill's secret team feeding him with information about the nation's weakness, and laboured to defend against Russia's threat to the West at sea in the 1950s.

Lord Zuckerman has for a long time proclaimed against the production of more nuclear weapons, and their proliferation, and has repeatedly stated that the Soviet military threat has been greatly exaggerated.

Soon after the Cuban missiles crisis and his visit to Kennedy, Mountbatten softened to Khrushchev's thaw, and wanted to send a naval goodwill mission to Russia. All thought of his likely 'unpopularity' in Russia, which he had expressed to Ernie Bevin, had now quite disappeared. When Prime Minister Kosygin invited him to the celebrations for the thirtieth anniversary of the defeat of Germany, Mountbatten accepted eagerly. He made nostalgic tours of the palaces in Moscow and Leningrad, delighting his hosts with accounts of grand banquets, visits to the opera, and games with his beautiful young cousins.

Long before this visit in 1975, Mountbatten had turned against the concept that nuclear war was an acceptable consideration. According to Zuckerman, he had studied the arguments. These were, of course, the arguments of Zuckerman, whose influence was immense to the end of Mountbatten's life.

One of Churchill's great attributes was that he was always prepared to listen to advice. He was also very selective and wise in the choice of his advisers. Mountbatten ranged more widely, especially when he was old and retired. One to whom he listened more than most was his son-in-law, Lord Brabourne. According to Mountbatten, it was Lord Brabourne who persuaded him to embark soon after his retirement on an enormously long and profitable series of television films called *The Life and Times of Lord Mount-batten*. It took three years to make, and provided Mountbatten with a great deal of satisfaction. It certainly left out very little in a long and eventful life.

The growth of Mountbatten's vanity was something to which many people have contributed, if only because it was such an easy way to please him. To some, Mountbatten's vanity and egocentricity were irritating and in poor taste. It is sad, accurate, important and not uncharitable to state that the hard core of the Royal Navy in the upper echelons found these characteristics of his distasteful. Churchill treated Mountbatten's vanity indulgently and with humour, sometimes acid-tinged. The royal family were always indulgent about it and never took it seriously.

When a title was being sought for a book about his mother and father, and difficulties in getting it right were being experienced, Mountbatten turned to the Queen and Prince Philip for suggestions. 'Why not just call it "Lord Mountbatten's Parents"?' Prince Philip suggested, with a show of innocence. The redeeming factor is that Mountbatten joined in the laughter.

Without the slightest trace of self-consciousness, Mountbatten allowed his private secretary, who wrote the text of the picture album he prepared before his death, to describe him as 'still handsome in spite of his years', and much more equally ridiculous flattery.

Although he had once been fearful of becoming a megalomaniac, Mountbatten's vanity went largely unchecked. The closest members of his family might have tried to tame it (his mother actually did try, with no success) if they had not been able to laugh at it to his face. His sense of humour, as always, was his salvation.

His pride in his twelve-part autobiographical television series knew no bounds, and he could quote at any time the number of times it had been shown in various countries throughout the world. He also took great satisfaction in dubbing himself in the German and French versions. It was while he was in Paris preparing the French script in 1972 that the Duke of Windsor telephoned and invited his cousin to dinner.

The Duke's health was already failing, and he had recently suffered debilitating treatment for a tumour in his throat. Mountbatten remained blithely unaware of any coolness towards him by his old friend, but the Duke was determined to discover the reason why Mountbatten had not attended his wedding all those years ago.

The Duchess fretted at all the nostalgic talk about old times as shipmates, and the goings-on on board the *Renown* fifty years earlier. Then, when the women withdrew, the Duke posed the question. Mountbatten answered that it was because he had never been asked, although he had offered to stand as best man. The Duke was at first disbelieving, then contrite and forgiving and full of promises to make amends. The friendship that Mountbatten had never known had been broken, was spliced. They saw one another the following day, but never again.

After a harrowing visit from the Queen when he was already dying, the Duke of Windsor died of throat cancer on 28 May 1972: almost certainly the fourth English king to die from smoking in this century. 'He was my best friend all my life,' Mountbatten said on BBC radio at the time of his funeral.

When the Duke of Windsor died, Harold Wilson was Leader of the Labour Party. His admiration for Mountbatten has already been mentioned. The four preceding Prime Ministers, Churchill, Eden, Macmillan and Home, all admired Mountbatten, too, though not without reservations. Churchill claimed from time to time that he loved him. But it was really only the intermittent outpourings of guilt-tinged sentiment. Only one of these men loved him, and did not mind his vanity. 'He was such a sweet man,' said Harold Macmillan. 'He was slightly childish, with a sort of simple mind. He boasted a lot. But that didn't matter. That wasn't important. What did matter was that he was a charming character.'[3]

The old story about always driving to naval dockyards, when living ashore, in a large, expensive car, his Hispano-Suiza or Rolls-Royce, compounding the sin by having a special emblem on the bonnet, was often cited by his fellow officers as proof of his vanity and bad taste. The emblem was of a signal rating with his arms positioned at the alphabetical sign, the right arm straight up with the flag in hand and the left arm horizontal from the shoulder.

To the lower deck, on the other hand, this was proof that he identified with them. One of them wrote on the day of Mountbatten's murder – 'the saddest day of '79' – that 'he gave loyalty and received loyalty in return' and that the bonnet emblem 'was accepted as an honour to the signalmen ratings who served under him'.[4]

Mountbatten's vanity had many origins, but the most important was his need to excel. When he did not win, or when he was crossed, he was not such pleasant company. His temper was not flattering to him, his voice suddenly became harsh, peremptory and arrogant. But he was not rancorous, and like most great men he rarely harboured grudges.

He was nowhere more competitive than on the polo field. He could not bear to be beaten, and his language was as bad as any player's – which is to say, in polo, very bad. In a vital finals in the inter-Regimental Tournament with the 12th Lancers on 11 July 1936, his Royal Naval Polo Team were beaten 6–4. It was hard to take.

'We were leading 3 goals to 1 at the end of the 4th chukka,' he said in excuse, 'and to save a certain goal the 12th Lancers committed a serious foul and knocked over our No. 1's pony. The penalties awarded were, first, a free hit at goal, which I converted, making the score 4–1, and, second, an opponent of higher handicap to retire unless our injured player was fit to continue. He elected to go on, although his left leg was broken, with the inevitable result that the 12th Lancers caught us up and eventually beat us.'[5]

Thirty-seven years after the event, Mountbatten was still nursing this defeat like an old wound. At the time, the *Daily Telegraph*'s polo correspondent merely reported that 'the Lancers showed themselves to be much the better side'.

Mountbatten's tact, when needed, was boundless. He was also a very kind man. But it was possible for both to be overcome by his vanity. An ADC to the Governor of Bombay, who had been badly wounded in Burma, recalls Mountbatten's visit. ''43 or '44?' Mountbatten asked about the date of his action. The officer told him proudly that he had been fighting there since 1942.

Mountbatten then said, 'One thing I have never understood. You had about the same number of troops we have now. Perhaps we have a little more in the air and a few West Africans. But you still couldn't do the job we're doing now.'

The officer recalls today: 'To hear such a grossly inaccurate and hurtful remark from a man in his position is almost unbelievable, but every word became indelibly imprinted on my mind. I returned and rejoined my fellow ADCs, and caused consternation among them as apparently I had gone quite white.'[6]

Another officer commanding the Governor-General's Guard at Viceregal Lodge in New Delhi in October 1947 recalls the trouble he had in satisfying Mountbatten's demands with the daily ceremonial guard with pipes and drums. The guard consisted of a Gurkha officer and twenty. Mountbatten had just returned with his host from visiting his princely estate where a far larger guard had received them. Mountbatten demanded the same size guard for the Prince and himself. 'The manpower was just not available,' said the officer. 'He was most annoyed about it and showed impatience at once.'[7] Ceremonial equality was the last thing Mountbatten ever wanted to fail on, and rarely did.

Mountbatten's preoccupation with detail correctness bedevilled him all his life, but increased with the years. He could spot a misplaced minor decoration at one hundred yards, and would go to great trouble to establish, say, whether his guest was ex-RAF or ex-RAFVR in order to greet him wearing the right tie. One of his staff at the Ministry of Defence said, 'He'd go on for hours trying to work out how many guns ought to salute a CDS when there was a pile of work on his desk.'

It is hard to believe that there were not more important things to be done on the night before Mountbatten left to take up command in South-East Asia than to draw phoenixes. But perfection was always the first priority; perfection for the satisfaction that it gave him, and perfection in order that he could not be faulted.

This writer once suggested laughingly that his dog Kimberley was slightly overweight, and received a very sharp denial: 'Exactly right!' An old American friend who visited him a few weeks before his death told him that he had just learned that the reply to an invitation to a reception for a fellow historian and an authority on wartime resistance, M.R.D. Foot, had been sent by Mountbatten's office in error to the Leader of the House of Commons, the Right Honourable Michael Foot. 'Dickie seems to have lost his sense of humour,' said the American later, reporting Mountbatten's stony response to the 'joke'.

Failure and inefficiency on his part, and the Japanese, were the only subjects about which Mountbatten never laughed. But, as a rule, his light touch, his quick repartee, the sheer certainty of pleasure, stimulus and laughter were always present. The spirit of liveliness, the knowledge that *he* was going to enjoy himself, was heady to experience. One could feel this even at a distance. It was one of his great qualities.

When Mountbatten was in his seventies, women continued to fall under his spell, and his charm was as powerful as in the 1920s. And his need to have women about him was equally strong. Besides the women of the royal family, from Princess Anne to the aged but marvellously bright Princess Alice, Countess of Athlone (and of course the Queen herself, with whom he spent as much time as they could both spare), he made many new young friends, including Prince Charles's girlfriends, who often stayed at Broadlands, and whose numbers and variety made Mountbatten exclaim in mock dismay. Without exception, he made a great fuss of them.

He also kept up with older women friends, like Yola Letellier and Barbara Cartland. Barbara Cartland knew him for fifty years, and very well for the last five. She said, 'Wherever he was, in whatever company on whatever occasion, you at once felt his magnetism. He was the personification of leadership – everything was suddenly marvellous when he was there. He was so knowledgeable on every possible subject, so quick-minded, and – oh – so amusing! People forget his humour – and he was one of the most amusing men I ever knew. But never, never maliciously funny, because he was one of the kindest men alive.'[8]

Mountbatten and Barbara Cartland usually met at least once a week, and during those last years she would stay at Broadlands, and he at Camfield Place. They wrote a novel together in the last months, and she even succeeded in putting him on her vitamin diet. He claimed he felt marvellously improved in health by it, and he became one of her best proponents.

Like Prince Philip, Mountbatten preferred to be in control of things, in the broadest and narrowest sense. He nearly always drove his own cars until the last ten years or so, often with his chauffeur at his side. He drove (and often dented) his own cars before World War II, liked to be at the helm of his boats, even liked driving his trains.

'Placing his suitcase in a first-class carriage of the 6.04 pm train for Ashford,' observed an amazed eye-witness, 'he walked in front of me accompanied by a station official, went up to the engine driver, climbed into the cabin and remained there. When my train came alongside his near New Cross, I saw that Lord Mountbatten was driving the packed train, while the driver was just a bystander.'[9]

The stories of Mountbatten's remarkable memory for faces are legion. It is a quality cultivated by many members of the royal family, but none of them has developed it to such a fine degree as Mountbatten. He said he ruined his memory by overwork during the war, and it is true that in the 1930s he needed only a week to learn the names of every member of a destroyer's company – say two hundred.

His powers of recognition remained almost uncanny. At the airfield at Habbaniyah in Iraq in 1943, when Mountbatten was on his way to take up his appointment as Supremo, ten pilots of the Communications Flight, with Air Vice-Marshal Chapier de Crespigny, lined up to greet him. 'The aircraft stopped,' one of them recalled, 'the door opened, and down stepped Lord Louis in naval uniform, followed by half a dozen of the most beautiful Wrens.'[10]

Twenty-two years later, in the spring of 1965, the same pilot was at Labuan when Mountbatten as Chief of Defence Staff made a tour of the service bases in Sarawak and Malaysia. On leaving, he was climbing up the boarding steps of his famous Comet when he turned and came down again. 'Gathered dignitaries wondered what had gone awry – as I did. He walked twenty yards along the ranks to me and asked me where I had served in Burma. . . .' Mountbatten had recognized not only his Burma Star, but his face.

This power of recall certainly kept his subordinates up to the mark. Mountbatten himself remembered an investiture in Assam during the Burma campaign. 'A man of the 1st Burma Rifles came forward for his

Military Medal,' he said. 'I recognized him at once, and turned to his Colonel. "This man received his MM from the Viceroy at Imphal."

'The Colonel turned white and apologized. I asked him why he had been brought up again, and the Colonel said that his regiment was not on parade last time. I told him, "I don't mind him being brought up again, but I think I ought to have been told." This went rocketing around the troops!'

Mountbatten's thrift was less widely known. At its worst (failure to pay a debt without considerable nagging) it was aggravating. It could also be 'counter-productive', to use one of the favourite words he learned from his elder son-in-law, and it was amusing to hear him on the long-distance telephone for many minutes seeking a modest discount on a modest product. Although he felt he always had to travel first class, he encouraged his family to travel economy, and they often did, nipping in to his more exclusive part of the cabin for a chat from time to time.

This care with money was instilled in him from his earliest days, mainly from his mother, not because his parents were poor – although they were not very rich – but because of the Victorian ethic of thrift and economy handed down directly from the Queen herself. At school and at Osborne, Mountbatten was always on the lowest scale of pocket money, and was encouraged to take every care with his clothes.

A companion to Princess Beatrice, Queen Victoria's last daughter who married Mountbatten's uncle, Prince Henry of Battenberg, recounted to her niece how she helped keep the young Dickie's clothes in order. Once the boy asked her, 'Please can you make new collars for these shirts from the tails?' Which, she thought, revealed early signs of thrift and inventiveness.[11]

When one Admiral, Sir Arthur Pedder, who knew Mountbatten well, heard of his death, he exclaimed, 'Good God, what was he doing placing himself at that risk with his family?' The world was soon to learn that he was protected by minimum security. It was the same through all the years when he was famous, as Chief of Combined Ops, as Supreme Commander, even as Viceroy when hundreds were being assassinated daily about him.

A retired Major in the Intelligence Corps, G.P. Bartholomew, told of his horror on first arriving at Mountbatten's HQ at Kandy, to find 'Supremo' living not in the well-protected military establishment but in the Queen's pavilion, protected by a two-foot-high brick wall and (during daylight hours only) a Royal Marines sentry at the door, playing the part of butler.

This officer soon discovered that Mountbatten did not consider security, so he organized some NCOs to enter the pavilion at night and leave cigarette tins about the place marked 'BOMB'.

After this, Major Bartholomew was allowed to take some modest security action, without Mountbatten's knowledge, because it was well known by his staff that he detested it. At a reception, Mountbatten approached the Major and said, 'I understand you want to improve the security here. Well, I'm not going to have sentries in army boots thumping around the place keeping everyone awake.'

Mountbatten was assured that there was no question of that, and was invited out on to the lawn, with its beautiful flowers and scattered shrubs. 'There are the sentries, sir.'

The Major had placed sentries with dark brown faces and jungle green uniforms among these shrubs, each with a line of sight to his neighbour. Even at short range, Mountbatten could not identify them.

'Well, if *that's* all you want to do,' he said grudgingly, 'go ahead. But do you really think the Japs would think me a worthwhile target?'

The Major, it seems, was 'not prepared for such a breath-takingly modest question'.[12]

Was it really modesty – at Kandy, New Delhi, Singapore, Classiebawn Castle – that led Mountbatten to disregard security risks? It could also have been stupidity, arrogance, rashness or blind courage. It was not any of these alone, though nearest the last. It was a kind of lofty fatalism, a Prince's belief that his destiny was laid down when another name – that of Francis Albert Victor Nicholas – was etched into that Hessian family tree with its roots in Charlemagne, and no power on earth except God's could disturb its course.

Mountbatten on his destroyer's bridge, racing blindly up fjords and over minefields, handling a machine-gun against diving Stukas, striding up to the Arakan front or into a mob of frenzied zealots, was governed in his mind and conduct and in his physical stance by the tradition of timeless chivalry in which fear played no part. A prince with a bodyguard indeed!

It was all very splendid and very medieval. But it could be tragically wasteful of human life. When questioned about his personal security in Ireland, he is known to have asked, 'Do you really think the IRA would think me a worthwhile target?'

As always, he took it for granted that his family and those who served him should show equal fearlessness, or fatalism, for to hint at safety measures was to hint at caution. So, whether it was marching into a rioting, hysterical mob with his wife and daughter at his side, or through a minefield with the lives of two hundred men at risk, or – as an obvious target for assassins – pottering about with his family in an old launch looking for lobsters, everyone had to be prepared to share the dangers. And that was that.

Speed – speed in reaching decisions, speed in all his activities, from polo to driving cars, destroyers and speed-boats – was essential to his style of living. From the dreamy little boy with his white mice, who fell over things, who emanated charm but from whom little was expected in the way of achievement, there developed in adolescence this 'swashbuckling dynamo', as he was once called.

The more Mountbatten loved being known for his fast pace in everything, the faster he became, with 'Full Speed Ahead, both engines!' rung down to the engine room. His record time of one hour fourteen minutes for driving from Brook House in London to the dockyard gates at Portsmouth was widely known. It was a record he loved to quote, adding that it must be remembered that it was done in a car with rear-wheel brakes only, on rough and narrow roads.

He could cite the speed of all his victories in *Shadow II*, and adored reading in the newspapers about his reputation for getting on with things.

> We all admire the energy and enterprise of Lord Louis Mountbatten, who has many of the buoyant qualities of the Prince of Wales. His polo players are situated normally at Portsmouth. He is therefore buying an aeroplane to get them to and from the matches in time. Five fast cars are not swift enough. What his friends are wondering is whether he is going to have the ponies strapped on underneath, so that men and mounts can come together.

That was in 1929. In India in 1947, and on a less light-hearted level, his speed in negotiating the transfer of power had not diminished one knot; nor in 1966 during his investigations into prison security and reform, when Lord Longford found him 'too much in a hurry', with the result that 'prison reform was probably put back twenty-five years'.[13]

Mountbatten's love of speed, his reputation for swift decision-making, his vanity and boasting, his preoccupation with ceremonial and ritual, uniforms, orders, decorations and genealogy, even his practice of winning by any means, fair or almost foul – all these characteristics were judged as vulgar, irritating, or engagingly lovable. The better you knew him, the more tolerant you became of them. He was, as Harold Macmillan said, 'a simple man' fundamentally.

But it is wrong and unjust to deny him his enormous positive qualities, his compassion and kindness, the fullness of his love so that he saw humanity as one. His obsession with detail in his professional life was open to criticism, but it also led to a concern in detail for the sufferings of others, so that some injury or loss of which he had heard would be remembered and enquired about months or years later.

If he was not widely known for his financial generosity, he was generous above what most of us have ever met in anyone else in other ways. Many writers have been impressed by his willingness to give his time, and his con-

cern that they should get everything right. He would read passages of manuscript, proofs, write forewords, correct detail and give interviews, all with
care. Elizabeth Longford recalled a long session with him when she was
writing her book about the House of Windsor. The following day she was
invited back, bringing a tape recorder this time, so as to be sure that she
had got everything right.[14]

There was no need for Mountbatten to tell Churchill at Quebec that he
had a congenital weakness for believing that he could do anything. Churchill
knew that already, or he would not have made the proposal. He had long
ago seen in Mountbatten the qualities of his own younger days – courage,
the possession of a radical and experimental mind, the seeming self-confidence so that no obstacle was insurmountable, no convention unbreakable,
and no one unpersuadable. He did not always win. Mohammed Ali Jinnah
beat him, and so did the 12th Lancers. But victory over Mountbatten was
a very rare event.

Mountbatten was not always sharply discriminating. He chose some lightweight advisers and sometimes took lightweight advice about lightweight
matters. But so great was his charm and attraction, his position and rank,
that he also attracted some brilliant advisers; and Mountbatten had a canny
instinct for taking their advice over really important decisions, for example
at the abdication crisis, at Suez, and at Cecil King's suggestion that he should
become a dictator. Only in India was he poorly advised, and this led to great
tragedies and loss of life, and to the major error in coming home for the
royal wedding in the middle of it all.

Any historical judgment on Mountbatten will be bound to show that his
inspiration to achievement was greater than his actual achievement. His
power to lift spirits, to draw the best out of people, has been experienced
by thousands and is undeniable. The aura of greatness about him never failed
to inspire, and, in his presence, you could physically feel the adrenalin rising
when he became enthused or determined. His charm and humour, the speed
and agility of his mind, were a revelation every time you met him.

The roll of tangible achievement is not so impressive, however. His
detractors could make out a negative list. He did not win a victory at sea.
The enemy frequently damaged his ships, and finally sank him. He is, quite
unfairly, remembered as Chief of Combined Operations for the Dieppe raid
rather than for laying the foundations for the successful invasion of Europe.
Certainly, the 14th Army cleared Burma of the enemy, but it was denied
a great invasion and land victory, just as the admirals were denied a great
Eastern sea victory by the dropping of the atom bombs. The fates of war
were not on his side: yet one more parallel with his father.

Then, he encouraged the demand for independence of once-colonial or

Imperial nations at a speed that satisfied even the Americans, divided India and transferred power in some twenty weeks. Later, he deprived the three British services of their independence and forced them to become one.

So much for the negative side, and it would be unjust to his memory to ignore it. It is certainly unfair that it is more difficult to define convincingly his positive contributions to the winning of the war, and the creation of a freer and more compassionate society since. His energy and the quality of his mind made a great contribution to the creation of the will to win. He deserved that tribute from the the war leaders on D-Day. He deserved to be credited with the saving of India from the Japanese armies just as much as with the granting of independence to the sub-continent.

Mountbatten's love of America, and the Americans' love of him, was a monumental war-winning factor. Who else could have welded together such a disparate number of difficult nationalities into a great Army? Roosevelt loved him, MacArthur admired him, even Stilwell judged him to be a Limey who would actually fight.

Mountbatten's contribution to the British monarchy has also been immense, as the Queen has testified. She and Prince Philip loved him and relied upon his advice on a thousand occasions. His relations with Prince Charles were even closer and more affectionate, and the Prince is the first to underline the extent of his debt for advice, guidance and friendship.

Mountbatten was a passionate believer in the importance and value of the family unit, and through the years of the so-called generation gap had no trouble in bridging it with all his grandchildren, although he could be as fierce and firm with them as a ship's commander with a recalcitrant rating.

His numerous and widespread family loved him in return. Only with the Queen Mother was there a small shadow of reserve, still traceable forty years later to Mountbatten's close friendship with the man whose failure to do his duty forced her own husband on to the throne, and caused him to die prematurely.

Like all his emotions, his grief at the death of his friends and relations was extraordinarily intense. He was distraught at the loss of his only brother, at the death of his sister, the Queen of Sweden, in 1965, and of his eldest sister Alice.

Alice had spent her last years in a suite on an upper floor of Buckingham Palace, living very quietly after her sometimes tumultuous and tragic life. Unlike some women, the Queen loved having her mother-in-law living with her. 'The Queen,' said Mountbatten, 'was the only person who could speak to her in her normal voice and make herself completely understood – every word. My sister was completely normal at the end. People simply couldn't believe it when they met her. During the war, Dolla [her daughter Theodora] had sent to her in Greece a diamond and sapphire cross worth about £10,000 as she knew that her mother, living in a community of nursing sisters, was very poor. She took it straight to the church, hung it round the Virgin's neck and said, "I give this to you."

'But twenty years later at Buckingham Palace she had more influence on the Queen than anyone. The Queen adored her and she adored the Queen. She is fond of her mother, but got on infinitely better with my sister.'

After the inevitable childhood ailments, Mountbatten enjoyed marvellous health for all his life. Like his mother, he regarded illness as a sign of inefficiency. At the autopsy, his organs were found to be in excellent condition, and he was pronounced as having been a very fit man for his years. In 1970 his heart was temporarily suspect and he went into hospital for tests. Within twenty-four hours he had discharged himself, impatient with the whole tiresome business and proclaiming himself never fitter.

He tended to pick up the common cold more easily than most people, but he never took any notice of them beyond using up a great number of linen handkerchiefs. As an old man, the only thing he complained about, if questioned closely, was a tendency to vertigo, and it annoyed him greatly if he should suffer a mild attack when in public. To the end, Mountbatten took plenty of exercise and continued to satisfy his voracious appetite. When he was at Broadlands, he always rode for two hours in the morning, often with a young local girl, with whom he chatted amiably and ceaselessly about life and the world.

Many people have suggested that the manner of Mountbatten's death was as he would have wished it. He dreaded senility and old age. He died, after all, in what his assassins claimed was a war; and no death could have been more spectacular nor aroused such world-wide sensation. The headlines could not have been bigger and blacker, and that would have amused and pleased him.

He also liked the coincidences and ironies of history. He did not know it, but in 1972 his private secretary predicted that he would either linger on into miserable old age, or go out 'with a bang' in about eight years. And it is a considerable coincidence and irony that Mountbatten, who liked most to be remembered for what he did in India, was assassinated by politico-religious fanatics in another divided, strife-torn land at almost exactly the same age as his old friend, Mahatma Gandhi. In their own way, they were both martyrs.

CHRONOLOGICAL TABLE

Chronological Table of the Life of Admiral of the Fleet the Earl Mountbatten of Burma, KG, PC, GCB, OM, GCSI, GCIE, GCVO, DSO, FRS, Hon. DCL, Hon. LLD

Born Frogmore House, Windsor	25 June 1900
Christened Albert Victor Nicholas Louis Francis (Prince Louis of Battenberg)	17 July 1900
Educated mainly at home but also Macpherson's Gymnastic School, Sloane Street, London	Jan. 1905–Nov. 1909
Mr Gladstone's Day School, Eaton Square	Nov. 1909
Locker's Park preparatory boarding school	Sept. 1910–March 1913
Osborne Naval Training College	May 1913–Nov. 1914
Royal Naval College, Dartmouth	Nov. 1914–June 1916
Appointed Midshipman, serving in Admiral Sir David Beatty's flagship HMS *Lion*	July 1916–Feb. 1917
Transferred to HMS *Queen Elizabeth*, Beatty's Grand Fleet flagship	Feb. 1917–June 1918
Name and title changed to Lord Louis Mountbatten	June 1917
Promoted Sub-Lieutenant, briefly visits Western Front	July 1918
Appointed HM submarine *K6* briefly; then second-in-command and First Lieutenant HMS *P31*	July 1918
Cambridge University as undergraduate	Oct. 1919–March 1920
World cruises with HRH Prince of Wales in HMS *Renown*	March–Oct. 1920 Oct. 1921–June 1922
Promoted Lieutenant	1920
Engaged Edwina Ashley	14 Feb. 1922
Married St Margaret's, Westminster	18 July 1922
Appointed HMS *Revenge*	1923
Signal School, Portsmouth, and Royal Naval College, Greenwich	1924–6

Patricia Mountbatten (now Countess Mountbatten of Burma) born	14 Feb. 1924
Reserve Fleet Wireless and Signals Officer	1926
Assistant Fleet Wireless and Signals Officer, Mediterranean Fleet	1927–8
Promoted Lieutenant-Commander	1928
Signals and Wireless Officer, 2nd Destroyer Flotilla	1928–9
Senior Wireless Instructor, Signals School, Portsmouth	1929–31
Pamela Mountbatten (now Lady Pamela Hicks) born	1929
Fleet Wireless Officer, Mediterranean Fleet	1931–3
Promoted Commander	1932
Appointed HMS *Daring* in command	1934
Appointed HMS *Wishart* in command	1935
Admiralty Naval Air Division	1936
Promoted Captain in command HMS *Kelly* and 5th Destroyer Flotilla	1939
On active service, English Channel, Atlantic, North Sea (Norwegian campaign) and Mediterranean (Battle of Crete). *Kelly* damaged several times, and sunk	23 May 1941
Awarded DSO	1940
Appointed Commodore and Chief Adviser Combined Operations Command, and subsequently Chief of Combined Operations and member of British Chiefs of Staff, with rank of Acting Vice-Admiral	1941–3
Dieppe raid	19 Aug. 1942
Quebec Conference, when appointed Supreme Allied Commander South-East Asia Command with rank of Acting Admiral and courtesy ranks of General and Air Marshal	Aug. 1943–6
Battle of the 'Admin. Box'	Feb. 1944
Accepts Japanese surrender at Singapore	12 Sept. 1945
Elevated to title of Viscount, and reverts to rank of Rear-Admiral	1945
Viceroy of India	March–Aug. 1947
Governor-General of India	Aug. 1947–June 1948
Created 1st Earl Mountbatten of Burma	1947
Flag Officer Commanding 1st Cruiser Squadron, Mediterranean Fleet	1948–9
Promoted Vice-Admiral	1949
Fourth Sea Lord	1950–2
C-in-C Mediterranean Fleet, and C-in-C Allied Forces Mediterranean from 1953	1952–4
Promoted Admiral	1953

Appointed Personal ADC to the Queen   1953
First Sea Lord   18 April 1955
Promoted Admiral of the Fleet   1956
Chief of UK Defence Staff and Chairman of Chiefs of Staff
Committee (CDS)   1959–65
Appointed Colonel of Life Guards, Colonel Commandant of
Royal Marines, etc.   1965
Died   27 Aug. 1979

CHAPTER NOTES

All unattributed quotations by Lord Mountbatten, and anecdotes recounted by him, originate in taped or noted conversations with the author at various dates between 1972 and 1978, and are not individually cited.

Conv. = conversation

Corres. = correspondence

Chapter 1 The Boy Sailor

1. R. Hough, *Louis and Victoria: the First Mountbattens* (Hutchinson, 1974) p. 111.
2. Conv. Lady Pamela Hicks.
3. Royal Archives, Windsor.
4. Victoria Milford Haven (V.M.H.) (Princess Louis of Battenberg) to Miss Nona Kerr, 14 April 1903.
5. Hough, p. 219.
6. *Ibid*, p. 218.
7. *Ibid*, p. 220.
8. *Ibid*, p. 220.
9. W.S. Churchill, *The World Crisis*, Vol. I (Butterworth, 1923), p. 212.
10. Hough, p. 279.
11. *Ibid*, p. 300.
12. M. Gilbert, *Winston S. Churchill*, Vol. III (Heinemann, 1971), p. 149.
13. HRH The Duke of Windsor, *A King's Story* (Cassell, 1951), p. 108.
14. V.M.H. to Nona Kerr, 30 Oct. 1914.

Chapter 2 The Golden Couple

1. Hough, pp. 319–20.
2. *Ibid*, p. 320.
3. V.M.H. to Nona Kerr, 7 June 1917.
4. Hough, p. 325.
5. *Ibid*, p. 340.
6. Windsor, p. 106.
7. *Ibid*, p. 152.

8. J. Terraine, *The Life and Times of Lord Mountbatten* (Hutchinson, 1968), p. 35.
9. Windsor, p. 159.
10. Hough, p. 342.
11. *Ibid*, p. 333.
12. M. Masson, *Edwina Mountbatten* (Jarrolds, 1958), p. 66.
13. Windsor, p. 164.
14. *Ibid*, p. 171.
15. *Ibid*, p. 178.
16. Masson, p. 66.
17. *Ibid*, p. 76.
18. Hough, p. 344.
19. *Ibid*, p. 344.
20. Conv. Barbara Cartland.

Chapter 3 Family Affairs

1. Conv. Vice-Admiral Sir Charles Hughes Hallett, KCB, CBE.
2. *Ibid*.
3. Conv. HRH Princess Alice, Countess of Athlone.
4. Masson, p. 57.
5. Conv. B. Cartland.
6. Corres. Mountbatten to Captain Andrew Yates, MVO, RN (Retd), 13 Oct. 1926.
7. *Ibid*.
8. Corres. Commander P. du Cane, CBE, RN (Retd), 22 Feb. 1980.
9. A.J.P. Taylor, *Beaverbrook* (Hamish Hamilton, 1972), p. 308.

10. Cited R. Murphy, *The Last Viceroy* (Jarrolds, 1948), p. 63.
11. Conv. Lt-Commander P.K. Kemp, OBE, RN (Retd).
12. Masson, p. 99.
13. Hough, p. 347.
14. B. Boothroyd, *Philip: An Informal Biography* (Longmans, 1971), p. 70.
15. Conv. HRH Prince Philip Duke of Edinburgh, KG, KT, OM, GBE, PC.
16. Conv. HM Queen Elizabeth The Queen Mother.
27. Masson, p. 97.
18. Conv. HRH Princess Alice.
19. Conv. Rt Hon. Julian Amery, PC, MP.
20. Boothroyd, p. 68.
21. Conv. Kemp.
22. Conv. HM Queen Elizabeth II.

Chapter 4 Signals of Danger

1. Terraine, p. 56.
2. Conv. Vice-Admiral H.T. Baillie-Grohman.
3. Corres. Rear-Admiral J.G. Maclean.
4. Masson, pp. 109–10.

Chapter 5 The Kelly at War

1. Harold Nicolson, *Diaries & Letters 1939–45*, ed. N. Nicolson (Collins, 1967), pp. 47–8.
2. Churchill, I, p. 477.
3. C. de Wiart, *Happy Odyssey* (Cape, 1950), p. 174.
4. K. Poolman, *The Kelly* (Kimber, 1954), p. 133.
5. Corres. H.V. Rogers.
6. Corres. Lt C.J. Jones, MBE, RN (Retd).
7. Corres. Commander the Rt Hon. Allan Noble, KCMG, DSO, DSC, DL, RN (Retd).
8. Corres. P. Watson, DSM.

Chapter 6 Combined Operations

1. J.W. Wheeler-Bennett, *King George VI: His Life and Reign* (Macmillan, 1958), p. 397.
2. Boothroyd, p. 24.
3. *Chips: the Diaries of Sir Henry Channon* (Weidenfeld 1967), p. 287.

4. Boothroyd, p. 12.
5. Hough, p. 373.
6. Conv. Lady Pamela Hicks.
7. Boothroyd, p. 39.
8. N. Coward, *Future Indefinite* (Heinemann, 1954), p. 208.
9. Taylor, p. 815.
10. Coward, p. 209.
11. *Ibid*, p. 211.
12. Terraine, p. 83.
13. Conv. and corres. Dr Martin Gilbert, MA.
14. Channon, p. 328.
15. Hough, p. 379.
16. B. Fergusson, *The Watery Maze* (Cape, 1961), p. 89.
17. Conv. Hughes Hallett.
18. *Ibid*.
19. Churchill, IV, p. 178.
20. Conv. Hughes Hallett.
21. Conv. and corres. Kemp.
22. Corres. C. Trent Thomas.

Chapter 7 'Supremo' I

1. Churchill, V, p. 73.
2. R. Lewin, *Churchill as War Lord* (Batsford, 1974), p. 214.
3. Churchill, V, p. 73.
4. By the official historian of the Royal Navy in World War II, Captain Stephen Roskill, CBE, DSC, RN (Retd), *vide* his *Churchill and the Admirals* (Collins, 1977).
5. Churchill, V, p. 82.
6. D.C. James, *The Years of MacArthur*, Vol. II (W.H. Allen, 1975), p. 362 (citing the *Ohio State Journal*).
7. Churchill, V, p. 269.
8. A. Eden, *The Reckoning* (Cassell, 1965), p. 404.
9. Corres. Edward Ivermee.
10. Corres. G. Francis.
11. B. Tuchman, *Sand Against the Wind: Stilwell and the American Experience in China 1911–45* (Macmillan, 1971), p. 471.
12. de Wiart, p. 251.
13. *Ibid*, p. 238.
14. *Ibid*, p. 255.
15. Conv. and corres. Major R.A. Cooper, MC.
16. Churchill, V, p. 365.
17. *Ibid*, p. 365.
18. *Ibid*, p. 497.
19. Churchill, VI, p. 186.

Chapter 8 'Supremo' II

1. Corres. Major A.W.M. Dickie.
2. Churchill, VI, pp. 538–9.
3. Conv. Amery.
4. F. Williams, *A Prime Minister Remembers* (Heinemann, 1961), p. 49.

Chapter 9 Viceroy

1. Corres. Captain R.C. Todhunter, RN (Retd).
2. Conv. Rt Hon. Lord Butler of Saffron Walden, KG, PC, CH, MA.
3. Hansard, March 1947.
4. Conv. Amery.
5. Hansard, March 1947.
6. Williams, p. 208.
7. *Ibid*, p. 209.
8. A. Campbell-Johnson, *Mission with Mountbatten* (Jarrolds, 1951), p. 68.
9. A. Wavell, *The Viceroy's Journal* (Oxford University Press, 1973), pp. 432–3.
10. *Ibid*, p. 433.
11. *Ibid*, p. 433.
12. Corres. R. Walker, CBE.
13. Corres. Arthur E. Gilbert.
14. L. Mosley, *The Last Days of the British Raj* (Weidenfeld, 1961), p. 63.
15. Masson, pp. 206–7.
16. Conv. Rt Hon. Lord Hailsham of St Marylebone, PC, CH, FRS.
17. Conv. Rt Hon. Sir Harold Wilson, KG, PC, OBE, MP.
18. Conv. Butler.
19. Campbell-Johnson, p. 106.
20. Wavell, p. 434.
21. Terraine, p. 157.

Chapter 10 First Sea Lord: The Summit

1. Conv. and corres. Sir John Lang, GCB, CB.
2. Conv. HM The Queen.
3. Conv. HM Queen Elizabeth The Queen Mother.

4. Conv. HRH Princess Alice.
5. Conv. HRH Prince Philip.
6. Corres. Rev. H.I. Clutterbuck.
7. Conv. Kemp.
8. Corres. Vice-Admiral Sir Arthur Pedder, KBE, CB.
9. *Ibid*.
10. Conv. Lang.
11. *Ibid*.
12. Conv. Rt Hon. Harold Macmillan, PC, OM, FRS.
13. Conv. Butler.
14. Conv. Wilson.
15. Conv. Rt Hon. The Earl of Longford, KG, PC.
16. Conv. Hailsham.
17. Conv. Macmillan.
18. Conv. Kemp.
19. Conv. Macmillan.
20. Conv. Amery.
21. Conv. Wilson.
22. Conv. Lang.
23. Corres. Mrs A.F. Whitehead.
24. Conv. Amery.
25. Conv. Amery and corres. Gilbert.
26. Corres. T. Jeacock.

Chapter 11 Retirement

1. Corres. Desmond de Silva.
2. Corres. and conv. Lord Cudlipp, and his book *Walking on the Water* (Bodley Head, 1976).
3. Conv. Macmillan.
4. Corres. L.J. Lennocks.
5. Corres. W.R.M. Maxwell.
6. Corres. Mountbatten.
7. Corres. Lt-Colonel J.A.I. Fillingham, OBE.
8. Conv. B. Cartland.
9. Corres. Mrs Denise Silvester Carr.
10. Corres. Eric A.C. Berfoot, DFC.
11. Corres. Mrs Margaret Wade.
12. Corres. Major G.P. Bartholomew.
13. Conv. Lord Longford.
14. Conv. Countess of Longford, CBE.

ACKNOWLEDGMENTS

The author wishes to thank Their Majesties Queen Elizabeth II and Queen Elizabeth The Queen Mother, His Royal Highness The Prince Philip, Duke of Edinburgh and his sisters Princess Margarita of Hohenlohe-Langenburg and Princess George of Hanover, and Her Royal Highness Princess Alice, Countess of Athlone, for their reminiscences about Lord Mountbatten's parents and about Lord Mountbatten himself, when I was working on the family history and dual biography of the first Marquis and Marchioness of Milford Haven. Their contributions were so generous that much of what they told me appears here for the first time.

Other people, too many to list by name, have helped with reminiscences and, through their personal knowledge of Lord Mountbatten and their friendship with him, have also been able to check information. Hundreds more answered my public appeal for reminiscences, and I am grateful to everyone who responded with contributions ranging from important information and anecdotes, to small details which have helped me to form a more complete and accurate portrait of Lord Mountbatten.

I must, however, single out for my thanks the following who have been especially kind and forthcoming: Julian Amery, Sir Arthur Bryant, Lord Butler, Barbara Cartland, Lord Cudlipp, Dr Martin Gilbert, Lord Hailsham, Vice-Admiral Sir Charles Hughes Hallett, Lieutenant-Commander Peter Kemp, Sir John Lang, the Earl and Countess of Longford, Harold Macmillan, Professor Arthur J. Marder, Vice-Admiral Sir Arthur Pedder, Tom Pocock, Lady Soames, Sir Herbert Thompson, Sir Harold Wilson and Captain A. V. S. Yates.

My thanks are offered also to the staff of the RUSI, Cirencester and London libraries, to Douglas Matthews, Librarian of the London Library, for the index, and to Jackie Gumpert for her swift and accurate typing.

INDEX

(Ranks and titles are generally the highest to be attained)

Margaret ('Peg'), Princess Louis of (*née* Geddes), 88
May, Princess of, 14
Hewitt, Admiral H. Kent, USN, 153
Hicks, David, 2, 242
Hicks, Lady Pamela (*née* Mountbatten; M's younger daughter): at Classiebawn, 2; mother's strictness with, 72; birth, 81; evacuated to New York, 118; on mother's not gossiping 139; post-war reunion, 204; character, 204; goes to India, 213; in Malta, 233; friendship with princesses, 242; marriage and children, 242, 256
Hitler, Adolf, 109, 111, 120, 127, 142
Hohenlohe-Langenburg, Margarita, Princess of, 59
Home, Alexander F. Douglas-Home, Baron, 264
Hopkins, Harry, 151, 154
Hore-Belisha, Leslie, 1st Baron, 118
Hughes Hallett, Admiral Sir Charles, 65, 148-9
Hughes Hallett, Admiral Sir John ('Jock'), 148, 154-6

Illustrious, HMS, 126, 144, 162
Imphal, 187-9
India: Prince of Wales' 1921 tour of, 53-7; M's love for, 54-5; end of imperialism in, 202-3; M appointed Viceroy, 207-10; transfer of power in, 210-13, 215-20, 225-30, 270; partition, 220-21, 229-30; princely states, 221; independence, 221-3, 230, 272; M as Governor-General of, 221-2; casualties, 222-3
Indo-China, 196
Invergordon mutiny, 1931, 91-2
Irène, Princess, *see* Prussia
Ismay, General Hastings ('Pug'), 164, 208, 214
Itagaki, Lieutenant-General S., 200
Italy, 106, 126-7, 161, 183

Jackal, HMS, 125, 129
Jacob, Brigadier (*later* General Sir) Ian, 163, 170
Jaipur, Maharajah of, 226
James, Audrey, 44, 48-9
Japan: 1922 visit to, 58, 202; naval rearmament, 58; naval air arm, 108; casualties, 155, 197; in World War II,

168-9; and Burma war, 186-8; war in China, 190-91; atomic bombing of, 195, 198; 1945 defeat of, 197-8; atrocities, 202
Javelin, HMS, 125
Jellicoe, Admiral of the Fleet John Rushworth, 1st Earl, 27, 29, 36-7, 146
Jinnah, Mohammed Ali, 212, 215, 218, 220-21, 227-8, 271
Joel, David, 65
Joint Intelligence Committee, 142
Jowitt, William Allen, Earl, 232
Jupiter, HMS, 125
Jutland, Battle of, 1916, 35, 172

Kandahar, HMS, 130
Kandy, Ceylon, 191-2, 268-9
Kashmir, HMS, 129-30, 132-3
Kelly, HMS: M wears badge from, 3, 6, 115; sunk, 3, 6, 131-5, 140-42; M commands, 112-14; luxury cabin in, 112, 114; armaments, 115; Noël Coward bases film on, 115, 140-41, 143; early wartime actions, 116-17, 121-2; torpedoed by E-boat, 122-4; recommissioned, 126-7; in Crete action, 129-31; Reunion Association, 135, 260
Kelvin, HMS, 119
Kemp, Lieutenant-Commander Peter, 77-8, 157, 238, 248
Kennedy, John Fitzgerald, 253-4, 262
Kent, George, Duke of, 82, 89, 113; killed, 160, 170
Kent, Marina, Duchess of, 84, 89, 113
Keyes, Admiral of the Fleet Roger John Brownlow, 1st Baron, 72-3, 145-7, 149, 220
King, Cecil, 261, 271
King, Admiral Ernest J., USN, 153, 166, 169, 182, 189
Kipling, HMS, 129-30, 133-4
Kitchener, Field-Marshal Horatio Herbert, 1st Earl, 25, 30, 33
Knatchbull, Nicholas (M's grandson), 2, 4
Knatchbull, Norton Louis Philip (M's grandson), 225-6
Knatchbull, Timothy (M's grandson), 2, 4, 6
Kohima, 187, 189

Lambe, Admiral Sir Charles Edward, 79, 244
Lang, Sir John, 233, 239-41, 250
Langtry, Lillie, 13, 66

LORD MOUNTBATTEN AND THE ROYAL FAMILY

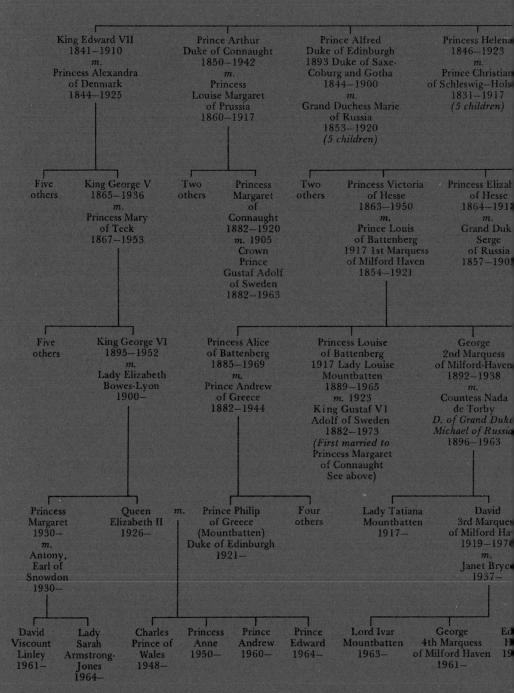

Note: Children not shown in order of ages, but see date of birth.